PENNSYLVANIA GOVERNMENT AND POLITICS

Understanding Public Policy in the Keystone State

Thomas J. Baldino and Paula A. Duda Holoviak

THE PENNSYLVANIA STATE UNIVERSITY PRESS

UNIVERSITY PARK, PENNSYLVANIA

Library of Congress Cataloging-in-Publication Data

Names: Baldino, Thomas J. (Thomas Joseph), author. | Duda Holoviak, Paula A., author.
Title: Pennsylvania government and politics : understanding public policy in the keystone state / Thomas J. Baldino and Paula A. Duda Holoviak.
Description: University Park, Pennsylvania : The Pennsylvania State University Press, [2024] | "Keystone books." | Includes bibliographical references and index.
Summary: "A comprehensive study of Pennsylvania government and politics. Includes commentary from interviews with over sixty individuals who served, participated in, or covered the state's political system"—Provided by publisher.
Identifiers: LCCN 2023047268 | ISBN 9780271097428 (hardback) | ISBN 9780271096797 (paperback)
Subjects: LCSH: Public administration—Pennsylvania. | Pennsylvania—Politics and government.
Classification: LCC JK3641 .B35 2024 | DDC 320.4748—dc23/eng/20231113
LC record available at https://lccn.loc.gov/2023047268

The Pennsylvania State University Press is a member of the Association of University Presses.

It is the policy of The Pennsylvania State University Press to use acid-free paper. Publications on uncoated stock satisfy the minimum requirements of American National Standard for Information Sciences—Permanence of Paper for Printed Library Material, ANSI Z39.48–1992.

PENNSYLVANIA GOVERNMENT AND POLITICS

KEYSTONE BOOKS

Keystone Books are intended to serve
the citizens of Pennsylvania. They are
accessible, well-researched explorations
into the history, culture, society, and
environment of the Keystone State as
part of the Middle Atlantic region.

To my brother, Paul,
whose selfless gift of life
will forever be remembered.—T.J.B.

To my late father, Peter P. Duda,
the consummate local politician,
who instilled in me a great love for all things Pennsylvania.

And to my late husband, Peter,
and my sons, Vladimir and Alexander,
for all their love and support.—P.A.D.H.

Contents

Illustrations

Tables

Acknowledgments

Bringing this book to publication has taken far longer than either of us ever imagined when we first discussed the project in the spring of 2015. It's said that it takes a village to raise a child; for this book, it took a small town to bring it to life. We wish to recognize and thank all those who provided encouragement and assistance. Whatever knowledge or enjoyment future readers may derive from our work is a direct result of the collective wisdom and encouragement that we received from those who appear below; we, however, accept full responsibility for the book's shortcomings.

Dean Paul Riggs of the College of Arts, Humanities and Social Sciences at Wilkes University along with Professor Kyle Kreider, Chair of the Division of Behavioral and Social Sciences, provided invaluable assistance to Tom, as well as Andrea Rizzo, administrative assistant to the Division. At the Farley Library, Dean John Stachacz and Reference Librarian Brian Sacolic were always ready to help locate and acquire books and other materials unavailable in the collection. His undergraduate research assistants, Christie O'Brien and Evan Sedor, attended several interviews, took notes and transcribed them while also tracking down data and difficult sources. Three graduate assistants, who were made available for short periods by Dean Riggs, were also helpful in locating data and sources: they were Karley Stasko, Jacob Hebda and Andree Rose Catalfamo. Emeritus Professor of History Diane Wenger generously read chapter 1 twice, suggesting the inclusion of frequently overlooked peoples and clarifying important events. Colleagues in the Political Science Department, Kyle Kreider and Benjamin Toll, read chapters and gave thoughtful suggestions, while former colleague Gary Aichele kindly gave of his time and expertise reviewing chapters and providing his expertise on the constitutional matters. Former student Jeffrey A. Clukey, senior staff to Republicans on the House Appropriations Committee, generously instructed his old professor on nuances of the appropriations process. Nicole Rademan, clerk to a Superior Court judge, patiently explained difficult legal questions as well as assisted in locating several court decisions. Claire Gauthreau and Chelsea Hill of the Center for Women and Politics at Rutgers University were gracious in providing their data on women in the Pennsylvania legislature.

We both wish to acknowledge our friends and colleagues across Pennsylvania who share our interest in the state's politics and offered encouragement and assistance in various ways as we toiled away: Christopher Borick, Professor of Political Science, Muhlenberg College; Michael Cassidy, former state representative and adjunct professor at Temple University; Jonathan Johnson, senior policy analyst, Center for Rural Pennsylvania; John Kennedy, Professor of Political Science, West Chester University; J. Wesley Lecrone,

Professor of Political Science, Widener University; Joseph McLaughlin, former Director of Temple University's Institute of Public Affairs and its bipartisan Center on Regional Politics; Joseph Melusky, professor of political science, St. Francis University; and Berwood Yost, professor of political science and director of the Franklin and Marshall Poll.

Our heartfelt thanks and appreciation is extended to all those who agreed to be interviewed. Their insightful comments, humorous anecdotes, and extensive experience significantly enriched the book. We also gratefully acknowledge the three reviewers whose thoughtful critiques substantially improved our work.

To Jenna Lipowski, graduate assistant to Kutztown's MPA program, we owe a special thank you for her extensive research, editing and formatting of graphics and tables.

Our thanks to the Penn State University Press for agreeing to publish our book. Managing editor Alex Ramos and editorial assistant Maddie Caso, as well as copy editor John Morris, were unwavering in their support. But we also must recognize Kathryn Bourque Yahner, our former editor at PSU Press, who patiently guided us through most of the manuscript's completion. Without her, we know that this book might never have made it into print.

Finally, we wish to thank our families. Aside from simply dealing with our distractedness and complaints about being overworked, their love sustained us over the project's long gestation. Peter's encouraging words while battling cancer were an inspiration, while Vladimir and Alexander patiently accepted their mom's busy schedule, while also accompanying her on numerous research trips across the commonwealth. Sandy's contributions went beyond patience with her absent-minded husband. She volunteered to help transcribe data and compile tables and charts and read chapters as an educated layperson, offering suggestions on how to make my sometimes dense prose more accessible. At those moments when my spirit wavered, her reassuring words kept me focused and grounded. She may not be excited to learn about the next book project, but I take comfort knowing that she will always be there for me.

Introduction

Contemporary politics and policy-making in the commonwealth of Pennsylvania are the products of its formal and informal governmental institutions as well as the unique personalities of the men and women who participate in its political arena. As William Penn stated in his preface to the First Frame of Government of Pennsylvania (1682), "Governments, like clocks, go from the motions men give them, and as governments are made and moved by men, so by them are they ruined too. Wherefore governments rather depend upon men than men upon governments."[1]

Penn correctly concluded that people create governments, which require maintenance by the people. Those constructing governmental institutions bring with them their history, cultural heritage, and diverse personal experiences. They hoped that what they fashioned would endure. It is a testament to the skills of Pennsylvania's founders that their government has endured for over 340 years, leading us to conclude that whatever the current turmoil that swirls within its political system, its foundation remains solid.

Our goal in this book is to present a clear, cohesive, and, we hope, engaging explanation of how Pennsylvania's government and politics work to an audience of political amateurs and professionals, students, and citizens. Combining the elements noted above—institutions, processes, and personalities—we present the material and attempt to answer interesting questions that our audience may ask. For example, How are laws made? How are our tax dollars spent? What, if anything, makes the Keystone State's political culture unique? How has its long history contributed to the development of America's basic constitutional rights and privileges?

To answer these questions, we draw on a variety of primary and secondary sources. Primary sources include legislative documents, constitutional texts, court decisions, and government agency records. News articles, historical texts, and previous research on Pennsylvania politics and government comprise the secondary sources. The sources are complemented by personal interviews with former and current elected officials, appointed and career administrative officials, party leaders, lobbyists, directors of research agencies and nongovernmental associations, and prominent political commentators and reporters.

We also employ a theme to bring coherence to our book: institutionalism. In political science, institutionalism, as a theoretical perspective, posits that one must understand institutions if one is to understand governments, because their norms, rules, and structures profoundly shape a political system's behavior and its ability to function. By applying this perspective to Pennsylvania's institutions, both formal and informal, we hope to demonstrate how significant they are for maintaining democracy. To understand the ins and outs of Pennsylvania's political system, therefore, one must understand its institutions, as they have held the commonwealth together for over three centuries. Though periodically tested by natural disasters, social upheavals, political corruption, and pitched political conflicts, these institutions provided stability, allowing the state to weather each challenge. In response to each crisis, Pennsylvanians modified their institutions, notably by constitutional amendments but also via legislation, so that the state would be better prepared to confront future crises. Recent events, however, have severely tested the Keystone State's institutions. Together, the COVID pandemic and the 2020 presidential election placed extraordinary burdens on the institutions such that they tore at their very fabric: the governor and his administration's authority were repeatedly challenged, the General Assembly battled with the governor and its own deep internal divisions were exposed to the public, the legitimacy of court decisions was questioned and the public's trust in the courts eroded, the parties became more intensely at odds than at any time since the Civil War, and whatever faith the people had in political journalists to report the news objectively appeared to vanish. While we believe that Pennsylvania's institutions will withstand these latest tests, we leave it to our readers to form their own opinions.[2]

With institutionalism as our theme, each chapter opens with an introduction that gives an overview of the chapter's subject, followed by an explanation of the subject's significance and function within the state's political system. The subject's role and its powers or influence are next considered. Finally, specific policy examples are woven within the discussion of current issues along with the interviews to expose the "why" behind Pennsylvania's policy and electoral choices.

Pennsylvanians and many historians consider the commonwealth to be the birthplace of America's government. Therefore, we begin with a chapter that traces Pennsylvania's historical development from the time of William Penn, through four frames of government, the state's first constitution, the Civil War and Reconstruction, and two World Wars, ending with the 1968 constitutional revisions. Chapter 2 explores Pennsylvania's political culture with an eye toward regional and rural and urban differences. Chapter 3 introduces the reader to elections and how they function, as well as three informal institutions: political parties, interest groups and their lobbyists, and news media. Chapter 4 surveys the state's legislature: the General Assembly. We consider who its members are, how they came to be elected, and the legislature's structure and operation, as well as the consequences of the assembly's actions. Chapter 5 describes the duties and functions of the state's chief executive, while chapter 6 fleshes out the remainder of the executive branch and the state's many administrative offices. Chapter 7 reviews Pennsylvania's unified judicial system: its organization, membership, and place within the political system. Chapter 8 places Pennsylvania within the federal system by discussing the tensions between states' rights and federal powers. Chapter 9 captures the complexity of Pennsylvania's local government system, including its sixty-seven counties and numerous municipalities. Lastly, chapter 10 presents a case study of the struggles and policy choices that confronted Pennsylvania's political system during the COVID-19 crisis and the 2020 presidential election. These simultaneously occurring events placed inordinate pressure on the state's political institutions that, upon examination, revealed their strengths and weaknesses.

We trust that our efforts to present a full and colorful portrait of the Quaker State will cause the reader to become more attuned to the state's politics and perhaps decide to participate beyond voting. As Penn noted, governments depend upon the people, but simply observing the government is not supporting it. Active involvement is required.

NOTES

1. US History, Pennsylvania, https://www.ushistory.org/penn/quotes.htm.
2. For a fuller understanding of institutionalism, see Kingdon, *Agendas, Alternatives, and Public Policies*; Peters, *Institutional Theory in Political Science*; Lowndes and Roberts, *Why Institutions Matter*.

BIBLIOGRAPHY

Cater, Douglass. *Power in Washington, DC: A Critical Look at Today's Struggle to Govern in the Nation's Capital*. New York: Random House, 1964.

Heclo, Hugh H. "Issue Networks and the Executive Establishment." In *The New American Political System*, edited by Anthony King, 87–107. Washington, DC: American Enterprise Institute, 1978.

Kingdon, John. *Agendas, Alternatives, and Public Policies*. 2nd ed. New York: Longman, 1995.

Lowndes, Vivien, and Mark Roberts. *Why Institutions Matter: The New Institutionalism in Political Science*. London: Red Globe Press, 2013.

Peters, B. Guy. *Institutional Theory in Political Science: The New Institutionalism*. 4th ed. Northampton, MA: Edward Elgar, 2019.

Ripley, Randall, and Grace Franklin. *Congress, the Bureaucracy, and Public Policy*. 5th ed. Pacific Grove, CA: Brooks/Cole, 1991.

Skok, James E. "Policy Issue Networks and the Public Policy Cycle: A Structural-Functional Framework for Public Administration." *Public Administration Review* 55, no. 4 (1995): 325–32.

CHAPTER 1

Pennsylvania History

In this chapter we present an overview of the Keystone State's history, emphasizing its politics. While we do not ignore social and economic developments, we focus on those that affected the state's political climate and contributed to constitutional change. By learning the historical context, the reader will be better prepared for material encountered in later chapters.

Since William Penn received his proprietary colony in 1681, Pennsylvanians have had nine documents that established governments and protected citizens' freedoms: four frames of government and, since statehood, five constitutions. While the size and scope of the governments created under each document varied considerably, one constant was a statement of rights that included freedom of religious thought and practice; in reality, however, intolerance toward non-Christians was never completely eliminated.

Variations in each of Pennsylvania's five constitutions reflected the social and political tensions present in the state and, quite often, the nation at the time each was adopted. The legislative, executive, and judicial branches, the government's formal institutions, experienced the most dramatic alterations. They were the targets of the people's ire, and the citizens modified those institutions to bring about different public policies. As we describe below, the first constitution was radical in that it placed most power in the legislature, the people's branch, and severely reduced the role of the executive, a reaction against the proprietors. Later reforms focused on the legislature, while the last constitutional revisions focused on the judiciary.

Amendments ratified between constitutions also significantly affected institutions: for example, the recent amendments limiting the governor's power to declare emergency disaster declarations. Divided governments in the next decade will likely bring more amendments, with serious consequences for the state's institutions.

NATIVE AMERICANS AND THE EARLIEST EUROPEANS

Before European settlers came to the territory that would become Penn's Woods, indigenous people had occupied the land for millennia. Archeologists have identified seven distinct tribes, based on their languages and cultures, that roamed over or lived in the region between AD 1000 and 1500. Many were strictly hunter-gatherers, others practiced agriculture, while others engaged in both. For over five hundred years, tribes merged with each other if they found their populations dwindling, but they also fought each other, as well as invading peoples, with the victorious absorbing those captured into the tribe.[1]

By the time of first contact, sometime in the sixteenth century, the Algonquian people, who called themselves the Lenni-Lenape (the "real" or "original" people) and whom the English later called the Delaware, lived in the region on either side of the Delaware River to the West Branch of the Susquehanna River and from lower New York south to Delaware. The northernmost tribe of the Lenni-Lenape was the Munsee, with the Unami below them and the Unalachtigo farthest south. The Conestoga, part of the Susquehannock people, inhabited southeastern Pennsylvania. The Shawnee were scattered across the state's center, while the Nanticokes lived along the Susquehanna's East Branch and as far south as the present Maryland border. Out west, the remnants of the Erie and Monongahela peoples as well as the Wyandottes were the major tribes.

Much uncertainty surrounds who made first contact with Native Pennsylvanians and when they did so. One theory is that Giovanni da Verrazano, commissioned by the French to explore the New World, encountered the Munsee in 1524 in New York Bay, and a second is that the Conestoga met John Smith in 1608 when he sailed into the Chesapeake Bay. The precise point of contact is less important than its consequences. While the Natives discovered value in the goods offered in trade by the Europeans, such as metal pots, glass beads, and blankets, which they exchanged for beaver and other animal pelts, they could not anticipate the suffering that would befall them when the Europeans brought diseases such as smallpox to the New World. Without any natural immunities or effective treatments, viruses killed thousands, perhaps as much as 75 to 95 percent of the Natives in affected tribes. Through all their suffering, Natives continued trading furs for European goods, while also sharing their knowledge of the land, its resources, and crops such as, maize (corn), beans, squash, and tobacco.[2]

As their interactions extended over decades, Europeans learned that tribes had forms of government that, superficially, appeared similar to monarchical regimes, because all the tribes had chiefs whom the Europeans considered kings. With deeper understanding, however, the governments are revealed to be dramatically different. For example, the Delaware had chiefs who governed following the will of the people rather than authoritatively. Their system more closely resembled a representative than a monarchical system.

A more elaborate form of Native government was found among the original Five Nations of the Haudenosaunee—the Iroquois League or confederation—composed of the Mohawks, Oneidas, Onondagas, Cayuga, and Seneca. (A sixth tribe, the Tuscarora, joined the League early in the 1700s.) Though the Iroquois tribes dwelled mostly in New York, their travels and trading expeditions brought them into frequent contact with Native Pennsylvanians, sometimes leading to wars, which the Iroquois frequently won. As with the Delaware, each tribe was led by a chief, who was instructed by its people during council meetings attended by *all* tribal members sitting in concentric circles, with the chief in the center, elders closest to the chief, then men, with the women and children farthest out. Discussion continued until the chief determined the tribe's will. There were also formal procedures for diplomacy, initiating wars, and settling conflicts. Each tribe sent its delegates to League council meetings, where decisions regarding all the tribes were made.[3]

Historians have debated the extent to which Native governmental structures directly or indirectly influenced the drafters of the US Constitution. Some argue that the Iroquois Confederacy was a model for America's federal system. Others contend that the inspiration was provided by philosophers like Hume rather than Indian tribal rules. Without definitive evidence the argument cannot be settled, but it is clear that the Natives did have relatively sophisticated governments and that some of the Framers were aware of them.[4]

CONTACT WITH EUROPEANS

Across North America, European explorers, traders, and later settlers established relationships with the Native peoples they encountered. The French in Canada became friends with the Hurons, enemies of the Iroquois. The English allied with the Susquehannocks, while the Dutch made treaties with the Lenni-Lenape. Sadly, for the Natives, Old World rivalries were visited upon the New World. The tribes came to view their European allies' enemies as their enemies as well as the enemy's Native ally. These relationships proved critical in the nation's and Pennsylvania's development.[5]

The Great Powers' conflicts spread to America as they sought to derive riches from the new land while depriving their enemies of the same. Dutch claims date from 1609, when Henry Hudson, exploring in their name, sailed to what the Dutch called New Amsterdam. Dutch trappers were also known to have visited the Delaware Water Gap area shortly thereafter. Hans Christiansen and Adrian Block built an outpost on Manhattan Island in 1613, only to be driven out by the English, who also claimed it. Around the same time, Cornelius May sailed around the Delaware Bay and into New Jersey. The Dutch government chartered the West India Company in 1621, which sent Dutchmen to build a colony at Fort Nassau, on the east side of the Delaware River across from the future site of Philadelphia. By 1629, Samuel Bloomaert and Samuel Godyn became the first landowners in the lower Delaware Bay, while a different group of Dutch settlers sailed to Lewes Creek and established Swanendael in 1631; however, the community was massacred in 1632. A supply ship discovered the tragedy and left a small group to rebuild.[6]

In 1630, Sweden, emboldened by its military success in Europe, established the New Sweden Company to extend its influence to America. Swedish settlers led by Peter Minuit landed in the Delaware Bay in 1638, bought land from the Natives, and built Fort Christiana (near today's Wilmington) in the New Sweden colony. When Minuit died, the Queen named Peter Ridder as governor in 1640, but when the colony failed to prosper, Ridder was succeeded by Johan Printz, a much more ambitious individual, who improved the colony's fortunes and expanded Swedish influence up the Delaware River to Tinicum Island (near Philadelphia), where a fort was built.

But the English contested each of the Swedish settlements, claiming title to everything north of their Virginia holdings. To rebuff the English advances, the Swedes allied with the Dutch, led by Peter Stuyvesant, and together they built additional forts north along the Delaware and Schuylkill Rivers. The alliance did not last long, however, as Stuyvesant turned on the Swedes and attacked them. Following a short, bloodless campaign, Swedish General Johan Clauson Rising surrendered his forts to the Dutch in 1655. Though Rising departed that year, a number of Swedes and Finns, who had accompanied the Swedes, remained under Dutch rule to continue working the land.[7]

The English claims in America can be traced to their settlements at Jamestown, Virginia, in 1607 and the Plymouth colony in 1620 along with explorers, such as Captain John Smith, who traveled to the Delaware Bay as early as 1608. The Duke of York claimed the area that would become Pennsylvania and Delaware around 1664, eventually turning them over to King Charles II. Military actions were necessary, however, especially against the Dutch and the French, before the English actually controlled the claimed lands. New Amsterdam first fell to the English in 1664 to become New York, but the area changed hands several times, as the Anglo-Dutch wars dragged on until 1674, when the Treaty of Westminster settled the conflict, leaving all of New Netherlands, including New Amstel, the southernmost Dutch outpost, under English rule.

Extending their influence southward from Canada, the French built a series of forts along Lake Erie and farther inland, including Fort Duquesne, at the confluence of the Allegheny and Monongahela Rivers in 1754. During the French and Indian War, the French, faced with losing the garrison to the English, burned it down in 1758. By 1760, the English had constructed Fort Pitt on the same site, which thus became the first English settlement in western Pennsylvania.[8]

WILLIAM PENN AND THE FOUNDING OF PENNSYLVANIA

Admiral William Penn had a distinguished naval career, served in Parliament, and acquired substantial wealth and a number of powerful friends, including King Charles II, who was in debt to the admiral for a considerable sum. As executor and heir to the estate when the admiral died in 1670, his eldest son, William, should have easily transitioned into his father's businesses and circle of friends. However, William Jr. joined the Society of Friends, having been converted during his short time studying at Oxford. Like other Quakers, Penn was persecuted for his beliefs, spending time in prison. Following his father's death, William became a Quaker missionary, traveled to the Netherlands and Germany, and wrote *The Great Case of Liberty and Conscience*, in which he argued for tolerance of all religious beliefs.

Determined to create a utopian community in the New World founded on religious freedom, Penn approached King Charles II in 1680 for the rights to the land west of the Delaware River as payment of the debt owed to his father. The land's monetary value would also aid Penn's precarious financial situation, for he had accumulated substantial debt. His petition was reviewed by the Privy Council, and following negotiations with the Duke of York and Lord Baltimore, whose land claims were affected by Penn's request, Penn's proprietary charter was officially proclaimed on April 2, 1681. The charter made Penn the sole proprietor with full governing powers but with some rights retained by the Crown.

Before setting off for his utopia, Penn worked on recruiting people of all faiths, especially Quakers, from Germany, England, Ireland, and Wales who sought religious freedom to immigrate to Penn's Woods. Rhineland Germans were particularly eager to acquire land and economic freedom as well as religious liberty.[9] They were later joined by Scots-Irish and French Huguenots. Penn also concluded an agreement with the Duke of York to take possession of the Lower Counties—New Castle, Kent, and Suffolk, which later would become Delaware—outlined plans for the commonwealth's government, and wrote *The Conditions and Concessions*, which outlined his intentions for how the colony should be settled, its relations with the Natives, and much more.[10]

During this time, Penn also sent his cousin, William Markham, to Pennsylvania. Arriving in June 1681, Markham, under orders from Penn, formed a temporary governing council and local courts that would be replaced by the constitution Penn was preparing. Sailing on the *Welcome*, Penn finally arrived at New Castle on October 27, 1682, and promptly proclaimed his First Frame (Constitution) of Government. It contained a governor, who presided over a seventy-two-member council that performed the three major functions of government: legislative, executive, and judicial. There was also a two-hundred-member assembly that could accede to or reject bills proposed by council. Voting for council and assembly members was restricted to freemen, defined as men who owned fifty acres or possessed property worth fifty pounds. The Frame essentially ensured Penn control over his colony by retaining the landowners' support and by recruiting candidates for office. From his first headquarters in Upland (near what is now Chester, Pennsylvania), he oversaw the elections of the first council and assembly. During its first meeting in December 1682, the council and assembly passed the Great Laws, which infused Quaker values into the commonwealth's legal system. They guaranteed protections for religious practice; eliminated oaths and the death penalty, except for murder and treason; ensured that jury trials were held for civil and criminal cases; and required that only Christians be eligible to hold public office.[11]

Penn quickly realized that his frame had a problem, namely the excessive size of both council and assembly. On April 2, 1683, he announced his Second Frame. This one had an eighteen-member council and a thirty-six-member assembly. Each of the three original counties, Philadelphia, Bucks, and Chester, elected six members to the council and twelve members to the assembly. The proprietor also consented not to act in any public capacity without the approval of the council, a significant concession of power to council.[12]

Penn also negotiated a treaty with Delaware chief Tamanend in the winter of 1682 at Shackamaxon and signed it under the Treaty Elm, often depicted in romanticized paintings, to ensure continued peaceful relations with the tribe. Tamanend reportedly said, "We will live in peace with Onas [Penn] and his children for as long as the sun and moon shall endure."[13]

Penn returned to England in 1684 to thwart Lord Baltimore's claims to the Lower Colonies, which Penn succeeded in holding by order of King James II in 1685. But Penn's close ties to James II proved costly. The Glorious Revolution replaced Catholic King James with Protestants King William and Queen Mary. In 1688, King William had Penn charged with treason. Penn was acquitted but quickly rearrested on the same charge. Unable to return to Pennsylvania, Penn selected John Blackwell as deputy governor, but this appointment did not sit well with the commonwealth's residents, especially its Quakers, and they resisted any attempt by Blackwell to exercise his authority. Frustrated, Blackwell submitted his resignation to Penn in April 1689.

Charged yet a third time with treason by King William, Penn was once again prevented from traveling to Pennsylvania. To make matters worse, the King also ordered that Pennsylvania become part of New York because Pennsylvania's assembly refused to defend itself or pay for its defense as England warred with France. When the charge was dropped, Penn appealed to Queen Mary for his reinstatement as Pennsylvania's proprietor, which she granted in August 1694, once he promised to take financial responsibility for the colony's defense.

During Penn's absence, the commonwealth fell into disarray. The Lower Counties resisted Pennsylvania's effort to rule them but were unsuccessful in achieving independence. The Pennsylvania Assembly named Thomas Lloyd, who led the resistance against Blackwell, to be Pennsylvania's deputy governor. But New York governor Benjamin Fletcher had appointed William Markham to serve as *his* deputy in Pennsylvania in 1692 after King William placed the colony under Fletcher's jurisdiction. The political unrest also upset the Quaker community. In 1690, George Keith, a reactionary who formed the Christian Quaker faction, publicly called for Quakers to remove themselves from politics, causing a schism that left the Society of Friends in turmoil.[14]

The colony's growing political divisions became obvious in 1696 with the appearance of a Third Frame of Government, also known as Markham's Frame. Drafted by the assembly and accepted by Markham, who remained as deputy with Penn's endorsement after Penn was restored as proprietor, the frame created a bicameral legislature. The council had two members from each county, while the assembly had four from each. Members of both chambers were elected by freemen to a one-year term, and both chambers could propose legislation; however, only the council held executive and judicial authority.[15]

Because the assembly passed the frame as a piece of legislation, its legitimacy as a proper frame was challenged by some Quakers, who refused to accept it; they held their own elections under the Second Frame's rules. To further complicate matters, Penn refused to endorse the Third Frame, declaring that he alone had the power to alter the commonwealth's government. When Penn returned in 1699, he announced new elections to be held under the 1683 (Second) Frame, but the assembly resisted. Penn then declared that he would govern the colony without a frame, which he did from June 7, 1700, to October 26, 1701.

During this period, Penn managed to restore some order. He dismissed Markham as deputy and removed David Lloyd as the commonwealth's attorney general. He settled boundary issues with neighboring colonies, settled land disputes, and provided for the colony's defense, among many other things. Notably, he appointed a nine-member advisory council, composed of his supporters, wealthy, urban Quakers, with John Logan as its chair. Logan became leader of the Proprietary faction, which backed Penn, arguing that the proprietor was the foundation of power. In opposition was the Popular faction. Led by David Lloyd and composed of poor, rural Quakers, they believed that the assembly reflected the people's will and therefore was the true source of the government's legitimacy. And for a short time, starting in the early eighteenth century, a third faction emerged made up of non-Quakers and called the Churchmen. They were Anglicans and loyalists to the Crown, headed by Judge Robert Quary, who sought to have Penn's charter revoked so Pennsylvania could become a royal colony. A fourth potential faction remained unengaged: the colony's German population. As their numbers increased, especially later in the eighteenth century, their distinctive customs and language drew the attention of the other factions' leaders, who feared that the Germans might complicate an already contentious political scene should they choose to participate. Some notables, including Franklin, also worried that Germans might come to dominate the population.[16] As forerunners of traditional American parties, the factions that would emerge in the 1790s wrestled over the colony's control, and as they did so, Penn's dream of a utopian community dissolved.[17]

With the Third Frame discredited, the assembly drafted the Fourth Frame, the Charter of Privileges, which Penn reluctantly signed in 1701 and which remained in effect until the Revolution. The Frame granted many more powers to the voters, but the franchise remained restricted to freemen, while continuing to extend religious freedom to most people; Jews and Muslims were denied this freedom and others.[18] Full legislative authority was vested in a unicameral assembly composed of four members elected annually from every county that could propose legislation and set its own rules, but the proprietor or his governor retained the right to veto legislation. The governor became an independent executive with the sole authority to name members to the council, which transitioned into his advisory body. Both the proprietor and the Crown were expressly recognized as holding the power to veto laws passed by the assembly. There was also a state judicial branch with appointed judges; magistrates and other minor court officers were elected by their respective county's voters. Finally, the commonwealth's three "lower counties," which eventually became Delaware, were permitted their own legislature.[19]

THE CONSTITUTION OF 1776

Events between 1701 and 1776, notably the French and Indian War (1753–63), Pontiac's War (1763), and the King's Proclamation of 1763, which banned colonial settlements west of the Alleghenies and placed all trade with the Natives under the Crown's control, shuffled and divided earlier political alliances and the competing factions' names and membership. The Gentlemen's faction, with William Allen as its leader, replaced the Proprietary faction, drawing its constituents from wealthy, urban Anglicans and Scots-Irish Presbyterians on the frontier. Continuing to support the proprietor's interests, it also advocated for creating new counties for the western settlers and for the colonial government paying for the defense of those settlements against both the French and Native peoples.[20]

Benjamin Franklin emerged as the head of the Country faction, which supplanted the Popular faction. Reflecting Quaker values, it opposed the Penn family's financial interests as well as military expenditures, any use of force against the Natives, and the addition of new counties. Eventually, the question of separation from or loyalty to England became the ultimate issue dividing the citizens, with Franklin and the County faction supporting independence and Allen and many Gentlemen remaining faithful to the Crown.[21]

The pronouncement of the Declaration of Independence necessitated that Pennsylvanians draft their first constitution in the spring of 1776. Considered by many historians to be the most radical state constitution in the new United States, it was written by the new Radical faction, which supported the war and favored strong, independent states with a government directly controlled by the people. Translating their views into a government, they enlarged the electorate by adding all free, male taxpayers, regardless of race, and their sons over the age of twenty-one who had lived in the state for one year.[22] It retained a unicameral legislature that met once each year and whose members were elected annually. Lawmakers could serve four out of every seven years and were required to take an oath that they believed in God. The assembly had extensive powers, including appointing the state treasurer. And as in the frames that preceded it, a Declaration of Rights was included.[23]

In place of a strong, single executive, the convention invented a twelve-member Executive Council, with one member from each county and the city of Philadelphia and one of its members elected as president on an annual basis by a vote of the council *and* the assembly. The council was authorized to implement state laws and to grant and appoint state judges and administrators, except the treasurer, but it was denied veto power over acts of the assembly. Command of the state militia was assigned to the council president.[24]

The constitution's anomaly was a Council of Censors composed of twenty-four members, two from each of the eleven counties and Philadelphia. Its authority was limited to monitoring the behavior and performance of state officials and to identifying violations of the constitution. With a two-thirds vote it could call for a convention to consider amendments to the constitution.[25]

Judges were appointed for seven years, but only Supreme Court justices were eligible for reappointment. Twelve trial courts were established, one for each county and Philadelphia, as well as common pleas, orphans, and other specialized courts. Judges could be removed at any time by the assembly for misbehavior.[26]

THE CONSTITUTION OF 1790

Though most popular with the Radicals, who by 1788 had become the Constitutionalists, the 1776 constitution quickly lost favor with a majority of the people, but it was most vocally opposed by a faction variously known as the Moderates, Anticonstitutionalists, and Republicans. Despite holding majorities in the assembly, the Radicals were unable to govern effectively, especially in matters involving the state's economy, taxation, and the war. Tensions mounted between the Radicals, who controlled the state militia, and the Continental Army's commanders. Following a deadly riot instigated by the Radicals in Philadelphia in October 1779 over the authority of General Benedict Arnold, the public's trust in the Radicals dissipated. The Republicans, who had warned of mob rule under the Radicals, slowly gained seats in the assembly until they attained a majority; John Dickinson's election as commonwealth president marked the end of Radical rule. The Radicals must be remembered, however, for their greatest achievement: on March 1, 1780, a majority of the assembly, composed of both Radicals and Republicans, voted to abolish slavery.[27]

The debate over the ratification of the US Constitution produced two new national factions, the Federalists, who supported ratification, and the Anti-Federalists, who opposed it. Both had followers in Pennsylvania. The commonwealth's Federalists, formerly the Moderates/Republicans, called for a meeting to write a new state constitution, which was held in Philadelphia in November 1789 and dominated by Federalists. The constitution, ratified in 1790, created a General Assembly that was modeled on the US Congress. The House had sixty to one hundred members elected annually, while the Senate had eighteen members elected to four-year terms, approximately one-quarter of whom were elected every year. Seats were reapportioned every seven years among the counties based on the number of taxpaying citizens. The Assembly retained its supreme legislative authority and continued to appoint the state treasurer.[28]

The Executive Council and Council of Censors were replaced by a unitary executive: a popularly elected governor with a three-year term, who could serve only nine out of every twelve years. The governor had the authority to appoint all cabinet members except the treasurer (who was named by the assembly), other supervisory officers, all state judges, and other court officers without senatorial confirmation; call special sessions of the assembly; grant pardons and reprieves; deliver a state of the state message; and veto legislation, though the veto was subject to an override by a two-thirds vote of both houses of the assembly.[29]

The state was divided into judicial circuits, each consisting of three to six counties, for appeals from trial courts. Judges could be removed by impeachment. It also had a bill of rights; however, property ownership remained a voting qualification, with the residency requirement increased from one to two years.[30]

The 1790 constitution was a victory for the Federalists and their values, but more importantly, it ensured Pennsylvania's place within a properly functioning federal system. During the years it was in effect, the state's population grew and its economy expanded, though its political divisions widened.

THE CONSTITUTION OF 1838

A national party realignment followed the 1800 presidential election; Jefferson's Democratic-Republicans displaced Adams's Federalists as the nation's majority party. Pennsylvania experienced political upheaval as well. The Democratic-Republicans won a majority in the assembly and the governorship in 1799 and thereafter dominated state governments and most county governments through the 1830s and beyond, leaving the Federalists only marginally competitive until they vanished in the 1820s.

When a single party dominates for a long period, it eventually experiences fractures. In Pennsylvania, divisions appeared after Simon Snyder's gubernatorial win in 1808. His followers, referred to as "New School" Democrats, favored drafting a new constitution in order to limit the governor's and state courts' powers, spending more money on infrastructure projects, adding more protective national tariffs, and later supporting Andrew Jackson for US president. The "Old School" Democrats, led by Michael Leib and William Duane, disagreed with Snyder's people on every point except tariffs.

By 1824, more fissures were occurring within the Democratic-Republican Party. The Family faction, so named because its two leaders, George Dallas of Philadelphia and William Wilkins of Pittsburgh, were related by marriage, succeeded the Old School Democrats. Concurrently, Old School Democrats and the Federalist Party's remnants merged, becoming the Amalgamation Party. The Family Party enjoyed more statewide electoral successes than the Amalgamation Party between 1824 and 1838; however, Jackson's eight years in the White House contributed to the complete splintering of Jefferson's former party in the state and nation. The Family Party became a branch of Jackson's new Democratic Party, while all those who opposed him—the Amalgams, National Republicans, and Anti-Masons[31]—formed the Anti-Jackson Party, which itself divided after 1832 into the Whigs and the Anti-Masons. Ultimately, Jackson's Democrats dominated the Keystone State's government until 1860.

In 1825, the voters approved a referendum to replace the 1790 constitution, but no action was taken until 1837, when a convention was held. Elected delegates were evenly split among the Democratic, Whig, and Anti-Mason Parties. After deliberating for seven months, the gathering produced a constitution that was ratified by the voters in 1838.

The Democrats' main objective during the convention, consistent with the party's orthodoxy, was to reduce the governor's extensive authority. His power to appoint judges and cabinet secretaries was curtailed by requiring Senate confirmation, while county row officers, such as coroners, sheriffs, clerks, and recorders of deeds and wills, were removed from the governor's purview and made elective, thereby devolving authority to the local level. The governor's term remained three years, but an incumbent could serve only six out of every nine years. Other executive powers were retained.[32]

The legislature's powers were also slashed. The assembly was forbidden to grant divorces by act, grant new state bank charters (a particularly sensitive issue for the Jacksonians), renew existing charters without public notice, grant private corporate charters lasting more than twenty years, and delegate its power of eminent domain to other entities.[33]

The judiciary, a secondary Democratic target, saw judges' terms revised. Supreme Court justices were limited to fifteen years, the president judge's term in all counties was cut to ten years while all other judges' terms were shortened to five years. Justice of the peace was made an elected position with a five-year term.[34]

Suffrage rules were modified so that taxpaying citizens had to reside in the state for only one year to vote in state elections and ten days in their voting district for local offices. The previous constitution's ambiguous language on suffrage was removed and replaced with a clear statement that limited the vote to White citizens. Given the state's history of extending the franchise to all male taxpayers, including Blacks, this was a major step backwards.[35]

Provisions for a less cumbersome amendment process were added. A majority of both houses was required to vote on an amendment in two successive legislative sessions, accompanied by public advertising. An amendment then had to be placed before the voters in a referendum where a majority vote was required to adopt. Subsequently, the 1838 constitution was amended four times: in 1850 to permit the election of all judges; in 1857 to fix the House's size at one hundred, to change the method of electing its members from multimember to single-member districts, and to restrict the assembly's power to borrow money and create new counties; in 1864 to provide for absentee voting by Pennsylvanians serving in the Union army and a few more limitations on the assembly's authority; and in 1871 to make state treasurer an elected office.[36]

Economic and social forces were changing the commonwealth in the years after the Civil War. The GOP controlled the state almost continuously from 1861 through the 1940s. This stretch of one-party rule witnessed yet another party rupture, as Republicans split between the Stalwarts, or Regular Republicans, led by Simon Cameron, a wealthy businessman who was Lincoln's secretary of war, a US senator, and eventually the boss of the state's Republican Party machine, and the Liberals, who were first headed by Governor Andrew Gregg Curtin and later by Alexander McClure, a state senator. Cameron prevailed, as he was an astute politician and better able to direct patronage in the form of government jobs and contracts to his supporters to retain their votes.

Muckrakers' reporting fed public outrage over widespread corruption in both the executive and legislative branches, as Republicans used their power to advance the interests of their friends in the business community, particularly the coal, steel, railroad, and banking industries. By 1871, demand was so intense for constitutional reform that even John Geary, Cameron's handpicked governor, supported a constitutional convention. It convened in 1872, with its work ratified by the voters in 1873.[37]

Republicans held a majority of the convention's 133 elected delegates, but they crafted a constitution that responded to most of the criticisms directed at state government, particularly the legislature, while also allowing Cameron's machine to operate freely. The new document required that the General Assembly meet biennially rather than biannually, reducing the need for special sessions, where much of the alleged mischief occurred. The House was doubled in size to two hundred, while the Senate was increased from thirty-three to fifty. The reapportionment of seats, a sensitive issue for the state's growing urban centers, was set to follow the decennial US census, but limits were placed on the number of senators from cities. Philadelphia, for example, with one-fifth of the state's population, could have no more than one-eighth of the Senate's seats.

There were twenty-seven specific provisions that limited the legislature's powers and formalized its procedures. Among them were new requirements that all laws be passed as bills, that bills be considered in committee before a floor vote was taken, that there be three readings on three different days before a floor vote on a bill, and that appropriations bills have clearly stated purposes. One important substantive restriction was that any state tax must be *uniformly* applied, a provision that was continued in future constitutions, complicating efforts in the twentieth century to adopt a graduated income tax.

The executive branch was reorganized with the governor's term extended to four years but without possibility of reelection. An elected lieutenant governor was established, with a four-year term and no chance for reelection. The people were permitted to directly elect the secretary of the treasury, secretary of internal affairs, and auditor general, while the secretary of the commonwealth, secretary of public instruction, and the attorney general were converted to appointment by the governor. The governor's veto power was strengthened by requiring an override vote by two-thirds of all members of both houses rather than two-thirds of those members present and voting at the time. The governor was also given the line-item veto for appropriations bills, but the power to pardon was constrained with the creation of a pardon board. Finally, the governor was permitted to call special legislative sessions for narrowly defined subjects.

Judges for all courts were made elected positions, incorporating an amendment to the 1838 constitution. The Supreme Court's size was increased from five to seven justices and their tenure extended to twenty-one years but with no possibility for reelection. The court's original jurisdiction was narrowed significantly so that most of its cases would be heard on appeal.

Reformers insisted that autonomy for local communities be secured by constitutional language, so a new, lengthy section was included to protect local governments from state interference. As local governments' legal status had heretofore not been recognized in any previous constitution, the 1873 document specifically enumerated traditional county officers such as clerk of court and sheriff while adding new ones such as county commissioner, treasurer, and auditor.

Perhaps most significantly, given public protests over the failure to grant ballot access to free Black men during the 1837 convention, the franchise was extended to Black men, and property and wealth requirements were removed for all men; women remained without the vote.

The 1873 constitution served the state reasonably well through World War II, but thereafter its antiquated elements were so evident that it required several amendments; the most important, adopted in 1959, required the legislature to meet annually to keep pace with the state's growing economy and diversifying society, but it also limited its ability to pass major laws, except in even-numbered years.[38]

THE CONSTITUTION OF 1968

The Quaker State prospered in the post–World War II years, particularly under Republican governor William Scranton (1963–1967); the economy boomed and the unemployment rate fell below 3 percent. The healthy economy removed it as an issue during the 1966 gubernatorial election, permitting Republican candidate Raymond Shafer to center his campaign on reforming the state's constitution. Once again party divisions, this time among the Democrats, helped Shafer's cause. The Democratic Party endorsed state senator Robert P. Casey Sr., but he was defeated in the primary by businessman Milton Shapp. Shafer easily won the election. In March 1967, Shafer proposed a limited constitutional convention—that is, a convention whose scope of work would be restricted to specific articles of the 1873 document. The idea, which received endorsements from popular governors George Leader (D) and William Scranton and US senators Hugh Scott (R) and Joseph Clark (D), was approved by the people in a referendum on May 16, 1967.

Officers for the 1967–68 convention included future governors Republican Raymond Broderick and Democrat Robert P. Casey Sr., Republican Party leader Frank A. Orban, and famed novelist James Michener. After months of meetings, studies, and deliberations, the convention produced seven proposals to place before the voters.

The first and second proposals centered on the General Assembly. The Senate's size remained at 50, but the House's number was increased to 203. The Assembly's reapportionment would follow the decennial US Census and be conducted by a Reapportionment Commission composed of five members: the House and Senate's majority and minority leaders, with the fifth member and chairperson selected by the four.

The third and fourth proposals addressed state finances. The commonwealth's untenable debt situation in the mid- to late 1960s precipitated calls to reform Pennsylvania's finances and provide limits on borrowing linked to tax revenues. Included as well were provisions for auditing the state's finances and a requirement for a balanced budget.[39]

Proposal 5 dealt with taxation. Recommendations included granting state and local tax exemptions for certain property classes such as public utilities, but "in lieu of local taxation, a portion of the gross receipts tax imposed by the state . . . will be allocated to local governments on a fair and equitable basis"; permitting the General Assembly to allow local taxing authorities to extend tax exemptions—for example, the real estate tax—to needy citizens, but only if the local governments were reimbursed by the state for any losses suffered from such exemptions; and allowing the General Assembly to "provide for exemptions or special taxing provisions to be applicable for a limited period of time, generally at the option of local taxing authorities, to encourage rehabilitation of deteriorating areas, and promoting industrial and housing development."[40] The last proposal's adoption led to the creation of Keystone Opportunity Zones and other such tax-forgiveness programs intended to spur development in economically struggling communities or within cities.

Proposal 6 addressed issues related to local governments by granting to all forms of county and municipal governments the right to adopt a home rule charter. (See chapter 9 for details.) Some reforms were also made to county government offices such as county treasurer, county coroner, and county surveyor. Other provisions allowed local governments to enter into cooperative agreements, such as councils of government (COGs), for the delivery of common services, and for annexation of and consolidation with other willing local municipalities. Debt limits were placed on local governments, but the right of public authorities to finance municipal projects using issuing bonds was preserved.[41]

The convention's final proposal addressed the judiciary. Changes were made to court administration, structure, and financing, specifically creating a unified court system, centrally administered and financed by the state, rather than continuing to have counties pay for their courts. The Pennsylvania Supreme Court was assigned responsibility for administering the new unified judicial system.[42]

The amendments were ratified by popular vote in 1968, and in 1972 the legislature declared the amended 1873 constitution to be the commonwealth's constitution of 1968. The constitution has been amended forty-eight times since 1968. Between 1971 and 2003, article I, sections 6, 9, 10, and 14 were amended a total of seven times to expand the rights of the accused to align with US Supreme Court decisions. Additionally, in 1971 Pennsylvanians added section 27 to article I, which guaranteed "the right to clean air, pure water, and to the preservation of the natural, scenic, historic and esthetic values of the environment." Attorney general was made an elected office by amendment to article IV, section 4.1 in 1978, with the amendment taking effect in 1980. The last three were approved in May 2021: one limited the governor's power to declare an emergency, another authorized the legislature to extend or terminate a gubernatorial emergency declaration by simple resolution, and a third prohibited the denial or abridgment of a person's rights because of the person's race or ethnicity.[43]

CONCLUSION

Unlike many states that choose to retain their founding documents for hundreds of years and amend them when necessary, Pennsylvanians have disposed of frames and constitutions with some regularity (an average of once every thirty-eight years), as well as amending them with some frequency. Such treatment of the state's basic law may appear insensitive and perhaps disrespectful. We believe instead that it demonstrates Pennsylvanians' willingness to identify and correct problems in order to ensure that their government accurately reflects their needs and desires. In the coming chapters, we explain and analyze the major elements of the 1968 constitution as well as the components of the state's political system, its parties, is interest groups, and the media that contribute to its proper functioning.

NOTES

1. Richter, "First Pennsylvanians"; Klein and Hoogenboom, History of Pennsylvania, chap. 1; Witthoft, Indian Prehistory.
2. Richter, "First Pennsylvanians"; Grumet, Historic Contact.
3. Wallace, Indians in Pennsylvania; Sipe, Indian Chiefs.
4. See Grinde and Johansen, "American Societies"; Richter, Ordeal of the Longhouse; Tooker, "United States Constitution"; Tooker, "Rejoinder to Johansen."
5. See Richter, "First Pennsylvanians."
6. See Klepp, "Encounter and Experiment"; Weslager, New Sweden on the Delaware.
7. See Acrelius, History of New Sweden.
8. See Klepp, "Encounter and Experiment."
9. The authors are indebted to Diane Wenger, Emeritus Professor of History, Wilkes University, for this insight. Additionally, German-speaking people accounted for as much as one-third to three-fifths of the colony's non-Native European population by 1776.

10. See Bronner, *William Penn's Holy Experiment*; Illick, *Colonial Pennsylvania*.
11. See Illick, *Colonial Pennsylvania*.
12. See Miller and Pencak, *Pennsylvania*, 16–35.
13. See Sharpless, *Quaker Experiment in Government*.
14. See Shepherd, *History of Proprietary Government in Pennsylvania*.
15. Ibid.
16. See Splitter, "Germans in Pennsylvania Politics"; Tully, "Englishmen and Germans"; Wenger, "Pennsylvania German Communities."
17. See Sharpless, *Quaker Experiment in Government*.
18. See Morais, *Jews of Philadelphia*; Whiteman, *History of the Jews of Philadelphia*.
19. Miller and Pencak, *Pennsylvania*, 66–67.
20. It should be noted that upon Penn's death in 1718, the proprietorship was bequeathed to his male children. However, Hannah Callowhill Penn, Penn's wife, quietly acted as proprietor after her husband suffered several strokes between 1712 and 1718, and then openly as proprietor while serving as the guardian for her minor sons until her death in 1726.
21. See Hutson, *Pennsylvania Politics*.
22. By 1780, Blacks accounted for approximately 5 percent of the state's population, most of whom lived in Philadelphia. There were also about six thousand slaves; however, in 1780 the state passed America's first abolition law. See Turner, *Negro in Pennsylvania*; Brown, *Negro in Pennsylvania History*; Williams, "Regimentation of Blacks."
23. Branning, *Pennsylvania Constitutional Development*, 14–15.
24. Ibid., 15.
25. Ibid., 15–16.
26. Ibid., 15.
27. Klein and Hoogenboom, *History of Pennsylvania*, 109–11.
28. Branning, *Pennsylvania Constitutional Development*, 19–20.
29. Ibid., 18–19.
30. Ibid., 20.
31. The Masons were a fraternal organization whose wealthy members held high governmental positions as well as owning large businesses. The Anti-Masons believed Masons to be America's aristocracy, secretly controlling everything in the country, and they sought to expose them and return control to the people.
32. Branning, *Pennsylvania Constitutional Development*, 29–30.
33. Ibid., 30.
34. Ibid.
35. Ibid., 26. See also Smith, "End of Black Voting Rights in Pennsylvania"; Nash, *Forging Freedom*.
36. Branning, *Pennsylvania Constitutional Development*, 31–33.
37. See Klein and Hoogenboom, *History of Pennsylvania*; Branning, *Pennsylvania Constitutional Development*, chap. 4.
38. Klein and Hoogenboom, *History of Pennsylvania*, 357–60.
39. Pennsylvania Constitutional Convention, *Constitutional Proposals Adopted by the Convention*, 8–15.
40. Ibid., 16–17.
41. Ibid., 19–25.
42. Ibid., 26–50.
43. The legislature placed the question to the voters on November 7, 2017, to amend article VIII, section 2(b)(vi) of the Pennsylvania Constitution, which permitted the legislature to allow taxing authorities to exempt some of a home's assessed value used to determine real estate taxes. Taxing authorities like school districts that used the exemption effectively lowered their constituents' property taxes.

BIBLIOGRAPHY

Acrelius, Israel. *A History of New Sweden*. Philadelphia: Historical Society of Pennsylvania, 1876.

Arnold, Andrew B. *Fueling the Gilded Age: Railroads, Miners, and Disorder in Pennsylvania Coal Country*. New York: New York University Press, 2014.

Baldino, Thomas J. "Vare Brothers Machine." In *Political Parties and Elections in the United States: An Encyclopedia*, edited by Sandy Maisel, 1171. New York: Garland, 1991.

Barry, John M. *The Great Influenza: The Story of the Deadliest Pandemic in History*. New York: Penguin Books, 2018.

Beers, Paul B. *Pennsylvania Politics, Today and Yesterday: The Tolerable Accommodation*. University Park: Pennsylvania State University Press, 1980.

Branning, Rosalind L. *Pennsylvania Constitutional Development*. Pittsburgh: University of Pittsburgh Press, 1960.

Bronner, Edwin B. *William Penn's "Holy Experiment": The Founding of Pennsylvania, 1681–1701*. New York: Columbia University Press, 1962.

Brown, Ira V. *The Negro in Pennsylvania History*. Philadelphia: Pennsylvania Historical Society, 1970.

Churella, Albert J. *The Pennsylvania Railroad*. Vol. 1, *Building an Empire, 1846–1917*. Philadelphia: University of Pennsylvania Press, 2013.

DiGaetano, Alan. "Urban Political Reform: Did It Kill the Machines?" *Journal of Urban History* 18, no. 1 (1991): 37–67.

Fineman, Herbert. "Looking Back on the Legislative Modernization Movement in Pennsylvania: Remarks of Herbert Fineman, Former Speaker of the Pennsylvania House of Representatives, Given at the Annual Meeting of the Pennsylvania Political Science Association, April 4, 2003." Introduction and commentary by Michael E. Cassidy. *Commonwealth* 12, no. 5 (2003): 87–110.

Grinde, Donald, Jr., and Bruce Johansen. *Exemplar of Liberty: Native Americans and the Evolution of Democracy*. Los Angeles: American Indian Study Center, University of California, 1991.

Grumet, Robert S. *Historic Contact: Indian People and Colonists in Today's Northeastern United States in the Sixteenth Through Eighteenth Centuries*. Norman: University of Oklahoma Press, 1995.

Hoffecker, Carol E., Richard Waldron, Lorraine E. Williams, and Barbara E. Benson, eds. *New Sweden in America*. Newark: University of Delaware Press, 1995.

Hutson, James H. *Pennsylvania Politics, 1746–1770: The Movement for Royal Government and Its Consequences*. Princeton: Princeton University Press, 1972.

Illick, Joseph E. *Colonial Pennsylvania: A History*. New York: Charles Scribner's Sons, 1976.

———. *William Penn, the Politician*. Ithaca: Cornell University Press, 1965.

Johansen, Bruce. "American Societies and the Evolution of Democracy in America, 1600–1800." *Ethnohistory* 37 (1990): 279–90.

Johnson, Amandus. *The Swedish Settlements in the Delaware Valley, 1638–1664*. Philadelphia: Swedish Colonial Society, 1911.

Klein, Philip S., and Ari Hoogenboom. *A History of Pennsylvania*. 2nd and enlarged ed. University

Park: Pennsylvania State University Press, 1980.

Klepp, Susan E. "Encounter and Experiment: The Colonial Period." In Miller and Pencak, *Pennsylvania*, 47–100.

Licht, Walter. "Civil Wars: 1850–1900." In Miller and Pencak, *Pennsylvania*, 203–56.

McCaffery, Peter. *When Bosses Ruled Philadelphia: The Emergence of the Republican Machine, 1867–1933*. University Park: Pennsylvania State University Press, 1993.

McLarnon, John M., and G. Terry Madonna, "Dilworth, Clark, and Reform in Philadelphia, 1947–1962." *Pennsylvania Legacies* 11, no. 2 (2011): 24–31.

McLaughlin, Joseph P., Jr. "The Pennsylvania General Assembly Before and After the 1968 Legislative Modernization Commission: A Brief History." Lecture, Members' Symposium, Pennsylvania General Assembly. Harrisburg, PA, February 28, 2011.

———. *The Pennsylvania General Assembly Before and After the 1968 Legislative Modernization Commission: The Evolution of an Institution*. Vol. 1 of *The Temple Papers on the Pennsylvania General Assembly*. Philadelphia: Temple University, 2012.

———. "Remembering Herbert Fineman: Speaker." Eulogy, August 16, 2016.

———. "Testimony on House Bill 260, Providing for a Unicameral Legislature." Public Hearing, House Democratic Policy Committee, Philadelphia Convention Center, April 6, 2010.

———. "Thoughts on Political Reform in Pennsylvania." Paper presented at the Pennsylvania Political Science Association meeting, Harrisburg, March 26, 2010.

———. "Yo, Ed! It's Groundhog Day!" Lecture delivered to University of Pennsylvania Urban Studies Class, January 2013.

Miller, Randall M., and William Pencak, eds. *Pennsylvania: A History of the Commonwealth*. University Park: Pennsylvania State University Press, 2002.

Morais, Henry S. *The Jews of Philadelphia: Their History from Earliest Settlement to Present Time*. Ithaca: Cornell University Press, 2009.

Nash, Gary B. *Forging Freedom: The Formation of Philadelphia's Black Community, 1720–1840*. Cambridge, MA: Harvard University Press, 1988.

Olien, Roger M., and Diana Davids Olien. *Oil and Ideology: The Cultural Creation of the American*

Petroleum Industry. Chapel Hill: University of North Carolina Press, 2000.

Peckham, Howard H. *Pontiac and the Indian Uprising*. Detroit: Wayne State University Press, 1947.

Pennsylvania Capitol Preservation Commission. "The History of Pennsylvania's Early Capitols." http://cpc.state.pa.us/history/the-history -of-pennsylvanias-early-capitols.cfm.

Pennsylvania Constitutional Convention. *Constitutional Proposals Adopted by the Convention*. Harrisburg: Commonwealth of Pennsylvania, 1968.

Pennsylvania Economy League of Greater Pittsburgh. "The Economic Impact of the Coal Industry in Pennsylvania." Report prepared for the Pennsylvania Coal Alliance, March 2014.

Pew Center for the States. *Pennsylvania*. http://www.pewcenteronthestates.org/states _rankings.aspx?abrv+PA.

"Railroads of Pennsylvania." Pennsylvania Historical and Museum Commission. http://www .phmc.state.pa.us/portal/communities /railroads/history.html.

Richter, Daniel K. "The First Pennsylvanians." In Miller and Pencak, *Pennsylvania*, 3–46.

———. *The Ordeal of the Longhouse: The Peoples of the Iroquois League in the Era of European Colonization*. Chapel Hill: University of North Carolina Press, 1992.

Sharpless, Isaac. *Political Leaders in Proprietary Pennsylvania*. New York: Hyperion, 1919.

———. *A Quaker Experiment in Government: A History of Quaker Government in Pennsylvania, 1682–1783*. Philadelphia: Ferris and Leach, 1902.

Shepherd, William R. *A History of Proprietary Government in Pennsylvania*. 1896.

Sipe, C. Hale. *The Indian Chiefs of Pennsylvania*. Butler, PA: Ziegler, 1927.

Skocpol, Theda, and Vanessa Williamson. *The Tea Party and the Remaking of Republican Conservatism*. Oxford: Oxford University Press, 2012.

Smith, Eric Ledell. "The End of Black Voting Rights in Pennsylvania: African Americans and the Pennsylvania Constitutional Convention of 1837–1838." *Pennsylvania History* 65, no. 3 (1998): 279–99.

Splitter, Wolfgang. "The Germans in Pennsylvania Politics, 1758–1790: A Quantitative Analysis."

Pennsylvania Magazine of History and Biography 122, no. 1/2 (1998): 39–76.

Steffens, Lincoln. *The Shame of the City*. New York: Compass Books, 2020.

Tooker, Elisabeth. "Rejoinder to Johansen." *Ethnohistory* 37 (1990): 279–90.

———. "The United States Constitution and the Iroquois League." *Ethnohistory* 35 (1988): 305–36.

Tully, Alan. "Englishmen and Germans: National-Group Contact in Colonial Pennsylvania, 1700–1755." *Pennsylvania History* 45, no. 3 (1978): 237–56.

Turner, Edward R. *The Negro in Pennsylvania: Slavery—Servitude—Freedom, 1639–1861*. Washington, DC: American Historical Association, 1911.

Wallace, Paul A. W. *Indians in Pennsylvania*. 2nd ed. Harrisburg: Pennsylvania Historical and Museum Commission, 1981.

Weber, Michael. *Don't Call Me Boss: David Leo Lawrence*. Pittsburgh: University of Pittsburgh Press, 1993.

Wenger, Diane, and Simon J. Bronner. "Communities and Identities: Nineteenth to the Twentieth Centuries." In *Pennsylvania Germans: An Interpretive Encyclopedia*, edited by Simon J. Bronner and Joshua R. Brown, 53–76. Baltimore: Johns Hopkins University Press, 2017.

Weslager, C. A. *New Sweden on the Delaware, 1638–1655*. Wilmington, DE: Middle Atlantic Press, 1988.

Whiteman, Maxwell, and Edwin Wolf. *The History of the Jews of Philadelphia from Colonial Times to the Age of Jackson*. Philadelphia: Jewish Publication Society, 1975.

Williams, Oscar R. "The Regimentation of Blacks on the Urban Frontier in Colonial Albany, New York City and Philadelphia." *Journal of African American History* 63, no. 4 (1978): 329–38.

Witthoft, John. *Indian Prehistory of Pennsylvania*. Harrisburg: Pennsylvania Museum and Historical Commission, 1965.

Woodard, Colin. *American Nations: A History of the Eleven Rival Regional Cultures of North America*. New York: Penguin Books, 2011.

CHAPTER 2

Pennsylvania's Political Culture and Political Geography

The Keystone State's contemporary political culture is not easily described or summarized, and it is a source of fascination and frustration for all who study it. It is the culmination of five centuries of immigrant peoples, each arriving with their own rich and diverse culture, as well as contributions from the state's Native peoples. The Swedes, Finns, Dutch, French, English, and Germans of the seventeenth century were joined later by Irish, Welsh, Scots, Italians, Greeks, and Poles. They settled across the state's forty-six thousand square miles of mountains, valleys, and plains, expanding Penn's original commonwealth westward. Though united as a political entity—first as a colony and then as a state—it was decades after statehood before a majority of its residents shared a distinctly Pennsylvania identity or character. Some observers of the Quaker State's historical development, however, have argued that even to this day, its residents don't appear to fully understand or appreciate their uniqueness as Pennsylvanians. When asked, "Where are you from?" Pennsylvanians are more likely to offer their hometown rather than their home state, as would most Texans, for example.[1] One could also infer confusion over the state's identity from listening to General Assembly debates, where finding common ground among lawmakers of the same party, let alone different parties, on noncontroversial bills can often be exceedingly frustrating.[2]

In this chapter, the state's natural and political geographies are presented first because Pennsylvania's topography affects almost every aspect of the state, from how people speak and the foods they enjoy to their political views and their economic and social relationships. Political culture is then introduced with a description of the concept and its usefulness as an approach to understanding Pennsylvania's politics and government.

POLITICAL GEOGRAPHY

Before embarking on any discussion of the state's political geography, one must first understand the commonwealth's physical geography, climate, and natural resources as they influence its economy, communication patterns, and population dispersion.

The commonwealth of Pennsylvania, one of four commonwealths in the United States along with Kentucky, Massachusetts, and Virginia, is situated in the Mid-Atlantic region and benefits from a temperate climate. Because of its strategic location among the thirteen original states, it was nicknamed the Keystone State, and it has certainly lived up to that moniker, particularly during the country's first 150 years, as a transportation, industrial, commercial, and banking hub. While advances in transportation and communication as well as America's westward expansion have reduced the strategic importance of Pennsylvania's physical location, a Brookings study described the state as "a demographic 'bridge' between midwestern states like Ohio and eastern states like New Jersey and Maryland—states that are more diverse both economically and demographically."[3] Since the 1960s, the Quaker State has frequently been clustered with upper midwestern states, New York, New Jersey, and New England as part of the Rust Belt, so called because the region experienced an exodus of large manufacturing enterprises to the South and overseas that left behind rusting factories. Pennsylvania's struggle to recover economically from the loss of heavy industries continues to shape the state's economy and politics in the twenty-first century.

Moving east to west, Pennsylvania's major rivers—the Delaware, Schuylkill, Susquehanna, Allegheny, Monongahela, and Ohio—guided the Native peoples and the earliest colonists in locating settlements. For example, the state's two largest cities, Philadelphia and Pittsburgh, were established on rivers: Philadelphia on the Delaware, which then expanded west to the Schuylkill, and Pittsburgh at the confluence of the Allegheny, Monongahela, and Ohio Rivers. Differences among rivers' navigability greatly affected industrial and commercial growth.

The Appalachian Mountains, which include the Blue Mountains on their eastern front and the Allegheny Mountains on the western front, run northeast to southwest through the state's midsection. People who settled in its many valleys, especially those distant from large towns and major cities, were isolated, developing their own customs and patterns of speech. One consequence is that Pennsylvania is considered "one of the most linguistically rich [states] in the country," with at least five and as many as eight distinct dialects within its borders.[4]

By dividing the state, the Appalachians directly affected its social and economic growth. As we were informed by Mr. Jon Delano, "Western Pennsylvania looks west rather than east." Pittsburgh and the cities west of the Alleghenies have more in common with the Midwest than the East Coast, because travel and commerce are easier headed west than east. The rivers flow west, and the distances to midwestern cities are shorter than to Philadelphia, New York, or Boston. "The moderate conservativism of western Pennsylvania is more like that of Ohio and the rest of the Midwest than it is to eastern Pennsylvania." Moreover, he added, "For years, Philly looked down on Pittsburgh. People didn't leave Philly to go to Pittsburgh, but people from the Midwest moved to Pittsburgh. East coast liberalism never made it across the mountains to Pittsburgh and western Pennsylvania."[5]

Pennsylvania's natural resources fueled America's industrial revolution, bringing jobs to many and great wealth to a few. The extraction processes, however, scarred the land, contaminated the water, and generally despoiled the environment. For example, coal literally powered American industry and heated its homes through the nineteenth and well into the twentieth centuries, with Pennsylvania leading the nation in coal production for decades.[6] Anthracite coal was plentiful in the state's northeastern region, while bituminous coal was abundant in the southwest. Yet for all the economic benefits that the nation and Pennsylvania derived from coal, the state suffered from acid water runoff from the mines, which polluted lakes, streams, and rivers and killed fish and plant life. Culm and waste coal removed during mining were piled high around the mines, blighting landscapes and polluting the air and water. Large-scale coal mining in the northeast effectively ended in 1959 with the Knox mine disaster,[7] and though coal mining continues in the southwest, the number of mines and quantity of coal removed are drastically lower in 2021 compared to their high points in 1920.[8]

Coal's importance as an energy and heating source was displaced by oil beginning in the 1860s, with Pennsylvania at the forefront of oil's development. Native Americans in western Pennsylvania were well aware of oil seeping naturally from the ground, but it was not until the 1850s that businessmen Samuel Kier and George Bissell founded the Pennsylvania Rock Oil Company and hired Edwin Drake to drill for oil in the vicinity of Oil Creek. On August 27, 1859, Drake struck oil near Titusville, and over the next twenty years the Rock Oil Company drilled wells that pumped millions of barrels a year, peaking at thirty-one million in 1891. With oil's discovery in California, Ohio, Texas, and Oklahoma, and the consolidation of most oil-drilling and refining companies under John D. Rockefeller's Standard Oil Trust in 1882, the state's prominent role in oil production was dramatically eclipsed, though wells continue to operate today, producing high-quality, light, sweet crude oil.[9]

Oil's discovery necessitated dramatic improvements in the state's transportation system: the construction of a railroad network and the supporting infrastructure to move the oil to refineries in the Midwest and along the East Coast. A series of short lines built by small companies in the 1860s and '70s eventually were consolidated into a few large companies such as the Pennsylvania Railroad.[10] By the turn of the twentieth century, railroading had become a major industry and a source of great wealth for people like Matthias Baldwin, Alexander Cassatt, Asa Packard, and John Edgar Thompson.[11]

Natural gas deposits in the Marcellus Shale formation in northeastern and southwestern Pennsylvania were long known to geologists, but it was not until 2008 that gas drilling began. The desire for a more environmentally friendly fossil fuel, coupled with natural gas's rising price on the world market, made the costly extraction process—hydraulic fracturing, or fracking—financially and technically feasible. Fracking requires few wells but demands large quantities of water at each well site. Combined with chemicals, the fluid is pumped into the ground at high pressure, breaking rock and allowing gas to escape. Since fracking began, Pennsylvania has been among the leading natural gas–producing states along with Texas and Louisiana.[12] The state's economy benefitted enormously as many businesses and homeowners switched from coal or oil to gas, thereby lowering their energy costs and generating fewer greenhouse gases. Proximity to the wells led Royal Dutch Shell to locate a large cracking plant in western Pennsylvania that transforms gas into plastic pellets, bringing hundreds of jobs to the region and new tax revenue.[13] But, like coal, Marcellus Shale gas has negatively impacted the environment, as fracking fluid has contaminated groundwater, escaped methane gas fouls the air at well sites, and gas pipeline construction disturbs farmlands and residential communities.[14]

A moderate climate and good soil have made agriculture a significant component of the state's economy. Forty-eight of the state's sixty-seven counties are classified as rural and are home to many farms. Raising livestock accounts for approximately 70 percent of agricultural production, while greenhouse nurseries, corn, hay, soybeans, and other vegetables, along with apples, grapes, peaches, and mushrooms, complete the agricultural economy.[15]

The Quaker State's industrial base has changed since 1950. While the state was once known for producing steel, textiles, railroad engines and cars, and oil and refining chemicals, many of these industries have relocated or closed, replaced by pharmaceutical and medical research facilities, technology companies, distribution centers, and white-collar businesses connected to the "knowledge economy," found mostly in and around Philadelphia, Pittsburgh, and State College. Though Pennsylvania was once among the nation's leading and innovative economies, more recently it "has gone flat, and the state has scaled back public investment in its most significant innovation resources," despite its major research universities and "capable technology-based economic development programs that operate across the state."[16]

In April 2020, the US Census Bureau estimated Pennsylvania's population at 13,002,700, making it the sixth largest in the country, but from 1820 to 1970 it ranked either second or third. With slow population growth between 1960 and 2021, Pennsylvania lost thirteen House seats, dropping from thirty to seventeen, thereby weakening the state's political influence in Washington.[17]

Approximately 82 percent of the commonwealth's inhabitants are White, 12 percent Black, 7.6 percent Latinx, 3.7 percent Asian, 2 percent more than two races, and 0.4 percent Native American. Women slightly outnumber men, 52 percent to 48 percent. More than 60 percent hold a high school degree or higher, while approximately 30 percent have a college degree or more. The state, however, suffers from a "brain drain," as young people, educated in the state's many colleges and universities, have departed for jobs elsewhere.[18]

The state's median age is 40.7, making its population the seventh oldest in the country. By age cohort, approximately 23 percent are under 20; 26 percent are between 20 and 39; 26 percent are between 40 and 59, and 26 percent are 60 and older. An aging, slowly growing population places greater demand on government for services while reducing tax revenue since Pennsylvania does not tax pensions, Social Security, or other retirement income. The state's oldest residents are not evenly distributed across its counties, with more senior residents in rural counties, especially in central and western Pennsylvania. The commonwealth's greatest population growth has been in the Philadelphia and Pittsburgh metropolitan areas, with Berks, Centre, Lehigh, and Northampton Counties trailing behind. Adams, Lancaster, and York Counties, which border Maryland, added people who commute to the Washington, DC, metropolitan area, comparable to the Pocono Mountain counties—Pike and Monroe—which experienced rapid population gains after 9/11 as people departed the New York City metropolitan region for safety and more affordable homes. Many commuted daily to New York City for years, but both counties' populations declined slightly between 2010 and 2020.

Turning to Pennsylvania's political geography, longtime observers often speak of the "T," a shorthand for how Republican and Democratic voters are dispersed across the state. Democrats are concentrated in Philadelphia, Allegheny, Erie, Luzerne, and Lackawanna Counties, while Republicans dominate the central swath and the entire northern tier. Though merely a shorthand, it visually depicts how citizens voted for much of the twentieth century. In interviews with six respected journalists, each agreed that the T remains, but they were quick to note that changing voter preferences since 1990 had distorted the T's appearance.[19] For example, in the southeast, voters in Delaware, Chester, Montgomery, and Bucks Counties began slowly trending Democratic in the 1990s after reliably voting Republican for local, state, and national candidates since 1860. From the New Deal, voters in the southwest corner were reliably Democratic until around 2000, when the counties ringing Allegheny gradually shifted Republican when voting for national and some statewide offices, even as Allegheny remained loyal to the Democrats. Centre County along with the Lehigh Valley counties have been trending Democratic since 2008, while during the same period Luzerne and Lackawanna Counties, once consistently Democratic, appear to be slowly shifting Republican. Voting patterns for local offices in all of these counties have not consistently mirrored those of state and national races, however, as old partisan loyalties die hard.

The T also captures the commonwealth's urban-rural division. The state's two largest cities are found in the southern corners. They once boasted heavy industries that employed unionized labor, which voted consistently Democratic since 1936 as part of FDR's New Deal coalition. More recently, they and their varied populations have been homes to the knowledge economy: educational institutions, tech companies, law firms, banking, and major research hospitals. The state's rural, predominantly White voters, employed in agriculture, small businesses, and tourism, remain steadfastly loyal to the party of Lincoln, holding fiscally and socially conservative opinions and viewing Philadelphia suspiciously.

"Philly" has always been the state's largest city and its major economic engine with a population of over 2 million in 1950 and approximately 1.5 million in 2020. But the city's

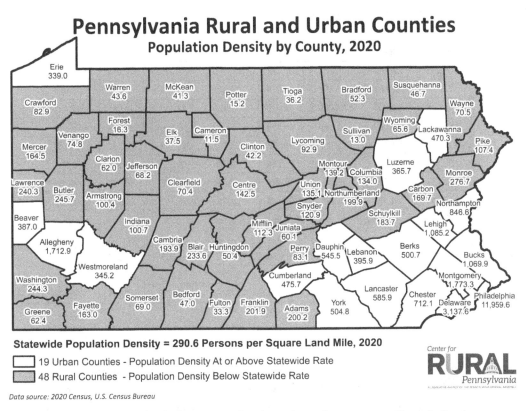

Pennsylvania Rural and Urban Counties
Population Density by County, 2020

Erie 339.0
Warren 43.6
McKean 41.3
Potter 15.2
Tioga 36.2
Bradford 52.3
Susquehanna 46.7
Wayne 70.5
Crawford 82.9
Forest 16.3
Elk 37.5
Cameron 11.5
Wyoming 65.6
Lackawanna 470.3
Pike 107.4
Venango 74.8
Clinton 42.2
Lycoming 92.9
Sullivan 13.0
Mercer 164.5
Clarion 62.0
Jefferson 68.2
Montour 139.2
Columbia 134.0
Luzerne 365.7
Monroe 276.7
Lawrence 240.3
Butler 245.7
Armstrong 100.4
Clearfield 70.4
Centre 142.5
Union 135.1
Northumberland 199.9
Snyder 120.9
Carbon 169.7
Northampton 846.6
Beaver 387.0
Indiana 100.7
Mifflin 112.3
Juniata 60.1
Schuylkill 183.7
Lehigh 1,085.2
Allegheny 1,712.9
Cambria 193.9
Blair 233.6
Huntingdon 50.4
Perry 83.1
Dauphin 545.5
Lebanon 395.9
Berks 500.7
Bucks 1,069.9
Westmoreland 345.2
Cumberland 475.7
Montgomery 1,773.3
Washington 244.3
Somerset 69.0
Bedford 47.0
Fulton 33.3
Franklin 201.9
Adams 200.2
York 504.8
Lancaster 585.9
Chester 712.1
Delaware 3,137.6
Philadelphia 11,959.6
Fayette 163.0
Greene 62.4

Statewide Population Density = 290.6 Persons per Square Land Mile, 2020

☐ 19 Urban Counties - Population Density At or Above Statewide Rate
▨ 48 Rural Counties - Population Density Below Statewide Rate

Data source: 2020 Census, U.S. Census Bureau

Center for
RURAL
Pennsylvania
A LEGISLATIVE AGENCY OF THE PENNSYLVANIA GENERAL ASSEMBLY

MAP 2.1 Pennsylvania rural and urban counties. Population density by county, 2020. Center for Rural Pennsylvania: A Legislative Agency of the Pennsylvania General Assembly.

needs and problems—poverty, crime, housing, and mass transit, for example—when presented in the General Assembly, have not always been received sympathetically by rural legislators.[20]

Pittsburgh, however, the state's second-largest city (population approximately 677,000 in 1950 and 300,000 in 2020), is perceived more favorably by Pennsylvania's rural residents, despite its racial diversity and knowledge-based economy.[21] Like Philadelphia, the Steel City and the rest of Allegheny County have been dependably Democratic since 1936, with unionized workers at its base. The bedroom counties surrounding Allegheny, namely Beaver, Butler, Armstrong, Westmoreland, and Washington, were also once steadfastly Democratic, but with fewer coal mines, steel factories, and other heavy industries, union membership declined and blue-collar Democrats slowly transitioned to voting for Republican candidates beginning in 2000, accelerating thereafter.

The state's other largest cities, except for Altoona, remain predictably Democratic bastions despite their declining populations. Altoona has a history of supporting Republican candidates notwithstanding its many unionized blue-collar workers. Nearby Johnstown, despite suffering severe job losses, remained Democratic even as Cambria County trended Republican.

Table 2.1 Population change for a sample of Pennsylvania cities, 1950–2020

City	1950	1960	1970	1980	1990	2000	2010	2020	% Change 1950–2020
Allentown	105,233	109,551	109,871	103,758	105,090	106,632	118,032	125,845	+1.0%
Altoona	76,844	69,084	63,115	57,078	51,881	49,523	46,320	43,963	-43%
Bethlehem	66,340	75,055	72,686	70,419	71,428	71,239	74,982	78,034	+1.0%
Chester	66,039	63,063	56,331	45,794	41,856	36,854	33,972	34,150	-48%
Erie	130,803	136,136	129,285	119,123	108,718	103,717	101,786	94,831	-27%
Harrisburg	89,544	78,870	68,061	53,264	52,376	48,950	49,528	50,099	-44%
Johnstown	63,232	53,636	42,476	35,496	28,134	23,906	20,978	18,411	-71%
Lancaster	63,744	59,674	57,690	54,725	55,551	56,348	59,322	58,039	-.09%
Philadelphia	2,071,605	1,971,239	1,988,165	1,722,894	1,616,326	1,517,550	1,526,006	1,603,797	-23%
Pittsburgh	676,806	597,745	558,066	454,971	395,895	334,563	305,704	299,434	-46%
Reading	109,230	98,061	87,643	78,686	78,380	81,207	88,082	95,112	-13%
Scranton	125,536	110,273	102,696	88,117	81,805	76,415	76,089	76,328	-39%
Wilkes-Barre	76,826	63,068	58,856	51,551	47,523	43,123	414,989	44,328	-42%

Source: Compiled by authors from U.S. Census data.

To explain the partisan differences across the different areas of the Quaker State that result in the T, one must understand how race, religion, education, age, and a region's political culture (discussed below) affect voters' party allegiance. Of the state's sixty-seven counties, the Republican Party holds a voter registration majority in forty-eight, all of them rural, defined as having a population density of fewer than 284 people per square mile. But

Table 2.2 Presidential votes for a sample of Pennsylvania cities

City	2008		2016		2020	
	D	R	D	R	D	R
Allentown	29,545	10,047	23,713	11,013	28,338	13,332
Altoona	3,835	3,701	2,688	5,189	7,210	12,516
Bethlehem	5,626	3,065	4,915	3,234	6,494	3,748
Chester	14,267	958	12,847	859	7,407	693
Erie	14,331	3,313	22,437	12,395	24,878	13,534
Harrisburg	18,092	2,584	15,575	2,265	15,897	2,712
Johnstown	4,987	2,925	3,246	3,167	3,501	3,424
Lancaster	16,912	5,169	15,888	4,729	18,288	5,791
Philadelphia	574,930	113,260	584,025	108,748	603,790	132,740
Pittsburgh	253,643	159,578	114,847	31,805	125,949	33,831
Reading	20,648	4,578	19,189	4,626	16,456	6,113
Scranton	20,931	10,121	17,692	8,245	19,943	11,419
Wilkes-Barre	9,571	4,881	6,488	5,632	8,164	5,806

Source: Compiled by the authors from state, county, and city election data sites.

rural counties contain only 27 percent of the state's total population (see map 2.1).[22] Rural counties' voters tend to be older, Whiter, and largely Christian and have fewer college graduates among them, precisely the demographic characteristics that political scientists identify as likely to prefer Republican candidates in the twenty-first century.[23] Traditional Republicans tend to value smaller, less intrusive government, low taxes, and laissez-faire capitalism and champion individual initiative.

Republicans thoroughly dominated Pennsylvania's politics from 1860 through 1936, winning most federal, state, and local elections, including in Philadelphia and Pittsburgh. Indeed, Philly's Vare Brothers machine was noted by Lincoln Steffens for its corruption and efficiency in delivering votes for its candidates.[24] But the Great Depression devastated the Keystone State's economy and created opportunities for Democrats. Though Roosevelt carried the nation in 1932, Pennsylvanians did not join the New Deal bandwagon until the 1936 election. In subsequent federal and state elections, the T slowly emerged, with Republicans retaining support in rural areas as Democrats expanded their ranks among blue-collar workers, people of color, Catholics, and Jews in urban centers. By 1968, when Pennsylvanians narrowly supported Humphrey over Nixon, the T was complete.

Republicans remained competitive in the state after 1936, however, because their base also included the new suburban counties surrounding Philadelphia, namely Bucks, Montgomery, Chester, and Delaware. After World War II, White, middle-class city residents migrated to those counties in great numbers, expanding their populations. Many of those new residents joined the Republican Party, which had dominated their county and local governments. The four suburban counties were Republican strongholds until the 1990s, when, in the presidential and the occasional statewide race, they slowly began trending Democratic. With the rise of the Tea Party movement in 2010, Philly's suburban voters' disenchantment with the Republican Party accelerated, with Democrats eventually gaining majorities on all four counties' governing bodies by 2020.

Pittsburgh's suburban counties, Washington and Westmoreland, experienced a transition in the opposite direction. Reliably Democratic until the mid-1980s, they gradually shifted their allegiance to GOP candidates in federal and then state elections, so that by 2020 each had a majority of its voters registered as Republican.

A dramatic example of the T's electoral impact is the 2002 gubernatorial race between Democrat Ed Rendell and Republican Mike Fisher. Rendell carried only eighteen of sixty-seven counties but won 53.4 percent of the vote, as the former Philly mayor's popularity in the city and its suburbs helped him handily carry the five southeastern counties, along with the traditional Democratic areas beyond the T. For any statewide Democratic candidate to overcome the Republican geographical advantages in the T, the Democrat must do very well in the party's strongholds in the southern corners, particularly the southeast because of its larger population. Current wisdom advises that a Democratic candidate in a typical statewide race must emerge from all the southeastern counties with at least a five-hundred-thousand-vote lead. All other things being equal, such a large advantage should overwhelm the Republican candidate's support within the T. Democrat Hillary Clinton narrowly lost the state to Donald Trump in the 2016 presidential election in part because she failed to reach that threshold.[25]

Pennsylvanians are serviced by eleven television markets: five that are shared with bordering states and six that are wholly within it. They tend to buttress partisan divisions. To be profitable, local TV news and entertainment producers reflect the tastes and values of their viewers, and as they do so, they reinforce existing social, cultural, and political values rather than challenge them. For example, Philadelphia's TV market, America's fourth largest, extends north to the city's suburbs and into the Lehigh Valley. It should not be surprising that the suburban counties' plus Berks, Lehigh, and Northampton counties' residents have more in common politically than people living outside Philly's coverage area. Likewise, the nation's 106th-largest television market, Altoona-Johnstown, which covers much of the central-western part of the T, binds the cities' residents culturally and politically with their rural neighbors in Elk and Cameron Counties rather than with the people of Pittsburgh less than one hundred miles to the west, who are served by the Steel City's media market.

On a lighter note, loyalty to one of Pennsylvania's two professional sports markets also divides Pennsylvanians. Steelers, Pirates, and Penguins fans are more likely to be found in the western half of the state, while Eagles, Phillies, and Flyers enthusiasts are more prevalent in the eastern half. Similarly, devotees of the Quaker State's two famous convenience store chains—Wawa and Sheetz—are also mostly divided geographically: east and west, respectively.

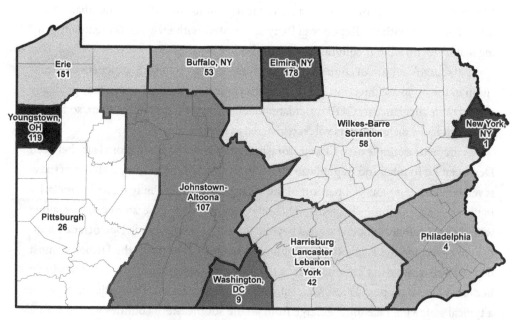

MAP 2.2 Map of media markets of Pennsylvania, 2020.

Attempts by various commentators to characterize the state's political culture have been memorable, if not exactly flattering. Perhaps the most oft-quoted description, and most reviled by its citizens, was delivered by James Carville, who in 1986, while working on the gubernatorial campaign of Democratic candidate Robert P. Casey Sr., said that "between Paoli [a Philadelphia suburb] and Penn Hills [a Pittsburgh suburb], Pennsylvania is Alabama without the Blacks.[26] (Such a description equates to the T described above.) Carville's portrayal was understood by many as a slur, but it contained grains of truth, as KKK chapters were active in several rural areas into the twenty-first century.

Equally unkind was a depiction offered in 2008 by then–presidential candidate Barack Obama: "You go into small towns in Pennsylvania and, like a lot of small towns in the Midwest, the jobs have been gone for 25 years and nothing has replaced them. . . . And it's not surprising then they get bitter, they cling to guns or religion or antipathy toward people who aren't like them or anti-immigrant or anti-trade sentiment as a way to explain their frustrations."[27] Adding insult to injury, two journalists, John Baer, formerly of the *Philadelphia Inquirer* and *Daily News*, and Brad Bumsted of the *Caucus* described Pennsylvania respectively as "the Land of Low Expectations" and a state with a "custom of corruption."[28]

While elements of truth exist in each description, none fully or fairly captures Pennsylvania's distinctive political culture. In this section, we explore the meaning of political culture, previous systematic efforts to identify that in Pennsylvania, and the factors that contribute to it in the present day.

For sociologists and anthropologists, culture is a concept that captures the norms, values, and customs that define a people. As adapted by political scientists, political culture identifies the dominant political beliefs, norms, and values held by the majority of a people that shape and support their political system, whether at the local, state, or national levels. For example, the vast majority of Americans believe in democracy, freedom, justice, and equality. These are key components of our national political culture, as reflected in the Constitution, that continue to inform debates on public issues today.

But Americans also are divided by two different understandings of what political systems should do. One view is that a political system is a marketplace in which free individuals, acting out of self-interest, bargain with other free individuals. Individuals alone navigate the market to successfully achieve their individual goals with government acting as the moderator, enforcing trade and business rules fairly on everyone without favoring any person or group. In this view, individual freedoms and rights are paramount and government does not act to enhance the lives of some citizens at the expense of others.

The other perspective sees the political system as a commonwealth in which people act collectively to achieve a common goal or goals identified by the people collectively. Government serves the people's will and facilitates cooperation among people to attain their goals. In this conception, community freedoms and rights are paramount and government acts to help all people attain basic goals.

Political scientist Daniel Elazar defined political culture as "the particular pattern of orientation to political action in which each political system is embedded." To explain differences in citizens' political behavior and their state governments' public policies, he theorized that the United States contained three political subcultures, operating concurrently at the state level within the national culture. He defined the three political cultures while incorporating the two different conceptions of political system.[29]

A moralist political culture is one in which the people conceive of themselves as a commonwealth. Collectively through government, people strive to improve the lives of all and advance their common interests. Government is viewed as a positive force to promote the general welfare, while politics is perceived as a noble activity in which all citizens are encouraged to participate honestly and selflessly. The needs of the community are advanced before those of the individual. Elazar argued that moralist political culture arrived in America with the Pilgrims, and he located moralist cultures mostly in New England, a few areas in the Mid-Atlantic states, the Upper Midwest, the Great Plains, and the Rocky Mountain and Western Coastal states.[30]

By contrast, in an individualist political culture, citizens see their democratic system pragmatically as a marketplace created "for strictly utilitarian reasons, to handle those functions demanded by the people" it serves. Such a culture promotes the individual's rights and needs over those of the community. Government may be used by individuals to advance their personal interests, even at the expense of the public's interest. It should come as no surprise that where individualistic culture prevails, government corruption is accepted as the price of doing business; it is, after all, a marketplace. The Mid-Atlantic states as well as the Lower Midwestern states and parts of the Great Plains, Alaska, and Hawaii were deemed by Elazar to possess individualist cultures.[31]

The last political culture is traditional, which Elazar found in the Deep South as well as parts of Texas, Oklahoma, Kansas, Missouri, New Mexico, Arizona, and Hawaii. In these places, citizens hold "an ambivalent attitude toward the marketplace coupled with a paternalistic and elitist conception of the commonwealth." The people accept a hierarchically organized society based on historically dictated norms in which certain people are naturally recognized as "the elite" while all others hold lesser positions in society. Government may act as a positive force in the community, but its role is limited to maintaining the existing social order. A subset of the elite occupies most positions within government and is acknowledged by the people as rightfully holding leadership positions. Political parties are much less important in traditional cultures because governments here are essentially dominated by one party.[32]

Elazar thought that the majority of Pennsylvanians shared values consistent with the individualist culture, except in parts of the northeast, where he detected areas of moralist culture, and in a few small pockets along the border with West Virginia and Maryland, where he identified traditional culture. His assessments were based on his reading of the state's history and his contemporaneous observations of how the state's residents and government officials practiced politics.[33]

The characteristic indicators of an individualist culture noted by Elazar are an intensely partisan environment in which the two major party organizations battle to control government not to advance the public's interest but to reward the party's followers should it win office; where the typical citizen holds government in low esteem and eschews politics, thinking of it as a sordid activity best left to professional politicians even as they accept government favors—patronage—dispensed by party leaders; where most citizens are apathetic, expect little from government, and prefer instead to be left alone to pursue their own objectives; and where the status quo is favored over change or reform.[34]

Another attempt to explain US political subcultures, Colin Woodard's *American Nations: A History of the Eleven Rival Regional Cultures of North America*, presents a wider variety of cultures than Elazar. Woodard found three of his cultures in Pennsylvania: the Midlands, New Yankeedom, and Greater Appalachian. The Midlands political culture reflects Quaker values of tolerance, community, striving for the common good, egalitarianism, and suspicion of government. It stretches across most of the state from Philadelphia to Pittsburgh.[35]

New Yankeedom's culture covers the northern tier and much of the northeast. This culture, introduced by the Puritans, favors the creation of a wholesome society using an active government that places the community's goals above those of the individual while seamlessly integrating new members into the community.

Pennsylvania's southwest quadrant, dominated by the Appalachian Mountains, is home to the Greater Appalachian culture, though it does not include Pittsburgh and its surrounding area. Its values mirror those of the immigrants from Northern Ireland, Scotland, and England who settled in the mountains: mistrust of government, distaste for aristocracy, and championing of individual initiative and rights.[36] Despite their idiosyncratic terminologies, Elazar and Woodard identified many of the same values in the Keystone State's culture, though they differed in locating their cultures within the state.

Elazar's analysis, despite criticism of his methodology and conclusions, continues to be cited because his insights remain relevant and consistent with those of contemporary political scientists and journalists. One may quibble with his terms, choice of indicators, and where he placed the cultures geographically, but the persistence of the political values that Elazar first identified in 1966 cannot be denied. In the following pages, we will examine the many facets of Pennsylvania's political culture.[37]

Consistent with the individualistic political culture that is found across most of the state, Pennsylvanians have displayed partisan sentiments since the American Revolution. Its citizens have divided along faction and party lines, with voters consistently identifying with and exhibiting loyalty to their respective parties. From the 1860s to the present, the majority of the electorate aligned itself behind either the Republican or Democratic Party.

While both parties have state organizations, the parties' actual power centers reside at the county and local levels, where most patronage opportunities are concentrated. In the largest cities and in some counties, local organizations were dubbed "machines" because they operated efficiently in distributing patronage and turning out their supporters for elections. Among the more notorious were Philadelphia's machines: the Republican Vare Brothers and its Democratic doppelgänger of the mid- to late twentieth century.[38]

The Quaker State exhibits many features of a strong two-party system, such as closed primaries, stringent ballot access rules that diminish the odds of minor parties appearing on a ballot, ballots that once permitted straight-ticket voting (see chapter 4), party labels adjacent to candidates' names on ballots (including for all judicial seats), and lax campaign finance rules.

Historically, when a Pennsylvania party held majorities in the General Assembly and occupied the governor's mansion, its leaders rewarded their faithful with government jobs and contracts in return for their votes—that is, patronage. By distributing the spoils of victory, the ruling party was much more likely to retain control of government while also enriching its leaders. Patronage was a legal and accepted practice for many decades even as it was condemned by good-government advocates for violating the public's trust that government should treat everyone equally. When patronage's excesses were exposed by muckrakers around the turn of the twentieth century, reformers pushed for transitioning the hiring process from patronage to merit appointment and for implementing objective procedures for awarding government contracts. Pennsylvania, however, was slow to adopt statewide reforms, tolerating party leaders and unscrupulous officeholders who continued employing patronage through much of the twentieth century. Eventually blatant corruption brought prosecutions and convictions and changes to state government practices, but not necessarily to county and city governments.[39]

Accepting government corruption as the price of doing business in the marketplace, as Elazar explained, is a by-product of an individualist culture, and Pennsylvanians appear to have a high tolerance for gross levels of government misconduct. From the financial improprieties during the construction and furnishing of a new state capitol in 1906–7 to the disgrace of the "kids for cash" scheme in 2009–10, the state's residents have shrugged off government scandals. The frequency, severity, boldness, and breadth of the misdeeds at the state, county, and local levels have been well documented. A recent study gave Pennsylvania an F and ranked it forty-fifth out of fifty states in level of corruption. It should come as no surprise, then, that tolerance of government corruption is noted by many as a feature of the state's political culture.[40]

Consistent with tolerating corruption, many Pennsylvanians mistrust their state government, and some also find county governments untrustworthy, with only local governments appearing to hold the confidence of most citizens. Governments closest to the people, such as townships and boroughs, are those that people regularly observe. They provide people's basic services, and people are more likely to personally know their elected officials, all of which engenders trust. And there is no shortage of local governments in the commonwealth, which has over 4,500 municipalities and special districts.[41]

A manifestation of persistent citizen mistrust is what Beers called "negativism": the tendency of the state's citizens and legislators to vote regularly against government reform.[42] Other writers have described this quality as "resistance to change,"[43] a preference for the status quo, and, most bluntly, an antireform mentality.[44] How else might one explain a 1963 referendum in which the voters rejected a proposal to allow the state's capital to be moved in case of a nuclear attack, or the legislature's failure to pass any significant reforms to the state's lobbying and campaign finance rules, which are among the nation's most lenient? Pennsylvanians appear to prefer the devil they know to the devil they don't.[45]

This is not to suggest that the state's voters are inflexible. Those Pennsylvanians holding Elazar's moralist or Woodard's New Yankeedom values have occasionally enticed a majority of their fellow citizens to join them in reform movements. For example, Governor Gifford Pinchot brought conservation to the state in the 1920s and '30s; Governor David Leo Lawrence championed civil rights, fair housing, and environmental legislation in the early 1960s; and the constitutional convention of 1967–68 modernized the state's government.[46] Similarly, reform movements, however short-lived, appeared periodically in Pittsburgh and Philadelphia in the 1950s through the 2010s.[47]

But the negativism/antichange/antireform element in the state's political culture is long-standing and runs deep, particularly when the subject is taxes. Among the earliest and most famous examples of Pennsylvanians' abhorrence of taxes were the Whiskey Rebellion of 1794 and Fries's Rebellion of 1798, both triggered by federal excise taxes. Many of the state's constitutions had provisions that placed limits on state and local governments' taxing authority, severely restricting their ability to raise revenue.[48]

The state's first income tax was levied in 1971 as a flat tax after the legislature initially passed a graduated income tax that was quickly challenged as unconstitutional and struck down by the state's high court for violating the constitution's uniformity clause: article VIII, section 1.[49] In addition to its regressive income tax, Pennsylvania generates revenue from sales and excise taxes, multiple lotteries, casino gambling, and user fees, and, at the local level, the much-hated property tax. If there is one constant issue in the Keystone State's history, it is the argument over taxes. It will move Pennsylvanians to action and, when coupled with their suspicion of government, trigger anger and votes against increasing or adding taxes.

Rejecting reform and preferring the status quo relate to another value that flows from the Quaker tradition as well as the moralist culture embedded in parts of the state— namely, Pennsylvanians' tendency toward moderation, their "indifference to extremes."[50] For example, from 1900 to the present, the majority of candidates elected to *statewide* offices, regardless of party, have been moderates rather than ideological extremists or radicals. (The same cannot be said for some US representatives and members of the General Assembly who are elected by district.) The state's legislature, judges, and Supreme Court justices rarely lead the nation in passing groundbreaking laws or issuing precedent-setting decisions, respectively, preferring instead to move incrementally. In many state rankings compiled by organizations that assess states' performance, Pennsylvania often can be found ranked between twentieth and thirtieth in the nation.[51]

Beyond Philadelphia and the city's immediate environs, many Pennsylvanians harbor a deep resentment toward the City of Brotherly Love,[52] which manifested as early as 1791, when the state capital was relocated from Philadelphia to Lancaster, and then to Harrisburg in 1812.[53] While citizens in other states may resent their largest cities—think New York City and New York, Chicago and Illinois, Detroit and Michigan—their relationships may not be nearly as strained. Interestingly, the resentment toward Philly does not carry over to Pittsburgh, the state's second-largest city. Reasons for the bitterness range from jealousy (the city's media presence exceeds the rest of the state) and resentment (those outside the city believe it receives a disproportionate share of state resources) to arrogance (Philadelphians look down on other Pennsylvanians) and racism (people of color are a majority of the city's population, while 82 percent of the state's entire population is White). Reasons aside, the anti-Philadelphia sentiment regularly affects the city and its residents when the General Assembly votes against the city's interest and when candidates who hail from the city run for statewide offices—they are more likely to lose compared to candidates who reside elsewhere. Additionally, candidates not from Philadelphia often invoke Philadelphia as a dog whistle to tap into the animosity harbored by voters beyond the city to gain support.[54]

Related to several previously discussed values is apathy. As Elazar theorized, people holding individualistic values find politics a sordid affair and much prefer to be left alone to pursue their lives rather than have government intrude on them. Many Pennsylvanians over the decades have exhibited apathetic political behavior. As Beers wrote, "The private contentment, social diversions, and benign environment of much of Pennsylvania's rural and small-town life only reinforce the indifference to politics. Boredom reigns in the dark, neglected underside of the vibrant partisanship that preoccupies other communities. . . . Pennsylvania's long-time passionate involvement with athletics . . . contrasts with its often slack-jawed approach to the responsibilities of citizenship in a democracy."[55] Specific examples of political apathy abound. For example, numerous elections post low turnouts. In presidential elections, normally those that generate the highest turnout, Pennsylvanians' turnout reached 70 percent of eligible voters in 1960 and nearly 68 percent in 2020, but generally averaged 56 percent between 1996 and 2020, placing the state slightly above the national average of 54 percent during this period. In nonpresidential, general elections, turnout is consistently poor, while turnout for primaries can be embarrassingly low, such as Bucks County's 15 percent turnout in the 2019 primary elections.[56]

CONCLUSION

The influence of the Quaker State's physical geography on its social, cultural, and economic development is widely accepted. Disagreement arises, however, over its effect on political culture and whether political culture shapes political institutions. By introducing the reader to the concept of political culture and several theories that explain Pennsylvania's political culture, we provide a lens through which one may interpret Pennsylvanians' political attitudes and behaviors, such as party affiliation, voting patterns, and policy positions. Political scientists have tested the heuristic value of political culture as an explanatory variable with mixed results, yet political culture remains a durable theory.[57]

As we discussed in the introduction, however, there are many approaches to understanding governments and political systems, one of which—institutionalism—we employ through the remaining chapters. Where appropriate, we offer an analysis using political culture to further explicate an issue.

NOTES

1. Beers, *Pennsylvania Politics*, 1–2.
2. See Madonna and Young, "Pennsylvania Paradox."
3. Frey and Teixeira, "Political Geography of Pennsylvania."
4. See Malady, "Where Yinz At"; Loviglio, "Philadelphians Have a Unique Accent"; Madej, "Phila.'s Shifting Dialect."
5. Jon Delano (reporter for KDKA-TV, columnist for *Pittsburgh Business Times*, and chief of staff to former US Rep. Doug Walgren), interview with the authors, August 10, 2016, by phone.
6. John Fell of Wilkes-Barre first burned coal for heat on an open-grate stove in 1808. See Pennsylvania Economy League of Greater Pittsburgh, "Economic Impact of the Coal Industry"; Arnold, *Fueling the Gilded Age.*
7. On January 22, 1959, while tunneling under the Susquehanna River, Knox Coal Company miners pierced the riverbed, flooding miles of the interconnected mines in the area and killing twelve men. See Berger, "Death Underground."
8. See Pennsylvania Economy League of Greater Pittsburgh, "Economic Impact of the Coal Industry."
9. See Olien and Olien, *Oil and Ideology*; Hopkins and Coons, "Crude Petroleum and Petroleum Products."
10. See Churella, *Pennsylvania Railroad.*
11. See "Railroads of Pennsylvania."
12. See U.S. Energy Information Administration Report, "U.S. Natural Gas Production."
13. See Corkery, "Giant Factory Rises"; Colvin and Boak, "Trump Visits New Plant."
14. See Marusic, "Air Pollution from Fracking"; Levy, "Pennsylvania Opens Investigation."
15. See Pennsylvania Department of Agriculture, https://www.agriculture.pa.gov/Pages/Pennsylvania-Agriculture.aspx.
16. Maxim and Muro, "Ideas for Pennsylvania Innovation."
17. U.S. Census Bureau.
18. See Vu, "States Work to Plug 'Brain Drain'"; Rothermel, "When We End the Brain Drain"; John Baer (columnist, *Philadelphia Daily News* and *Philadelphia Inquirer*), interview with the authors, May 25, 2016, by phone.
19. Baer, interview; Brad Bumsted (reporter, the *Caucus*), interview with the authors, May 25, 2016, by phone; Delano, interview; Borys Krawczenick (reporter, *Scranton Times Tribune*), interview with the authors, May 24, 2016, by phone; Robert Swift (reporter, *Times Shamrock*), interview with the authors, May 24, 2016, by phone.
20. In an interview with an experienced Harrisburg journalist who covered state government but

requested anonymity, June 1, 2016, by phone. The journalist said that the city's representatives in the legislature think that the rest of the state "is suspicious of the city." See also McLaughlin, "Yo, Ed! It's Groundhog Day!"

21. Delano, interview; experienced journalist, who requested anonymity, interview.

22. See Center for Rural Pennsylvania website, https://www.rural.palegislature.us/rural _urban.html.

23. See, for example, Campbell et al., *American Voter*.

24. See Steffens, *Shame of the City*; Baldino, "Vare Brothers Machine"; Barry, *Great Influenza*, 198–209, 324–30.

25. Galston, "Why Hillary Clinton Lost Pennsylvania"; Malawskey, "Where Hillary Clinton Lost Pennsylvania."

26. Brown, "Extreme Make-Over." The original quote is presented here but has been shortened and modified to "Pennsylvania is Philadelphia and Pittsburgh with Alabama (or Kentucky or Mississippi) in between."

27. Smith, "Obama on Small Town Pennsylvania."

28. See Baer, *On the Front Lines*; Bumsted, *Keystone Corruption*.

29. Elazar, *American Federalism*, 109, 115–18.

30. Ibid., 117–18.

31. Ibid., 115–17.

32. Ibid., 118–19.

33. Ibid., 125.

34. Ibid., 120.

35. See Woodard, *American Nations*.

36. Ibid.

37. For example, see Hero and Tolbert, "Racial/Ethnic Diversity Interpretation"; Nardulli, "Political Subcultures in the American States"; Mondak and Canache, "Personality and Political Culture"; Wirt, "'Soft' Concepts and 'Hard' Data."

38. For example, see Baldino, "Vare Brothers Machine"; McLarnon and Madonna, "Dilworth, Clark, and Reform"; McCaffery, *When Bosses Ruled Philadelphia*.

39. See Baer, *On the Front Lines*; Beers, *Pennsylvania Politics*; Bumsted, *Keystone Corruption*.

40. See Baer, *On the Front Lines*; Beers, *Pennsylvania Politics*, 30–33; Bumsted, *Keystone Corruption*; Madonna and Young, "Continuity and Change"; Ecenbarger, *Kids for Cash*; Lavelle, "Pennsylvania Gets F Grade."

41. Zhorov, "Why Does PA Have So Many?"

42. Beers, *Pennsylvania Politics*, 11.

43. Madonna and Young, "Continuity and Change."

44. See Baer, *On the Front Lines*; Bumsted, *Keystone Corruption*; Madonna and Young, "Continuity and Change."

45. Beers, *Pennsylvania Politics*, 11.

46. See Weber, *Don't Call Me Boss*.

47. See, for example, DiGaetano, "Urban Political Reform."

48. Miller and Pencak, *Pennsylvania*, 147–48.

49. See *Amidon v. Kane*, 444 Pa. 38 (1971); Swift, "State Tax Hike."

50. See Beers, *Pennsylvania Politics*; Madonna and Young, "Continuity and Change."

51. See Ginley, "Grading the Nation"; Tierney, "Do You Trust Your State Government?"; De Haldevang, "Which US State?"; Pew Center for the States, *Pennsylvania*.

52. See Baer, *On the Front Lines*; Beers, *Pennsylvania Politics*; Madonna and Young, "Continuity and Change."

53. See "The History of Pennsylvania's Early Capitols," Pennsylvania Capitol Preservation Commission, http://cpc.state.pa.us/history /the-history-of-pennsylvanias-early-capitols .cfm.; McLaughlin, "Yo, Ed! It's Groundhog Day!"

54. See Baldino and Featherman, "Has Philadelphia Lost Its Political Muscle?"; Hanna and Seidman, "He's a Liar"; Evans, *Making Ideas Matter*.

55. Beers, *Pennsylvania Politics*, 3.

56. For examples, see McCrone, "Philadelphia Voter Turnout Wasn't High"; Pennsylvania Department of State, Voting and Election statistics, https://www.dos.pa.gov/VotingElections /OtherServicesEvents/VotingElection Statistics/Pages/VotingElectionStatistics.aspx.

57. For example, see Erickson, McIver, and White, "State Political Culture."

BIBLIOGRAPHY

Arnold, Andrew B. *Fueling the Gilded Age: Railroads, Miners, and Disorder in Pennsylvania Coal Country*. New York: New York University Press, 2014.

Baer, John. *On the Front Lines of Pennsylvania Politics: Twenty-Five Years of Keystone Reporting*. Charleston, SC: History Press, 2012.

Baldino, Thomas J. "Vare Brothers Machine." In *Political Parties and Elections in the United States: An Encyclopedia*, edited by Sandy Maisel, 2:1171. New York: Garland, 1991.

Baldino, Thomas J., and Sandra Featherman. "Has Philadelphia Lost Its Political Muscle?" Paper presented at the Pennsylvania Political Science Association meeting, April 1990.

Beers, Paul B. *Pennsylvania Politics, Today and Yesterday: The Tolerable Accommodation*. University Park: Pennsylvania State University Press, 1980.

Berger, Lauren. "Death Underground: The Knox Mine Disaster." *Pennsylvania Center for the Book*. https://pabook .libraries.psu.edu/literary-cultural -heritage-map-pa/feature-articles /death-underground-knox-mine-disaster.

Brown, Carrie Budoff. "Extreme Makeover: Pennsylvania Edition." Politico, April 1, 2008. https://www.politico.com/story/2008 /04/extreme-makeover-pennsylvania -edition-009323.

Bumsted, Brad. *Keystone Corruption: A Pennsylvania Insider's View of a State Gone Wrong*. Philadelphia: Camino Books, 2013.

Campbell, Angus, Phillip E. Converse, Warren E. Miller, and Donald E. Stokes. *The American Voter*. Chicago: University of Chicago Press, 1960.

Churella, Albert J. *The Pennsylvania Railroad*. Vol. 1, *Building an Empire, 1846–1917*. Philadelphia: University of Pennsylvania Press, 2013.

Colvin, Jill, and Josh Boak. "Trump Visits New Plant in Western Pa." *Philadelphia Inquirer*, August 14, 2019.

Corkery, Michael. "A Giant Factory Rises to Make a Product Filling Up the World." *New York Times*, August 12, 2019.

Ecenbarger, William. *Kids for Cash: Two Judges, Thousands of Children and a $28 Million Kickback Scheme*. New York: New Press, 2013.

Elazar, Daniel J. *American Federalism: A View from the States*. 3rd ed. New York: HarperCollins, 1984.

Erickson, Robert S., John P. McIver, and Gerald C. Wright. "State Political Culture and Public Opinion." *American Political Science Review* 81, no. 3 (2014): 797–813.

Evans, Dwight. *Making Ideas Matter: My Life as a Policy Entrepreneur*. Philadelphia: University of Pennsylvania Press, 2013.

Frey, William H., and Ruy Teixeira. "The Political Geography of Pennsylvania: Not Another Rust Belt State." Brookings Policy Brief, April 2008.

Galston, William A. "Why Hillary Clinton Lost Pennsylvania: The Real Story." Brookings, November 11, 2016, https://www.brookings .edu/blog/fixgov/2016/11/11/why-hillary -clinton-lost-pennsylvania-the-real-story.

Ginley, Caitlin. "Grading the Nation: How Accountable Is Your State?" Center for Public Integrity, November 10, 2015. https://public integrity.org/politics/state-politics/grading -the-nation-how-accountable-is-your-state.

De Haldevang, Max. "Which US State Is Most Corruption Prone? Look Away, North Dakota." quartz.com, October 11, 2018. https://qz.com /1419802/which-state-is-most-prone-to -corruption-heres-a-ranking.

Hanna, Maddie, and Andrew Seidman, "'He's a Liar': Hot Debate over Education in Pa. Governor's Race." *Philadelphia Inquirer*, August 17, 2018.

Hero, R. E., and C. J. Tolbert. "A Racial/Ethnic Diversity Interpretation of Politics and Policy in the States of the U.S." *American Journal of Political Science* 40, no. 3 (1996): 851–54.

Hopkins, G. R., and A. B. Coons. "Crude Petroleum and Petroleum Products." *Statistical Appendix to the Minerals Yearbook, 1932–33*. [Washington, DC]: US Bureau of Mines, 1934.

Lavelle, Marianne. "Pennsylvania Gets F Grade in 2015 State Integrity Investigation: An Entrenched Culture of Malfeasance." Center for Public Integrity, November 9, 2015. https://www.publicintegrity.org/2015/11 /09/18507/pennsylvania-gets-f-grade-2015 -state-integrity-investigation.

Levy, Marc. "Pennsylvania Opens Investigation into 350-Mile Gas Pipeline." nbc10Philadelphia .com, March 12, 2019. https://www.nbc philadelphia.com/news/local/pennsylvania -investigates-gas-pipeline/175380.

Malady, Matthew J. X. "Where Yinz At." Slate, December 14, 2017. http://www.slate.com /articles/life/the_good_word/2014/04 /pennsylvania_dialects_from_pittsburghese _to_philadelphia_speak_the_keystone.html.

Malawskey, Nick. "Pennsylvania's Dialects Are as Varied as Its Downtowns—and Dahntahns." Pennlive.com, November 29, 2011.

Marusic, Kristina. "Air Pollution from Fracking Killed an Estimated 20 People in Pennsylvania from 2010–2017." *Environmental Health News*, June 5, 2020, https://www.ehn.org/fracking -pennsylvania-deaths-2646154025.html.

Maxim, Robert, and Mark Muro. "Ideas for Pennsylvania Innovation." Brookings, August 2019.

McCaffery, Peter. *When Bosses Ruled Philadelphia: The Emergence of the Republican Machine, 1867–1933*. University Park: Pennsylvania State University Press, 1993.

McCrone, Brian X. "Philadelphia Voter Turnout Wasn't High. It Was Worse in the Suburbs." nbc10Philadelphia.com, May 22, 2019. https://www.nbcphiladelphia.com/news/local/have-a-problem-with-philadelphia-voter-turnout-its-worse-in-the-suburbs/172790.

McLarnon, John M., and G. Terry Madonna. "Dilworth, Clark, and Reform in Philadelphia, 1947–1962." *Pennsylvania Legacies* 11, no. 2 (2011): 24–31.

McLaughlin, Joseph P., Jr. "Yo, Ed! It's Groundhog Day!" Lecture delivered to University of Pennsylvania Urban Studies Class, January 2013.

Miller, Randall M., and William Pencak, eds. *Pennsylvania: A History of the Commonwealth*. University Park: Pennsylvania State University Press, 2002.

Mondak, Jeffery J., and Damarys Canache. "Personality and Political Culture in the American States." *Political Research Quarterly* 20, no. 10 (2013): 1–16.

Nardulli, Peter. "Political Subcultures in the American States: An Empirical Examination of Elazar's Formulation." *American Political Research* 18, no. 3 (1990): 287–315.

Olien, Roger M., and Diana Davids Olien. *Oil and Ideology: The Cultural Creation of the American Petroleum Industry*. Chapel Hill: University of North Carolina, 2000.

Pennsylvania Economy League of Greater Pittsburgh. "The Economic Impact of the Coal Industry in Pennsylvania." Report prepared for the Pennsylvania Coal Alliance, March 2014.

Pew Center for the States. *Pennsylvania*. http://www.pewcenteronthestates.org/states_rankings.aspx?abrv+PA.

"Railroads of Pennsylvania." Pennsylvania Historical and Museum Commission. http://www.phmc.state.pa.us/portal/communities/railroads/history.html.

Rothermel, Jonathan C. "When We End the Brain Drain, We Become the Keystone State Again: An Opinion." *Pennsylvania Capital Star*, March 18, 2019.

Smith, Ben. "Obama on Small Town Pennsylvania: Clinging to Religion, Guns, Xenophobia." Politico, April 11, 2008. https://www.politico.com/blogs/ben-smith/2008/04/obama-on-small-town-pa-clinging-to-religion-guns-xenophobia-007737.

Steffens, Lincoln. *The Shame of the City*. New York: Compass Books, 2020.

Swift, Robert. "State Tax Hike Raises Fairness Issue." *Scranton Times Tribune*, June 22, 2009.

Tierney, John. "Do You Trust Your State Government?" *Atlantic*, May 12, 2014.

U.S. Energy Information Administration Report. "U.S. Natural Gas Production Grew Again in 2019, Increasing by 10%." https://www.eia.gov/todayinenergy/detail.php?id=43115.

Vu, Pauline. "States Work to Plug 'Brain Drain,'" Pew Stateline, July 25, 2007. https://www.pewtrusts.org/en/research-and-analysis/blogs/stateline/2007/07/25/states-work-to-plug-brain-drain.

Weber, Michael. *Don't Call Me Boss: David Leo Lawrence*. Pittsburgh: University of Pittsburgh Press, 1993.

Wirt, Frederick W. "'Soft' Concepts and 'Hard' Data: A Research Review of Elazar's Political Culture." *Publius* 21, no. 2 (1991): 1–13.

Woodard, Colin. *American Nations: A History of the Eleven Rival Regional Cultures of North America*. New York: Penguin Books, 2011.

Zhorov, Irina. "Why Does PA Have So Many Local Governments?" whyy.org, September 16, 2014. https://whyy.org/articles/why-does-pa-have-so-many-local-governments.

CHAPTER 3

Elections, Parties, Interest Groups, and the Media

Elections are the lifeblood of representative democracies, the mechanism by which citizens choose those who represent them in government. In Pennsylvania, citizens elect members to all three branches: the General Assembly (legislative); the governor, lieutenant governor, attorney general, treasurer, and auditor general (executive); and judges at every level of the court system from minor courts to Supreme Court justices (judicial).

Political parties recruit candidates for office, organize their campaigns, raise money, and mobilize voters who share the parties' values and policy positions. If a party's candidates win, they are expected to use their offices to implement the party's agenda. Pennsylvania's two major parties, Republican and Democrat, have been rivals since 1856, and though they win most elections, other parties occasionally appear and contend for statewide and local offices.

As a large and diverse state, it should come as no surprise that Pennsylvania has no shortage of groups representing the full panoply of interests found elsewhere in the nation as well as those that are idiosyncratic to Pennsylvania. The largest interest groups are wise to the ways of Harrisburg and adept at influencing state government using their in-house lobbyists or hiring from among the many professional lobbyists (aka government relations specialists) occupying offices around the capital. Interest groups play a vital role in state politics, as they present their organizations' positions to government's elected and appointed officials as well as its bureaucrats, hoping to affect public policy.

Finally, political journalists, like parties and interest groups, provide an essential function in liberal, representative democracies. They serve as the public's eyes and ears, reporting to citizens their governments' accomplishments and shortcomings, helping citizens to hold their government accountable. Reporters ask questions of those in office that citizens would ask if they had the time and expertise to camp out in their capital, county seat, or city hall. In the following pages, we consider these four critical components of Pennsylvania's political system.

Elections are essential for democracies, and with over forty-six hundred governmental entities Pennsylvanians have ample opportunities to cast their votes. Though article VII of the state's constitution contains its electoral rules, most regulations and procedures are found in the commonwealth's Registration and Election Codes.[1]

To vote in the Quaker State, one must be at least eighteen years old, a US citizen for one month, and a state resident for ninety days preceding a statewide election and sixty days preceding a local election. These criteria were interpreted in 1971 to apply to university students who register to vote at their schools.[2] Registering to vote was simplified in 2015, when Pennsylvania adopted online registration.

In 2019, the General Assembly passed Act 77, which made significant changes to registration and voting procedures, including shortening the deadline to register from thirty to fifteen days before an election, eliminating the need to offer an excuse to receive a mail ballot, allowing voters to request placement on a list to receive mail ballots automatically for every election, extending the deadline for the receipt of mail ballots from 5:00 pm on the Friday before election day to 8:00 pm on election day, eliminating the straight-ticket ballot option (only seven states offered this), and providing money to assist counties with the purchase of secure voting systems that create a paper trail.[3] Neither party was particularly happy with all the changes, especially Democrats, who insisted that dropping straight-ticket ballots would suppress the vote among poorer, less-educated citizens, but the bill was passed by a large bipartisan majority. Democratic Governor Wolf wrote, "While I understand the concerns about eliminating the straight party ticket option, this bipartisan bill creates the most significant improvements to our elections in more than 80 years. Pennsylvania has gone from collectively being the state least friendly to voters to a national leader in voting and election security reforms."[4] Following the 2020 presidential election and the unsubstantiated claims by President Trump that mailed ballots contributed to massive voter fraud that caused him to lose, Republican lawmakers have attacked Act 77 as unconstitutional. Bills to repeal the law have been introduced, as have bills to eliminate specifically drop boxes for mail ballots and no-excuse mail ballots.[5] This matter is treated more fully in chapter 10.

Pennsylvania holds its gubernatorial election every four years in even-numbered years that are not presidential election years, for example, 2014, 2018, and 2022. All other general elections for executive offices—attorney general, treasurer, and auditor general—are held in presidential election years. All judicial elections for appellate, common pleas, minor court judges, and municipal general elections take place in odd-numbered years.

Primary elections are held in mid-May prior to a November general election, except for presidential primaries, which take place in late April before the presidential general election. Pennsylvania is one of the nine states that employ a closed primary, in which voters must register in a party and then can vote only for the candidates of that party.

Though a closed primary prevents voters who register as "independent" from participating in *any* party's primary, it does prevent crossover voting and raiding, which are possibilities in open primary systems. Crossover voting occurs when citizens registered in one party cast ballots in a different party's primary, while raiding takes place when voters of one party intentionally cast their ballots for the weakest, most beatable candidate of the opposition party. According to its advocates, closed primaries promote strong parties by enhancing party loyalty and make it easier to mobilize voters, but they also clearly benefit the two *major* parties. As Republicans and Democrats control the General Assembly, there is little reason to expect that either party will support a switch from a closed to open primary system. One bill was offered in 2009, and it failed to generate support; however, Senate hearings were held on SB 690 of 2021 in April of 2022, and this had bipartisan cosponsors. A previous version of this bill passed the Senate in 2021 but stalled in the House.[6]

Pennsylvania imposes term limits of eight years (two terms) on all of its executive offices, a change included in the 1968 constitution. It replaced the four-year (one-term) limit in the 1873 constitution. Members of the General Assembly are not term-limited. Judges at all levels serve ten-year terms, at the conclusion of which they must stand for retention or retire, except judges of minor courts (courts of limited jurisdiction)—namely, district judges and Philadelphia municipal court jurists—who have six-year terms. Judges may stand for retention without limit until they reach a mandatory retirement age of seventy-five, at which point they may request senior status and serve in that capacity until age seventy-eight.

Initiative, Referendum, and Recall

Pennsylvania is one of the few states that does not allow its citizens extensive access to the tools of direct democracy: initiative, referendum, and recall. However, there are several exceptions. One is to amend the constitution, described in article XI. Only the General Assembly may propose an amendment, and the proposed amendment must be tailored to address only one subject.[7] It must pass both chambers by a simple majority vote in two consecutive legislative sessions, and then be placed on the ballot at least three months after the second General Assembly vote. A simple majority vote of the electorate is necessary to approve. A rejected amendment may not be reconsidered for five years.[8]

Article VIII, section 7, clause 3 requires that the General Assembly place questions of public indebtedness—borrowing money—before the electorate; a simple majority vote is required to incur debt.

The constitution permits any local government—city, town, county, borough, or township—that adopts home rule (see chapter 8) to include in its home rule charter provisions for initiative and referendum but not recall. Only seven counties, as well as seventy-six municipalities, have adopted home rule, though not all have incorporated initiative or referendum into their charters.

Finally, school boards must hold referenda if they seek property tax increases higher than the Act 1 index. Following public outrage, especially among senior citizens, over large property tax increases to fund public education, the General Assembly responded by passing Act 1 of 2006. School districts may raise their property taxes no more than the Act 1 index, which is calculated for each school district every fiscal year. The index's formula includes changes in wages statewide and school employee compensation costs nationwide. If a school board proposes a higher tax increase than the Act 1 index permits, the school board must place the question before its constituents for approval by a majority vote.

Registration and Turnout

Participation in the commonwealth's many elections requires that citizens meet eligibility criteria discussed above and be registered. As table 3.1 reveals, the percentage of the state's voting age population (VAP) that is registered has exceeded 80 percent since 2000, but the percentage of those casting ballots is approximately 20 percent less over the same period. Tables 3.1 and 3.2 use data from presidential elections, which typically generate the highest turnouts. Since 1960, Pennsylvania has ranked between twenty-third and thirty-seventh among all states in turnout for presidential elections.[9]

In other elections turnout declines, with the lowest turnouts found in primary elections. Reasons for unimpressive turnout include the state's previously stringent registration rules, the difficulties of voting absentee, and general voter apathy toward primaries. As some of these barriers were lowered with Act 77 of 2019, discussed above, turnout appears to be increasing. Heightened partisanship since the 2016 presidential election also has contributed to higher turnout rates since 2018, especially among younger voters.[10]

Campaign Finance

Most states regulate, to some degree, how candidates raise money for their campaigns by restricting who or what can contribute to candidates and in what amounts, but Pennsylvania's campaign finance laws are among the least restrictive in the country; the last major campaign finance law was passed in 1937.[11] The Keystone State is one of eleven states that permit individuals to make unlimited contributions to candidates, one of nineteen that allow parties to give without limit to candidates, and one of thirteen that place no restrictions on contributions by political action committees (PACs) to candidates.[12] Moreover, there are no rules that restrict how candidates may use contributions, including for personal use, or that require itemized expense reports.[13] Investigative journalists found that state political campaigns "spent $3.5 million from 2016 to 2018 without disclosing what they were buying."[14] Pennsylvania does, however, prohibit direct contributions to candidates

Table 3.1 Pennsylvania's voter demographics, 1932–2020

YEAR	Total population	Voting age population (VAP)	Total registered voters	% of VAP registered	% of VAP actually voting
1932	9,764,000	5,441,000	2,749,488	50.5	52.5
1936	9,767,000	5,718,000	4,044,187	70.7	71.8
1940	9,896,000	6,103,000	4,060,883	66.5	66.8
1944	9,214,000	6,423,000	3,755,533	58.5	59.1
1948	10,287,000	6,709,000	3,654,623	54.5	55.4
1952	10,503,000	6,870,000	4,562,058	66.4	66.7
1956	10,972,000	6,928,000	5,025,208	72.5	66.1
1960	11,319,000	6,998,000	5,687,837	81.3	71.5
1964	11,319,000	7,157,000	5,728,359	80.0	67.4
1968	11,780,000	7,311,000	5,599,364	76.6	64.9
1972	11,800,000	8,073,000	5,871,902	72.7	54.9
1976	11,845,000	8,383,000	5,749,660	68.6	55.1
1980	11,860,000	8,653,000	5,754,287	66.5	52.7
1984	11,820,000	8,786,000	6,193,702	70.5	55.1
1988	11,850,000	8,914,000	5,875,943	65.9	50.9
1992	12,050,000	9,007,000	5,993,002	66.5	55.1
1996	12,220,000	9,085,000	6,805,612	74.9	49.6
2000	12,280,000	9,166,000	7,781,997	84.9	53.6
2004	12,390,000	9,318,000	8,366,663	89.8	61.9
2008	12,570,000	9,471,000	8,755,588	92.4	63.5
2012	12,770,000	9,910,224	8,508,015	85.9	58.1
2016	12,778,000	10,018,510	8,722,977	87.1	61.0
2018	12,810,000	10,141,082	8,609,880	84.9	79.0
2020	13,002,700	10,186,170	8,906,295	87.4	67.9
2022	12,972,008	10,222,313	8,618,386	84.3	52.5

Source: Compiled by the authors from U.S. Census, PA Department of State and Vital Statistics website, and Curtis Gans, *Voter Turnout in the United States, 1788–2009* (Washington, DC: Congressional Quarterly Press, 2010).

from unions and corporations, but there are no barriers to a corporation's officers and employees or individual union members from contributing to their corporation's or union's PAC. Similarly, corporations and unions may spend unlimited amounts to influence elections as long as neither coordinates its political expenditures with a candidate's campaign organization.[15]

Historically, the state's lax campaign finance rules supported an environment that fostered corruption. From the days of Simon Cameron, Matthew Quay, and Boies Penrose in the late nineteenth and early twentieth centuries to John Perzel, Bill DeWeese, and Vince Fumo in the twenty-first century, the commonwealth has witnessed more than its fair share of scandals.[16] Though reformers in both major parties have pursued legislation to limit who

Table 3.2 Party registration, 1932–2020

Year	Total Registered Voters	% Registered Democrat	% Registered Republican	% Registered Independent/Other
1932	2,749,488	21	75	4
1936	4,044,187	42	54	4
1940	4,060,883	43	56	1
1944	3,755,533	41	58	1
1948	3,654,623	38	61	1
1952	4,562,058	40	59	1
1956	5,025,208	45	53	1
1960	5,687,837	49	49	1
1964	5,728,359	50	48	1
1968	5,599,364	49	50	2
1972	5,871,902	51	46	3
1976	5,749,660	55	42	4
1980	5,754,287	53	41	5
1984	6,193,700	55	40	5
1988	5,875,943	52	43	5
1992	5,993,002	51	43	6
1996	6,805,612	49	43	8
2000	7,781,997	48	42	10
2004	8,366,663	48	41	12
2008	8,755,588	50	37	13
2012	8,508,015	50	37	13
2016	8,722,977	48	38	14
2018	8,609,880	48	38	14
2020	8,906,295	46	39	15
2022	8,618,386	46	40	11

Source: Compiled by the authors from PA Department of State website.

can contribute as well as carefully proscribe how contributions may be used, no significant changes to the 1937 law have been made. In 2011, newly elected governor Tom Corbett, formerly the state's attorney general, who prosecuted members of the General Assembly for corruption, proposed modest revisions, but his suggestions failed to advance as legislators appeared reluctant to modify campaign rules that benefited their reelections.[17] In 2019, a group of Democratic senators introduced S215, a bill to limit contributions from contractors doing business with the state; as of publication the bill had stalled. Also in 2019, Senator Costa offered a reform bill "that would set limits on political contributions, increase transparency and ban candidates from using campaign cash for their personal benefit," and though then–Senate Majority Leader Scarnati tweeted his general support for the bill, as of publication the bill had not advanced.[18]

Legal experts, academics, and good government advocates also bemoan the weak penalties that accompany violations of the state's lenient rules as well as the small staff with a tiny budget in the secretary of the commonwealth's office responsible for oversight and enforcement. Most campaign finance reports (60 percent) were filed on paper rather than online, further burdening the staff. Reformers note paper filing's inefficiencies, yet bills to require all reports to be submitted online have languished. Despite the many calls for campaign finance reform, serious change appears unlikely in the foreseeable future.[19]

POLITICAL PARTIES

Political parties have been active in Pennsylvania since 1776, when the Republicans, who later became the Federalists, battled the Constitutionalists, who transitioned into the Anti-Federalists and later the Democratic-Republicans, over the ratification of the state's first constitution.[20] In subsequent years, other parties waxed and waned until 1856, when the Republican and Democratic Parties were firmly established as the state's major parties.

From 1861 to 1955, Republicans dominated Pennsylvania's electoral arenas. As shown in table 3.3, Democrats won the governorship only three times and held a majority in the General Assembly only once during those ninety-four years. During the same period, Democrats managed to gain a majority in one legislative chamber for at least one term only seven times. A more competitive balance emerged in the late 1950s, with the two parties alternating gubernatorial control and the three executive offices with some regularity. Since the 1990s, however, because of gerrymandering and the state's political geography, Republicans have held a majority in both houses of the General Assembly more frequently than Democrats.

But the Republican and Democratic Parties of the twenty-first century are ideologically different from what they were in previous decades. Moreover, significant divisions within the two parties materialized, first among Republicans in 2009 and later among Democrats, that shattered what cohesiveness both parties had earlier enjoyed. The Republican's Tea Party faction emerged nationally in reaction to President Obama's legislative achievements, principally the Affordable Care Act, and his executive actions, and in Pennsylvania as a backlash against eight years of Democratic governor Ed Rendell's policies. The Tea Party's agenda diverged dramatically from traditional Republican orthodoxy. As economic populists, they sought to move the party further to the right. They believed that the federal and state governments had become too powerful, imposed too many taxes, spent too much to help undeserving people—namely, the young, illegal immigrants, and "freeloaders" (the unemployed) who accepted welfare checks, food stamps, and free housing. They hoped to bring down the business and political elites who controlled government to return power to the masses.[21]

Table 3.3 Party control of executive and legislative branches

Year	Governor	House D	House R	House Other	Senate D	Senate R	Senate Other	U/D*
1933	Pinchot (R)	65	140	3	7	43	0	U
1935	Earl (D)	117	89	2	19	31	0	D
1937	Earl (D)	154	54	0	34	16	0	U
1939	James (R)	129	79	0	23	27	0	D
1941	James (R)	126	82	0	18	32	0	D
1943	Martin (R)	76	132	0	18	32	0	U
1945	Martin (R)	99	109	0	18	32	0	U
1947	Duff (R)	38	170	0	16	34	0	U
1949	Duff (R)	91	117	0	15	35	0	U
1951	Fine (R)	88	120	0	20	30	0	U
1953	Fine (R)	98	110	0	18	32	0	U
1955	Leader (D)	112	98	0	24	26	0	D
1957	Leader (D)	84	126	0	23	27	0	D
1959	Lawrence (D)	108	102	0	22	28	0	D
1961	Lawrence (D)	109	101	0	25	25	0	U**
1963	Scranton (R)	102	108	0	23	27	0	U
1965	Scranton (R)	116	93	0	22	28	0	D
1967	Shafer (R)	99	104	0	23	27	0	U
1969	Shafer (R)	107	96	0	23	27	0	D
1971	Shapp (D)	113	90	0	26	24	0	U
1973	Shapp (D)	96	107	0	26	24	0	D
1975	Shapp (D)	114	89	0	30	20	0	U
1977	Shapp (D)	118	85	0	30	20	0	U
1979	Thornburg (R)	100	103	0	28	22	0	D
1981	Thornburg (R)	100	103	0	24	26	0	U
1983	Thornburg (R)	103	100	0	23	27	0	D
1985	Thornburg (R)	103	100	0	23	27	0	D
1987	Casey (D)	102	101	0	24	26	0	D
1989	Casey (D)	104	99	0	23	27	0	D
1991	Casey (D)	107	96	0	24	26	0	D
1993	Casey (D)	105	98	0	25	25	0	U**
1994	Casey (D)	105	98	0	24	26	0	D***
1995	Ridge (R)	101	102	0	21	29	0	U
1997	Ridge (R)	99	104	0	20	30	0	U
1999	Ridge (R)	100	103	0	20	30	0	U
2001	Ridge/Schweiker (R)	99	103	0	20	30	0	U
2003	Rendell (D)	93	110	0	21	29	0	D
2005	Rendell (D)	93	110	0	20	30	0	D
2007	Rendell (D)	102	101	0	21	29	0	D

		House			Senate			
Year	Governor	D	R	Other	D	R	Other	U/D*
2009	Rendell (D)	104	99	0	20	30	0	D
2011	Corbett (R)	91	112	0	20	30	0	U
2013	Corbett (R)	92	111	0	23	27	0	U
2015	Wolf (D)	83	120	0	20	30	0	D
2017	Wolf (D)	82	121	0	16	32	0	D
2019	Wolf (D)	93	110	0	21	28	1	D
2021	Wolf (D)	90	113	0	21	28	1	D
2023†	Shapiro (D)	102	101	0	22	28	0	D

*Unified or Divided control of both branches
**With a tie in the Senate, the lieutenant, a Democrat, casts tiebreaking votes.
***A Democratic senator switched parties, giving Republicans control of the chamber.
†Information as of March 2023.

In the 2010 election cycle, Tea Party voters helped Republicans retake the US House and elected their own candidates to seats previously occupied by traditional Republicans. In Harrisburg, the GOP captured the House and the governor's mansion and held the Senate with the Tea Party's support. Its candidates, however, challenged Republican incumbents in primaries for seats in the General Assembly. In an extraordinary case in 2014, Scott Wagner, a Tea Party leader, orchestrated a write-in campaign against an incumbent state senator in York County and won. Once in office, he pushed successfully to replace the Republican majority leader, Dominic Pileggi, with someone more conservative. Four years later, he received the Republican Party's endorsement for governor and defeated two other candidates in the primary, but ultimately lost the general election to incumbent Democratic governor Tom Wolf.

Between 2012 and 2016, the Tea Party as a distinct national entity faded away, even as its adherents continued to support economically populist, socially conservative candidates running for seats in the General Assembly. With Donald Trump's arrival in the GOP's presidential primary in 2016, they found a champion who spoke to their values while adding an America First foreign policy. Their support in the general election was essential in securing Trump's victory in Pennsylvania, as well as later electing populist conservative Republicans, such as Representative Russ Diamond and Senators Cris Dush and Doug Mastriano, to the General Assembly. As their numbers in the assembly increased, they became vocal and active opponents of Wolf's legislative agenda, which is addressed more fully in chapter 10.

Fissures appeared in the Democratic Party's ranks nationally after 2010, partly in reaction to the Tea Party's success and partly due to Democrats who believed President Obama was not advancing a sufficiently liberal agenda. Labeled Progressive Democrats, they aimed to shift the Democratic Party's programs further to the left. When Democrats regained control of the House in 2019 and then the Senate in 2021, their members in Congress, led by Senators Bernie Sanders and Elizabeth Warren and Representative Alexandria Ocasio-Cortez, pressed for "Medicare for All," or government-provided health insurance, an aggressive environmental agenda called the Green New Deal, immigration reform, and more. In Pennsylvania, progressives mobilized at the county and local levels, sometimes identifying themselves as Justice Democrats or the Working Families Party, where they sought to take control of the party's committees by having their candidates win in the party's primaries for state and local offices. Though not as widely successful as the progressives were in New York in terms of winning many seats in the legislature, Philadelphia's progressives celebrated when their candidate, Larry Krasner, was elected as the city's district attorney in 2016 along with several city council seats.

More fundamentally, the internal party discord was a manifestation of the widening ideological gulf within the electorate. Differences over public policies between Democrats and Republicans were subsumed by deeply felt, personal animosity toward one's opponents. What political scientists once described as affective political polarization became inadequate to capture the extraordinary emotional antipathy each side felt toward the other, leading some to explain the phenomenon as sectarian polarization. The consequences for Pennsylvania's government and politics are explored in some detail in chapter 10.[22]

Though the Democratic and Republican Parties have appeared on ballots in every election since 1856, other parties have materialized from time to time when the major parties failed to respond adequately to voters' needs. For example, the Prohibition Party advocated ending the sale of alcohol, while the Socialist Labor Party emerged to protect industrial workers' rights. The Quaker State has also entertained the American Independent, Communist, Constitution, Consumer, Green, Libertarian, Patriot, and Reform Parties. However, only the Constitution, Libertarian, and Green Parties have run candidates for statewide offices with any regularity since the 1950s.[23]

In the next few pages, we review the organization and leadership of the major parties, the parties' viability in the electorate, and the parties' control of government offices over time.

Organization and Leadership

The Republican and Democratic Party organizations are very similar. Both parties' foundations are their county organizations. A county's party is empowered by its state party to create its own rules, but those rules must conform to the state party's principles. Traditionally, county parties are organized by precincts that are located within wards, which collectively report to the county committee. In both parties, precinct captains, ward leaders, and county committee members are elected only by registered members of their party to four-year terms in gubernatorial election years. The county chairpersons, who are elected by their county committees, automatically become members of their respective state party committees. Additional state committee members are elected by registered party members in each county during gubernatorial election years. Each party has a formula to determine the number of additional state committee members elected by county, which is based on the number of registered party voters in a county. Both parties' rules require that when a county is permitted to elect more than one state committee member, those members must be balanced between women and men.

State party chairpersons, vice-chairs, and treasurers are elected to four-year terms by their respective state party committees; the chair and vice-chair must be of different sexes. Both parties require regular meetings of their state committees, during which the committees determine party's platforms and decide whether to endorse any candidates running in the primaries or to withhold endorsements, among other things.

Controversies swirled around both parties' state committee chairpersons recently, ending with the resignations of Democrat Marcel Groen in 2018, who was replaced by Nancy Mills, and Republican Val DiGiorgio in 2019, who was succeeded by Bernadette Comfort and then by Lawrence Tabas. While disputes within the parties over leadership positions or candidate endorsements are not unusual, it is rare for them to draw extensive media attention, as both of these cases did.

It is far more typical for state party chairs to be seen publicly as the party's spokespeople, cheerleading for candidates, fundraising, and criticizing the opposition. As we learned from our interviews with recent party chairs, however, their functions change somewhat when the governor is of their party. Mr. T. J. Rooney, Democratic chair from 2003 to 2010, recalled that he was the liaison between the state committee and Governor Rendell, who had little time or tolerance for the state committee. Mr. Rooney speculated that Rendell did not understand the dynamics within the state committee, and that it was his job to balance the diverse interests from across the state to "keep things from blowing up" in the governor's face.[24] Similarly, Mr. Alan Novak, Republican chair from 1996 to 2004, described his position with Governor Ridge as the "'cabinet secretary' for party matters," a facilitator with the county chairs, who devoted much time to strengthening the county organizations.[25] Mr. Novak saw himself not as a dictator but as a motivator and consensus builder, while Mr. James Burns, Democratic chair from 2010 to 2015, tried to "bring people to the table" so that every person and group in the party had an opportunity to present their positions.[26]

Behind the scenes, state chairs assist in recruiting candidates for office, fundraising, settling policy differences within the party, resolving conflicts of various kinds at the county level, and overseeing the state committee's staff, which assists the party's candidates at all levels as they campaign for office. All the chairs stressed the need to find the best candidates, devoting considerable time to recruitment. Raising money for the party and for candidates was also time-consuming, especially with the changes in federal regulations. In the past, all the money raised flowed into state party offices, which then distributed money to individual candidates across the state. Today, however, campaigns are "segregated": each campaign has its own fund and raises much of its own money.[27]

According to the party chairs, campaigns have changed significantly with the advent of the internet, social media, and "bifurcated" campaigns—that is, campaigns not against a single opponent but against multiple opponents: the opposing candidate and every outside group supporting that candidate.[28] Campaigns were once straightforward but are now more complex due to "the 24/7 news cycle, social media and *Citizens' United*. In the old days, you'd fight with your dukes up—two fists—against your opponent. Now, you need to fight like an octopus. You need to be a lot nimbler."[29] Mr. Rooney's insights were echoed by the other chairs, who also bemoaned the loss of face-to-face contact with voters to social media, the rise of super PACS, and partisanship's increasing intensity, which each attributed to gerrymandering, which occurs when a party draws district boundaries to ensure that it wins as many legislative seats as possible. When a district contains a large majority of a party's voters, the primary election becomes more important than the general and contributes to electing more ideologically extreme candidates.

A distinctive type of party organization, the party machine, appeared in America and Pennsylvania late in the nineteenth century. Party machines were best known for securing voter loyalty through patronage: awarding government jobs and contracts to the party's supporters. The country's most recognized machine was New York City's Tammany Hall, though the Republican Vare Brothers' organization, which controlled Philadelphia for decades, also acquired a national reputation.

Other Pennsylvania communities also had machines. For example, Reading, from about 1895 to the late 1930s, was dominated by the Socialist Party;[30] Erie first had a Republican machine from the mid-1880s to the 1950s, when it was replaced by a Democratic one.[31] During roughly the same period, Republican machines ran Luzerne and Lackawanna Counties and their respective cities, Wilkes-Barre and Scranton, until being supplanted by Democrats.[32] Delaware County and its major city, Chester, were ruled "with an iron fist" by Republicans and their machine, the "War Board," from 1869 to 2019, though the machine was losing steam by 2000.[33] While the heyday of political machines has passed, the legacy of powerful organizations distributing benefits to its followers lingers.

State parties' platforms are, for the most part, consistent with those of their national parties.[34] For the Democrats, expanding access to health care, pocketbook issues like higher wages and jobs, education funding, reproductive rights, and preserving the environment are among their priorities.[35] Republicans call for strengthening security for Americans at home and abroad, restoring opportunities for everyone so that they may achieve the American dream, reforming and improving local educational opportunities, "protecting the sanctity of marriage and the rights of the unborn,"[36] and reducing the size and scope of government. Mr. Novak added that he and Governor Ridge promoted improving the technical sophistication of the state's farmers by creating a life science grant program to stimulate university-based research, because agriculture was the state's largest industry.[37]

Party platforms are documents that theoretically have the wholehearted support of every party member, but the reality is much different. Pennsylvania's Democrats and Republicans differ internally on some important issues, based on whether a party's members live in urban or rural areas. For example, Democrats in rural counties and small towns are more likely to back gun rights and oppose abortion, while Republicans in large cities and their suburbs are more likely to prefer commonsense gun control, support abortion rights to varying degrees, and be more tolerant of diversity. The party chairs we interviewed each stressed the difficulty of holding their parties' different factions together. For both Democrats and Republicans, the differences among Philadelphians, Pittsburghers, and members from the smaller cities and rural areas can be quite dramatic.[38]

An anomalous yet interesting bipartisan event is the Pennsylvania Society's annual meeting held in December at the Waldorf Astoria Hotel in New York City. Founded in 1899 by Pennsylvanians living in New York to unite "all Pennsylvanians at home and away from home in bonds of friendship and devotion to their native or adopted state," the organization incorporated in 1903 as "the Pennsylvania Society" and in the years since "has sponsored scores of historical and social functions . . . to remind them [its members] of Pennsylvania's vital and long-standing leadership in the economic and industrial life of the nation."[39] The Society's noble goals aside, its annual weekend-long meeting attracts luminaries from both parties and provides the Quaker State's political, civic, and business leaders, interest groups, and lobbyists opportunities for fundraising, networking, and socializing while candidates for statewide offices test their viability.[40] The spectacle of lavish parties attended by the state's elite has been a rich information source for Pennsylvania's political reporters at least since the 1950s, though its political significance may be waning.[41]

Party in the Electorate

Republicans ruled the Keystone State almost continuously from 1860 to 1934, holding all statewide elected offices, majorities in both houses of the legislature, and both US Senate seats and carrying the state for their presidential candidates. The Great Depression and FDR's victory in 1932 foreshadowed Democratic victories in 1934, when the party took the governor's office, the state house, and a US Senate seat. Thereafter, the two parties alternated control of state offices and the General Assembly for several decades (see appendix A for historical data on statewide elected offices).

Democratic electoral successes, however, did not translate into voters registering with the party. Registration figures presented in table 3.1 indicate that Democrats did not achieve parity with Republicans until 1960, a balance that persisted until the early 1970s.[42] Thereafter, Democrats acquired more Pennsylvanians' loyalty until the early 1990s, at which point voters registering as independent or with minor parties increased. (Recall that those registering independent under the state's closed primary system are shut out of voting in any party's primary election.) And by 2022, voters switching their registrations from Democratic to Republican resulted in the Democratic registration advantage shrinking to under one million voters. Additionally, a Franklin and Marshall College poll conducted in 2021 found that Pennsylvanian voters were more likely to identify as Republican than Democrat.[43]

Registration figures do not tell the whole story, however. Voter surveys conducted about twenty years apart suggest that party registration is not fully predictive of how Pennsylvanians will vote. It appears that registered Democrats are somewhat more likely to nominally affiliate with the Republican Party than registered Republicans are with the Democratic Party.[44]

Statewide registration numbers also conceal the differences in voter allegiance across Pennsylvania. Recall our discussion of political geography in chapter 2. Republican strength remains in the T. However malformed the T has become in the twenty-first century, it remains mostly rural and less populated than the urban and suburban areas, where Democrats tend to be heavily concentrated. Though Democrats hold an overall registration edge, however narrow and shrinking, their challenge in statewide elections was and remains mobilizing their supporters to get to the polls, something that the Republican Party generally does better than Democrats. Political science research has found that those aged eighteen to twenty-five, people of color, low-income individuals, and people without a college degree are less inclined to vote; voters who match these characteristics are also more likely to support Democratic candidates, if they decide to vote, which challenges the party's ability to mobilize them.[45]

In nearly all Pennsylvania's cities, but especially Philadelphia and Pittsburgh, Democrats have outnumbered Republicans by as much as nine to one in the twenty-first century.

Table 3.4 Actual party orientation compared with nominal party affiliation of Pennsylvania voters

		Nominal party affiliation							
Date		**Republican**		**Democrat**		**Ind. or other**		**Total**	
October 2019		**Number**	**Column %**	**Number**	**Column %**	**Number**	**Column %**	**Number**	**Column %**
Actual	ID as R	154	89	20	9	24	39	198	44
Party	ID as Ind	11	6	18	8	17	29	46	10
Orientation	ID as D	9	5	180	82	19	32	208	46
	Total	174	38	218	48	60	13	452	100
July 1998									
Actual	ID as R	165	90	21	11	22	49	208	50
Party	ID as IN	8	4	14	7	11	24	33	8
Orientation	ID as D	11	6	154	81	12	27	177	42
	Total	184	44	189	45	45	11	418	100

Source: B. A. Yost, "Disappearing Democrats: Rethinking Partisanship Within Pennsylvania's Electorate," *Commonwealth* 12 (2003): 77–86. Data from Franklin and Marshall Poll and the Center for Politics and Public Affairs.

At the same time, Republicans in nearly all the forty-eight rural counties outnumbered Democrats by two-to-one or more since at least 2000.[46] It is in the suburbs and the exurbs of Pittsburgh and Philadelphia, where party loyalty remains fluid, that statewide races are won or lost, as these areas hold more independents and voters are more weakly committed to their parties than elsewhere in the state.

Party in Government

From 1860 to the 1930s, the Republican Party controlled the legislative and executive branches and held the most seats on the courts. Our analysis begins in 1932, with the nation in the throes of the Great Depression and voters nationally turning to Democratic candidates. Consider appendix B. Pennsylvanians supported Republican Hoover over the winning candidate, Democrat Franklin D. Roosevelt, in the 1932 presidential election, bucking the national shift. Hoover's coattails extended to Republicans running for treasurer and auditor general that year. (Two years earlier, foreshadowing continued Republican strength in the state despite the pain inflicted by the Depression, the GOP's candidates, Gifford Pinchot and Philip Dewey, captured the offices of governor and secretary of internal affairs, respectively.) But in 1934 Pennsylvanians reversed course, electing Democrats Guffey, Earle, and Logue to the US Senate, governorship, and secretary of internal affairs, respectively. In 1936, Pennsylvanians joined voters nationally to reelect FDR and two other Democrats seeking statewide offices: Ross as treasurer and Roberts as auditor general. The presidential coattail effect for both parties' candidates continued with only two exceptions—Truman in 1948 and Nixon in 1972—until Reagan's 1980 election. Thereafter, down-ballot statewide candidates could not expect to benefit from the success of its party's presidential candidate. The 2020 elections were an example: Biden carried the state, but only Democrat Josh Shapiro succeeded in winning the attorney general's office, while two other Democrats lost the auditor general and treasurer's offices.

Control of the governorship and other row, or executive branch, offices—namely, the lieutenant governor (not listed in the table),[47] treasurer, auditor general, secretary of internal affairs,[48] and attorney general[49]—oscillated between the parties from 1930 to 2022. Republicans held the governorship twelve times (ten different men) and Democrats eleven times (eight different men). In the state's history, no woman has held the office. Notably, after the 1968 constitution permitted the governor to seek reelection, every incumbent governor was reelected until 2014, when Republican governor Tom Corbett lost to Democratic challenger Tom Wolf. And in 2022, for the first time a two-term incumbent governor's party successfully retained the office when Democrat Josh Shapiro was elected following eight years of Governor Wolf.

Because governors are not elected simultaneously with any other row offices—except lieutenant governors and secretary of internal affairs, an office eliminated in 1968—it is impossible to consider gubernatorial candidates' coattail effect.[50] A close examination of appendix B reveals that gubernatorial election results presaged presidential and row office victories two years later in twelve out of twenty-three elections from 1930 to 2020 by carrying either the presidency or a majority of row offices or both. Democratic governors experienced this phenomenon eight times and Republicans five, hinting that Pennsylvania voters were satisfied with the governor's performance and were willing to reward his party. In the other eleven elections, the results suggest that the winning gubernatorial candidate's personal appeal was more important than his party affiliation, as voters two years later rejected his party's row office or presidential candidates.

From 1933 to 2023, Republicans dominated both chambers of the General Assembly for fifty years, while Democrats did so for only ten years (refer to table 3.3). In the remaining twenty-eight years, the General Assembly was split between the parties, with Democrats holding a House majority twenty-two times and Republicans twenty-four times. When the legislature was divided, there were fourteen sessions (twenty-eight years) in which the difference in seats between the majority and minority parties was five or fewer; this slim margin appeared most frequently from 1967 to 2009.

Republicans held the Senate majority in forty sessions (seventy-eight years); during the same period, Democrats were limited to just eight sessions (sixteen years). Slim majorities of five or fewer seats separated the parties in eighteen sessions (thirty-six years), most often from 1953 to 1994.

Pennsylvanians experienced unified government—that is, one party controlling both the executive and legislative branches—forty-four times (eighty-six years) from 1933 and 2021. Republicans led unified governments sixteen times, while Democrats did so only six. Between 1943 and 1953, three Republican governors, Martin, Duff, and Fine, enjoyed large legislative majorities, but from 1995 to 2003 under Governor Ridge, the Republican House majority was five or fewer seats. The Republican Senate majority was considerably larger, however. There were no periods of eight or more years during which Democrats led unified governments; however, during six of the eight years of Governor Shapp's administration—1971 to 1977—Democrats held both the House and the Senate.

In the period under study, the number of divided governments and unified governments with slim legislative majorities suggests that the state's electorate was relatively balanced between the Democratic and Republican Parties. Much of the state's vast rural area and small towns consistently elects Republicans, providing the GOP with a majority of its state representatives and senators. The Democrats' most loyal voters, by contrast, are concentrated in the state's densely populated metropolitan areas. Since the Democratic Party's emergence as a serious competitor in the 1930s, it has succeeded in winning statewide offices more frequently than it has gained majorities in one or both chambers of the General Assembly, producing divided governments. When gerrymandering is factored in, a party can secure legislative dominance without receiving a majority of the statewide vote, which contributes to divided government or small majority party margins in the legislature. If recent elections are predictive, Pennsylvanians can anticipate many more years of divided government.

INTEREST, SPECIAL INTEREST, OR PRESSURE GROUPS

Any group that advocates its agenda before any branch of government to influence public policy is an interest, special interest, or pressure group. And while people form groups for many reasons, not all groups become politically engaged. Circumstances motivate a group's members to turn to government, particularly when a change in public policy adversely affects its members. But since most people do not feel the need to formally join even a single group, their interests are less likely to be heard by government.

Political scientists have identified four reasons why people join groups, based on the benefits derived from group membership: solidary groups, in which members build relationships and network; material groups, from which members seek tangible benefits such as product discounts, vacation packages, or specialized insurance; purposive groups, through which members collectively advocate for a cause; and informational groups, from which members receive training or legal or technical assistance, share research findings, and attend specialized conferences. Groups may provide more than one type of benefit to their members.[51]

Interest groups have been active in the Quaker State since the Republic's earliest days. The first constitution's drafters considered interest groups so important that they included the right to petition the government in section 20 of article I, the Declaration of Rights. While interest groups in Pennsylvania form and disband regularly, a group's emergence indicates an issue's importance at the time. Moreover, their increased numbers, especially since the mid-twentieth century, correlate with the growth and diversity of Pennsylvania's population and economy. Though it is impossible to provide an exact number of politically active interest groups, we estimate at minimum 230 groups in 2019.[52] With so many interest groups, it is quite likely that most citizens' interests are virtually represented, and since no interest is necessarily more special than another, the objective of any politically active group is to ensure that its members' needs are considered by the government ahead of other groups. As one lobbyist put it, "If you're not at the table, you're on the menu." He went on, "What separates the successful interest group from unsuccessful ones is the preparation that goes into making the pitch to a legislator: how much research is done, how carefully the argument is made, and then connecting it to the member's constituents."[53]

From our interviews with lobbyists and lawmakers, the most oft-mentioned, influential groups in the capital are the teachers' union (PSEA), trial lawyers (PTLA), doctors (PAMED), the PA Chamber of Business and Industry, the Insurance Association of PA, the PA Bankers Association, and the National Rifle Association (NRA). More recently, the Marcellus Shale Coalition, the Roman Catholic Church, and the gaming industry—individual casinos and its associations (the PA Video Gaming Association and the American Gaming Association)—and PennFuture, an environmental organization, have been active as the state considers legislation affecting each group. For example, sexual abuse by clergy, uncovered after a two-year investigation by the attorney general in August 2018, prompted the Catholic Church to lobby unsuccessfully against legislation extending the time period for abuse victims to bring lawsuits. Similarly, the Shale Coalition mobilized successfully to block Governor Wolf's calls for an extraction tax in each of his annual budget proposals during his time in office.

There was consensus among the lobbyists interviewed that the most difficult interests to represent are social issues, such as LGBTQ rights, abortion and birth control, gun rights, and, surprisingly, access to alcoholic beverages. The Quaker State is one of only two states (the other is Utah) that operates its own liquor stores while it licenses beer sales to private enterprises. While most residents favor privatizing alcohol sales, the union representing state store employees opposes the idea. Lobbying firms usually associated with liberal and conservative causes are found representing both sides of this issue, which contributes to the logjam in moving privatization bills through the General Assembly.[54]

A wide range of tools is available to interest groups, several of which do not require professional assistance. When the General Assembly is in session, nearly every day groups demonstrate in the Capitol's main lobby to attract media coverage and lawmakers' attention. Group members then disperse to visit their solons' offices to discuss their issues. Universities, nurses, car dealers, wholesale beer distributors, and adults with special needs are among the many groups whose members have appeared in the Capitol.

A group may also mobilize its members to contact their legislators by phone, texts, email, social media, or handwritten letters to educate them about the group's agenda. Social media was identified by all the lobbyists we interviewed as an effective tool for influencing legislators. Mr. Michael Acker, Mr. Gene Barr, and Mr. Dennis Walsh, lobbyists all, noted how the General Assembly's members are significantly more accessible to the public than in the past, such that legislators can easily be overwhelmed with texts, Facebook posts, and the like.[55] Elected officials are more likely to respond favorably to personal appeals from constituents, often referred to as grassroots lobbying, than from other, more impersonal requests, known as astroturf lobbying. The Pennsylvania NRA is frequently identified as among the most effective in using grassroots lobbying to stymie firearms regulations.

Also available to a group with sufficient resources and legal representation is litigating in federal and state courts to compel the state or a local government to either fulfill a responsibility or cease an activity that a group believes aids or harms its members. Six poor school districts, for example, sued in state court in 2014 to create a more equitable funding formula for all public schools,[56] while truckers failed in their federal court action to reverse the state's use of PA Turnpike toll revenue to fund other state roads and the PA State Police.[57]

Campaign contributions have historically been used to gain an elected official's attention, though not necessarily ensuring success in winning the official's support. Even under Pennsylvania's relatively lax campaign finance rules, it is illegal to exchange something of value for a vote on a bill or an executive action. As Mr. James Vaughan of the PSEA related, money contributions don't buy votes, but if a group helps a member reach office, especially a member who shares the same values as the group, the assistance will likely improve the group's opportunity to access the member.[58] Groups do not require professional assistance to contribute as long as they are aware of the regulations, but with professional guidance, contributions can be strategically placed, thereby eliciting benefits over time.

Larger interest groups, especially business and professional organizations, are likely to form political action committees (PACs), which are legal entities whose purpose is to raise and spend money in the political arena on behalf of a group's members. PAC contributions, like other sources, are loosely regulated in the Keystone State. But some groups, like the PA Chamber of Commerce, separate their PAC contributions from their lobbying activities. As we were informed by Mr. Barr, the chamber's PAC contributions are distributed to members who regularly voted with the chamber's position on bills, as opposed to enticing members' support with contributions.[59]

An interest group may also present a sympathetic lawmaker with a bill, drafted by the group's lawyers and experts, that delivers exactly what a group desires from the legislature, whether special tax treatment, regulatory relief, or extending government protection. Such a bill is known as model legislation, and though the bill may be modified by the representative or amended as it moves through the process, it ensures that an interest group's goals are foregrounded in the bill. Interest groups of all persuasions present model legislation, particularly when the subject matter is complex or technical. For example, the American Legislative Exchange Council (ALEC) is a conservative think tank that is widely recognized for successfully crafting model legislation that it shares with state lawmakers around the country, including Pennsylvania, who then introduce them as their own bills.[60]

Interest groups may also retain lobbyists, aka government relations specialists, as employees, or contract with professional lobbying firms, or both; however, lobbying is an activity that, unfortunately, is poorly perceived and generally misunderstood by the public. Lobbying's history in Pennsylvania is long and, at times, sordid. For example, in the early twentieth century, lobbyists for the railroad, steel, oil, coal, and banking industries were frequently seen roaming the Capitol's halls and were well known, especially to Republican leaders. Indeed, seats in the Senate chamber on either side of the dais were reserved for Harry Davis and William Reiter, lobbyists for Sun Oil and the Pennsylvania Railroad, respectively, who were referred to as the fifty-first and fifty-second senators.[61] Joseph R. Grundy, president of the Pennsylvania Manufacturing Association for thirty-three years, was active in state politics in the mid-twentieth century, during which he "wielded virtual veto power over the dominant Republican Party" and led to the coining of the term "Grundyism."[62]

In the early twenty-first century, convicted felons and former legislators such as Democratic House majority leader Bill DeWeese, Democratic House whip Mike Veon, Republican speaker John Perzel, Republican Senate majority leader Joseph Loeper, and Democratic chair of the Senate Appropriations Committee Vincent Fumo all registered as lobbyists after completing their prison sentences. Pennsylvania does not ban convicted felons from lobbying; though attempts have been made to do so, all failed, further tarnishing honest lobbyists' reputations and contributing to the public's suspicion of their work.[63]

We learned from our interviews that lobbying has changed in Harrisburg with the advancements in technology and communications noted above, but also because of one person's efforts and a specific event. Former state representative Steve Wojdak founded S. R. Wojdak and Associates, now Wojdak Government Relations, in 1977, and until his death in 2015 he was a highly respected and much sought-after lobbyist, who enhanced lobbying's reputation by "hiring talented professionals . . . and used their information and analyses to convince legislators and other public officials that his clients' interests were compatible with the public interest."[64] Many of those we interviewed—lawmakers, fellow lobbyists, and journalists—noted Mr. Wojdak's legacy: modernizing and professionalizing government relations in Harrisburg.

The event that changed lobbying was the General Assembly's 2005 midnight vote to dramatically raise members' salaries.[65] Public outrage over both the method and size of the salary increase triggered a tsunami at the polls, where legislative and party leaders as well as senior incumbent members—the old guard—either resigned or were swept from their seats in a primary or the general election. They were replaced by populists, who had little or no political experience and were far less likely to heed their party leaders, deferring instead to their constituents' wishes. As Mr. Walsh related, these new members ran under a microscope, with everything they did immediately appearing online, 24/7. This fractured the parties internally and made compromise across the parties nearly impossible, passing any bills extremely arduous, and lobbying much more difficult.[66]

Governors, cabinet officials, and lawmakers regularly confront issues about which they require information to inform their decisions. A lobbyist provides decision-makers evidence gathered by a client's experts to present the client's position favorably. When multiple lobbyists representing clients with opposing views present their positions, government officials are better informed. All five of the lobbyists we interviewed stressed honesty and integrity as essential personal qualities to gain the trust of those they lobby.

Besides the traditional method of meeting officials individually, contemporary government relations firms also mount public relations campaigns to educate the public or a legislator's constituents about their clients' priorities. The objective is to convince constituents that the client's position should be the constituents' position and then have the constituents contact their legislator to support that position. As Mr. Walsh described it, influencing a member's vote is a campaign in which "lobbying is a tactic in a broader strategy. The more the public can be informed and educated, the more successful the effort [to gain the member's support] will be."[67]

An interest group may employ several lobbyists. For example, AIG (insurance) has had as many as seven lobbyists, 84 Lumber and Altria (tobacco) as many as thirteen, the PA Medical Society nine, and the PA Hospital and Health Systems Association eleven.[68] The Pennsylvania Association of Government Relations, the lobbyists' professional association and itself an interest group, counts 158 members, though not all of them are lobbyists and many are lobbying firms rather than individuals. Well over 1,400 people have registered as lobbyists with the state. We consider fifteen firms to be the most recognized professional lobbying operations in Harrisburg.[69]

Pennsylvania imposes rules on lobbyists, but like campaign finance regulations, they are widely perceived as lax compared to other states, despite Act 2 of 2018, which stiffened penalties for failure to comply.[70] Indeed, lobbyists with whom we spoke believe that Pennsylvania's lobbying rules have changed, but not significantly. As one related, the state's laws "are focused on reporting not prohibiting behaviors or tactics."[71] Another suggested that the rule changes haven't dramatically affected professional lobbyists' work because they *are* professionals,[72] while another added that "the new rules are for the better. More lobbying is occurring, but things are still accomplished. People want to avoid the appearance of impropriety, so disclosure is important."[73]

As of 2018, lobbyists, lobbying firms, and principals, defined as those who employ lobbyists, must register electronically with the state and give standard identifying information: name, address, phone numbers, and the nature of the business. Lobbying firms must also provide a list of the principals they represent. A $300 registration fee is collected for each firm and independent lobbyist, but the House Government Oversight Committee has recommended eliminating the fee.[74] Principals must file quarterly expense reports that contain their lobbyists' names, subject matter about which they lobbied, and all costs associated with their lobbying during the quarter. By contrast, lobbyists are not required to identify the legislators they contact or bills on which they lobby or their positions on issues or submit expense reports, unless they represent an exempt entity and the total expenses exceed $2,500 for the quarter. When expense reports are submitted, expenditures are not itemized but instead aggregated under general headings like "direct and indirect communications." While expense reports are publicly available, the state's website is slow and cumbersome, and most state audits of expense reports are confidential. Reformers and the House Government Oversight Committee have called for greater transparency.[75]

Former public officials or public employees must not lobby their former employers on any matter for at least one year after leaving their positions, a "cooling off" period intended to mitigate the harm of the "revolving door," the practice of lobbyists and public officials regularly changing places.[76] Sitting legislators, however, are not required to disclose any contact they have with lobbyists. Moreover, there are no specific restrictions on lawmakers representing the interests of any individual or group before the legislature, except where obvious conflicts of interest arise.

Legislators must disclose any gifts, whether meals, travel on private planes, or tickets to sporting or cultural events, resorts, or professional conferences worth more than $250 in total from a single lobbyist, individual, or group. Gifts from family members and personal friends are exempt. After assuming office in 2015, Governor Wolf, by executive order, banned all executive branch employees, appointed and civil service, from accepting gifts in any amount from anyone other than family members and close friends.[77]

Despite government reformers' best efforts to make lobbying more transparent and to limit any group's ability to gain untoward influence over elected officials, two lobbying firms' practices since 2008 have provoked controversy among professional lobbyists and drawn the ire of mostly Democratic lawmakers. The lobbying firms Long, Nyquist and Associates, which services the Senate, and Maverick Strategies, which deals with House candidates, also operate LN Consulting (Long, Nyquist) and Red Maverick Media (Maverick), which manage election campaigns for Republicans seeking Senate and House seats, respectively. Additionally, Maverick Strategies controls Maverick Finance, a fundraising business available to its clients. Both firms also oversee political action committees (PACs): Long, Nyquist has Better PA PAC, while Maverick has Strategy PAC. In the General Assembly in 2017, 11 of 34 Republican senators' campaigns were run by Long, Nyquist, while 57 of 121 GOP House members' campaigns were run by Red Maverick Media. That a single firm can assist a candidate's campaign and then lobby that same person, now a legislator, on behalf of the firm's clients is akin to "double dipping" and appears inappropriate at best and unethical at worst, though not illegal. Attempts to ban the practice have stalled in the General Assembly as recently as 2017.[78]

Those who object to these practices, such as Democratic representative Brandon Neuman, contend that "lobbyists have a defined benefit for what they do for their clients—and it should be totally separate from campaigns. . . . It's a public-perception issue and it's a good government issue." Adav Noti of the Campaign Legal Center in Washington, DC, said that firms that engage in both activities present "more or less the same ethical issues that you have when you have lobbyists in general who are making campaign contributions or otherwise helping officials in office. If you have somebody that's helping a candidate get elected, then when they do come around to lobby that candidate, they're going to have more access and influence than other people who are active on the same issue."[79]

Responding to such concerns, Ray Zaborney, founder of Maverick Strategies, stated that he goes to great lengths to separate the political and lobbying parts of his businesses and that he did not believe his dual services gave him any advantages. "People whose campaigns I've worked on have opposed me vigorously. And there have been times when people who I tried to defeat helped me on an issue. Legislators are strong enough to stand up for what they believe in." Mike Long of Long, Nyquist made similar arguments, but from a legal perspective. "Courts have been clear that lobbyists are carrying out the right to petition the government for folks who have retained their services. Equally, you can't ban folks from being involved in campaigns, because courts have found that it is protected activity."[80]

We end this section as we began it: interest groups and lobbying have been around since American independence, and will be with us into the future. Access to state government is guaranteed in article I, though the rules under which they operate and the methods they employ will continue to evolve, as evidenced by a flurry of bills introduced in the House and Senate in the fall of 2021 intended to make lobbyists' work more transparent.[81]

THE MEDIA

At the turn of the twentieth century, journalists covering Pennsylvania's government came exclusively from the state's largest newspapers, working out of offices in the Capitol rotunda's mezzanine that looked like the set of *The Front Page*. The occupants were men who nurtured relationships with the Capitol's denizens, also mostly men, learning their interests, foibles, and relationships with fellow members, party leaders, and lobbyists, which they exploited to gain access to important information that fed their columns. Though the offices look essentially the same today, save for laptops and cells having replaced typewriters and rotary phones, there are fewer reporters toiling there. More women are in their ranks, and they come from television, radio, and online news organizations as well as newspapers. More importantly, journalists' relationship with government officials has changed from personal to professional.

Pennsylvania has witnessed a gradual decline in the number of daily newspapers as more people have turned to the internet and social media for news. Most cities and towns today are lucky to have one daily paper when once they had two or more independently owned publications. For example, the *Philadelphia Inquirer* and the *Daily News* are owned by the same organization; the *Pittsburgh Post-Gazette* and the *Pittsburgh Tribune-Review* continue as independent publications, but the "*Trib*" moved entirely online in 2016; and Harrisburg only has the *Patriot News* and its online counterpart, PennLive, leaving Wilkes-Barre as the only city with two separate papers: the *Citizens' Voice* and the *Times Leader*. Fewer newspapers with smaller circulations and less revenue than in the past translates to fewer reporters covering state government.[82]

Pennsylvania's television stations in the largest media markets—namely (in order of Nielsen ranking), Philadelphia, Pittsburgh, Harrisburg/Lancaster/York/Lebanon, Wilkes-Barre/Scranton/Hazelton, Altoona/Johnstown/State College, and Erie—once had dedicated reporters in Harrisburg, but no longer. And only Philadelphia's and Pittsburgh's all-news radio stations, KYW-AM and KDKA-AM, respectively, retain a news presence in the capital.

With fewer reporters assigned to the Capitol beat, citizens miss out on vital information about what their government does and therefore are less able to hold those in government accountable. Fortunately, since the turn of the twenty-first century several news services have appeared, providing information and engaging in investigative or accountability reporting. Capitolwire, founded in 1999 as an online subscription news service, gathers information on all aspects of state government. Its ownership has changed hands several times, but it remains a trusted news source. The Caucus, a weekly online publication based in Harrisburg that appeared early in the twenty-first century, conducts in-depth investigations on state government and public policy questions. And Spotlight PA is a team of investigative reporters based in Harrisburg with a mission to produce "nonpartisan investigative journalism about Pennsylvania government and urgent state-wide issues" who describe themselves as "an independent watchdog unafraid to dig deep, fight for the truth and take on the powerful to expose wrongdoing and spur meaningful reform."[83] It receives funding from foundations and works in partnership with the *Philadelphia Inquirer*, the *Pittsburgh Post-Gazette*, the *Harrisburg Patriot-News*, and the Caucus. Its articles appear in papers across the state.

When asked what changes they observed over their many years covering Pennsylvania government, the seven journalists we interviewed noted the internet and social media's impact on reporting. A breaking story is so rapidly disseminated that their editors and the public may learn of it as reporters do. Their publications' online components require material nearly 24/7, which means they have much less time, as individuals, to provide rich context for a story.[84] Most claimed that covering state government is somewhat easier than twenty years ago, because sunshine and freedom of information laws as well as government's posting material online give them greater access to documents, except for information related to campaign finance, lobbying, and legislators' expenses.[85]

Among the issues most frequently covered are tax reform (particularly income and property), campaign finances, and corruption. And when asked who among the many elected officials they found most interesting, Governor Ed Rendell was named by all. Several mentioned US senator Arlen Specter, governors Richard Thornburgh and Robert P. Casey Sr., state senator Vincent Fumo, and state representatives Bill DeWeese and Mike Veon.[86]

CONCLUSION

In this chapter, we presented three informal institutions—political parties, interest groups, and the media—and one formal institution—elections—that are essential to any fully functioning democracy. Integrated thoroughly into Pennsylvania's political system, they remain vibrant components despite the changes each has experienced over time. Party organizations have evolved, as have their campaign methods and platforms, but they rarely fail to recruit and run candidates for office. Similarly, access to the franchise has expanded since 1776 even as rule adjustments recently adopted may make voting more difficult for some citizens. And interest groups have continued to press their agendas uninterrupted over more than three hundred years, even as their causes and tactics have changed. Finally, journalists assigned to report on the Keystone State's politics have transitioned from print to radio to television to social media. Though their numbers have declined in Harrisburg and county seats, they remain committed to delivering the news professionally to their readers.

In the coming chapters, we turn our attention to other formal political institutions, namely the legislature, the governor, the bureaucracy, and the courts. In these chapters, the relevance of the four components discussed here will become more apparent.

NOTES

1. There are several excellent books that analyze Pennsylvania elections. See Kennedy, *Pennsylvania Elections*; Lamis, *Realignment of Pennsylvania Politics*; Treadway, *Elections in Pennsylvania*.
2. A 1971 opinion issued by the state attorney general. *Pennsylvania Manual*, vol. 119, 2009, 7-3.
3. Late-arriving absentee ballots in the 2018 elections were not counted at eleven times the national average. See Lai, "Primary Landslide."
4. See Murphy, "Pa. Gov. Tom Wolf."
5. A bill, SB 1200, to eliminate the use of drop boxes for mailed ballots passed the Senate on April 12, 2022, on a near-party-line vote. Other bills are in the legislative pipeline as well as a court challenge. See chapter 10.
6. See Frank, "Proposed Law"; Jackson, "Pa. Senate Panel."
7. A constitutional amendment dealing with victim's rights known as Marcy's Law was challenged prior to the vote because the amendment included multiple issues. A Commonwealth Court judge allowed the election to occur, but ruled that the votes not be tallied until a full hearing on the matter was held. Scolforo, "Judge: Referendum Votes."
8. Article XI also includes provisions for introducing and passing an amendment in an emergency.
9. See U.S. Election Project website, http://
www.electproject.org. Also, the national average turnout using VAP was approximately 55 percent.
10. See Lai, "Nov. Voter Turnout."
11. See Couloumbis et al., "Pennsylvania State Lawmakers Are Hiding."
12. See National Conference of State Legislatures, https://www.ncsl.org.
13. See Couloumbis, Bumsted, and Janisch, "Pennsylvania State Lawmakers Are Hiding"; Janesch and Couloumbis, "Pa. Lawmakers Hand Out Millions."
14. Janesch and Couloumbis, "Pa. Lawmakers Hand Out Millions."
15. See federal decisions in *Citizens United v. FEC*, 130 S.Ct. (2010), and *SpeechNow.org v. FEC*, No. 08-5223 (D.C. Cir. 2010), which removed restrictions on independent campaign expenditures.
16. See Beers, *Pennsylvania Politics*; Bumsted, *Keystone Corruption*; Baer, *On the Front Lines*.
17. See Davies, "Building Trust Starts with Campaign Reform."
18. Janesch and Couloumbis, "Citing *Spotlight/PA Caucus* Probe."
19. Bumsted and Janesch, "Here's What Pa. Lawmakers Can Do."
20. Miller and Pencak, *Pennsylvania*, 103.
21. See Skocpol and Williams, *Tea Party and the Remaking of Republican Conservatism*.

22. For a more complete discussion of sectarian polarization, see McCoy and Somer, "Toward a Theory of Pernicious Polarization"; Graham and Svolik, "Democracy in America?"; Drutman, *Breaking the Two-Party Doom Loop*; Layman et al., "Secularism and Political Behavior"; Mason, *Uncivil Arguments*; Cohn, "Why Political Sectarianism Is."

23. The Constitution Party advances socially conservative as well as small government policies. The Libertarian Party's positions are consistent with the national Libertarian Party's platform of free market capitalism and maximum protection of individual liberties. The Green Party advocates for policies that protect the environment. For additional details on these parties, see their respective websites.

24. T. J. Rooney (former Pennsylvania State Democratic Party chair), interview with the authors, July 1, 2016, by phone.

25. Alan Novak (former Pennsylvania State Republican Party chair), interview with the authors, July 6, 2016, by phone.

26. James Burns (former Pennsylvania State Democratic Party chair), interview with the authors, September 9, 2016, by phone.

27. Novak, interview.

28. Rooney, interview.

29. Ibid.

30. See Engle, "Gilded Age of Reading"; Andrews, "Gilded Age in Pennsylvania."

31. See Gabriel, "How Erie Went Red"; Goodheart, "Swing County, Swing State."

32. See Beers, *Pennsylvania Politics*; Wolensky, Baldino, and Hepp, "Remaking Municipal Government?," 6.

33. See editorial, "Only One Pennsylvania Governor"; Bate, "In Historical Win."

34. See the Pennsylvania Democratic and Republican Party websites for their complete platforms.

35. Rooney, interview; Burns, interview; Marcel Groen (state Democratic Party chair), interview with the authors, July 6, 2016, by phone.

36. See the Republican state party platform.

37. Novak, interview.

38. Interviews with all of the party chairpersons.

39. Pennsylvania Society webpage, https://www.pasociety.com/history.

40. Brennan, "At Pa. Society."

41. See Beers, *Pennsylvania Politics*.

42. For an excellent discussion of partisan realignment in the state, see Lamis, *Realignment of Pennsylvania Politics*.

43. See Yost, "Changing Party Identities."

44. Yost, "Disappearing Democrats."

45. See Prysby, *Rich Voter, Poor Voter*; Yost, "Changing Partisan Identities."

46. See *Pennsylvania Manual* for party registration numbers by county.

47. The lieutenant governor was elected separately from the governor until the 1968 constitution, when the office was joined with a party's gubernatorial candidate in general elections only. Candidates for lieutenant governor run for their party's nomination apart from the gubernatorial candidates. At no time between 1930 and 1960 were the governor and lieutenant governor from different parties, something which happened several times between 1874, when the office was established, and 1960.

48. The office of secretary of internal affairs was created in the constitution of 1873 and eliminated in the constitution of 1968, with the last secretary elected in 1966. Secretaries were elected to a four-year term in the same year as the governor, but unlike the office of governor, the office was not term-limited.

49. The attorney general was appointed by the governor until 1978, when attorney general was made an elected office by constitutional amendment. The first attorney general was elected in 1980. Republicans held the office for thirty-two years—1981 to 2013—until Kathleen Kane became the first Democrat and woman to be elected.

50. During the period under study, successful gubernatorial candidates appeared to assist the internal affairs candidates of their party in every election except 1962, when Democratic incumbent secretary Genevieve Blatt retained her office despite Republican gubernatorial candidate William Scranton Sr.'s victory.

51. See Walker, *Mobilizing Interest Groups in America*.

52. Our estimate is based on figures from the article by Woodall, "Who Has the Most Lobbyists." We excluded individual companies or entities employing lobbyists and included all public and private organizations presenting a *group*'s concerns in Harrisburg.

53. Gene Barr (president and CEO, formerly vice president for government affairs, Pennsylvania Chamber of Business and Industry), interview with the authors, July 11, 2016, by phone.

54. Michael Acker (partner, Triad Strategies), interview with the authors, June 29, 2016, by phone.

55. Acker, interview; Barr, interview; Dennis Walsh (government relations specialist with the Bravo Group), interview with the authors, June 9, 2016, by phone.

56. The Pennsylvania Association of Rural and Small School Districts filed suit in Commonwealth Court in 2014 representing six poor, rural school districts. With the support of the Public Interest Law Center and a private law firm, their case was finally heard before Commonwealth Court judge Jubelirer, with a decision likely in the spring of 2022. See https://www.pubintlaw.org /cases-and-projects/school-funding -lawsuit/.

57. The Owner-Operator Independent Drivers Association, joined by the National Motorist Association, filed suit in 2018 against the PA Turnpike Commission and several other parties. The US Court of Appeals for the Third Circuit found for the Turnpike Commission. See https://www.lehighvalleylive.com/news /2019/08/appeals-court-hands-truckers -defeat-in-pennsylvania-turnpike-toll -lawsuit.html.

58. James Vaughan (executive director, PSEA, formerly the organization's director of government relations), interview with the authors, August 9, 2016, by phone.

59. Barr, interview.

60. See https://www.alec.org. And for an excellent example of how an interest group develops and coordinates with legislators to present model legislation, see Couloumbis, "How a Lobbyist Can Pen a Bill."

61. See Wise, *Legislative Process*, 64; Beers, *Pennsylvania Politics*, 192. There are also tales of lobbyists in Pennsylvania and Illinois cueing lawmakers how to vote by pointing to their eye for "aye" and their nose for "no." Shared with Baldino in emails from Michael Cassidy about this practice in the Pennsylvania Senate and Joseph McLaughlin in the Illinois legislature.

62. King, Cassidy, and Foreman, "Interest Groups"; see also Beers, *Pennsylvania Politics*.

63. See Bumsted, "Lawyer Wants to Stop Convicted PA Lawmakers"; Erdley and Zwik, "Convicted Lawmakers Enjoy Access as Lobbyists"; Bumsted and Janesch, "Insider Access."

64. Joseph McLaughlin (former lobbyist with Wojdak Associates), interview with the authors, August 18, 2016; see also Vargas and Moran, "Pa. Lobbyist Was the 'King of Clout,; McLaughlin, "Remembering Steve Wojdak"; Baer, "Lobbyist's View."

65. Additional information on this subject can be found in chapter 4 on the legislature.

66. Acker, interview; Walsh, interview; Mary Young, PhD (director of government relations for the Association of Independent Colleges and Universities of Pennsylvania [AICUP]), interview with the authors, July 8, 2016, by phone.

67. Walsh, interview.

68. See https://www.pennlive.com/news /2016/04/who_has_the_most_lobbying _powe.html.

69. They are: Bravo Group, Buchanan Public Relations, DT Firm, Emerald Strategies, Greenlee Partners, K and L Gates, Gmerek Government Relations, Inc., Long Nyquist + Associates, Maverick Strategies, Milliron and Goodman Government Relations, Novak Strategies, Pugliese Associates, Ridge Policy Group, Triad Strategies, and S. R. Wojdak and Associates. All have offices in Harrisburg, but a few have their main offices in Philadelphia or Pittsburgh.

70. See NCSL website on lobbying regulations, https://www.ncsl.org/research/ethics /lobbyist-regulation.aspx. See also Simmons -Ritchie, "Pa.'s Lobbying Law Got Tougher in 2018"; a Sunlight Foundation study gave Pennsylvania a C rating.

71. Dennis Walsh (government relations specialist with the Bravo Group), interview with the authors, June 9, 2016, by phone.

72. Acker, interview.

73. Vaughan, interview.

74. See House Government Oversight Committee Report on lobbying.

75. Ibid.

76. The restriction does not apply to attorneys because of a PA court decision: *Shaulis v. PA State Ethics Commission*, 574 PA 680, 833 A. 2nd 123 (2003).

77. Executive Order 2015-01—Executive Branch Employee Gift Ban, January 20, 2015.

78. Couloumbis and Navratil, "Pennsylvania Lobbyists Also Help Elect Lawmakers."

79. Ibid.

80. Ibid.

81. On October 13, 2021, four bills were introduced in the Senate to make lobbying in the Capitol more transparent: SB 801, 802, 803, and 804. On June 10, HB 1602 was introduced,

followed on October 25 by HB 1599, 1600, 1601, 1603, 1605, 1606, 1607, 1608, 1609—all with the express purpose of making particular features of lobbying transparent.

82. Baer, interview; Bumsted, interview. Both specifically mentioned fewer journalists as a problem.

83. See Spotlight PA Mission Statement.

84. Baer, interview; Bumsted, interview.

85. Baer, interview; Bumsted, interview; Peter Jackson (retired AP reporter), interview with the authors, June 1, 2016, by phone; Krawczeniuk, interview; Swift, interview.

86. Baer, interview; Bumsted, interview; Jackson interview; Krawczeniuk, interview; Swift, interview.

BIBLIOGRAPHY

Andrews, J. Cutler. "The Gilded Age in Pennsylvania." *Pennsylvania History* 34, no. 1 (1967): 1–24.

Baer, John. "A Lobbyist's View on Why So Many Hate Lobbyists." *Philadelphia Inquirer*, May 6, 2018.

———. *On the Front Lines of Pennsylvania Politics: Twenty-Five Years of Keystone Reporting.* Charleston, SC: History Press, 2012.

Bate, Dana. "In Historical Win, Democrats Take Delaware County Council in a Clean Sweep." WITF, November 6, 2019. https://www.witf.org/2019/11/06/in-historic-win-democrats-take-delaware-county-council-in-a-clean-sweep.

Beers, Paul B. *Pennsylvania Politics Today and Yesterday: The Tolerable Accommodation.* University Park: Pennsylvania State University Press, 1980.

Brennan, Chris. "At Pa. Society, Silence Is the Bigger Answer." *Philadelphia Inquirer*, December 9, 2019.

Bumsted, Brad. *Keystone Corruption: A Pennsylvania Insider's View of a State Gone Wrong.* Philadelphia: Camino Press, 2013.

———. "Lawyer Wants to Stop Convicted PA Lawmakers from Lobbying." *Citizens' Voice*, September 5, 2014.

Bumsted, Brad, and Sam Janesch. "Here's What Pa. Lawmakers Can Do to Close the Loopholes in Campaign Finance Law." Lancaster Online, October 27, 2019. https://lancasteronline.com/news/politics/heres-what-pa-lawmakers-can-do-to-close-the-loopholes-in-campaign-finance-law-theyve/article_f1822f18-f757-11e9-b939-b3f91105d3cd.html.

———. "Insider Access." *Citizens' Voice*, August 20, 2017.

Cohn, Nate. "Why Political Sectarianism Is a Growing Threat to American Democracy." *New York Times*, April 19, 2021.

Couloumbis, Angela. "How a Lobbyist Can Pen a Bill." *Philadelphia Inquirer*, April 17, 2022.

Couloumbis, Angela, and Liz Navratil. "Pennsylvania Lobbyists Also Help Elect Lawmakers." *Philadelphia Inquirer*, September 17, 2017.

Couloumbis, Angela, Mark Wereschagin, Brad Bumsted, Paula Knudsen, and Sam Janesch. "Pennsylvania State Lawmakers Are Hiding Millions in Campaign Spending. And It's All Legal." Spotlight PA and the Caucus, October 22, 2019. https://www.inquirer.com/news/pennsylvania/spl/pa-election-hidden-campaign-spending-spotlight-pa-20191022.html.

Davies, Paul. "Building Trust Starts with Campaign Reform." *Philadelphia Inquirer.* January 22, 2011.

Drutman, Lee. *Breaking the Two-Party Doom Loop: The Case for Multiparty Democracy in America.* Oxford: Oxford University Press, 2020.

Editorial. "Only One Pennsylvania Governor Called Delaware County Home." *Delaware County Daily Times*, January 23, 2019.

Engle, Rob. "The Gilded Age of Reading, Pennsylvania and the Rise of the Socialist Party." Berks County Historical Society Paper.

Erdley, Debra, and Kevin Zwik. "Convicted Lawmakers Enjoy Access as Lobbyists." *Pittsburgh Tribune-Review*, July 17, 2017.

Frank, Howard. "Proposed Law Would End Pennsylvania's Closed Primaries." *Pocono Record*, June 16, 2009.

Gabriel, Trip. "How Erie Went Red: The Economy Sank, and Trump Rose." *New York Times*, November 12, 2016.

Gans, Curtis. *Voter Turnout in the United States, 1788–2009.* Washington, DC: Congressional Quarterly Press, 2010.

Goodheart, Jessica. "Swing County, Swing State." *American Prospect*, November 8, 2019.

Graham, Matthew J., and Milan W. Svolik. "Democracy in America? Partisanship, Polarization and the Robustness of Support for Democracy in the United States." *American Political Science Review* 114, no. 2 (2020): 392–409.

Jackson, Kent. "Pa. Senate Panel Considers Open Primaries." *Philadelphia Inquirer*, April 22, 2022.

Janesch, Sam, and Angela Couloumbis. "Citing *Spotlight/PA Caucus* Probe, Top Lawmaker Pushes Limits on Campaign Donations, Stricter Disclosure Rules." https://www.spotlightpa.org. October 25, 2019.

———. "Pa. Lawmakers Hand Out Millions in Public Contracts to Law Firms That Fill Their Campaign Coffers." *Philadelphia Inquirer*, October 13, 2021.

Kennedy, John J. *Pennsylvania Elections: Statewide Contests from 1950–2012.* Rev. ed. Washington, DC: University Press of America, 2014.

King, Michael R., Michael E. Cassidy, and Jeff Foreman. "Special Interests in Pennsylvania Politics." Unpublished book chapter, 1994.

Lai, Jonathan. "November Voter Turnout Has a Message." *Philadelphia Inquirer*, December 3, 2019.

———. "A Primary Landslide: The Votes Not Cast." *Philadelphia Inquirer*, October 23, 2019.

Lamis, Renee M. *The Realignment of Pennsylvania Politics Since 1960: Two-Party Competition in a Battleground State.* University Park: Pennsylvania State University Press, 2009.

Layman, Geoffrey C., David E. Campbell, John G. Green, and Nathanael Gratias Sumaktoyo. "Secularism and Political Behavior." *Public Opinion Quarterly* 85, no. 1 (2021): 79–100.

Mason, Lilliana. *Uncivil Arguments: How Politics Became Our Identity.* Chicago: University of Chicago Press, 2018.

McCoy, Jennifer, and Murat Somer. "Toward a Theory of Pernicious Polarization and How It Harms Democracies: Comparative Evidence and Possible Remedies." *Annals of the American Academy of Political and Social Sciences* (January 2019).

McLaughlin, Joseph P., Jr. "Remembering Steve Wojdak." Eulogy, June 8, 2015.

Murphy, Jan. "Pa. Gov. Tom Wolf: Election Reform Bill 'Removes Barriers to the Voting Booth.'" PennLive.com, October 29, 2019.

Miller, Randall M., and William Pencak. *Pennsylvania: A History of the Commonwealth.* University Park: Pennsylvania State University Press, 2002.

Pennsylvania House Government Oversight Committee Report on Lobbying. https://www.legis.state.pa.us/WU01/LI/TR/Reports/2019_0001R.pdf.

Prysby. Charles. *Rich Voter, Poor Voter, Red Voter, Blue Voter: Social Class and Voting Behavior in Contemporary America.* New York: Routledge, 2020.

Scolforo, Mark. "Judge: Referendum Votes Won't Be Tallied." *Citizen's Voice*, October 31, 2019.

Simmons-Ritchie, Daniel. "Pa.'s Lobbying Law Got Tougher in 2018. But It Still Falls Short in Exposing Influence." *Philadelphia Inquirer*, February 17, 2020.

Skocpol, Theda, and Vanessa Williamson. *The Tea Party and the Remaking of Republican Conservatism.* Oxford: Oxford University Press, 2012.

Sorauf, Frank. *Party and Representation.* New York: Atherton Press, 1962.

Spotlight PA Mission Statement. https://www.spotlightpa.org/about/mission.

Sunlight Foundation study. https://sunlightfoundation.com/2015/08/12/how-transparent-is-your-states-lobbying-disclosure.

Treadway, Jack M. *Elections in Pennsylvania: A Century of Partisan Conflict in the Keystone State.* University Park: Pennsylvania State University Press, 2005.

Vargas, Claudia, and Robert Moran. "Pa. Lobbyist Was the 'King of Clout,'" *Philadelphia Inquirer*, June 3, 2015.

Walker, Jack. *Mobilizing Interest Groups in America.* Ann Arbor: University of Michigan Press, 1991.

Wise, Sidney. *The Legislative Process in Pennsylvania.* Washington, DC: American Political Science Association, 1971.

———. *The Legislative Process in Pennsylvania.* 2nd ed. Harrisburg: Commonwealth of Pennsylvania, 1984.

Wolensky, Robert P., Thomas J. Baldino, and John H. Hepp III. "Remaking Municipal Government? Charter Reform in Wilkes-Barre, Pennsylvania, 1968–2001." *Pennsylvania History: A Journal of Mid-Atlantic Studies* 73, no. 4 (2006): 446–79.

Woodall, Candy. "Who Has the Most Lobbyists." PennLive, May 20, 2019.

Yost, B. A. "Changing Party Identities." Issue #17. Center for Opinion Research, January 27, 2022.

———. "Disappearing Democrats: Rethinking Partisanship Within Pennsylvania's Electorate." *Commonwealth: A Journal of Political Science* 12 (2003): 77–86.

CHAPTER 4

The Legislative Branch

The General Assembly

William Penn established the Pennsylvania Assembly on December 4, 1682, to approve the colony's "First Frame of Government" (its constitution), and it has met continuously in one form or another ever since, making it America's longest-serving legislature.[1] For over 340 years, the General Assembly's transformation from a unicameral to bicameral, part-time to full-time, amateur to professional, and relatively small to significantly larger institution has been remarkable. In this chapter, we examine Pennsylvania government's first branch: its modernization, its members and how they are elected, its operational rules and procedures, its relations with the executive branch, and the challenges it faces going forward. And in the process, we reveal the critical importance of this institution's place as the keystone of the Keystone State.

MODERNIZING THE GENERAL ASSEMBLY, 1968–2020: A BRIEF HISTORY

To fully appreciate the reasons for and means by which the General Assembly changed, we must explain how and why the legislature functioned before 1968, beginning with the 1873 constitution. Pennsylvania's legislature, like others in the post–Civil War period, was plagued by corruption, as the state's major industries exercised untoward influence over it. By adopting the 1873 constitution, citizens assumed that institutional transformation could be achieved by banishing wrongdoing from the Capitol's halls. They expected that institutional reforms would lead to laws benefitting people rather than immense holding companies and corporations. The revisions increased the size of the House from one hundred to two hundred and the Senate from twenty-five to fifty, assuming that with so many more lawmakers, industry lobbyists would be unable to sway enough votes to pass their favored bills. The governor's line-item veto over spending bills was strengthened with a two-thirds vote in both chambers required to override it, in the expectation that the veto would end the legislature's wasteful spending. By creating a lieutenant governor to oversee the Senate as well as to succeed the governor, reformers assumed the lieutenant governor would cast tiebreaking votes and, as presiding officer, obstruct questionable legislation on the floor. Biennial legislative sessions were mandated, meaning fewer sessions and less time for legislative mischief. Also included were technical provisions that restricted subjects from the legislature's purview, like banning "the introduction of amendments to bills that contradicted the original purpose of the bill; writing ambiguous appropriations bills; and habitually sloughing over the required three readings of all bills."[2]

Unfortunately, scandalous and criminal activities continued, notably the financial improprieties surrounding the construction of the new Capitol in 1905.[3] Thereafter, the General Assembly muddled along as a part-time, unprofessional, and significantly weakened institution inadequate to meet its constitutional responsibilities.

Attempts to reinvigorate the legislature's stature occurred again in 1959 and 1967 using constitutional amendments. The 1959 amendment permitted the legislature to meet annually but restricted even-numbered year sessions to bills dealing only with revenue and appropriations and odd-numbered years to all other legislation.[4] Subsequently, the General Assembly engaged in pitched battles with governors over budgets. Seven of the ten budgets between 1959 and 1968 were late by an average of ninety-four days.[5]

The 1967 amendment allowed the General Assembly to meet continuously during its two-year term without restrictions on the types of legislation that it could consider in any year; required that every bill be referred to a committee and that bills be printed and distributed to all members in advance of floor votes; mandated that each bill passed have a single subject matter reflected in the bill's title, except for appropriations bills and codifying legislation; and compelled all bills to have three readings in each chamber and that all amendments be printed and distributed to members before the final vote, at which time the members' yeas and nays must be recorded.[6]

The 1967 Constitution Convention incorporated the 1959 and 1967 amendments' provisions but went further in addressing the General Assembly's shortcomings. Though the convention was restricted to amending only four areas—the judiciary, state finance, local government, and legislative reapportionment—the delegates' decisions in the latter area affected the General Assembly profoundly—namely, by fixing the House's size at 203 and the Senate's at 50.[7]

In the early 1960s, the state government's deficiencies had become a source of public derision, driving voters' support for a constitutional convention and ultimately to ratify a new constitution. At the same time within the General Assembly, modernizing the institution had gained momentum, culminating in a proposal—HR 207—jointly sponsored by majority leader Lee Donaldson (R, Allegheny) and minority leader Herbert Fineman (D, Philadelphia) to create a bipartisan study commission that was adopted overwhelmingly by both chambers.[8] The Commission on Legislative Modernization was composed of twelve members appointed by House and Senate leaders, with novelist James Michener and Theodore Hazletter Jr., president of the Mellon Charitable and Educational Trust, elected as cochairs.[9] The Commission engaged the services of academic scholars and management consultants to study the legislature's operations, and in January 1969, after extensive hearings with testimony from business and labor leaders, the press corps, and good government advocates such as the League of Women Voters, the Commission issued a 204-page report, *Toward Tomorrow's Legislature,* containing fifty-eight recommendations.[10] The major recommendations included:

1. Strengthen the committee system by providing for fewer committees with parallel jurisdictions in both houses, increase accountability (public meetings, recorded votes), adequately fund committee activities, expand committee roles in oversight of executive agencies, and establish committee staffing for both majority and minority parties.
2. Improve legislative facilities and amenities, including member offices and committee meeting rooms.
3. Increase legislative salaries commensurate with added legislative duties.
4. Expand the role of the House and Senate ethics committees and require the disclosure of financial and other campaign information by legislators.
5. Establish uniform and standard accounting practices in the legislature in combination with annual audits.
6. Hire additional staff to assist members with the development of legislation, constituency work, and dissemination of information to constituents and the press and develop uniform personnel policies and job qualifications.[11]

Though the report's many recommendations were not fully implemented as written, most were eventually achieved in full or in part because of Speaker Herbert Fineman's leadership from 1969 to 1972 and 1975 to 1977. Known as the "father of the modern Pennsylvania legislature" and "architect of legislative reform," Fineman studied the changes occurring in other states, scoured research published by the National Conference of State Legislatures (NCSL), and took seriously a 1971 report on enhancing state legislatures issued by the Citizens Conference on State Legislatures.[12] Working across the aisle, he accomplished the following: improved members' salaries, empowered committees to engage in more oversight, provided members and committees with offices and staff (though staff hiring was partisan rather than bipartisan as recommended), hired staff based on experience and expertise rather than solely on party loyalty, reduced the number of standing committees but added an ethics committee, opened committee hearings to the public, limited a committee chair's power to block legislation from floor consideration, increased minority party representation on committees to better reflect the party ratio in the House, and devised "an innovative system that divided the legislative schedule into 'committee weeks' and 'floor weeks,'" which reduced committee hearing and floor vote conflicts and allowed for greater committee scrutiny of bills. Not to be outdone, the Senate eventually adopted many of the same reforms.[13]

Additional changes over several decades further modernized the General Assembly, such as creating new agencies to assist with financial analyses. We consider these improvements below.

LEGISLATORS: WHO THEY ARE, THEIR COMPENSATION, AND HOW THEY ARE ELECTED

The 1968 constitution's article II vests the state's legislative power in a General Assembly of two chambers, a Senate and a House of Representatives, making the Keystone State one of forty-nine with a bicameral legislature. Only Nebraska's is unicameral. Legislative elections are held every two years, in even-numbered years, for the entire House and half of the Senate.

Senators, who must be twenty-five at the time they assume office, are elected to four-year terms, while representatives serve two-year terms and must be twenty-one when sworn into office. Both must be US citizens, be state residents for four years, and live in their respective districts for one year prior to election as well as during their service in the legislature. They must not have been convicted of serious crimes, hold any other public office, or work another full-time job while in office.

The General Assembly's membership has never mirrored the state's demographic profile in terms of its percentages of women, Blacks, or other minorities, though some gains have occurred since the 1990s, especially for African Americans. For example, the state's population has been approximately 50 percent women for much of its history, yet women held only 31.6 percent of the seats in 2023, the highest percentage since 1923, placing Pennsylvania thirtieth among all states.

FIG. 4.1 Women in the House, 1933–2023.

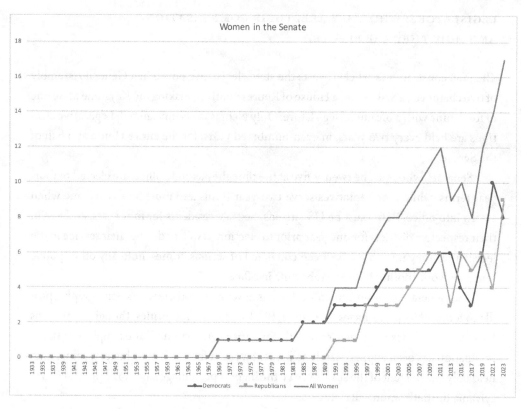

FIG. 4.2 Women in the Senate, 1933–2023.

The low numbers in the nineteenth and twentieth centuries were caused by women not holding the franchise and later the paucity of women seeking office; however, though more women candidates have run since the 1980s, few women candidates are successfully elected to the General Assembly. Why? Research suggests that nationally, women confront more obstacles than men when entering politics. For example, family obligations, such as caregiving and domestic responsibilities, impose a higher cost on women than men. Women experience lower levels of political ambition and face less encouragement to seek office even when they have equal or better qualifications than men. Insufficient experience serving in lower offices contributes to lower name recognition when standing for state-level positions. Party leaders, who are mostly men, are less likely to recruit women, and when they do, they fail to adequately support them compared to men, particularly with regard to money and connecting women to donors.[14] Additionally, Pennsylvania voters in the aggregate rarely choose women candidates running for *statewide* offices: only ten women were elected between 1954 and 2022, and none were women of color. The state has never had a female governor or US senator. Moreover, only eleven women have ever been elected to the US House from Pennsylvania, with five of the seventeen members in 2023 being women.[15]

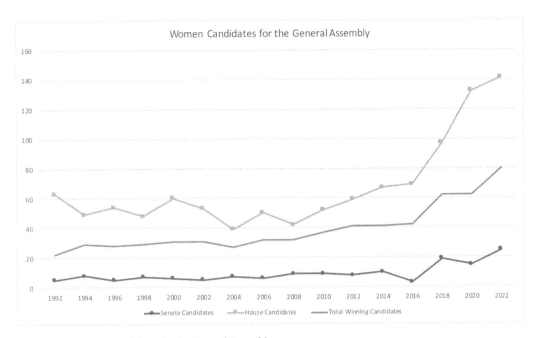

FIG. 4.3 Women candidates for the General Assembly, 1992–2022.

African Americans have fared somewhat better than women in winning legislative seats, especially since the 1990s. Figure 4.4 shows that Blacks currently hold twenty-eight seats, or about 11 percent of the total, closely mirroring the 11 percent of Pennsylvanians who are African American. A closer examination of the graph reveals that few Blacks were elected to the General Assembly prior to 1960, and until 1935, all were Republican, a result of African American voters' loyalty to the party of Lincoln. Most Blacks elected since 1937 have been Democrats, with the majority coming from districts in Philadelphia, Allegheny, and Delaware Counties, where the percentage of African American voters is relatively high compared to the rest of the state. Members of the Pennsylvania Legislative Black Caucus have expressed their concern and desire to have more African Americans elected from the state's other counties. According to political practitioners, Black candidates should "do the Barack Obama thing—put together the Black votes, establish a white core and create a special ethnic appeal."[16]

Lawmakers of other racial and ethnic minorities, such as Latinos/as and Asians, roughly 4 percent and 8 percent, respectively, of the population, comprise 1 percent or less of the General Assembly's membership. As the numbers suggest, the intersectional challenges faced by candidates of color who are also women are daunting when compared to White men.[17]

One may ask if achieving equality in descriptive representation in the General Assembly should be a goal—that is, whether the percentage of women and people of color in the assembly should precisely reflect their numbers in the general population. The answer

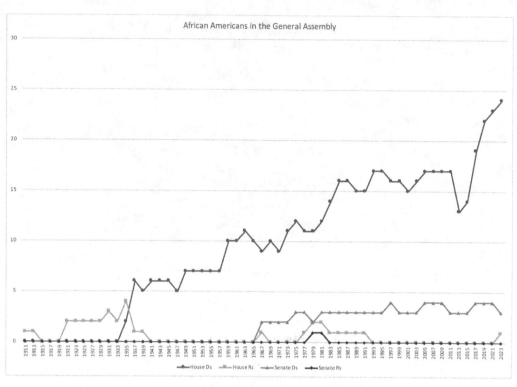

African Americans in the General Assembly

FIG. 4.4 African Americans in the General Assembly, 1911–2023.

from members of underrepresented groups is yes. They contend that issues important to their members are much more likely to be brought to the legislature's attention when they are seated in the assembly. For women, issues like health and child care, education, and pay equity are more likely to be addressed, while for people of color, issues like civil rights, fair employment, crime, and housing are more often presented. Again, national research on this subject indicates that descriptive representation often results in better substantive representation.[18]

Before transitioning to a full-time professional legislature, Pennsylvania's lawmakers overwhelmingly failed to self-identify as full-time legislators. "Only 20 legislators called themselves full-time in 1960. By 1970, 49 were full-time, and by 1990, the number rose to 178 out of 203 members of the House."[19] The same trend was found in the Senate.[20] By 2020, most members acknowledged lawmaking as their profession, but two events—the July 2005 pay raise vote and the 2007 Bonusgate scandal—altered the General Assembly's composition and members' perceptions of their job and the institution. By 2020, a number of senior members had retired or been defeated in primary or general elections, replaced by people somewhat younger, reflecting more gender and racial diversity, from occupations other than law, and more ideologically partisan.[21]

The Keystone State's solons are well compensated compared to those in other states. In 2020, the average salary was $90,335 along with a $178 per diem paid for session days (permitted under article II, section 8), should a member opt to take it, while leaders' salaries were as much as 30 percent higher, ranking Pennsylvania's wages third nationally behind California and New York.[22] Controversies may arise when members vote to increase their salaries, though raises only take effect when the next General Assembly assumes office. For example, in 2005, lawmakers voted to increase their pay 16 percent and leaders' pay by over 30 percent. Members rescinded the raise following weeks of public outrage.[23] Subsequently, members have accepted salary increases under the 1995 Public Officials Compensation Act, which automatically raises their pay by a percentage equal to the Consumer Price Index.[24]

The substantial per diems noted above have been questioned as excessively generous, but even more controversial are the funds available to all members in the "accountable accounts."[25] Representatives receive $20,000 annually plus $4,000 for postage, while senators collect at least $40,000 and $20,000 from the Postage and Communications Expense Account. These funds have covered meals and hotel rooms for legislators and staff, domestic and foreign travel to conferences and training sessions, and other business expenses. Investigative journalists have requested legislators' detailed spending reports under the Freedom of Information Act but have been consistently frustrated because many reports "contained vague descriptions of expenses or had redactions that made it impossible to see their purposes. The redactions primarily concealed whom legislators were meeting with and why." Lawmakers argue that article II, section 15 protects their information as "privileged," meaning they can refuse to provide detailed accounting of the approximately $360 million that each year funds the legislative branch. Following a series of investigative reports by Spotlight and the Caucus, the Senate began issuing monthly expense reports online for its members in the fall of 2021. Yet further digging by reporters uncovered additional spending on legal expenses between 2019 and 2020 in which the purposes, reasons, and the legislators' names were intentionally redacted.[26]

All General Assembly members are elected from single-member districts. Article II, section 16, states: "The Commonwealth shall be divided into 50 senatorial and 203 representative districts, which shall be composed of compact and contiguous territory as nearly equal in population as practicable. Each senatorial district shall elect one Senator, and each representative district one Representative." Between 1875 and 1968, the House's size fluctuated between 200, as required by the 1873 constitution, and 210, a consequence of multimember districts and the requirements that every county have at least one House seat and no county have more than four. (In the Senate, each county was mandated at least one senator, but no county could have more than one-sixth of all Senate seats, a provision designed to weaken Philadelphia county's influence.)[27] The 1968 constitution eliminated multimember districts and the guaranteed House seat for every county. The new criteria made Pennsylvania's rules consistent with the US Supreme Court's *Baker v. Carr* and

Reynolds v. Sims decisions, which mandated that districts have equal populations, be contiguous, and be relatively compact.[28]

In 1962, the General Assembly drafted and passed a reapportionment proposal that followed the 1874 constitution's guidelines, and it was signed by the governor. That plan was challenged before the Pennsylvania Supreme Court, which rejected it in *Butcher v. Bloom* (1964), requiring the legislature to redraw its districts. When the General Assembly failed to comply, the state's Supreme Court issued a second ruling in *Butcher v. Bloom II* (1966), imposing districts that resulted in ten rural counties losing their House seats.[29] More importantly, the redistricting turmoil stoked support for the 1967 constitutional convention, which directly addressed reapportionment's mechanics. The delegates removed the governor from the process entirely while relegating the assembly's role to naming four of the five members to a new Legislative Reapportionment Commission. The House and Senate majority and minority party leaders, or their designees, each appointment a commissioner. The four commissioners then have forty-five days to select a chairperson. If they fail to agree, which happens frequently because of partisan differences, the entire Supreme Court has thirty days to appoint the chair.

For the 1970 and 1980 Reapportionment Commissions, the Supreme Court's nominees were not considered partisan, and both reapportionments proceeded smoothly. But beginning in 1990, the court's choice for a chair, and the process itself, became mired in controversy. Supreme Court justices, like all state judges, are chosen through partisan elections. The party that holds the court's majority names a chair from the party or someone whose political orientation aligns closely with it. Thus, the Commission's final membership usually favors one party, and the districts it designs improve the party's odds of winning a majority of them.

Once all commissioners are seated and have received the US census data, the commission has ninety days to issue a reapportionment proposal, followed by a thirty-day period for comments and corrections, at which point the newly drawn districts are used to elect the next General Assembly. The Quaker State is one of just four that employs a "political commission," while ten others have independent commissions, and in the remaining states the legislatures devise the districts.[30]

Recall that the General Assembly retains responsibility for crafting the state's US House districts. A redistricting plan must pass both chambers before it is submitted to the governor for his signature or veto. In times of divided government, the redistricting process can become contentious, while during periods of unified government the procedure appears less heated but is more likely to produce gerrymandered districts, as happened in 2001 and 2011, when unified Republican governments crafted the congressional maps. The 2001 plan was challenged in federal court on grounds that it violated the US Constitution's article I, one-person-one-vote clause and the Fourteenth Amendment's equal protection clause. Voting 5–4, the US Supreme Court in *Vieth v. Jubelirer* rejected the appellant's claims because it could not find a judicial solution to what it viewed as a political question, leaving the newly drawn districts in place.[31]

With more sophisticated technology and better voter demographic data, the Republican's 2011 map was a gerrymandering masterpiece. As Pennsylvania's House delegation fell from nineteen to eighteen members, the plan's malformed districts resulted in Republican candidates winning thirteen seats in the 2012 election despite Democrats holding a large voter registration edge and their candidates winning more votes statewide than Republicans. (One particularly oddly shaped district, the seventh, attracted national scorn for looking like the Disney character Goofy kicking Donald Duck.) Frustrated, the League of Women Voters and other groups sued in Pennsylvania's Commonwealth Court, challenging the map as a violation of the *state* constitution's one-person-one-vote provision. On January 29, 2017, that court ruled in *League of Women Voters, et al. v. the Commonwealth of Pennsylvania* that the map was constitutional, but on appeal to the state Supreme Court on February 7, 2018, the court declared the redistricting plan an illegal partisan gerrymander, reversed the Commonwealth Court's decision, and ordered the General Assembly to issue a new plan, while simultaneously naming Stanford law professor Nate Persily to assist the court in creating a new map should the legislature fail to deliver an acceptable plan.[32]

Failing in the state high court, Republican legislative leaders went to *federal* court with the same case to prevent the Pennsylvania Supreme Court from imposing its map, but the US Supreme Court issued a curt decision in *Michael Turzai et al. v. League of Women Voters et al.* refusing the request.[33] Subsequently, the Republican General Assembly submitted a remedial redistricting plan to Democratic Governor Wolf, who rejected it. On February 19, 2018, the Supreme Court adopted Professor Persily's map by a four-to-three vote. Republicans appealed again to the US high court, which refused to intervene in the case on March 19. The November 2018 congressional elections proceeded with the court's map, resulting in the eighteen seats splitting evenly between Democratic and Republican candidates. Frustrated, Republicans introduced a motion to impeach the four Democratic justices who voted to impose the new districts, but as of publication no further impeachment actions had been taken.[34]

The Keystone State's lawmakers from both chambers enjoy an unusually high reelection rate, should they choose to seek reelection. In most years since the 1980s, most have. Between 1900 and 1980, 84 percent and 89 percent of House and Senate incumbents, respectively, were reelected, with the percentages increasing to over 95 percent in both houses by 2018.[35] In the 2020 elections, five out of six districts were considered noncompetitive.[36]

Facing such daunting odds, it is unsurprising that few people appear willing to challenge incumbents. In the 2016 election, half of all incumbents ran unopposed.[37] In the twenty-first century, incumbents most fear primary opponents, especially if the challenger is more ideologically extreme than the incumbent. An incumbent may also be unseated if the incumbent is tainted by scandal or the district has been redrawn to disadvantage the incumbent's party.[38]

Nonetheless, incumbents enjoy many advantages over their challengers beyond gerrymandered districts that improve the probability of their reelection, including name recognition, the ease with which they can raise campaign money, the ability to provide constituent services, and the Quaker State's version of an earmark: WAM, walking around money.

Pennsylvania legislators spend considerable time and money striving to meet their constituents' needs, and in the process, remind voters of their labors. In so doing, they establish name recognition among their constituents so that on election day the average voter is much more likely to see and positively remember the incumbent's name.[39] Each of the eight legislators we interviewed emphasized the importance of serving their constituents, a sentiment captured by former president pro tempore Robert Jubelirer: "A lawmaker's first priority is to his district's constituents."[40] Senator Lisa Baker noted that "the function of a senator's office is to solve problems for individual constituents, elected local officials and communities. . . . That creates goodwill, which helps at election time."[41]

All lawmakers meet regularly with constituents in their district and Capitol offices to hear their concerns and assist with obstacles they encounter in dealing with state or local governments. Referred to as constituent service, this enhances the incumbent's name recognition.[42] Another practice popular with both party's legislators is hosting community events, such as senior citizens' issue forums, health fairs, document shredding, or seminars on gun laws, boating rules, and the like. Most activities, which may be scheduled at any time, even in the weeks preceding an election, are paid from the legislature's budget, though some may be funded by gifts from interested businesses or friends. Critics argue that these activities are a waste of taxpayers' money and advantage incumbents unfairly, while lawmakers respond that their constituents benefit from these free services.[43]

Money is essential to candidates, even more so for challengers, yet incumbents generally outraise and outspend their opponents by wide margins.[44] One reason for this disparity is obvious: contributors generally prefer to support candidates who are likely to win and they know incumbents' reelection rates.[45] In 2010, 90 percent of interest group contributions went to incumbents of both parties.[46] But also recall chapter 3's discussion of the state's lax campaign finance laws, which do not limit the amounts that candidates may raise (one of eleven states) and place no restrictions on how campaign funds are spent (one of two states). Incumbents can and do raise tens of thousands of dollars to intimidate potential candidates from even filing to run, and should an opponent enter a race, incumbents heavily outspend challengers, usually ensuring victory.[47]

Once campaign funds are raised, a candidate may expend the money for any purpose, including personal use or establishing "zombie PACs." Spotlight PA and the Caucus conducted a yearlong investigation into lawmakers' use of campaign funds. Between 2016 and 2018, the journalists could not fully trace approximately $3.5 million donated to House and Senate candidates, because expenses were listed under general headings and candidates submitted their unitemized credit card bills for reimbursement. "Charges included foreign trips, sports tickets, limos, lavish dinners, fine wines and liquor, country club memberships and a DNA test kit."[48] Following the article's publication, bills were introduced to address the problems, but as of 2021 there have been no changes to the rules on spending campaign funds.[49]

Defeated or retiring incumbents may choose to spend their remaining campaign money on themselves for expenses such as snow removal, exterminating, or "flagpole repair," or establish a "zombie PAC," which is a political action committee formed by a seemingly dead campaign that directs money to other candidates.[50] No legislation has yet been passed to prevent these actions.

The last incumbent advantage worth noting flows from constituent expectations that Pennsylvania's lawmakers will "bring home the bacon"—that is, direct state money to their districts to ensure that their districts receive their fair share of state dollars, a practice with a long history in the Quaker State. Originally known as public improvement grants, they appeared as a response by lawmakers to petitions from constituents "to secure funds for a long list of local community needs." Like other legislative leaders, Representative Samuel E. Hayes Jr. considered his colleagues' requests to fund district improvement projects year-round, because he realized that "representatives knew their districts better than desk-bound bureaucrats in Harrisburg."[51]

Sometime in the late twentieth century, a public improvement grant became known as WAM—walking around money—Pennsylvania's version of an earmark. An earmark or WAM is akin to pork-barrel spending—that is, government appropriations distributed to legislators' districts to benefit their constituents and enhance their legislative accomplishments. In the Keystone State, WAMs were inserted into appropriations bills or an agency's budget that targeted money to specific lawmakers' districts for specific purposes, like constructing a park or community center, which aided legislative leaders in securing members' votes. WAMs were also placed within agencies' budgets, which were controlled by legislative leaders and used to entice their members' votes.

WAMs were reimagined in the 1980s during Republican governor Thornburgh's administration. In collaboration with Democratic majority leader James Manderino, Thornburgh set aside funds for the four legislative caucuses to be distributed at caucus leaders' pleasure to their members for district projects.[52] Party leaders gained leverage over members to influence their votes on difficult bills, and in return, members demonstrated to constituents their skill at bringing projects home, as Representative Dwight Evans explained. WAM funding began small but grew over time, later joined by the Redevelopment Assistance Capital Program, or RACP, an invention of Thornburgh's secretary of legislative affairs, Rick Stafford, "as a means to finance the Philadelphia Convention center in 1986. They differ from WAMs in several important aspects: Applicants for the money must raise a matching amount and undergo an extensive review by budget officials. The state borrows the money through bond issues, and so these expenditures aren't included as part of the state operating budget. The rationale for borrowing the money is that the projects carry long-term benefits."[53]

While the RACP program and its successor, the Economic Growth Initiative grant, continued receiving funds under both parties' governors through 2020, grant amounts and project sizes varied considerably, from new museums to renovating a college's engineering labs.[54] They continue to be popular with lawmakers, though not among government reformers, who view the grants as insufficiently vetted and lacking transparency.

WAMs transitioned to the Department of Community and Economic Development (DCED) as a community-revitalization line in 1995, with a cursory review added, during Republican governor Ridge's administration. Minority Democrats called these grants "Ridgies." Though the community revitalization line was zeroed out in the 2009–10 budget, new lines magically appeared in the DCED budget for "community conservation and employment" and "cultural activities," demonstrating once again WAMs' resilience.[55] Millions of dollars continued to flow via WAMs to lawmakers' districts until Republican governor Corbett fulfilled a campaign promise and eliminated the grants in 2011; however, WAM-like provisions reappeared in transportation bills in 2012 and 2013, leading WAM critics to cry foul.[56] When Republican lawmakers inserted $7.2 million into the fiscal code, an obscure piece of legislation that accompanies the budget, for WAM-like projects of both parties' members, Corbett used his line-item veto to strike the funds.[57] Republican legislative leaders challenged the governor's veto in Commonwealth Court, arguing that the governor's press release was an insufficient "official legislative notification" and that his use of the line-item veto on the fiscal code was unconstitutional; the court ruled for the governor in 2015.[58] Unfortunately for Corbett and future governors, the state's highest court overruled the Commonwealth Court on a technicality, finding that a governor's press release was not sufficient legislative notification for his action, but the court did not rule on the constitutionality of the use of the line-item veto on the fiscal code.[59]

We were reminded that governors have their own WAMs funded from the state budget. One member recalled that during his first term in the House in 1971, "when Governor Shapp was working to gain House passage of Pennsylvania's first income tax, there was a steady stream of lawmakers being called to the governor's office. Why? To offer public improvement projects for a 'Yes' vote." In another instance, then-governor Robert P. Casey Sr. presented a large mock check, drawn from public funds duly appropriated by the House and Senate, to a Huntingdon County group for a drug-abatement project. When asked by Representative Hayes if the check was a WAM, Governor Casey admitted, "Yes, it's a Governor WAM."[60]

Though political parties are not formally included in the constitution, they play a critical role in the legislature's organization, leadership, and operation. Each chamber's majority party manages that chamber; it holds the leadership positions, fixes the legislative calendar, and determines which bills are considered. An appreciation of the parties' role in the General Assembly is, therefore, essential to fully understand it.

The lieutenant governor is the Senate's president, though the lieutenant governor may not be of the same party as the Senate's majority party, because the office is filled simultaneously with that of the governor. Lieutenant governors preside over the Senate at their discretion and may cast a vote on any question, when the chamber is tied, "except the final passage of a bill or joint resolution, the adoption of a conference report or the concurrence in amendments made by the House of Representatives" (article IV, section 4). Formally, the lieutenant governor's legislative role appears to be relatively unimportant, but in reality, the lieutenant governor's votes to break ties on procedural motions can significantly affect a bill's future.

During routine business and debates, the lieutenant governor rarely officiates; instead, the duties are exercised by the president pro tempore, a position elected by the entire Senate and won consistently by a member of the majority party (article II, section 9). Similarly, the House elects its constitutionally mandated leader, the speaker, from among its entire membership, and like the Senate, the majority party's candidate normally wins, except in one instance.[61] Beyond these constitutional positions, the assembly's other leaders are determined by party votes taken within each house's party caucus.

Table 4.1 presents the General Assembly's leadership. One can readily identify parallel positions across the chambers.[62] The speaker and president pro tempore formally administer their houses but informally head their parties within their chambers. Together with other elected party leaders, they compose each house's leadership team, while the minority party's leadership team is a mirror image of the majority party minus a speaker or president pro tempore. Technically, the speaker and president pro tempore appoint all majority committee chairpersons and committee members in their respective chambers, but functionally, the leadership teams assist in these decisions, while minority leaders and their teams name the minority committee chairpersons and their party's members to committees.

Majority party leaders, also referred to as floor managers, organize each session day's work schedule, chair their chamber's rules committee, and lead the party on the floor during debates, a task also done by minority leaders for their party. The whips are responsible for securing votes in support of their parties' position on bills as well as serving as information conduits between the leadership team and its backbenchers.

Table 4.1 Leadership offices in the General Assembly

	House Speaker	Party	Leadership	Senate President*	
				President pro tempore	
Majority leader	Minority leader			Majority leader	Minority leader
Majority whip	Minority whip			Majority whip	Minority whip
Caucus chair	Caucus chair			Caucus chair	Caucus chair
Caucus administrator	Caucus administrator			Caucus secretary	Caucus secretary
Policy Committee chair	Policy Committee chair			Policy Committee chair	Policy Committee chair
Appropriations Committee chair	Appropriations Committee chair			Appropriations Committee chair	Appropriations Committee chair

*The lieutenant governor is the Senate's president.
Source: General Assembly website.

Caucus chairpersons, administrators, and secretaries serve a party's caucus, which is the official party organization in each chamber and perhaps the General Assembly's most significant informal component. The appropriations committees are the most important standing committees in each house, because they consider not only budget and spending bills but *every* bill that affects the state's budget, even constitutional amendments, as advertising the amendments in the media expends money from the state budget.[63] Appropriation chairpersons are elected by their caucuses rather than appointed by leadership and play a crucial role in defending their parties' positions on fiscal issues.

Regardless of their titles, the goal of all leaders is to pass legislation that benefits Pennsylvanians, especially bills favored by their party's supporters, or to stymie bills offered by their opponents when they conflict with the majority's positions. Leadership strategies, however, are a function of whether one's party is in the majority or minority, a party's total seats in each house, whether the governor is of one's party, the partisan intensity at the time, and the tools available to secure members' votes. Obviously, the majority party has a distinct advantage in passing bills, but if the majority's size is trivial (fewer than five seats), then leaders must carefully negotiate with members who express unwillingness to toe the party line when called to vote on a bill. When WAMs or their facsimiles were available, both parties' leaders offered these incentives to wavering members to gain their votes. Representative Dwight Evans, former Democratic Appropriations Committee chair, referenced trading votes for members' projects as a good practice, because members knew their districts. WAMs helped to pass difficult bills and improved members' reelection prospects.[64]

In years past, leaders once punished members who consistently resisted supporting the party's legislative agenda by stripping them of chairmanships or committee assignments; today, such actions would be taken by a vote in the respective chamber's party caucus. With large majorities, leaders can tolerate a few defections without fear of losing a vote on an important bill. But when a party holds a majority by a single member, and one member switches parties during a legislative session, the consequence is dire: a party loses its majority and control of the chamber. In 1993, Republican Senator Frank Pecora, disappointed with his new district map, joined the Democrats, leaving the body 50–50; because the Democrats held the governorship, the lieutenant governor's vote gave them a bare majority. Democratic representative Tom Stish switched parties in 1995, giving Republicans a one-seat majority.[65] (Both party switchers lost their next election.) In 2019, Senator John Yudichak announced his departure from the Democratic Party over policy differences to become an independent, but he negotiated with Republicans to retain his seniority and caucused with them. His switch did not affect the Republicans' majority, but it made it more difficult for Democrats to capture the Senate in the future.[66]

The fate of any governor's agenda in the General Assembly depends upon whether the governor's party holds the majority in one or both houses and the governor's willingness to personally negotiate with lawmakers. Referencing table 3.3, during periods of unified government, governors expect to have a relatively easy time advancing their programs through the assembly. Internal majority party disagreements and governors who are aloof from the legislative process, however, have caused governors' bills to stall, as Governor Corbett learned, costing him reelection.[67] Of the lawmakers we interviewed who commented on governors' legislative involvement, Thornburgh, Ridge, Rendell, and Wolf were identified as governors willing, even eager, to negotiate with legislators, while Casey and Corbett were viewed as rigid or aloof.[68] Senate minority leader Jay Costa recalled Wolf attending budget meetings with his laptop open and running data analyses of budget options as an example of an attentive governor.[69]

When the governor's party lacks a majority in either house, minority leaders employ the few tools available to them to frustrate the majority, but ultimately only a gubernatorial veto can thwart it. Facing a Republican-dominated General Assembly, Democratic governor Wolf exercised the veto nine times during his first year but less frequently during the remaining years of his first term, principally because Republican leaders took Wolf's veto threats seriously rather than challenging him directly; however, Wolf issued far more vetoes in his second term, as GOP leaders pushed legislation related to election rules, COVID-19, and culture war issues.[70]

We wrote in chapter 3 about the increased partisan intensity since 2010, when both parties witnessed their endorsed moderate primary candidates lose to more ideologically extreme candidates who went on to win in the general election. These new members tend to resist direction from party leaders, because their victories were not dependent on their parties' endorsement, organization, or financial support, and so are less willing to be instructed by party leaders on how to vote.[71] Many of those we interviewed spoke of the difficulties that highly partisan members posed for conducting legislative business, perhaps best illustrated by Senator Robert Jubelirer's reflections as president pro tempore: "The current partisanship is unprecedented. . . . The middle has disappeared. There are more members being elected who don't want government or anything from government. They don't want anything so there are fewer members with whom one can negotiate. You can't move or change the votes of people who don't want something."[72]

Longtime observers of Pennsylvania's legislature often refer to the General Assembly's four-caucus system with fear or admiration as "King Caucus" or "the caucus culture" because each chamber's party caucuses wield extraordinary influence in the Capitol.[73] With a strong, disciplined two-party system for well over a hundred years, party caucuses evolved to become power centers, though differences exist across the caucuses resulting from tradition. Representative Samuel E. Hayes Jr. recalled, "Sometimes the two caucuses in the same chamber had more in common than the same party's caucus in the other house."[74]

The four caucuses' leaders regularly negotiate the substance of important legislation, leaving regular members waiting patiently to be instructed on how to cast their votes. It is also common for party leaders to request a break during floor deliberations to allow lawmakers to retreat to their caucuses, where strategy is discussed and members' votes secured before returning to the floor to vote. Since 2010, however, regular members have pushed back in caucus sessions against deals cut by their leaders if they believe their interests and those of their constituents are not adequately reflected in bills, as suggested by Senators Baker and Costa and Representatives Hayes and Pashinski.[75]

The caucuses can operate autonomously because of the assembly's informal rules and traditions and their funding, which comes from the legislature's budget. Every state budget contains a line that supports the entire legislative branch. Should the fiscal year end with a surplus in that line, it is placed into the Legislative Reserve Fund. As of 2020, the Reserve Fund totaled over $170 million.[76] In most years, the surplus's existence was never seriously questioned because it was relatively small, but during fiscally austere times, its mere existence has been criticized. Legislators from both parties, for example Senators Yudichak and Costa and Representatives Hayes and Pashinski, defended the surplus as important to maintain the General Assembly's independence from the governor. They argue that any governor could veto the legislature's budget line to extract concessions, leaving the branch defenseless; the surplus permits the legislature to continue functioning normally.[77] Critics argue the surplus is nothing more than a "slush fund" and should be dramatically lowered during financially challenging times.[78] In a balanced assessment, retired leader Samuel E. Hayes Jr. noted that the surpluses "are for the purposes of enabling the Legislature to discharge its constitutional responsibility without succumbing to corrosive pressure on the part of a governor. If the legislative surplus is not needed, it lapses. It remains as unspent revenues of the Commonwealth. It's not wasted."[79] After the caucuses' funding practices came under intense scrutiny from a grand jury and a legislative investigation in 2010, some funding and procedural adjustments were made. The four caucuses' influence on the legislative process continues, however.[80]

Since modernization, the General Assembly has been supported by professional and partisan staff totaling 2,358 in 2015, placing Pennsylvania third behind Texas and New York in staffing.[81] As with other aspects of the General Assembly, detractors claim staffing is excessive, wasteful, and arbitrarily distributed. Legislators counter that because there are 253 members serving over twelve million constituents, they need the help, as noted by several of our interviewees, namely Senators Jubelirer and Costa and Representatives Pashinski and Sturla. An analysis of House staffing published in 2010, however, gave credence to the uneven assignment of staff.[82]

Not all staff work directly for individual lawmakers and leadership. Many are employed by legislative service agencies (LSAs), units that provide the General Assembly with specialized services and information. They assist members in formulating bills, conducting research for potential legislation, and aiding lawmakers with data collection related to constituent concerns that could lead to legislation, but they are not directly involved in the legislative process. All LSAs, apart from the Independent Fiscal Office, Independent Regulatory Review Commission, and Legislative Reference Bureau, are overseen by committees from both parties and chambers, with the majority party usually holding more committee seats.

Table 4.2 Legislative service agencies*

Agency	Year created	Number of legislators on Oversight Committees by party and chamber
Legislative Reference Bureau	1909	None**
Local Government Commission	1935	Senate: 3 R and 2 D House: 3 R and 2 D
Joint State Government Commission	1937	Senate: 4 R and 2 D House: 4 R and 2 D
Legislative Budget and Finance Committee	1959	Senate: 3 R and 3 D House: 3 R and 3 D
Legislative Data Processing Center	1968	Senate: 3R and 2 D House: 3 R and 2 D
Joint Legislative Air and Water Pollution Control and Conservation Committee	1968	Senate: 4 R and 4 D House: 4 R and 4 D
Commission on Sentencing	1977	Senate: 1 R and 1 D House: 1 R and 1 D
Independent Regulatory Review Commission	1982	None**
Capital Preservation Committee	1982	Senate: 2 R and 2 D House: 2 R and 2 D
Center for Rural Pennsylvania	1987	Senate: 1 R and 1 D House: 1 R and 1 D
Independent Fiscal Office	2010	None**

*Number and names of agencies as of April 2023.
**Agency has no dedicated oversight committee.

The Legislative Reference Bureau (LRB), staffed almost entirely by lawyers, takes a legislator's rough draft of a bill, resolution, or amendment and converts it into formal legislative language. The Independent Fiscal Office provides economic analyses of budgets and policy proposals as well as revenue projections, while the Independent Regulatory Review Commission examines regulations from all commonwealth agencies (except the Game Commission and Fish and Boat Commission) to establish whether the agency has statutory authority to issue a regulation, establish whether the regulation meets the legislature's intent, and determine the regulation's economic, safety, and public health consequences.[83] The Legislative Budget and Finance Committee, at a member's request, produces a research report on a bill's economic impact. Its high-quality reports have earned it an excellent reputation.

While several agencies' purposes are obvious from their titles, for example Capitol Preservation, Rural Pennsylvania, Data Processing, and Conservation, others are more obscure. The Commission on Sentencing, for example, assists with creating coherent and fair sentencing guidelines by conducting studies within the state and across the country. The Joint Committee on State Government does research on statewide issues, and the Legislative Office for Research Liaison (LORL), which was funded by the House but was available to all members, conducted nonpartisan research on any topic. Its small, permanent staff was supplemented by faculty from affiliated Pennsylvania public and private universities who possessed expertise. LORL was decommissioned in 2013 when Republicans captured the House majority and claimed LORL's work was duplicative of other agencies or better served by existing partisan caucus staff.

Legislative issue caucuses are informal groups funded by the legislature and organized around a single issue, theme, or cause. Members join for many reasons, such as coalition-building around an issue, consciousness-raising within the legislature, and providing members with something concrete to which they can refer when constituents ask, "What have you done on this issue?" Issue caucuses can form and then vanish rapidly. Membership may be partisan or bipartisan, and unicameral or bicameral, depending on a caucus's objective. Table 4.6 presents a sample of issue caucuses from 2010 to 2020. Some among them have long histories, such as the Legislative Black Caucus, formed in 1973, while others have only recently appeared, such as the Taxpayers' Caucus, formed in 2015.

HOW A BILL BECOMES A LAW

Moving a bill through the General Assembly is similar to passing legislation in the US Congress. The constitution's article III presents the foundation, but House and Senate rules and traditions are also essential. The process we describe here is linear to ease comprehension, but in a typical session there are many bills moving through the process at different stages in both houses.

Table 4.3 Legislative issue caucuses*

Name	Partisan or Bipartisan	Unicameral or Bicameral
Arts and Culture	Bipartisan	Bicameral
Blue Green Caucus	Bipartisan	Unicameral (House)
Coal Caucus	Bipartisan	Bicameral
Community Pharmacy Caucus	Bipartisan	Bicameral
Common Sense Caucus	Partisan (R)	Unicameral (House)
Government Reform Caucus	Bipartisan	Bicameral
House Steel Caucus	Bipartisan	Unicameral (House)
Legislative Black Caucus	Bipartisan	Bicameral
Motorsports Caucus	Bipartisan	Bicameral
Northeast Legislative Caucus	Bipartisan	Bicameral
PA Safe Caucus	Partisan (D)	Unicameral (House)
Pro Life Caucus	Bipartisan	Unicameral (House)
Prayer Caucus	Bipartisan	Bicameral
Senate Manufacturing Caucus	Partisan (R)	Unicameral (Senate)
Taxpayers' Caucus	Bipartisan	Bicameral
Women's Health Caucus	Bipartisan	Bicameral
YMCA Caucus	Bipartisan	Bicameral

*Caucus names are as of April 2023.

Any member intending to introduce a bill or amendment must present it to the LRB to be drafted into appropriate language. Once prepared, the member files the bill with the House's chief clerk or the Senate's secretary. The bill is printed, assigned to a standing committee, and given a number, for example HB 47 or SB 213, depending on the chamber, that stays with the bill through its journey in that chamber unless amended, at which point it receives a new number. Traditionally, the member introducing the bill is its prime sponsor, who may also approach colleagues within the chamber from either party to sign on as cosponsors to improve the bill's chances for enactment. Cosponsorship, however, does not commit a legislator to voting for the bill. Representative Pashinski and Senator Baker indicated that it is not uncommon for a minority party member to introduce a bill only to discover that a majority party member soon introduces a very similar bill, leaving the original bill unlikely to advance.[84]

Assigning a bill to committee in each house is technically the speaker's and Senate president's responsibility; in fact, however, each chamber's majority party leadership team performs this task, while exercising considerable discretion, because even after modernization committee jurisdictions overlap.[85] For noncontroversial and personal bills, like naming a park or recognizing a constituent's accomplishments, the clerk or secretary automatically refers the bill to the appropriate committee, but the sponsor may request that a specific committee consider it. For major legislation, such as appropriations or gubernatorially

Table 4.4 Standing committees of the House*

Committee		Number of members by party
Aging and Older Adult Service		12 D and 9 R
Agriculture and Rural Affairs		12 D and 9 R
Appropriations		22 D and 15 R
Children and Youth		12 D and 9 R
Commerce		12 D and 9 R
Committee on Committees		9 D and 5 R
Consumer Protection, Technology and Utilities		12 D and 9 R
Education		12 D and 9 R
Environmental Resources and Energy		12 D and 9 R
Ethics		4 D and 4 R
Finance		12 D and 9 R
Game and Fisheries		12 D and 9 R
Gaming Oversight		12 D and 9 R
Government Oversight		5 D and 4 R
Health		12 D and 9 R
Housing and Community Development		12 D and 9 R
Human Services		12 D and 9 R
Insurance		12 D and 9 R
Judiciary		12 D and 9 R
Labor and Industry		12 D and 9 R
Liquor Control		12 D and 9 R
Local Government		12 D and 9 R
Professional Licensure		12 D and 9 R
Rules		18 D and 15 R
State Government		12 D and 9 R
Tourism and Recreational Development		12 D and 9 R
Transportation		12 D and 9 R
Veterans' Affairs and Emergency Preparedness		12 D and 9 R

*Information as of April 2023.

requested bills, party leaders are seriously involved in the bill's assignment to either a committee deemed friendly or hostile to the bill, thereby aiding the bill's passage or ensuring its defeat.[86] Tables 4.4 and 4.5 present the General Assembly's standing committees.

Once submitted to committee, a bill's fate rests in the chairperson's hands. At the majority chair's discretion, the committee "may dispose of a bill in the following ways": (1) "take no action," (2) "hold public hearing(s)," (3) "vote to defeat the bill in committee," (4) "report the bill to the chamber for action either with or without amendment."[87] Since modernization, the committees' place in the legislative process is secure, but its influence

Table 4.5 Standing committees of the Senate*

Committee		Number of members by party
Aging and Youth		7 R and 4 D
Agriculture and Rural Affairs		7 R and 4 D
Appropriations		15 R and 9 D
Banking and Insurance		9 R and 5 D
Communications and Technology		7 R and 4 D
Community, Economic and Recreational Development		9 R and 5 D
Consumer Protection and Professional Licensure		9 R and 5 D
Education		7 R and 4 D
Environment Resources and Energy		7 R and 4 D
Ethics		3 R and 3 D
Finance		7 R and 4 D
Games and Fisheries		7 R and 4 D
Health and Human Services		7 R and 4 D
Intergovernmental Operations		7 R and 4 D
Judiciary		9 R and 5 D
Labor and Industry		7 R and 4 D
Law and Justice		7 R and 4 D
Local Government		7 R and 4 D
Rules and Executive Nominations		11 R and 6 D
State Government		7 R and 4 D
Transportation		9 R and 5 D
Urban Affairs and Housing		7 R and 4 D
Veterans' Affairs and Emergency Preparedness		7 R and 4 D

*Information as of April 2023.

has waned. As Senator Yudichak noted, committees in the General Assembly are weak compared to those in the US Congress.[88]

Depending on leadership, party, chamber, and a bill's substance, a bill may receive only cursory treatment in committee, while other bills may receive full consideration: hearings, perhaps before a subcommittee held in locations outside the capital, where expert witnesses are invited, testimony may be subpoenaed, and hours of debate may occur, after which amendments are offered. Each party's members coordinate with their respective committee staff to prepare for hearings and final votes.

Democratic representative Pashinski related very different experiences on two committees. Human Services chairperson Republican representative DiGirolomo allowed all members to speak; bipartisanship was palpable. At state government, then chaired by Republican representative Daryl Metcalfe, only Republican bills were discussed and voted out; Democrats' bills were never debated.[89]

Should a chair deny a bill consideration before a committee, a bill may be extracted from that committee using a discharge petition, which requires that a majority of the chambers' members sign a petition. Discharge petitions are rarely successful, but if they are, bills go directly to the floor for debate.

After a bill leaves committee, tradition dictates that it travel to the chamber's party caucuses, where members, guided by the caucuses' chairpersons, discuss the bill and determine the party's position and what amendments to offer, if any. Minor bills may skip this step, but not major bills.

Arriving on the floor, the bill receives its "first reading" when the clerk or secretary reads the bill's title and number; no debate, votes, or amendments occur at this time. Majority leadership schedules the second and third readings to accommodate their priorities or their governor's, if of the same party. Tradition again requires that debate and amendments take place during the second and third readings, with amendments offered in the House only during third reading and in the Senate only during the second. At the conclusion of the third reading, each chamber debates and votes, with a majority necessary for passage: 102 in the House and 26 in the Senate. If passed, the bill moves to the other house, where it is considered at a date determined by the majority party. Should the bill pass both houses, it is signed by the speaker and Senate president and sent to the governor. If the bill does not pass both houses in exactly the same language, a conference committee is formed to reconcile the differences. The four caucus party leaders name their party's conference members with the majority party in a chamber receiving more seats than the minority party. Should the conference committee successfully negotiate a compromise bill, that bill is assigned a new number and returned to each house, where it is debated without possibility for amendments on the floor and voted on.

Article III, section 10 requires that all revenue (tax) bills originate in the House, but the Senate may offer amendments. The state's annual budget bill and any appropriations bills may begin in either chamber and, like revenue bills, are referred to the appropriations committees in each house for consideration before any floor vote. By law, a bill considered by any other committee that affects the state budget is also referred to the appropriations committees, but by tradition the appropriation committees consider nearly all significant bills, though they are not required to report these bills. The Independent Fiscal Office along with appropriation committees' staff analyze each bill and attach a fiscal note explaining its economic impact on state spending and revenue.[90] Former appropriations chair Dwight Evans provides a vivid description of the committee's work, its intricacies, and the personal politics at play behind the scenes in his book *Making Issues Matter*.[91]

The appropriations committees act as informal traffic cops for the General Assembly. Both parties' leaders understand that they can expect few bills to move through the committees unscathed—that is, without having their financial implications given serious scrutiny. As Mr. Atkinson described the committees, "[They're] where bills go to die."[92]

"Separated institutions sharing power" was political scientist Richard Neustadt's description of the federal government, a depiction that applies as well to Pennsylvania's government.[93] The legislative process includes the governor, and for the executive branch to function it requires the legislature's cooperation. As we discussed above and in chapter 3, when the same party controls both branches (unified government), relations between the two are more likely to be harmonious than when the parties split control (divided government), though this is not guaranteed. The state's constitution, like its federal counterpart, assumes that the branches will work collaboratively, but it cannot dictate the quality of the relationship.

As previously noted, all bills and concurrent resolutions must receive the governor's signature to become law. The governor has ten days after receiving a bill to sign it, and if the governor does not, and the General Assembly continues in session rather than adjourning, the bill becomes law. The governor may also choose to veto a bill but must explain the decision. Overriding the veto requires a two-thirds vote in both houses: 34 in the Senate and 136 in the House, numbers that are difficult to attain. If the General Assembly transmits a bill to the governor and it adjourns, the governor has thirty days to file an objection, a quasi-veto, with the secretary of the commonwealth, comparable to the US president's pocket veto, which cannot be overridden. The governor also has a line-item veto employed to strike individual items, or lines, from appropriation bills without vetoing the entire bill. As with other vetoes, the legislature can override them with a two-thirds vote in both houses.

The governor has the authority under article II, section 4, to call the General Assembly into a "special session" to study and debate solutions to pressing state issues. Individual members may also ask the governor to convene a special session, as happened in 2020 to address police reform.[94] The special session generally occurs during a regular legislative session, running concurrently. Party leaders may reserve part of a day or days to debate the special session's subject, but legislation on the subject need not ever pass. On very rare occasions, lawmakers are called to return to the Capitol after an adjournment for a special session. Since 2000 there have been fewer than six special sessions, most of which ended with few accomplishments other than demonstrating the governor's and perhaps the legislature's interest in a current issue, such as opioid addiction.[95]

Pennsylvania's budget battles have been monumental, whether the government is unified or divided, especially when the governor's taxing and spending priorities don't match those of the General Assembly's caucus leaders. Governors of both parties have experienced legislative resistance to their budgets, thereby missing the June 30 passage deadline by days, weeks, and even months, though none longer than Wolf's 2015 budget, which was six months overdue. Governor Rendell notably endured eight consecutive years of failing to have the General Assembly pass his budget on time. Eventually, both sides achieve some agreement to keep the government operating, but the public finds these stalemates frustrating, particularly when public services, like museums, parks, and access to the motor vehicle department, are suspended. Interestingly, however, neither governors nor lawmakers pay much of a political price for missing deadlines.[96]

The Senate has special authority to confirm the governor's cabinet secretaries as well as court vacancies the governor may need to fill before the next judicial elections are held. Typically, gubernatorial nominations are pro forma, with the nominees' hearings as opportunities for the candidates to reveal their knowledge and experience; however, nominees are occasionally rejected.[97]

Finally, the General Assembly is authorized to engage in oversight of executive branch departments and agencies—that is, they monitor operations to ensure that the bureaucracy is efficiently and effectively implementing laws. Oversight takes many forms, from occasional committee hearings in which lawmakers question agency heads about their work to sunset reviews where an agency's very existence is challenged. The Independent Regulatory Review Commission (IRRC) aids the legislature in assessing rules and regulations that a department or agency promulgates before they take effect. Under the 1981 Sunset Act, the Legislative Budget and Finance Committee was granted authority to examine "74 agencies to determine if they should be terminated or consolidated or simply improved."[98] Unfortunately, in practice, legislative committees allowed routine sunset reviews to lapse around 1991.[99]

LEGISLATIVE-JUDICIAL RELATIONS

The legislative and judicial branches share few constitutional powers, but where their authority does overlap is fundamental: lawmaking. The General Assembly passes bills, the governor signs the bills into laws and carries them out, and the courts determine their constitutionality. But when the legislature passes a bill that is of questionable constitutionality, it invites litigation, and "the paradox of constitutionality" is manifest.

Hypothetically, if the constitutionality of a bill under consideration is questioned by a lawmaker, the General Assembly's legal specialists investigate the question, and when no single, clear interpretation can be agreed upon, the majority presses its position, passes the bill, and it becomes law, if signed by the governor. Someone then challenges the new law in court, and the case works its way through the system to the Supreme Court, where it determines that the law is unconstitutional. The majority party then announces that the court has engaged in legislating from the bench. This is the paradox of constitutionality. Had it been more attentive to the constitutional questions initially raised, the legislature could have avoided the constitutional challenge rather than essentially inviting court action, revealing the paradox of constitutionality.[100]

In a similar vein, the General Assembly found itself challenged by the courts over its failure to pay close attention to the constitution's single-subject clause (article III, section 3), which requires that all bills contain only one subject. Over many years, the legislature incorporated large expenditures or major projects into innocuous bills to ease their passage, but they were superficially or tangentially related to the original expenditure or project. The courts, for unknown reasons, did not entertain challenges to this practice for decades. An example was Act 71 of 2004, the Pennsylvania Racehorse Development and Gaming Act. Initially, a bill was drafted to help rejuvenate the state horse racing industry, but instead the bill became the vehicle by which casino gambling was legalized. But by 2010, the courts began accepting challenges to this practice, aggressively striking down laws that were passed in violation of article III, section 3, even overturning laws passed decades earlier. As the courts removed this legislative sleight of hand, leadership also renounced this trick that had aided them in rounding up votes, thereby making the passage of major bills much more difficult.[101]

ETHICS

Pennsylvania's history is littered with political scandals, many involving the General Assembly, with money, power, or both at their roots. Recall that public demand for a new constitution in the early 1870s was prompted by muckrakers' stories of lawmakers whose votes were easily acquired by corporate lobbyists' generosity.[102] The turn of the twentieth century witnessed the humiliating investigation and eventually conviction of those who swindled the state of millions from cost overruns during the construction of the new Capitol Building. Republicans Matthew Quay and Boies Penrose served in the General Assembly between 1890 and 1920. Their machine firmly controlled the Keystone State, while engaging in reprehensible activities that never brought convictions.[103]

Corruption continued through the twentieth and into the twenty-first century, ensnarling Democrats and Republicans, from leaders to rank-and-file members in both houses. A sampling of those convicted includes speaker Herbert Fineman (D) in 1977 for buying votes and taking kickbacks; Henry "Buddy" Cianfrani (D), appropriations chair, in 1977 for hiring "ghost employees," that is, people hired for government positions who never actually worked; Representative Frank Serafini (R) in 1997 for perjury related to illegal use of his campaign fund; Representative Frank Gigliotti (D) in 2000 for extorting money from contractors to steer state work to their businesses; Senate Majority Leader F. Joseph Loeper (R) in 2000 for tax fraud related to unreported earnings; Representative Jeff Habay (R) in 2006 for using his legislative staff for campaign work; Representative Frank LaGrotta (D) in 2008 for hiring ghost workers; Senator Vincent Fumo (D), "the Vince of Darkness," widely regarded as among the most influential senators of his era, convicted in 2009 on 137 counts of fraud, conspiracy, tax evasion, and conspiracy in federal court; Senator Raphael Musto (D), indicted in 2010 for exchanging services for money, but who died before his trial; Senator Jane Orie (R) in 2012 for forgery and theft of services; and Senate president pro tempore Robert Mellow in 2012 (D) for mail fraud and tax issues.[104]

But the General Assembly's most dramatic contemporary scandal was uncovered in 2007 by the *Harrisburg Patriot News*: Bonusgate. Both parties' House leaders were discovered paying staffers for election work often done within the Capitol. Approximately $3.6 million in public money was distributed to legislative staff during the 2005–6 session, of which about $2.2 million went to Democratic aides. State prosecutors, led by then attorney general Tom Corbett, indicted and tried fifteen Democrats in 2009, including majority leader Bill DeWeese, whip Mike Veon, and thirteen staffers, and ten Republicans, among them speaker John Perzel, appropriations chair Brett Feese, and eight aides.[105] The grand jury impaneled by Corbett released a report in 2010 calling for reforms, such as eliminating WAMs, eliminating financial support for the four caucuses and leadership accounts, revising per diem reimbursement procedures, and reducing the legislature's size.[106] We consider these recommendations along with others in the next section.

The "Me-Too" movement brought attention to ethical and moral lapses occurring within the General Assembly that had long been ignored. In 2018, Representative Leanne Krueger-Braneky described the Capitol's culture as "the most misogynistic I've ever seen."[107] Since 2018, sexual harassment or abuse charges have been leveled by staff and women lawmakers against three members: Representative Nick Miccarelli (R), Representative Thomas Caltagirone (D), and Senator Daylin Leach (D), as well as rape charges against Representative Brian Ellis (R), but as of publication the General Assembly had yet to adequately address this issue despite a grand jury's recommendation.[108]

As angry as the public becomes when scandals are revealed, honest lawmakers—and the majority are honest and hardworking—feel frustrated. Quoting a senator: "I am experiencing personal fatigue. Scandals suck the oxygen out of the room, which drives [voter] turnout down."[109]

FUTURE CHALLENGES AND THE DEMAND FOR REFORM

Since 1999, the General Assembly's public approval has fluttered between 11 percent and 33 percent, below that of most governors, leaving the legislature's members, burdened by the scorn, to limp along with a crippled image (see table 4.6). Explaining the reasons for the institution's poor reputation may seem obvious: its history of scandals, inefficiencies, and questionable practices, such as WAMs. But we suggest that the fundamental cause lies in the state's political culture, which lawmakers have internalized. As discussed in chapter 2, the Keystone State's individualistic political culture views politics as a transactional enterprise—that is, a system in which participants seek personal gain rather than community

Table 4.6 Public opinion of the General Assembly's performance

Date	Excellent	Good	Only fair	Poor	Don't know*
Jan. 2016	1	14	41	39	6
Aug. 2013	0	11	54	29	6
Jan. 2010	0	16	51	23	10
Oct. 2009	1	14	48	30	7
Aug. 2009	0	18	58	20	4
June 2009	1	26	49	18	6
Aug. 2007	1	25	53	16	5
June 2007	1	25	46	21	7
Feb. 2007	1	23	48	18	10
May 2006	1	19	51	22	8
Sept. 2005**	1	21	47	22	8
Nov. 2003**	1	22	55	17	5
Feb. 2002**	3	33	49	7	9
July 1999**	2	33	49	10	6

*Figures are percentages.
**Questions asked of registered voters, except for those dates marked with ** when the question was asked of all respondents, regardless of registration status.
Source: Franklin and Marshall College Poll and the Center for Politics and Public Affairs.

benefits. Individualistic cultures tend to have strong parties that run the system, while average citizens generally are apathetic and tolerate corruption within it. If this is accurate, then repairing the General Assembly requires overhauling the state's political culture, an impossible task; however, a more realistic solution is revamping the institution's critical components to constrain lawmakers' inclination toward personal benefit. In the following paragraphs, we review reforms that target the assembly's infrastructure.

Reducing the legislature's size was proposed and dismissed during the 1967 Convention, yet the idea has reemerged almost every year since 2011, notably after scandals or journalists' reports about the General Assembly's expenses.[110] Proposals to shrink the House to 153 seats and the Senate to 45 assume that fewer members will mean fewer crimes and lower costs; however, fewer members leave the remaining lawmakers serving larger constituencies, likely inconveniencing citizens, and it is unlikely to discourage corruption. The Quaker State has the nation's third-largest legislature, supported by one of the largest staffs, yet as of 2020, no bill to diminish the size of either house has cleared the General Assembly.

In 2010, the House considered HB 260 to convert the General Assembly into a unicameral legislature like Nebraska's.[111] Like shrinking both houses, the bill sought to lower expenses, improve efficiency, and increase constituent accountability. With one house, citizens would have only one representative, who would draw intense scrutiny and, therefore, be less likely to engage successfully in dubious activities.[112] Arguments favoring retaining the bicameral structure claim that two houses slow the legislative process, allow-ing more deliberation and ensuring institutional stability.[113] While unicameralism has worked very well for Nebraska, it has a smaller, less diverse population than Pennsylvania, making direct comparisons difficult. The proposal did not advance.

We can consolidate several other suggested reforms into one question: Should Penn-sylvania's legislature be full-time and professional or part-time and amateur? Those arguing for the latter assume that having lawmakers meet several months every year (or several months every other year), be term-limited, and employ fewer staff would make them unable or less inclined to perpetrate unlawful acts.[114] We are unaware of any research that supports this conclusion; however, there is research that suggests that governors in states with part-time, term-limited, amateur legislatures have more power to shape budgets and are less likely to be checked effectively by their legislatures.[115] Recall that in the 1960s and '70s, modernizing the General Assembly—providing members with offices, phones, com-puters, staff, and better salaries—empowered the institution to challenge the governor in ways that it had previously been unable to. A wholesale movement to deprofessionalize the legislature now seems absurd to us; instead, we suggest a compromise: hold legislative sessions for four months each year, pro-rate lawmakers' total compensation, including per diem expenses, accordingly, and reduce legislators' individual office staff and the four party caucuses' staff, while retaining most committee and LSA personnel. This proposal would ensure that members have the technical support and infrastructure needed to remain pro-fessional to balance the governor's powers.

Finally, there have been many calls to eliminate personal financial gain as a motive for legislative service. Whether limiting campaign contributions' amounts, regulating how contributions may be spent, curtailing gifts from lobbyists, or stiffening penalties for rule violations, the flow of money, the "mother's milk of politics,"[116] into the system must be meaningfully regulated, not only to incentivize ethical behavior but also to restore public faith in the legislature. Lawmakers themselves have made only incremental changes to lobbying regulations and have avoided limiting campaign donations and controlling expenditures. If the General Assembly is unable or unwilling to advance real reforms in these areas, the electorate must directly pressure their lawmakers, particularly when they stand for reelection.

CONCLUSION

Pennsylvania's General Assembly, despite its shortcomings, is no better or worse than the legislatures in the other forty-nine states. As referenced at various places above, the Key-stone State's legislature has been ranked in the middle on many indexes, other than lobbying and campaign funding regulations. The overwhelming majority of its members competently and faithfully serve their constituents. We anticipate that the General

Assembly will adapt itself, however slowly, to meet the state's needs as its demographic profile and economy evolves. The legislature, as an institution, must play a vital role in the government if Pennsylvanians expect to retain a democratic political system.

NOTES

1. Kennedy, *Contemporary Pennsylvania Legislature*, 2.
2. *Pennsylvania Manual*, 1-22. See also McLaughlin, "Pennsylvania General Assembly"; Wise, *Legislative Process*, 2nd ed.; McLaughlin, *Pennsylvania General Assembly*.
3. *Pennsylvania Manual*, 1-23-2.
4. Jenkins Law Library.
5. McLaughlin, "Pennsylvania General Assembly," slide 2.
6. Jenkins Law Library.
7. For a fuller consideration of the size issue at the convention, see Fineman, "Looking Back," 99–100.
8. Ibid. See also McLaughlin, "Pennsylvania General Assembly."
9. See McLaughlin, "Pennsylvania General Assembly"; Wise, *Legislative Process*, 2nd ed.; McLaughlin, *Pennsylvania General Assembly*.
10. Fineman, "Looking Back," 100–101. For all fifty-eight recommendations, see Wise, *Legislative Process*, appendix 1.
11. King and Cassidy, "Pennsylvania Legislature," 7.
12. Fineman, "Looking Back," 87.
13. Ibid., 101.
14. See, for example, Schmedlen, *History of Women*; Brechenmacher, "Tackling Women's Underrepresentation"; Rosenthal, "Role of Gender in Descriptive Representation"; Carroll and Sanbonmatsu, *More Women Can Run*; Crowder-Meyer, "Gendered Recruitment Without Trying"; Dittmar, Sonbonmatsu, and Carol, *Seat at the Table*; Fox and Lawless, "Entering the Arena?"; Fulton and Dhima, "Gendered Politics of Congressional Elections"; Sanbonmatsu, "Legislative Party and Candidate Recruitment"; Sapiro, "Private Costs of Public Commitment." The authors are also indebted to Dr. Claire Gothreau for her expertise on this subject.
15. Sweet-Cushman, "Gendered Legislative Effectiveness."
16. Williams, "Pa. Legislature 'Dismal' in Racial Diversity"; see also Krupnikov and Piston, "Racial Prejudice, Partisanship."
17. See Brown and Gershon, *Distinct Identities*; Pennsylvania Census data taken from U.S. Census Bureau, https://www.census.gov/data.html.
18. See, for example, Sweet-Cushman, "Gendered Legislative Effectiveness"; Ditmer, *Seat at the Table*; Kidd et al., "Black Voter, Black Candidates"; Jacobsmeier, "From Black and White"; White, Laird, and Allen, "Selling Out?"; Grose, "Disentangling Constituency and Legislator Effects"; Little, Dunn, and Deen, "View from the Top"; Holman, Mahoney, and Hurler, "Let's Work Together."
19. Greenawalt and Madonna, "Pennsylvania General Assembly," 93. See also Kennedy, *Contemporary Pennsylvania Legislature*; King and Cassidy, "Pennsylvania Legislature."
20. King and Cassidy, "Pennsylvania Legislature," table 3.
21. See Couloumbis and Worden, "DeWeese: 7 Aides Ousted over Email"; Infield and Cattamiani, "Inside Bonusgate"; Bumsted and Erdley, "Shadows of Greed Darken State Capital."
22. See NCSL website for legislators' compensation, https://www.ncsl.org/research/about-state-legislatures/2019-legislator-compensation.aspx.
23. See Greenblatt, "How Lawmakers Can Raise Their Own Pay." Also, article II, section 8, forbids members from raising their own salaries, which explains why any pay raise vote must take effect with the seating of the next Assembly.
24. See Swift, "Shhh!"; Murphy, "Wolf to Sign Pay Freeze."
25. See, for example, Murphy, "Beyond Salaries."
26. See Couloumbis, Bumsted, and Janesch, "Scrubbed Senate Records Raise Concern"; Couloumbis, Bumsted, and Janesch, "Pa. Legislators Black Out Spending Details"; Couloumbis and Janesch, "Pa. Lawmakers Spend Millions."
27. McLaughlin, *Pennsylvania General Assembly*, 5.
28. *Baker v. Carr*, 369 U.S. 186 (1962); *Reynolds v. Sims*, 377 U.S. 533 (1964).
29. McLaughlin, *Pennsylvania General Assembly*, 7; *Butcher v. Bloom* 203 A.2nd 869 (PA 1964);

Butcher v. Bloom, 216 A. 2nd 457, 459 (PA 1966). See also Turzai, Corey, and Mann, "Protection Is in the Process," 353–402.

30. See Ballotpedia, https://ballotpedia.org/State-by-state_redistricting_procedures.

31. Vieth v. Jubelirer, 541 U.S. 267 (2004).

32. League of Women Voters v. Commonwealth, 645 Pa. 1, 178 A.3d 737 (2018).

33. Michael Turzai et al. v. League of Women Voters et al., 138 S.Ct. 1323 (2018).

34. See Ballotpedia, https://ballotpedia.org/Redistricting_in_Pennsylvania; Navratil, "Republican State Legislator Moves to Impeach."

35. See Kennedy, Pennsylvania Elections, 2nd ed.; Treadway, "Electoral Competition"; Turner, "Looking to Unseat a Pa. Lawmaker?"

36. See Janesch, "Who's Safe? Who's Not?"

37. Baer, "PA Lawmakers Close Their Eyes."

38. See Janesch, "Who's Safe? Who's Not?"; Treadway, Elections in Pennsylvania.

39. See Scolforo, "Helping Hand$?"; Cain, Ferejohn, and Fiorina, Personal Vote; Johannes, To Serve the People.

40. Robert Jubelirer (state senator and president pro tempore), interview with the authors, June 8, 2016, by phone.

41. Lisa Baker (state senator), interview with the authors, August, 11, 2015, in her district office, Dallas, PA.

42. See Scolforo, "Helping Hand$."

43. Swift, "Cost for Legislators' Community Events."

44. See Herrnson, Panagopoulos, and Bailey, Congressional Elections; Jacobson and Carson, Politics of Congressional Elections.

45. See Jacobson and Kernell, Strategy and Choice in Congressional Elections.

46. Jarrett and Strauss, "Best Capitol Money Can Buy."

47. See Herrnson, Panagopoulos, and Bailey, Congressional Elections; Jacobson and Carson, Politics of Congressional Elections.

48. Couloumbis et al., "Pennsylvania State Lawmakers Are Hiding."

49. Janesch, "Citing Spotlight PA/Caucus Probe."

50. Janesch, "Things That Go Cha-ching."

51. Email from Representative Sam Hayes to Baldino, September 22, 2020.

52. Evans, Making Ideas Matter, 104; see also Swift, "Future of WAMS Is Uncertain."

53. Evans, Making Ideas Matter, 104–5.

54. Swift, "Election Season Brings Bounty."

55. Ibid.

56. Couloumbis, "Walking Around Money Is Back."

57. Couloumbis, "Tucked into Spending Bill."

58. Scarnati et al. v. Wolf et al., 135 A. 3rd 200 (PA Commonwealth 2015); see also Esack, "Court Oks Ex-Gov. Tom Corbett's Budget."

59. Scarnati et al. v. Wolf et al., no. 3 MAP November 22, 2017.

60. Sam Hayes Jr. (former minority whip and leader), interview with the authors, July 18, 2016, by phone.

61. At the first meeting of the new House on January 2, 2007, Democrats held a one-seat majority, but its party leaders were unable to unite their members to support a Democratic speaker. In a clever maneuver, Democrats nominated Republican Dennis O'Brien after secretly negotiating with several Republicans. O'Brien was elected on a 105 to 97 vote, with six Republicans casting votes for O'Brien along with most Democrats, while three Democrats voted with most Republicans for outgoing Republican speaker John Perzel. O'Brien abstained from voting; he served two years as speaker. See Scolforo, "GOP Retains Speakership."

62. The House and Senate parliamentarians and chief clerks are appointed by and serve their respective constitutional leaders, the speaker and president pro tempore. The offices provide objective information and assistance to their superiors, especially the parliamentarians, whose rulings on motions and procedures during floor sessions affect the chambers' operation. See, for example, Manganaro, "Keeping House on an Even Keel."

63. David Atkinson (chief of state to state Senator Robert Jubelirer), interview with the authors, September 14, 2020, by phone.

64. See Evans, Making Ideas Matter.

65. Burton, "Colleagues: Switch Is Revenge."

66. Levy, "Yudichak's Defection Reverberates"; Seidman, "As State Splits."

67. See LaRosa, "Corbett Could Be First Governor to Lose."

68. Specifically, Senators Jubelirer, Costa, and Williams and Representatives Sturla and Hayes discussed governors in interviews with the authors.

69. Jay Costa (state senator and Democratic minority leader), interview with the authors, September 16, 2016, by phone.

70. Mahon, "How Gov. Tom Wolf Used His Veto Power." See also Coston, "Pa. GOP Answered Wolf's Vetoes."

71. See Wattenberg, *Rise of Candidate-Centered Politics*; Arbour, "Candidate-Centered Campaigns."
72. Robert Jubelirer (state senator and president pro tempore), interview with the authors, June 8, 2016, by phone.
73. Swift, "Caucus Culture Pervades Capitol."
74. Samuel E. Hayes Jr. (representative, majority whip, minority whip, and secretary of agriculture), interview with the authors, July 18, 2016, by phone.
75. Comments made during interviews.
76. Couloumbis and Bumsted, "PA Legislature Making Few Cuts."
77. Yudichak, Costa, interviews; Eddie Day Pashinski (representative), interview with the authors, August 17, 2015, in his district office, Wilkes-Barre, PA.
78. See Swift, "State Legislature Faces Controversy"; Baer, "Legislature Wallows."
79. Hayes, email to Baldino, September 22, 2020.
80. Martin, "What Is the Caucus?"
81. See National Conference of State Legislatures, https://www.ncsl.org/research/about-state -legislatures/staff-change-chart-1979-1988 -1996-2003-2009.aspx.
82. See Couloumbis and Worden, "Wide Disparity."
83. See IFO and IRRC websites.
84. Pashinski and Baker, interviews.
85. When the lieutenant governor's party is in the minority, tradition dictates that the lieutenant governor accedes to the president pro tempore's committee recommendations.
86. See Wise, *Legislative Process in Pennsylvania*, 2nd ed., 59–62; King and Cassidy, "Pennsylvania Legislature," 19.
87. King and Cassidy, "Pennsylvania Legislature," 20.
88. Yudichak, interview.
89. Pashinski, interview.
90. King and Cassidy, "Pennsylvania Legislature," 21.
91. See Evans, *Making Ideas Matter*.
92. Atkinson, interview.
93. See Neustadt, *Presidential Power*.
94. See Murphy, "PA House Speaker Calls."
95. Shaw, "Harrisburg Sets Special Session."
96. For a full explanation of the budget process, see Pennsylvania Office of the Budget website.
97. Esack, "PA Senate Rejects."
98. Wise, *Legislative Process in Pennsylvania*, 2nd ed., 96–101.
99. Atkinson, interview.
100. Ibid.
101. Ibid.
102. See Steffens, *Shame of the City*; Beers, *Pennsylvania Politics*.
103. Beers, *On the Front Line of Pennsylvania Politics*, 41–57.
104. Bonnor, "Guide to Pa.'s Long History"; see also Bumsted, *Keystone Corruption*.
105. See Couloumbis and Worden, "DeWeese: 7 Aides Ousted"; Infield and Cattamiani, "Inside Bonusgate"; Bumsted and Erdley, "Shadows of Greed."
106. Couloumbis and Infield, "Legislators Scoff at Report."
107. Knudsen and Bumsted, "Culture of Fear."
108. Ibid. See also Bumsted and McGoldrick, "Clearing a Path"; Bumsted and Knudsen, "Silent Treatment"; Gabriel, "As State Lawmaker Claims Abuse."
109. John Yudichak (state senator) interview with the authors, August 10, 2015.
110. See, for example, Bumsted and Knudsen, "Bloated Spending"; Swift, "State Legislature Faces Controversy"; Swift, "State Legislature Is Among Nation's Most Expensive."
111. See McLaughlin, testimony before the House Democratic Policy Committee.
112. Rosenthal makes many of these arguments in *Engines of Democracy*.
113. See McLaughlin, testimony on House Bill 260.
114. Pennsylvania does not limit legislative terms and requires a constitutional amendment to do so. No amendment had been offered for decades until March 2019 when two junior Republican representatives did so. See Murphy, "Term Limit Proposal."
115. See Squire, "Squire Index Update"; Barrilleaux and Berkman, "Do Governors Matter?"; Krupnikov and Shipan, "Measuring Gubernatorial Budgeting Power"; Kousser and Phillips, *Power of American Governors*.
116. Quote from Jesse Unruh, speaker of the California House and Democratic state party leader.

BIBLIOGRAPHY

Arbour, Brian. "Candidate-Centered Campaigns: Political Messages, Winning Personalities, and Personal Appeals." *Public Opinion Quarterly* 80, no. 3 (Fall 2016): 796–99.

Baer, John. "Legislature Wallows in Its Own Slush." *Philadelphia Inquirer*, March 22, 2017.

———. *On the Front Lines of Pennsylvania Politics: Twenty-Five Years of Keystone Reporting.* Charleston, SC: History Press, 2013.

———. "PA Lawmakers Close Their Eyes to Gerrymandering." *Philadelphia Inquirer*, March 6, 2017.

Barnes, Tiffany D., and Erin C. Cassese. "American Party Women: A Look at the Gender Gap Within Parties." *Political Research Quarterly* 70, no. 1 (2017): 127–41. http://www.jstor.org/stable /26384905 (accessed August 19, 2021).

Barrilleaux, Charles, and Michael Berkman. "Do Governors Matter? Budgeting Rules and the Politics of State Policymaking." *Political Research Quarterly* 56, no. 4 (2003): 409–17.

Bonnor, Theresa. "A Guide to Pa.'s Long History of Government Corruption." PennLive, May 22, 2019. https://www.pennlive.com/midstate /2016/07/capitol_corruption_parade.html.

Brechenmacher, Saskia. *Tackling Women's Underrepresentation in U.S. Politics: Comparative Perspectives from Europe.* Report. Carnegie Endowment for International Peace, 2018. http://www.jstor.org/stable /resrep16981.10 (accessed August 18, 2021).

Bumsted, Brad. *Keystone Corruption: A Pennsylvania Insider's View of a State Gone Wrong.* Philadelphia: Camino Books, 2013.

Bumsted, Brad, and Debra Erdley. "Shadows of Greed Darken State Capital." *Pittsburgh Tribune-Review*, November 18, 2007.

Bumsted, Brad, and Paula Knudsen. "A Culture of Fear." *Citizens' Voice*, March 11, 2018.

———. "Silent Treatment." *Citizens' Voice*, May 20, 2018.

Bumsted, Brad, and Gillian McGoldrick. "Clearing a Path." *Citizens' Voice*, September 8, 2019.

Burton, Cynthia. "Colleagues: Switch Is Revenge." *Philadelphia Inquirer*, January 2, 2007.

Cain, Bruce, John Ferejohn, and Morris Fiorina. *The Personal Vote: Constituency Service and Electoral Independence.* Cambridge, MA: Harvard University Press, 1988.

Carroll, Susan J., and Kira Sanbonmatsu. *More Women Can Run: Gender and Pathways to the State Legislatures.* New York: Oxford University Press, 2013.

Cassidy, Michael E., and Michael R. King. "Are We Really Doing More with Less? Reassessing Measures of Legislative Performance." Paper presented at the Annual Meeting of the Pennsylvania Political Science Association, April 9–10, 1999.

Coston, Ethan Edward. "Pa. GOP Answered Wolf's Vetoes with Constitutional Changes: The Strategy Is Here to Stay." *Philadelphia Inquirer*, January 17, 2022.

Couloumbis, Angela. "Tucked into Spending Bill, Special Funding." *Philadelphia Inquirer*, July 18, 2014.

———. "Walking Around Money Is Back, Critics Allege." *Philadelphia Inquirer*, December 1, 2013.

Couloumbis, Angela, and Brad Bumsted. "PA Legislature Making Few Cuts, No Promises to Tap Hefty Reserve as State Faces Massive Budget Shortfall." *PAPOST*, April 10, 2020. https://papost.org/2020/04/10/pa -legislature-making-few-cuts-no-promises -to-tap-hefty-reserves-as-state-faces-massive -budget-shortfall.

Couloumbis, Angela, Brad Bumsted, and Sam Janesch. "Pa. Legislators Black Out Spending Details." *Philadelphia Inquirer*, February 28, 2020.

———. "Scrubbed Senate Records Raise Concern." *Philadelphia Inquirer*, March 5, 2020.

Couloumbis, Angela, Mike Wereschagin, Brad Bumsted, Paula Knudsen, and Sam Janesch. "Pennsylvania State Lawmakers Are Hiding Millions in Campaign Spending. And It's All Legal." Spotlight PA and the Caucus, October 22, 2019. https://www.inquirer.com/news /pennsylvania/spl/pa-election-hidden-cam paign-spending-spotlight-pa-20191022.html.

Couloumbis, Angela, and Tom Infield, "Legislators Scoff at Report." *Philadelphia Inquirer*, May 26, 2010.

Couloumbis, Angela, and Sam Janesch. "Pa. Lawmakers Spend Millions of Tax Dollars on Private Lawyers but Often Don't Reveal Why." *Philadelphia Inquirer*, October 12, 2021.

Couloumbis, Angela, and Amy Worden. "DeWeese: 7 Aides Ousted over Email." *Philadelphia Inquirer*, December 18, 2007.

———. "Wide Disparity in Pennsylvania House Staffing." *Philadelphia Inquirer*, August 15, 2010.

Crowder-Meyer, Melody. "Gendered Recruitment Without Trying: How Local Party Recruiters Affect Women's Representation." *Politics and Gender* 9 (2013): 390–413.

Dittmar, Kelly, Kira Sanbonmatsu, and Susan J. Carroll. *A Seat at the Table: Congresswomen's Perspectives on Why Their Presence Matters.* New York: Oxford University Press, 2018.

Esack, Steve. "Court Oks Ex-Gov. Tom Corbett's Budget and Fiscal Code Cuts to Legislation." *Allentown Morning Call*, December 30, 2015. https://www.mcall.com/news/local/mc-pa-corbett-wolf-budget-cuts-20151230-story.html.

———. "PA Senate Rejects Tom Wolf's Nominee for State Police Commissioner." *Allentown Morning Call*, June 9, 2015. https://www.mcall.com/news/pennsylvania/mc-pa-marcus-brown-psp-senate-0608-20150608-story.html.

Evans, Dwight. *Making Ideas Matter: My Life as a Policy Entrepreneur*. Philadelphia: University of Pennsylvania Press, 2013.

Fineman, Herbert. "Looking Back on the Legislative Modernization Movement in Pennsylvania: Remarks of Herbert Fineman, Former Speaker of the Pennsylvania House of Representatives, Given at the Annual Meeting of the Pennsylvania Political Science Association, April 4, 2003." Introduction and commentary by Michael E. Cassidy. *Commonwealth* 12, no. 5 (2003): 87–110.

Fox, Richard, and Jennifer Lawless. "Entering the Arena? Gender and the Decision to Run for Office." *American Journal of Political Science* 48, no. 2 (April 2004): 264–80.

Fulton, Sarah A., and Kostanca Dhima. "The Gendered Politics of Congressional Elections." *Political Behavior* 43 (December 2021): 1611–37.

Gabriel, Trip. "As State Lawmaker Claims Abuse, Party Leaders Shield Her Colleague." *New York Times*, May 5, 2018.

Greenawalt, Charles E., II and G. Terry Madonna. "The Pennsylvania General Assembly— The House of Ill Repute Revisited." In *The Reform of State Legislatures and the Changing Character of Representation*, edited by Eugene W. Hickok. Lanham: University Press of America, 1992.

Greenblatt, Alan. "How Lawmakers Can Raise Their Own Pay in a Less Controversial Way." Governing, January 22, 2019. https://www.governing.com/topics/politics/gov-lawmaker-pay-raise-salary-legislature.html.

Grose, Christian R. "Disentangling Constituency and Legislator Effects in Legislative Representation: Black Legislators or Black Districts?" *Social Science Quarterly* 86, no. 2 (June 2005): 427–43.

Herrnson, Paul, Costas Panagopoulos, and Kendall L. Bailey. *Congressional Elections: Campaigning at Home and in Washington*. 8th ed. Washington, DC: Congressional Quarterly Press, 2020.

Holman, Mirya, Anna Mahoney, and Emma Hurler.

"Let's Work Together: Bill Success via Women's Cosponsorship in U.S. State Legislatures." *Political Research Quarterly*, no. 2 (June 4, 2021). https://journals.sagepub.com/doi/10.1177/10659129211020123.

Infield, Tom, and Mario F. Cattamiani. "Inside Bonusgate." *Philadelphia Inquirer*, December 24, 2009.

Jacobsmeier, Matthew L. "From Black and White to Left and Right: Race, Perceptions of Candidates' Ideologies, and Voting Behavior in U.S. House Elections." *Political Behavior* 37 (August 2015): 595–621.

Jacobson, Gary C., and Samuel Kernell. *Strategy and Choice in Congressional Elections*. New Haven: Yale University Press, 1983.

Jacobson, Gary C., and Jamie L. Carson. *The Politics of Congressional Elections*. 10th ed. New York: Rowman and Littlefield, 2020.

Janesch, Sam. "Citing Spotlight PA/Caucus Probe, Top Lawmaker Pushes Limits on Campaign Donations, Stricter Disclosure Laws." Spotlight PA, October 25, 2019. https://www.inquirer.com/news/pennsylvania/spl/pennsylvania-campaign-expenses-reform-bill-costa-20191025.html.

———. "Things That Go Cha-Ching in the Night." *Citizens' Voice*, March 10, 2019.

———. "Who's Safe? Who's Not?" Lancaster Online, February 4, 2020. https://lancasteronline.com/news/politics/whos-safe-whos-not-breaking-down-the-2020-pennsylvania-house-and-senate-contests/article_3f928aa4-43b1-11ea-87f7-4b7f7b149fca.html.

Jarrett, Jan, and Sandra L. Strauss. "Best Capitol Money Can Buy." *Philadelphia Inquirer*, February 11, 2010.

Jenkins Law Library. https://www.paconstitution.org/texts-of-the-constitution/1874-2/#A02S04-1959.

Johannes, John. *To Serve the People: Congress and Constituency Service*. Lincoln: University of Nebraska Press, 1984.

Kennedy, John J. *The Contemporary Pennsylvania Legislature*. New York: University Press of America, 1999.

———. *Pennsylvania Elections: Statewide Contests from 1950–2012*. 2nd ed. Lanham: University Press of American, 2014.

Kidd, Quentin, Herman Diggs, Mehreen Farooq, and Megan Murray. "Black Voters, Black Candidates, and Social Issues: Does Party Identification Matter?" *Social Science Quarterly* 88, no. 1 (March 2007): 165–76.

King, Michael R., and Michael E. Cassidy. "The Pennsylvania Legislature." Unpublished book chapter, 1994.

Kousser, Thad, and Justin H. Phillips. *The Power of American Governors: Winning on Budgets and Losing on Policy*. New York: Cambridge University Press, 2012.

Krupnikov, Yanna, and Spencer Piston, "Racial Prejudice, Partisanship, and White Turnout in Elections with Black Candidates." *Political Behavior* 37, no. 2 (2015): 397–418.

Krupnikov, Yanna, and Charles Shipan. "Measuring Gubernatorial Budgeting Power." *State Politics and Policy Quarterly* 12, no. 4 (2012): 438–55.

LaRosa, Mike. "Corbett Could Be First Governor to Lose Reelection in Pa. History." MSNBC, July 8, 2013. https://www.msnbc/hardball /corbett-could-be-first-governor-lose-re-elect.

Levy, Marc. "Yudichak's Defection Reverberates in the Senate." *Citizens' Voice*, November 24, 2019.

Little, Thomas, Dana Dunn, and Rebecca E. Deen. "A View from the Top: Gender Differences in Legislative Priorities Among State Legislative Leaders." *Women and Politics* 22, no. 4 (2001): 29–50.

Mahon, Ed. "How Gov. Tom Wolf Used His Veto Power." *PAPost*, December 31, 2019. https:// papost.org/2019/12/31/how-gov-tom-wolf -used-his-veto-power-in-2019.

Manganaro, John. "Keeping House on an Even Keel." *Philadelphia Inquirer*, July 5, 2011.

Martin, John P. "What Is the Caucus?" Philly.com, May 27, 2010. https://www.inquirer.com /philly/news/homepage/20100527_What_is _the_caucus_.html.

McLaughlin, Joseph P., Jr. "The Pennsylvania General Assembly Before and After the 1968 Legislative Modernization Commission: A Brief History." Lecture to Members' Symposium, Pennsylvania General Assembly, Harrisburg, PA, February 28, 2011.

———. *The Pennsylvania General Assembly Before and After the 1968 Legislative Modernization Commission: The Evolution of an Institution*. Vol. 1 of *The Temple Papers on the Pennsylvania General Assembly*. Philadelphia: Temple University Institute for Public Affairs, 2012.

———. Testimony Before the House Democratic Policy Committee.

———. Testimony on House Bill 260 Providing for a Unicameral legislature before the House Democratic Policy Committee, April 6, 2010.

Murphy, Jan. "Beyond Salaries, Taxpayers Also Pay to Feed, House State Lawmakers: A Look at Per Diems," PennLive, May 22, 2019.

———. "PA House Speaker Calls for Special Session for Police Reform; Challenging Times Provide Challenges for Opportunity." PennLive, June 9, 2020. https://www.pennlive .com/news/2020/06/pa-house-speaker-calls -for-special-session-on-police-reforms -challenging-times-provide-challenges-for -opportunity.html.

———. "Term Limit Proposal Seeks to Put an End to Career Politicians." PennLive, March 14, 2019. https://www.pennlive.com/news/2019 /03/term-limits-proposal-seeks-to-put-an -end-to-career-politicians-serving-in-pas -general-assembly.html.

———. "Wolf to Sign Pay Freeze for Lawmakers, Other." *Philadelphia Inquirer*, September 23, 2020.

National Conference of State Legislatures website. https://www.ncsl.org/research/about-state -legislatures/2019-legislator-compensation .aspx.

Navratil, Liz. "Republican State Legislator Moves to Impeach Four State Supreme Court Justices." *Philadelphia Inquirer*, March 20, 2018.

Neustadt, Richard. *Presidential Power and the Modern Presidents: The Politics of Leadership from Roosevelt to Reagan*. New York: Free Press, 1991.

Pennsylvania Manual, vol. 119, 2009, 1–22.

Pennsylvania Office of the Budget. https://www .budget.pa.gov/PublicationsAndReports /Documents/OtherPublications/Budget%20 Process%20In%20PA%20-%20Web.pdf.

Rosenthal, Alan. *Engines of Democracy: Politics and Policymaking in State Legislatures*. Washington, DC: Congressional Quarterly Press, 2009.

Rosenthal, Cindy Simon. "The Role of Gender in Descriptive Representation." *Political Research Quarterly* 48, no. 3 (September 1995): 599–611.

Sanbonmatsu, Kira. "The Legislative Party and Candidate Recruitment in the American States." *Party Politics* 12, no. 2 (2006): 233–56.

———. *Where Women Run: Gender and Party in the American States*. Ann Arbor: University of Michigan Press, 2006.

Sapiro, Virginia. "Private Costs of Public Commitments or Public Costs of Private Commitments? Family Roles Versus Political Ambitions." *American Journal of Political Science* 26, no. 2 (May 1982): 265–79.

Schmedlen, Jeanne H. *History of Women in the Pennsylvania House of Representatives, 1923–2001*.

Harrisburg: Pennsylvania House of Representatives, 2001.

Scolforo, Mark. "GOP Retains Speakership, but Perzel Ousted in Process." *Pocono Record*, January 3, 2007.

———. "Helping Hand$." *Citizens' Voice*, April 17, 2011.

Seidman, Andrew. "As State Splits, Dems See Hope to Win House." *Philadelphia Inquirer*, November 28, 2019.

Shaw, Colt. "Harrisburg Sets Special Session on Opioid Abuse." *Philadelphia Inquirer*, June 25, 2016.

Squire, Peverill. "A Squire Index Update." *State Politics and Policy Quarterly* 17, no. 4 (2017): 361–71.

Sweet-Cushman, Jennie. "Gendered Legislative Effectiveness in State Legislatures: The Case of Pennsylvania." In *Politiking While Female: The Political Lives of Women*, ed. Nicole Bauer, 137–57. Baton Rouge: Louisiana State University Press, 2020.

Swift, Robert. "Caucus Culture Pervades Capitol." *Citizens' Voice*, September 14, 2009.

———. "Cost for Legislators' Community Events Tops $200K." *Citizens' Voice*, November 7, 2016.

———. "Election Season Brings Bounty of State Generosity." *Citizens' Voice*, November 2, 2014.

———. "Future of WAMS Is Uncertain." *Citizens' Voice*, November 28, 2010.

———. "Shhh! It's Pay-Raise Time in Harrisburg." *Citizen Voice*, December 4, 2016.

———. "State Legislature Faces Controversy over Budget Surplus." *Citizens' Voice*, May, 21, 2012.

———. "State Legislature Is Among Nation's Most Expensive." *Citizen's Voice*, April 26, 2010.

Treadway, Jack. *Elections in Pennsylvania: A Century of Partisan Conflict in the Keystone State*. University Park: Pennsylvania State University Press, 2005.

———. "Electoral Competition for the Pennsylvania General Assembly, 1900–1988." Paper presented at the Annual Meeting of the Pennsylvania Political Science Association, April 11, 1996.

Turner, Fred. "Looking to Unseat a Pa. Lawmaker? Good Luck." *Citizens' Voice*, December 2, 2019.

Turzai, Mike, Rodney A. Corey, and James G. Mann. "The Protection Is in the Process: The Legislative Reapportionment Commission, Communities of Interest, and Why Our Modern Founding Fathers Got It Right." *University of Pennsylvania Journal of Legal and Public Affairs* 4 (2019): 353–402. https://scholarship.law.upenn.edu/jlpa/vol4/iss3/1.

Wattenberg, Ben J. *The Rise of Candidate-Centered Politics*. New York: Free Press, 1991.

White, Ismail K., Chryl N. Laird, and Troy D. Allen. "Selling Out? The Politics of Navigating Conflicts Between Racial Group Interest and Self-Interest." *American Political Science Review* 108, no. 4 (November 2014): 783–800.

Williams, Damon C. "Pa. Legislature 'Dismal' in Racial Diversity." *Philadelphia Tribune*, July 6, 2016.

Wise, Sidney. *The Legislative Process in Pennsylvania*. Washington, DC: American Political Science Association, 1971.

———. *The Legislative Process in Pennsylvania*. 2nd ed. Harrisburg: Commonwealth of Pennsylvania, 1984.

The Governor

A state governor's roles and responsibilities are many and varied. Chapter 5 details the powers as well as the limitations of the Pennsylvania governor. The institutional framework of the office is laid out in the Pennsylvania constitution, but the real power of the institution lies with the individual actor who inhabits the role. Across the United States, the governor holds the state's chief executive office and is responsible for both making and carrying out policy. The governor is a state's face and so holds both a practical and a symbolic role in state government. Lastly, governors are often seen as the heads of their parties, raising funds and working to ensure election of other local, state, and even national-level officials. The modern governor is a fairly powerful executive due in part to late twentieth-century reforms and to the governor's increased fiscal and intergovernmental responsibilities. However, unlike the president of the United States, governors must share power with other independently elected executive offices that they can neither control nor remove.[1]

US governors serve four-year terms in all but two states (New Hampshire and Vermont). All governors can serve more than one term, except in Virginia, and all states provide for the governor's removal via impeachment, with the exception of Oregon. There are no specific qualifications to become a state governor. Most states require a minimum age and a certain number of years of state residency, although a few have no formal provisions for US citizenship, age, or residency.[2] Who is most likely to become a state governor when the statutory requirements for office are so general? Historically, governors have risen through the ranks of the state legislature or other statewide elected offices, such as state attorney general, auditor general, or treasurer. Since 1980, governors have increasingly been elected from the US Congress.[3]

Table 5.1 provides an overview of the background of Pennsylvania's governors since the 1968 constitutional revisions. Between 1878 and 1968, many of Pennsylvania's governors were wealthy business entrepreneurs, lawyers, and judges.[4]

As a state's chief executive, a typical US governor is constitutionally vested with executive responsibilities and powers. For example, a governor can propose legislation. This is primarily done through the budget process and the state-of-the-state addresses. Additionally, like the US president, all governors possess the veto power over legislation. Forty-five states allow governors some form of line-item veto, whereby a governor can strike out or

Table 5.1 Pennsylvania governors under the constitution of 1968

Name	Start Term	End Term	Experience
Milton Shapp (D)	01/19/1971	01/16/1979	Business
Richard Thornburgh (R)	01/16/1979	01/20/1987	Asst. US attorney general
Robert Casey (D)	01/20/1987	01/17/1995	Auditor general
Thomas Ridge (R)	01/17/1995	10/05/2001	US congressman
Mark Schweiker (R)	10/05/2001	01/21/2003	County commissioner
Edward Rendell (D)	10/21/2003	01/18/2011	Mayor of Philadelphia
Thomas Corbett (R)	01/18/2011	01/20/2015	PA attorney general
Thomas Wolf (D)	01/20/2015	01/17/2023	Business
Josh Shapiro (D)	01/17/2023		Attorney general

Source: "Pennsylvania Governors 1951–2015," Pennsylvania Historical and Museum Commission, Pennsylvania Governors, http://www.phmc.state.pa.us/portal/communities/governors/1951-2015/index.html (accessed August 9, 2021).

change individual parts of bills, usually budget expenditures. Governors also appoint heads of state agencies, who can pursue policy initiated by the governor. Governors can make changes to the size and structure of the state bureaucracy. Lastly, governors can call for special legislative sessions to address pressing issues.[5]

Traditionally, governors have been the face of the state, promoting business and tourism and defending the state's interests in Washington. More recently, governors have been tasked with developing and expanding a state's economy by seeking international relationships with multinational corporations and foreign governments. Governors also serve as the spokesperson for the state in times of natural disaster, health emergency,[6] terror attack, or civil unrest. They are the state's National Guard's commander in chief. In this capacity, they can deploy the National Guard for any emergency, but primarily for disaster situations.[7] During Hurricane Sandy in 2012, both New Jersey governor Chris Christie and New York governor Andrew Cuomo mobilized the National Guard for protection of lives and property and to prevent looting in the hurricane-affected coastal areas. In all a total of 6,700 Guard troops were called up to active duty by governors in affected states.[8]

A recent analysis of the most pressing issues facing state governors found that the top five issues mentioned by governors in their state-of-the-state addresses were education, the economy, health care, corrections, and taxes. Eighty-eight percent of governors talked about education, and 72 percent of governors highlighted economic issues. Pension reform's importance in the addresses fell from 36 percent in 2011 to just over 18 percent in 2016. While education remains a perennial issue for state governments, increasingly health care and the opioid-addiction crisis dominate the policy agenda nationwide.[9]

What does it mean to be Pennsylvania's governor? In theory, the governor should be the most powerful elected official in the state, known as the "supreme executive power."[10] In reality, the governor is often as much a negotiator and mediator as an executive officer. The Pennsylvania constitution outlines the sole legal criteria to become governor: one must be at least thirty years old and a US citizen and have been a resident of the commonwealth for at least seven years.[11] Once elected, the governor is limited to two four-year terms but no more than eight year in office. The governor's powers, on paper at least, are a laundry list of duties from military to managerial. The governor is the head of the National Guard, appoints the cabinet and other executive offices with senatorial approval, convenes the General Assembly, and can grant pardons.[12]

The governor's duties can be divided into two parts: legislative, including budgetary and veto powers, and managerial, as the state's chief executive officer. Like most governors throughout the country, the Quaker State's governor prepares, approves, and implements the budget and approves and enacts state legislation. One of the governor's most powerful constitutional tools is the veto. Pennsylvania's governor also possesses the line-item veto in regard to the budget and may veto individual line-item appropriations within an entire budget bill. The legislature has the power to override all vetoes with a two-thirds vote of each chamber.[13]

The development of the modern Pennsylvania governorship and its powers can be traced to Pennsylvania's colonial roots. The Penn family served as both owners and governors of the commonwealth of Pennsylvania under the Charter of Privileges in the first half of the eighteenth century. The constitution of 1776 provided for a twelve-member elected supreme Executive Council. Each counselor served a three-year term. The members of the council along with the state General Assembly chose a president and vice president of the council to serve a one-year term. The Executive Council carried out executive activities such as the appointment of judges and the granting of reprieves and pardons. The president served as the commander in chief of the state militia. However, the president had no veto power, which meant the legislature (General Assembly) was the main source of political power.[14] It was not until the constitution of 1790 that the governor was granted supreme executive power. Governors served three-year terms. The longest tenure in office belongs to Governor Thomas Mifflin, who served three consecutive terms under the constitution of 1790, and the shortest to John C. Bell, who served only nineteen days in 1947 when he succeeded Edward Martin, who resigned to take a US Senate seat.[15]

Pennsylvania's governors during the first half of the twentieth century, prior to the Constitutional Convention of 1967, steered the commonwealth through a rapidly industrializing era, two world wars, and the Great Depression. These governors dealt with the influx of foreign immigrants to work in the steel mills and coal mines, the environmental issues posed by the very industrial development that made Pennsylvania a center of the nation's economy, and the social and demographic changes that accompanied economic growth and decline. The early twentieth century saw Pennsylvania become a leader in steel and coal production but at a cost to the state's forests, streams, and wildlife habitats. Into this void entered one of Pennsylvania's most influential governors, Gifford Pinchot, who has been described as both a maverick and a reformer. Governor Pinchot served two nonconsecutive terms as Pennsylvania's chief executive from 1923 to 1927 and again from 1931 to 1935. From an administrative and governing perspective, his commitment to a "dry" state foreshadowed the present-day Pennsylvania Liquor Code and a state-owned and operated liquor store system. To this day, municipalities still control the location of bars and state liquor stores. Pinchot was also responsible for the Pennsylvania Administrative Code, which created the first executive budget, the first budget office, and a pension system for state employees. Governor Pinchot appointed the first woman to serve as a cabinet-level official, Dr. Ellen Potter, as secretary of the Department of Welfare.[16]

His greatest contribution, however, was in the area of conservation of natural resources and state lands. During his first administration, the Department of Forests and Waters and the Sanitary Water Board were established. The Water Board was the first antipollution regulatory agency in the nation. He was also responsible for making the ruffed grouse, mountain laurel, and hemlock the state symbols. Pinchot's two terms in office were, however, also marked by labor turmoil and economic depression. The 1925 anthracite miners' strike led to a permanent decrease in coal's use for home heating and contributed to the coal industry's fifty-year decline. The Great Depression hit Pennsylvania particularly hard, with unemployment over 40 percent by the end of 1933. His second term was marked by a constant battle with the conservative state legislature for food and other emergency relief assistance for the unemployed, the blind, the elderly, widows, and orphans.[17]

Other twentieth-century governors made significant contributions to both the structure of Pennsylvania government and the social safety net resulting from the Great Depression and the post–World War II era. George Earle's administration (1935–39) was often referred to as the "Little New Deal." His administration was responsible for the creation of the PA Turnpike Authority and the Department of Public Assistance. His pro-union and unemployment policies mimicked the policies arising at the national level. During World War II and in the era of postwar prosperity, Governor Edward Martin (1943–47) advanced equalization of state aid for public schools, championed mine and factory safety, and made the Pennsylvania Historical and Museum Commission an independent agency reporting directly to the governor.[18]

The 1940s boom quickly faded as recession and unemployment took hold in Pennsylvania in the next decade. Governor John Fine (1951–55) faced both personal tragedy when his wife died in office and public stress as the commonwealth experienced the demands of the baby boom. Education spending, particularly for new schools and teachers' salaries, was one of this administration's priorities. Most notably, Governor Fine enacted a state sales tax in 1953, which remains a primary source of income for the commonwealth.[19]

Two other governors from the postwar era of one-term governors stand out as champions of civil rights and social reform. Governor George Leader (1955–59) was dubbed by writer Paul Beers "Mr. Clean"[20] because he pushed for inclusion of African Americans in the state Democratic party's ranks. He appointed the first Black cabinet member, Andrew Bradley, as budget secretary. He increased both basic and higher education funding levels and advanced the rights of the disabled.[21]

But Leader inherited a $58.2 million budget deficit from Fine and a state economy at its worst since the Great Depression. Unemployment in the state was 8.8 percent, and in the coal and steel regions was as high as 15 percent. His epic fourteen-month long battle with the General Assembly to raise taxes ended in victory in 1956 with a new 3 percent sales tax and a 1 percent increase in the corporate net income tax.[22]

Governor William Scranton (1963–67) made his mark on the national political scene with a failed run for the Republican presidential nomination in 1964. During his time in office, he called for a referendum on a state constitutional convention. His accomplishments included the creation of the Pennsylvania Council on the Arts and the William Penn Museum and additional money for schools, highways, and mass transit. Scranton managed to extend public school busing to parochial schoolchildren and to appoint the first Black appellate judge, Theodore Spaulding, to the Superior Court. He ended his career in public service with a stint as ambassador to the United Nations under the Ford administration.[23]

THE FIGHT FOR THE STATE INCOME TAX—
GOVERNORS SHAFER AND SHAPP

The last governor to serve under the constitution of 1874, Raymond Shafer (1967–71), bore the brunt of the state's financial crisis that precipitated the 1967 constitutional convention. When Governor Shafer took office, Pennsylvania was running a deficit of a million dollars a day. Shafer, who had never lost a political race in his career, was about to lose the biggest battle of his public life, the push for a state income tax. By 1969, Pennsylvania was $242 million in debt with no fiscal remedy in sight. Shafer succeeded in increasing spending for education and public assistance by raising the state sales tax to 6 percent. Despite having a legislative majority for his first two years in office, he failed to have his appointments confirmed, and he holds the record for the longest budget battle, a sixteen-month debacle that began in 1970. As a Republican, he championed a major protection for state employees by advocating for and signing Act 195, which allowed state employees to collectively bargain. Shafer is also credited with completing Pennsylvania's interstate highway system and addressing environmental issues with the creation of the Department of Environmental Resources. Shafer was, however, able to keep a campaign promise to revise and update the Pennsylvania constitution. Yet despite his accomplishments, his administration was marked by the inability to enact the state income tax.[24] As Shafer himself stated, "One of the greatest accomplishments [of our administration] was a new constitution for Pennsylvania. It has been highly acclaimed and a model for other states. . . . Our biggest disappointment was in not getting a one percent income tax in place."[25]

"The Knight in Tarnished Armor, Governor Milton Shapp,"[26] as he was later dubbed by Philadelphia journalist William Ecenbarger, entered office without a state budget in place and with a deficit of $2 million per day.[27] Shapp campaigned as the antipolitician and fought the political establishment and even his own Democratic Party, but he left office tainted by corruption within his administration. As Pennsylvania's first two-term governor, he faced a major natural disaster at the start of his first term. Hurricane Agnes hit Pennsylvania in June 1972, devastating the Keystone State, including the governor's mansion, which experienced flooding on its first floor. But tackling the state's fiscal mess proved to be a challenge for which Governor Shapp was much better prepared. Shapp achieved what no other Pennsylvania governor in the twentieth century could: the enactment of a state income tax.[28]

In the end, his accomplishments were numerous. In his first term, he called for the creation of the state's first lottery, the enactment of the Sunshine Law, and the formation of the Department of General Services to oversee state capital projects. In his second term, he formed the Department of Aging and ended sovereign immunity for the commonwealth. His fiscal and administrative accomplishments were unfortunately overshadowed by corruption within his own cabinet.[29] As former governor Leader commented in a 1992 roundtable, "He had the idea that as a businessman, he could run matters just by giving orders, and all would work out. . . . Milton Shapp got the leftovers, all the people money could buy and he got himself an organization of riffraff."[30]

ISSUES FOR PENNSYLVANIA GOVERNORS TODAY

The contemporary Pennsylvania governor enters office with an array of fiscal and administrative powers not available to nineteenth- and twentieth-century governors. Not restricted to a one-term limit since 1968, the state's governors now can pursue more expansive legislative agendas. Pennsylvania governors have advanced policy issues such as rights of the disabled, mental health initiatives, criminal justice reforms, and, under the Wolf administration, legalization of medical marijuana.[31] Armed with the power to generate revenue through taxation, the governor can use the budget to target policy areas such as expanded preschool or increased aid to state-owned universities. Supported by a large, professional executive staff, governors may engage with the public directly through social media, thwarting the General Assembly's agenda through direct personal appeals to the voters and presenting their factual cases for spending and their own legislative goals. Yet many modern Pennsylvania governors argue that the task of governing in the brave new world of constant and decentralized media coverage has become more difficult than ever before in the state's history. As Governor Rendell noted, "The ball is in the executive court."[32] But as Governor Wolf noted in regard to the rise of extreme partisanship in the American electorate, the ideological forces in the legislature and the lack of "institutions that aggregate interest together" make governing extremely demanding.[33]

CONTROLLING THE MESSAGE

In the days before the 24/7 news cycle and the existence of social media, a governor could rely upon a disciplined team of media and policy professionals to control his message and his image. Governor Thornburgh's press secretary, Paul Critchlow, a former print reporter with great credibility, worked closely with Rick Stafford in the governor's policy office to devise a media strategy that was consistent with the policy objective and supportive of the legislative process. Critchlow's stellar reputation allowed the Thornburgh administration some room to maneuver.[34] For example, when the Three Mile Island company representatives essentially lied about the gravity of the situation at the nuclear plant, the administration successfully conducted a series of press conferences to set the record straight.[35] As Governor Thornburgh stated in a 1985 interview, "A governor cannot command the television cameras free of editing the way a president of the United States can."[36] However, Thornburgh did communicate directly with the public to assuage rising fears at the height of the Three Mile Island disaster.[37]

You "gotta connect with your people" was how Governor Schweiker characterized the media's important role.[38] Governor Rendell agreed, adding that the media's task was to offer support and explanation, and he found the best way to connect with the public was to grant the media access.[39] Both Schweiker and Rendell readily admitted that social media was not an issue for their administrations.[40] Governor Corbett felt the media—in particular, the Harrisburg press—were very biased against him. He used Radio PA to get his message out.[41] Governor Wolf likewise expressed that "objectivity is missing in the press."[42] His administration actively sought to control its image through the use of interactive presentations on the state website, Facebook, and Twitter.[43]

HANDLING THE LEGISLATURE

The "separation of powers is not as clear as it should be or once was."[44] Contemporary Pennsylvania governors have consistently noted the increasingly partisan polarization of politics and the lack of legislative leadership control over the rank-and-file members of the legislature as factors making it difficult to legislate and govern. While "the ball is in the executive court," as Rendell put it, he acknowledged that the Pennsylvania House is increasingly controlled by ideology.[45] Governor Corbett found that individual personalities played a strong role in his relationship with the legislature, as they did when he was Pennsylvania's attorney general. "I was the political outsider, truly the outsider when I came in."[46]

Ultimately, the level of cooperation between the governor and the General Assembly comes down to a mixture of the governor's personal relationships with legislators and their staff and a certain degree of brinksmanship and strategy. Using the old poker adage "Know when to hold 'em, and when to fold 'em," Governor Rendell refused to fold on childhood education funding in the 2007–8 fiscal year and again during the prolonged budget debate in 2009.[47] Likewise, Governor Wolf vetoed sixteen bills in his first two years in office yet still managed to find common ground with the legislature on issues such as liberalizing regulations on beer and wine sales, legalizing ride-sharing companies in the state, and legalizing medical marijuana.[48]

MANAGING YOUR ADMINISTRATION

Lessons from the Shapp administration strongly suggest that governors should surround themselves with competent, loyal, and honest people. Governor Thornburgh sought three qualities in those he nominated for his cabinet: competence, confirmability, and the ability to avoid scandal. He did not want his cabinet members to become an issue that detracted from his agenda. He offered Helen O'Bannon, his secretary of welfare, as an example of a controversial cabinet member.[49] Secretary O'Bannon placed herself in direct conflict with a federal judge who had ordered the closing of Pennhurst, a state facility for the mentally challenged, and the placement of its residents into community-based group homes. US district judge Raymond Broderick threatened Secretary O'Bannon with contempt of court for her ongoing public defense of the state institution.[50] As Governor Thornburgh succinctly put it, a governor needs smart and loyal people "who speak in one voice" but who also create "no surprises" for the governor. Cabinet members need to be honest and direct with their boss.[51] Governor Rendell emphasized that quality people are essential just as much as geographical diversity. He deployed his cabinet members as communicators with the general public and state employees.[52] Similarly, Governor Corbett chose people who were "middle of the road and true blue" so that he knew what to expect from his subordinates[53]

Governor Wolf discussed the need to choose team players to prevent the silo effect,[54] which can result in a lack of communication between an organization's members and hinder effective decision-making. Yet his administration's critics noted that several of his original cabinet members and top advisory positions were filled with people who sought to achieve their own personal political agendas, especially Wolf's chief of staff, Katie McGinty, and his policy director, John Hangar.[55]

Being governor means juggling the daily responsibilities of governing while also prepar-ing for the unexpected. Governors have faced economic downturns, natural and manmade disasters, and unplanned events such as illness and death. In a post-9/11 world, modern governors are tasked with the routine security of their citizens. National security is no longer solely the federal government's concern; it has also become a state and local government priority. Governor Schweiker, who assumed the governor's office upon Governor Ridge's appointment to become the first secretary of homeland security in 2002, observed that governors "grow and manage through crisis."[56] He spoke from direct personal experience. As lieutenant governor, he assisted in responding to the infamous blizzard of 1996 and to the downing of Flight 93 in Shanksville, Pennsylvania, on Sep-tember 11, 2001. Later as governor, his leadership was tested when nine miners became trapped in the Quecreek Mine in July of 2002. As the *Pittsburgh Post-Gazette* reported during the disaster, Schweiker was the voice of calm and optimism during the mine's collapse and the miners' subsequent rescue. His everyman public persona served him well with both the national media and the local residents.[57] As Governor Schweiker said, "Big crisis is the one time you can show Pennsylvania that you can employ tactics and manage aggressively."[58]

But if a major crisis allows the governor to take center stage, it is the day-to-day affairs of governing that take a toll on a governor's approval ratings. As Governor Rendell stated, the annual budget negotiations with the General Assembly require the governor to

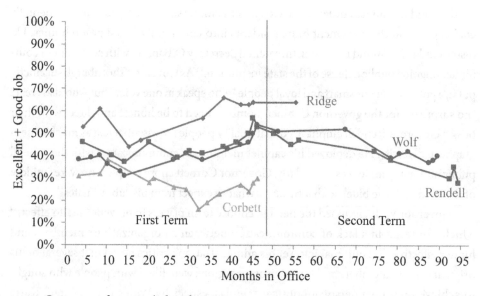

FIG. 5.1 Comparison of governors' job performance ratings. Source: Berwood Yost, 2021. Franklin and Marshall Poll, Center for Opinion Research, Floyd Institute for Public Policy, Franklin and Marshall College.

"understand how to make a deal."[59] Governor Rendell learned a few lessons during his first budget talks in 2003, when the legislature approved his entire budget proposal without any hearings. Governor Rendell had intended his initial budget proposal to be a "place-holder" until he submitted a more comprehensive spending plan, but the legislature called his bluff.[60]

Governor Wolf experienced his own lengthy struggle to pass his first budget, which hearkened back to the legislative confrontations of the Shafer administration. Governor Wolf's first budget was passed nine months into the fiscal year on March 28, 2015. It went into effect without his signature. By the end of his first year in office, his approval ratings were at 30 percent.[61]

THE BIGGEST CHALLENGES

Over four decades, Pennsylvania's governors faced common challenges over key issues that continue to confront the commonwealth. The governors we interviewed identified education funding, economic development, tax restructuring, pension crisis, environmental regulations, and judicial reform as the most significant, persistent problems facing the Quaker State. Fair and adequate funding for public education remains a perennial concern for Pennsylvania's governors and the General Assembly as it is linked to local property taxes and the state's contributions to local school district funding.[62] As Governor Corbett said, "We have an education funding issue in this state."[63] Governors Rendell and Schweiker agreed, pointing out Pennsylvania's "brain drain" while emphasizing their support for universal pre-K programs.[64]

At the same time, economic development remains the "eternal issue," in the words of Governor Schweiker.[65] Creating a more business-friendly environment in the commonwealth has drawn gubernatorial attention for decades, stretching from the inception of the Ben Franklin Partnership, which linked business, education, and industry during the Thornburgh administration, to the elimination of the capital stock tax in the first year of the Wolf administration.[66]

Lastly, addressing shortfalls in the state and local public employees' pension systems and fracking's future in the commonwealth loom large for the foreseeable future. Perhaps Governor Schweiker summed it up best. The job of being governor in Pennsylvania requires personality, style, a certain amount of strength and leadership. In the end, the governor must be dedicated to a "set of ideals that motivate you."[67] The need for state-level executive leadership in the twenty-first century is heightened by the most current health, economic, and environmental demands. Pennsylvania governors will continue to influence the future of the commonwealth at the same time that they deal with a host of unforeseen issues and crises.

CONCLUSION

The institution of governor in the commonwealth of Pennsylvania will continue to evolve. The institution may be altered by formal constitutional changes, but it will more likely be changed by the issues and challenges facing the commonwealth in the near future. The Pennsylvania governor will need to serve as a strong decision-maker in a rapidly evolving fiscal and political landscape. Both the institution and the actor will influence the power of the Pennsylvania governor.

NOTES

1. Bowman, Woods, and Stark, "Governors Turn Pro."
2. National Governors Association, "Governors' Powers and Authority."
3. Ferguson, "Governors and the Executive Branch."
4. "Pennsylvania Governors 1951–2015."
5. Council of State Governments, *Book of the States.*
6. Smith and Greenblatt, *Governing States and Localities.*
7. Ibid.
8. Willoughby, "State of the State."
9. Ibid.
10. PA constitution, article 4, section 2.
11. PA constitution, article 4, section 5.
12. PA constitution, article 4, sections 7–11, 16.
13. National Governors Association, "Governors' Powers and Authority."
14. Williams, "Influences of Pennsylvania."
15. "1861–1945."
16. "1776–1861"; "1861–1945."
17. "Governor Gifford Pinchot"; Beers, *Pennsylvania Politics.*
18. "Governor Edward Martin."
19. "Governor John Sydney Fine."
20. Beers, *Pennsylvania Politics,* 209.
21. "Governor George Michael Leader."
22. Beers, *Pennsylvania Politics;* "Governor George Michael Leader."
23. Beers, *Pennsylvania Politics;* "Governor William Warren Scranton."
24. Beers, *Pennsylvania Politics;* "Governor Raymond Philip Schafer."
25. Christ et al., "Pennsylvania Politics."
26. Beers, *Pennsylvania Politics,* 365.
27. Ibid.
28. Beers, *Pennsylvania Politics;* "Governor Milton Jerrold Shapp."
29. Beers, *Pennsylvania Politics;* "Governor Milton Jerrold Shapp."
30. Christ et al., "Pennsylvania Politics."
31. "Priorities for Pennsylvania."
32. Ed Rendell (former governor, district attorney, and mayor) interview with the authors, December 18, 2015, in his Philadelphia office.
33. Thomas Wolf (governor), interview with the author, March 22, 2016, by phone.
34. Richard Thornburgh, former governor, interview by the authors, July 22, 2016.
35. Ibid.
36. Behn, *Governors on Governing,* 136.
37. Ibid.
38. Mark Schweiker (former governor), interview with the authors, May 27, 2016, in his company office.
39. Rendell, interview.
40. Rendell, interview; Schweiker, interview.
41. Tom Corbett (former governor), interview with the authors, July 18, 2016, by Skype.
42. Wolf, interview.
43. Thomas Wolf, "About," Facebook, June 8, 2021, https://www.facebook.com/governorwolf/.
44. "Governor Wolf Signs."
45. Rendell, interview.
46. Corbett, interview.
47. Rendell, interview; "Rendell Signs"
48. Levy, "Pennsylvania's Huge GOP"; "Governor Wolf Signs"; Medical Marijuana Act.
49. Thornburgh, interview.
50. Geislmen, "Pa. Aide."
51. Thornburgh, interview.
52. Rendell, interview.
53. Corbett, interview.

54. Wolf, interview.
55. Giammarise, "What Defined"; Comisac and Zwick, "Wolf Year-One."
56. Schweiker, interview.
57. Gibbs, "Schweiker Makes Mark."
58. Schweiker, interview.
59. Rendell, interview.
60. Micek and Bull, "Rendell Budget."
61. Giammarise, "What Defined"; Comisac and Zwick, "Wolf Year-One."
62. Corbett, interview; Rendell, interview; Schweiker, interview; Wolf, interview; Thornburgh, interview.
63. Corbett, interview.
64. Rendell, interview; Schweiker, interview.
65. Schweiker, interview.
66. "Governor Richard Lewis Thornburgh"; Nicastre, "Wolf's First Year."
67. Schweiker, interview.

BIBLIOGRAPHY

Beers, Paul. *Pennsylvania Politics Today and Yesterday: The Tolerable Accommodation.* University Park: Pennsylvania State University Press, 1980.

Behn, Robert D., ed. *Governors on Governing.* Washington, DC: National Governors Association, 1991.

The Book of the States. Lexington, KY: Council of State Governments, 2018.

Bowman, Ann O., Neal D. Woods, and Milton R. Stark. "Governors Turn Pro." *Political Research Quarterly* 63, no. 2 (2008): 304–15. doi:10. 1177/1065912908328858.

Christ, Robert G., Genevieve Blatt, George M. Leader, Kenneth B. Lee, A. James Reichley, and Raymond P. Shafer. "Pennsylvania Politics and Government, 1950–1970: A Round Table Discussion." *Pennsylvania History* 59, no. 4 (October 1992): 297–309. http://www.jstor.org/stable/27773565 (accessed November 4, 2014).

Comisac, Chris, and Kevin Zwick. "Wolf Year-One Review, Parts 1, 2, 3 and 4." Capitolwire, April 4, 2016. capitolwire.com (accessed August 27, 2016).

"1861–1945: Era of Industrial Ascendancy." Pennsylvania Historical and Museum Commission, Pennsylvania History. http://www.phmc.state .pa.us/portal/communities/pa-history/1861 -945.html (accessed February 1, 2017).

Ferguson, Margaret. "Governors and the Executive Branch." In *Politics in the American States: A Comparative Analysis*, 11th ed., 235–74. Washington, DC: CQ Press, 2018.

———. "Rendell Signs Education Budget Preserving Pennsylvania's Academic Progress, Keeping Property Taxes Down." GANTNews, October 12, 2009. https://gantnews.com/2009/10/12 /rendell-signs-education-budget-preserving -pennsylvanias-academic-progress-keeping -property-taxes-down/amp/ (accessed May 23, 2017).

Geiselman, A. W., Jr. "Pa. Aide Stirs Ire of Judge." *Philadelphia Bulletin*, July 25, 1981. https:// digital.library.temple.edu/digital/collection /p15037coll7/search (accessed June 2, 2023).

Giammarise, Kate. "What Defined Tom Wolf's First Year in Office." *Pittsburgh Post-Gazette*, January 20, 2016. https://www.post-gazette .com/news/state/2016/01/20/Budget-fight -overshadows-Gov-Wolf-s-first-year-in-office /stories/201601200016 (accessed February 1, 2016).

Gibbs, Tom. "Schweiker Makes Mark as the Chief Spokesman." *Pittsburgh Post-Gazette*, July 26, 2002. http://old.post-gazette.com /localnews/20020728schweikerp4 .asp (accessed May 18, 2017).

"Governor Edward Martin." Pennsylvania Historical and Museum Commission, Pennsylvania Governors. http://www.phmc.state.pa.us /portal/communities/governors/1876-1951 /edward-martin.html (accessed August 9, 2021).

"Governor George Howard Earle III." Pennsylvania Historical and Museum Commission, Pennsylvania Governors. http://www.phmc.state.pa.us /portal/communities/governors/1876-1951 /george-earle.html (accessed August 9, 2021).

"Governor George Michael Leader." Pennsylvania Historical and Museum Commission, Pennsylvania Governors. http://www.phmc .state.pa.us/portal/communities/governors /1951-2015/george-leader.html (accessed August 9, 2021).

"Governor Gifford Pinchot." Pennsylvania Historical and Museum Commission, Pennsylvania

Governors. http://www.phmc.state.pa.us
/portal/communities/governors/1876-1951
/gifford-pinchot.html (accessed August 9, 2021).

"Governor John Sydney Fine." Pennsylvania Historical and Museum Commission, Pennsylvania
Governors. http://www.phmc.state.pa.us
/portal/communities/governors/1951-2015
/john-fine.html (accessed August 9, 2021).

"Governor Milton Jerrold Shapp." Pennsylvania
Historical and Museum Commission, Pennsylvania Governors. http://www.phmc.state.pa.us
/portal/communities/governors/1951-2015
/milton-shapp.html (accessed August 9, 2021).

"Governor Raymond Philip Shafer." Pennsylvania
Historical and Museum Commission, Pennsylvania Governors. http://www.phmc.state.pa
.us/portal/communities/governors/1951-2015
/raymond-shafer.html (accessed August 9, 2021).

"Governor Richard Lewis Thornburgh." Pennsylvania Historical and Museum Commission,
Pennsylvania Governors. http://www.phmc
.state.pa.us/portal/communities/governors
/1951-2015/richard-thornburgh.html (accessed
August 9, 2021).

"Governor William Warren Scranton." Pennsylvania
Historical and Museum Commission, Pennsylvania Governors. http://www.phmc.state.pa
.us/portal/communities/governors/1951
-2015/william-scranton.html (accessed August
9, 2021).

"Governor Wolf Signs Law Legalizing Ride-Sharing
Statewide." November 4, 2016. https://www
.governor.pa.gov/governor-wolf-signs-law
-legalizing-ride-sharing-statewide/ (accessed
May 23, 2017).

Levy, Marc. "Pennsylvania's Huge GOP Majorities
Could Test a Wolf Veto." Washington Times,
January 28, 2017. http://www.washingtontimes
.com/news/2017/jan/28/pennsylvanias-huge
-gop-majorities-could-test-a-wolf/ (accessed
May 27, 2017).

Medical Marijuana Act. P.L. 84, no. 16, April 17, 2016
(Pennsylvania, 2017). https://www.legis.state
.pa.us/cfdocs/legis/li/uconsCheck.cfm?yr
=2016&sessInd=0&act=16.

Micek, J., and J. Bull. "Rendell Budget Full of
Painful Cuts." Allentown Morning Call,
March 5, 2003. https://www.mcall.com

/news/mc-xpm-2003-03-05-3451633
-story.html.

National Governors Association. "Governors'
Powers and Authority." https://www.nga
.org/cms/home/management-resources
/governors-powers-and-authority.html
(accessed January 27, 2017).

———. "Pennsylvania: Past Governors Bios." nga.
org. http://www.nga.org/cms/home
/governors/past-governors-bios/page
_pennsylvania (accessed February 3, 2018).

Nicastre, Mark. "Wolf's First Year." Governor
.pa.gov. https://www.governor.pa.gov/blog
-looking-on-governor-wolfs-first-year
(accessed January 15, 2015).

"Pennsylvania Governors 1951–2015." Pennsylvania
Historical and Museum Commission, Pennsylvania Governors. http://www.phmc.state
.pa.us/portal/communities/governors/1951
-2015/index.html (accessed August 9, 2021).

"Priorities for Pennsylvania." Governor Tom Wolf.
July 19, 2021. http://www.phmc.state.pa.us
/portal/communities/governors/1951-2015
/milton-shapp.html (accessed June 2, 2023).

"1776–1861: Independence to the Civil War."
Pennsylvania Historical and Museum
Commission, Pennsylvania History. http://
www.phmc.state.pa.us/portal/communities
/pa-history/1776-1861.html (accessed
February 1, 2017).

"1681–1776: The Quaker Province." Pennsylvania
Historical and Museum Commission, Pennsylvania History. http://www.phmc.state.pa.us
/portal/communities/pa-history/1681-1776
.html (accessed February 1, 2017).

Smith, Kevin, and Alan Greenblatt. Governing States
and Localities: The Essentials. Washington, DC:
CQ Press, 2014.

Williams, Robert K. "The Influences of Pennsylvania's Constitution of 1776 on American
Constitutionalism During the Founding
Decade." Pennsylvania Magazine of History
and Biography 114, no. 1 (1988): 25–48.

Willoughby, Katherine. "State of the State
Addresses: Governors in the Hot Seat." CNN
.com. http://www.cnn.com/2013/07/13/wrld
/americas/hurrinace-sandy-fast-facts/
(accessed February 1, 2017).

CHAPTER 6

The Executive Branch

In this chapter we take an in-depth look at the offices and functions of the executive branch in Pennsylvania. The institutional structure of the executive branch influences both policy choices and policy impacts. The commonwealth's executive branch is composed of a mix of officials chosen by statewide elections and those chosen by the governor and confirmed by the state senate. This is in keeping with political traditions practiced across the United States. The governor's office is elected in every state, but great variation exists in the election of other offices. Across the country, executive positions such as lieutenant governor, attorney general, secretary of state, treasurer, state superintendent of education, and auditor general are elected statewide.[1] This chapter will explain the duties of the office of the lieutenant governor, the attorney general, the auditor general and treasurer, and the cabinet offices.

There are pros and cons to separately electing executive branch offices. One argument is that these officials can serve as a check on the governor's power. They also allow for greater voter participation in the management of state affairs. On the negative side, the politicization of essentially administrative offices can interfere with the functioning of state government and complicate efficient coordination among the governor's executive team.[2]

The most commonly elected executive branch office after governor is lieutenant governor. Forty-three states currently have lieutenant governors elected statewide, with New Jersey opting to add the office in 2009. The primary duty of the lieutenant governor is to be first in the line of succession. Since 1980, forty-two lieutenant governors have been called upon to serve as a state's governor after the resignation or death of a sitting governor. The reelection success rate for those lieutenant governors who then went on to seek reelection in the next special or regular election is 63 percent.[3] In 2021, Republicans in the General Assembly introduced a constitutional amendment to eliminate the office, claiming it is unnecessary and expensive. Before the 2022 election, however, the GOP controlled both legislative chambers, so the individual likely to be named to succeed a governor who could no longer fulfill the office's responsibilities would have been the House speaker or Senate president pro tempore, both Republicans.[4] As of January 2023, the Democrats control the House.

In twenty-five of the forty-three states with elected lieutenant governors, the lieutenant governor presides over the state senate as prescribed by the state's constitution. The statutory duties of the lieutenant governor range from none in Maryland, Mississippi, and New Jersey to more than thirty in Alabama, Texas, and Washington. But lieutenant governors can also gain duties and power through personal initiative or through special duties or appointments assigned by the governor. Post-9/11, many lieutenant governors took on oversight of homeland security issues. More recently, lieutenant governors have tackled issues such as opioid addiction, workforce development, and international economic development promotion for their states.[5]

The second most common statewide elected official is attorney general. This office is popularly elected in forty-three states. The attorney general engages in both civil and criminal litigation on behalf of the state. The attorney general may issue legal opinions to state agencies, engage in major criminal investigations, protect consumers from fraud, enforce environmental regulations through the legal process, and supervise charities and trusts within the state. Attorneys general have attracted some political controversy in recent years. They have been involved in incidences of sexual harassment, racial discrimination, drunk driving, and even fatal accidents. These problems tend to appear in their first term in office and are the result of poor political vetting and political inexperience.[6] Since 1984, the success rate for attorneys general who seek to become governor has been 11 percent, compared to the 22 percent of lieutenant governors who have won the governor's office.[7]

Secretaries of state round out the top trio of statewide officials, with thirty-nine of the fifty secretaries elected by the voters. The secretary of state is commonly in charge of the election process. Their role in elections includes supervising absentee ballots and early voting and maintaining online voter registration. The position came into the limelight during the 2020 presidential election with regard to voter fraud, election tampering, and voter identification laws. President Trump launched attacks on the secretaries of state in many key states, including Michigan, Nevada, and Arizona. In Pennsylvania, where state election law prevents the counting of absentee ballots until election day, Trump campaign officials targeted Secretary of State Kathy Boockvar as a partisan operative.[8] As a result of the 2020 electoral challenges, elections for secretary of state have become hotly contested across the nation. Recently both Democrats and Republicans have invested super PAC money in secretary of state elections.[9] The secretary of state was on the ballot in twenty-six states in 2022. With possible ramifications for the 2024 presidential election, outside groups such as iVote poured millions of dollars into these races.[10]

The Pennsylvania executive branch is made up of independently elected officials and appointed cabinet secretaries. Article IV of the Pennsylvania constitution establishes the Executive Department, which includes the offices of governor, lieutenant governor, attorney general, auditor general, and treasurer. The constitution also stipulates that the legislature can establish other offices as needed.[11] These include departments, agencies, and commissions, headed by administrators appointed by the governor and approved by the Senate. In addition, there are numerous commissions and public boards where the governor exercises minimal control. Several public corporations, such as the General State Authority, are not under the control of the governor, although the governor sits on the corporate board.[12]

The executive offices delineated in the Pennsylvania constitution are further governed by the Administrative Code, passed by the General Assembly in 1929. The Code established the organization of the various executive offices and sets their powers and fiscal duties. Examples of additional boards created by the legislature and added to the code include the Pennsylvania Turnpike Commission, the Civil Service Commission, the Milk Marketing Board, and the Pennsylvania Liquor Control Board (PLCB).[13] The governor also appoints six department heads to the Executive Board. Chaired by the governor, the Board oversees personnel policies, qualifications for employment in the executive branch, salaries, and employee bonding.[14]

PENNSYLVANIA'S LIEUTENANT GOVERNOR

The lieutenant governor is elected jointly with the governor every four years in nonpresidential election years. But candidates for lieutenant governor run separately from their parties' gubernatorial candidates in the primaries. It is thus possible for a party's gubernatorial and lieutenant governor candidates to hold different policy positions, have little in common personally, or worse, actually dislike each other.

According to the Pennsylvania constitution, the lieutenant governor's main duty is to serve as the president of the Senate. The lieutenant governor presides over the proceedings but is only able to cast a vote in the case of a tie. Even this tie-breaking vote is limited. For example, the lieutenant governor may not vote on the final passage of a bill or on a joint resolution.[15] The lieutenant governor is also the chairperson of the Board of Pardons.[16] Perhaps the most important responsibility of the lieutenant governor involves continuity of government. The lieutenant governor assumes the duties of the governor should the governor die, resign, or become incapacitated.[17]

Two lieutenant governors have assumed the office of governor in Pennsylvania's history. John Bell became governor when Edward Martin won election to the US Senate in 1947. Bell served as governor only for the final three weeks of Martin's term in office, making his governorship the shortest in Pennsylvania history. Mark Schweiker become governor in 2001 when Tom Ridge resigned to become the first secretary of homeland security in the George W. Bush administration.[18] Schweiker noted that during the transition period following Governor Ridge's resignation, the key was to have government operating normally.[19]

Perhaps one of the most dramatic temporary transfers of power occurred during the Casey administration. In June of 1993, Mark Singel became the commonwealth's acting governor while Governor Robert P. Casey Sr. underwent a rare heart-and-liver transplant. Mark Singel held the post of acting governor for six and a half months. During this time, he noted, "The moment I assumed the mantle of governor, there was a palpable burden. I was responsible for the commonwealth."[20] Singel realized the political implications of exercising too much power, but as he stated, "I wasn't just holding down the fort. I was aggressive but held myself back. While I wanted to make some legislative changes, I was wary."[21]

One example of a political decision that he was willing to make was on workers' compensation reform. Pennsylvania's businesses had long fought for changes to limit benefits and reduce premiums, which had risen by 24 percent in December of 1992. The AFL-CIO denounced the legislative package, but the reforms passed both chambers. The acting governor passed the bill on June 16 in his capacity as president of the Senate (lieutenant governor) and signed the bill into law on July 2, 1993, in his role as acting governor.[22] Lieutenant Governor Singel recently described his decision: "I signed it but the governor [Casey] would have vetoed it."[23]

The day-to-day activities of lieutenant governors are less dramatic than the duties of acting governor and are heavily determined by their relationship with their governor. Given their limited constitutional duties, lieutenant governors can take on many additional roles and duties as assigned. A number of lieutenant governors, including Kline, Scranton, Schweiker, and Singel, were designated by their governors to serve as chair of the Pennsylvania Emergency Management Agency (PEMA).[24] As Lieutenant Governor Mark Schweiker described it, PEMA was a place where he "could do some of the heavy lifting," especially during the floods of 1996 on the Susquehanna River and the downing of Flight 93 in Shanksville on September 11.[25] Likewise, Lieutenant Governor Singel noted that he handled all types of emergencies, earning him the title "Master of Disaster."[26] Lieutenant governors are often tasked with shepherding specific policy initiatives through the General Assembly or the bureaucracy. Mark Schweiker headed the "Weed and Seed" program to promote community-redevelopment efforts.[27] Mark Singel was the point person for the promotion of diversity through the Pennsylvania Humanities Council, vice-chairperson of the Economic Development Partnership Board, and head of the Energy Office. Not among the least of the lieutenant governor's duties is political campaigning and fundraising for both for the gubernatorial team and the party. Mark Singel may have summarized the role best: "You are about the business of being the best second in command that you can be.[28]

As lieutenant governor, John Fetterman changed the image of the office. While serving as chairperson of the Board of Pardons, Fetterman advocated for more commutations than any other lieutenant governor. He has also been a strong supporter of the legalization of recreational marijuana in the commonwealth.[29] But it is his personal style as the antipolitician that garnered the most media attention. Known for his "uniform" of black hoodies and cargo shorts, Fetterman as lieutenant governor portrayed himself as the everyman from small-town Pennsylvania. He rose to national prominence, first as the mayor of Braddock, a struggling former steel town near Pittsburgh, then as a spokesperson for the Democratic Party in the 2020 election and as the proponent of numerous progressive ideas such as single-payer health care.[30] In 2022 he was elected to the US Senate. Fetterman was not constricted by the limited structural role of the lieutenant governor in Pennsylvania.

The three other statewide elected offices in the commonwealth are attorney general, auditor general, and treasurer. Attorney general, the chief law enforcement office for the state, has been an independent elected office since 1980. The office offers legal advice to the governor and state agencies, represents the commonwealth in any lawsuits (for or against the state), provides consumer protection to the citizens of the commonwealth, and investigates and prosecutes any cases of government corruption or fraud, oversees all grand juries, and handles organized crime cases.[31] The former attorney general, now governor, Josh Shapiro saw his office as encompassing all these duties and more. Among the major tasks on his office's agenda was addressing what he described as "the number one public safety threat in Pennsylvania, heroin and opioids."[32] He also cited the need to "take on the big fights on behalf of Pennsylvania consumers," such as the Equifax credit security breach and the Sally Mae /Navient student loan scandals.[33] The Equifax security breach in 2017 resulted in the theft of personal data, including names and Social Security numbers, from 147.7 million Americans.[34] The Navient scandal involved mistakes in loan payment processing that cost borrowers additional loan-repayment fees and negatively affected their credit scores.[35] Shapiro's office sued Navient and was part of a nationwide settlement with Equifax in 2019.[36] Shapiro understood his responsibilities to include "protecting the rights and interests of all Pennsylvanians."[37] As a great believer in states' rights, then–attorney general Shapiro took the federal government to task on several issues, including the creation of a national standard for concealed carry permits and the status of the commonwealth's 5,900 DACA recipients.[38]

First on the former attorney general's list of tasks, however, was "restoring integrity to the office."[39] The Pennsylvania attorney general's office was the focus of many scandals. Former attorney general Ernie Preate served from 1988 until his resignation in 1995. A seasoned trial lawyer and a former district attorney from Lackawanna County, Preate was only the second elected attorney general of Pennsylvania. A master of public relations, he was a leading Republican candidate for governor in the 1994 election. But Preate had been under investigation since 1990 for illegal campaign contributions from video poker operators in Lackawanna County. After much public denial and accusations that the FBI and the Pennsylvania Crime Commission were engaging in a witch hunt motivated by ethnic bias against Italian Americans, Preate pleaded guilty to one count of federal mail fraud, ostensibly to prevent his brothers from being indicted as well. Preate resigned in 1995 and served a fourteen-month sentence in federal prison. After a five-year suspension, Ernie Preate had his law license reinstated, and he is once again practicing law in Lackawanna County.[40]

The most recent scandal to rock the office of attorney general involves the first woman and first Democrat to be elected to the office, Kathleen Kane. The long descent into perjury and obstruction of justice charges began when Kane leaked grand jury testimony to embarrass a state prosecutor, Frank Fina. Fina was believed to be the source of a story blaming

Kane for closing an investigation into corruption by Democratic lawmakers. In a series of plot twists, Kane lied under oath about the leak, eventually losing her license to practice law, all while remaining the attorney general. Kane was convicted in 2016 and sentenced to ten to twenty-three months in prison, but she remained free on bail while awaiting an appeal decision by the Pennsylvania Superior Court. Kane eventually served eight months of her sentence at the Montgomery County prison before she was released in July of 2019.[41]

The auditor general is dubbed the "chief fiscal watchdog of the commonwealth."[42] The office monitors all state funds for misuse, corruption, waste, and inefficiencies. The auditor general conducts audits of all state agencies, state-owned facilities, state liquor stores, school districts, municipal pension plans, nonprofit agencies receiving state funds, and even volunteer firefighters' relief associations. Only the state judiciary and the General Assembly, along with public school and public university building authorities, are not subject to the auditor general. The auditor general also conducts an analysis of the state's financial statements, known as a GAAP, or generally accepted accounting principles. This document is used by bond-rating agencies and investors to determine the financial condition of the commonwealth.[43]

The state treasurer is responsible for depositing, investing, and dispersing the commonwealth's money, including monitoring the fiscal health of the two major state retirement funds: the State Employee Retirement System (SERS) and the Public School Employee Retirement System (PSERS). The treasurer primarily invests in short-term US government securities in order to have quick access to state funds for meeting state obligations. Once converted to cash, this money is deposited into seventy financial institutions so the state can write checks. The treasurer also makes longer-term investments and oversees abandoned and unclaimed property such as bank accounts. Lastly, the treasurer's office administers the INVEST program, managing investments for local governments and nonprofits.[44]

As in the attorney general's office, the combination of fiscal responsibility and financial powers has led to corruption and scandals. In 1984, State Treasurer Bud Dwyer agreed to accept a $300,000 bribe in exchange for an accounting contract for Computer Technology Associates. While no money actually exchanged hands, the offer was enough to get Dwyer convicted of bribery charges in 1987. The day before his sentencing and on live television, Dwyer committed suicide with a handgun. His desperate act preserved his $1.2 million pension for his family, but it opened up a long debate on whether or not Dwyer was wrongly convicted.[45]

More recent scandals involving a state treasurer included charges of extortion and bribery, which led to the prosecution of not one but two state treasurers. Former treasurers Barbara Hafer and Rob McCord were charged with receiving illegal payouts from Philadelphia area businessman Richard Ireland. Ireland served as a finder in a "pay-to-play" scheme, providing campaign contributions and future job opportunities to government officials in exchange for state government contracts for his clients. Barbara Hafer received $675,000 in consulting fees after leaving office in 2005. This money was in addition to the $475,000 in campaign contributions she had also garnered. Hafer was convicted of lying to the FBI and the IRS regarding the consulting fees and was sentenced to thirty-six months' probation in October of 2017. McCord, who had aspired to become governor in 2014, was enticed by the same promise of campaign contributions and later cooperated with federal investigators, taping conversations and gathering text messages and emails to use in the case against Hafer. While all charges against Ireland were eventually dropped, McCord was sentenced to thirty months in prison in August of 2018.[46]

All of these scandals involving the executive branch cast a shadow on the ability of the offices to provide efficient and effective government services for the taxpayers. According to a 2015 study by the Center for Public Integrity, Pennsylvania received a failing grade in state integrity, including an F in civil service management, an F in state pension fund management, and a D in procurement. Pennsylvania has been ranked the fifth most corrupt state in the nation by the political blog FiveThirtyEight in terms of number of officials convicted.[47]

Act 120 of 2010 created the Independent Fiscal Office (IFO) to address issues related to economic forecasting for the Pennsylvania budget process. In addition to providing revenue projections, the IFO completes economic and fiscal analyses on a broad range of policy issues. For example, the IFO examines Pennsylvania's labor market, natural gas production, and the effect of various state tax credit programs. The IFO does not offer any policy recommendations. The key to the IFO is its nonpartisan, independent perspective. The IFO does not work for any party, nor does it work for one branch of government. The IFO seeks to create relationships between the various government agencies as well as nongovernmental institutions that serve the commonwealth.[48]

The IFO's revenue projections tend to be in line with the governor's office's official revenue projections. The IFO has highlighted some revenue and expenditure trends that will impact the commonwealth for the next two decades. Revenue will continue to lag as the number of working-age adults declines in the commonwealth and the number of retirees increases. The IFO projects that by 2025 the ratio of working adults to adults age sixty-five and older will be 2.6. This is a concern as the majority of the General Revenue Fund for the state is generated by the working population. Likewise, the IFO projects continued increases in mandatory expenditures related to pensions for teachers (PSERS) and state employees (SERS). Spending on human services (particularly health care), education, and corrections will continue to dominate state spending. An aging population means that Pennsylvania will see greater demand for services but lower sales and income tax growth. Spending will most likely continue to outpace revenues as older adults generate less sales tax income and as the population in general shifts from spending on taxable goods to nontaxable services like health care.[49]

Despite the many managerial and ethical issues facing Pennsylvania's executive branch, over eighty-four thousand state employees provide services ranging from criminal justice to human services to environmental regulation to education and the preservation of the commonwealth's history. Among state employees are administrators and professionals, skilled laborers, and protective services officers. Nearly fifty-nine thousand are unionized workers, and nearly thirteen thousand are managers. Roughly 70 percent of these positions are civil service—that is, merit appointments with protections. The average state salary is $55,450, and the average length of service of a state employee is twelve years, with 14.5 percent of the workforce drawn from minority groups.[50] This is the face of the commonwealth of Pennsylvania administrative branch. These are the people who continue the day-to-day operations of state government regardless of scandal and electoral politics.

The institutions of Pennsylvania's executive branch, both elected and appointed, will continue to impact the future of the commonwealth. Structural changes, such as making the secretary of state a statewide elected office, could change the nature of voting in the commonwealth and ultimately play a role in deciding close elections. However, the permanence of the rank-and-file employees of the various cabinet offices will continue to provide policy continuity from one gubernatorial administration to the next (table 6.1).

Table 6.1 Cabinet-level agencies

Department	Website
Department of Aging	https://www.aging.pa.gov
Department of Agriculture	https://www.agriculture.pa.gov
Department of Banking	https://www.dobs.pa.gov
Department of Community and Economic Development	https://www.dced.pa.gov
Department of Conservation and Natural Resources	https://www.dcnr.pa.gov
Department of Corrections	https://www.cor.pa.gov
Department of Education	https://www..pa.gov
Pennsylvania Emergency Management Agency	https://www.pema.pa.gov
Department of Environmental Protection	https://www.dep.pa.gov
Department of General Services	https://www.dgs.pa.gov
Department of Health	https://www.health.pa.gov
Department of Human Services	https://www.dhs.pa.gov
Insurance Department	https://www.insurance.pa.gov
Department of Labor and Industry	https://www.dli.pa.gov
Department of Military and Veterans Affairs	https://www.dmva.pa.gov
Department of Revenue	https://www.revenue.pa.gov
Department of State	https://www.dos.pa.gov
Pennsylvania State Police	https://www.psp.pa.gov
Department of Transportation	https://www.penndot.gov

1. Smith and Greenblatt, *Governing States and Localities.*
2. Ibid.
3. Skelley, "Stepping Up."
4. Scolforo, "GOP Faces Decisions"; Weissman, "Rep. Keefer Proposes"; Gerow, "Eliminate Pa.'s Second in Command?"
5. Greenblatt, "Lt. Governors on the Rise." National Lieutenant Governors Association (NLGA), September 23, 2021, http://www.nlga.us/ (accessed October 7, 2021); Skelley, "Stepping Up."
6. Greenblatt, "Why So Many Attorney Generals."
7. National Association of Attorneys General, October 5, 2021, http://www.naag.org/ (accessed October 7, 2021); Sabato, Center for Politics, April 22, 2010, http://www.centerforpolitics.org/crystalball/articles/ljs201000 42201 (accessed May 30, 2017); Smith and Greenblatt, *Governing States and Localities.*
8. Godmacher, Corasaniti, and Bogel-Burroughs, "Secretaries of State."
9. Smith and Greenblatt, *Governing States and Localities*; Jacobson, "Secretary of State Seats."
10. Schoutten, "Secretary of State Races."
11. Ibid., article IV, section 1.
12. *Pennsylvania Manual.*
13. Ibid., 391.
14. Pennsylvania Administrative Code of 1929.
15. PA constitution, article 4, section 4.
16. PA constitution, article 4, section 9.
17. PA constitution, article 4, section 13.
18. "Governor Mark Stephen Schweiker."
19. Mark Schweiker (former governor), interview with Holoviak, October 24, 2017.
20. Mark S. Singel (former lieutenant governor), interview with Holoviak, June 21, 2017, at his office, Harrisburg, PA.
21. Ibid.
22. Ibid.
23. Ibid.
24. *Pennsylvania Manual.*
25. Schweiker, interview.
26. Singel, interview.
27. Schweiker, interview.
28. Singel, interview; Singel, *Year of Change.*
29. Mayorquin, "Who Is John Fetterman?"
30. Friedman, "John Fetterman."
31. *Pennsylvania Manual.*
32. Shapiro, interview.
33. Ibid.
34. Ng, "How the Equifax Hack Happened."
35. Cowely and Silver, "Student Loan Collector Cheated."
36. "AG Shapiro Secures."
37. Joshua Shapiro (attorney general and gubernatorial candidate), interview with Holoviak, October 24, 2017, Harrisburg, PA.
38. Ibid.
39. Ibid.
40. Birkbeck, "Former Attorney General Fell"; Bumsted, *Keystone Corruption*; "Guide to Pa's Long History."
41. McCoy, "With Jail on Hold"; Bidgood, "Pennsylvania's Attorney General"; Thompson, "Whatever Happened"; McCoy, "Former AG Kane Released."
42. See https://www.paauditor.gov/about-the-department.
43. *Pennsylvania Manual.*
44. Ibid.
45. Bumsted, *Keystone Corruption*; Thompson, "Whatever Happened."
46. McCoy and Fazlollah, "Feds: Pa Treasurer Rob McCord"; Couloumbis, "Former Pennsylvania Treasurer Barbara Hafer"; Couloumbis, "Ex–Pa. Treasurer Rob McCord"; Thompson, "Whatever Happened."
47. Entin, "Ranking the States"; Lavelle, "Pennsylvania Gets F Grade."
48. See http://www.ifo.state.pa.us/about.cfm.
49. Renzi, "Independent View."
50. Pennsylvania Department of Administration, *Pennsylvania State Government Workforce Statistics.*

BIBLIOGRAPHY

The Administrative Code of 1929: Act of April 9, 1929, P.L. 177, and Amendments, Including Laws of 1963. Harrisburg: Legislative Reference Bureau, 1964.

"AG Shapiro Secures $600 Million from Equifax in Largest Data Breach Settlement in History." Pennsylvania Office of Attorney General. https://www.attorneygeneral.gov/taking -action/press-releases/ag-shapiro-secures -600-million-from-equifax-in-largest-data -breach-settlement-in-history/ (accessed September 17, 2021).

Bidgood, Jess. "Pennsylvania's Attorney General Is Convicted on All Counts." *New York Times*, August 15, 2016. https://www.nytimes.com /2016/08/16/us/trial-kathleen -kane-pennsylvania-attorney -general.html (accessed January 31, 2018).

Birkbeck, Matt. "Former Attorney General Fell from Grace in the Mid-1990's." *Pocono Record*, May 5, 2002. http://www.poconorecord.com /article/20020505/NEWS/305059999 (accessed January 18, 2018).

Bonner, Teresa. "A Guide to Pa.'s Long History of Government Corruption." PennLive, July 5, 2016. https://www.pennlive.com/midstate /index.ssf/2016/07/capitol_corruption _parade.html (accessed January 18, 2018).

Bumsted, Brad. *Keystone Corruption: A Pennsylvania Insider's View of a State Gone Wrong*. Philadel- phia: Camino Books, 2013.

Couloumbis, Angela. "Ex–Pa. Treasurer Rob McCord Gets 30 Months in Federal Prison." *Philadelphia Inquirer*, August 28, 2018. https://www.inquirer.com/philly/news /breaking/pennsylvania-treasurer-rob -mccord-prison-extortion-20180828 .html (accessed September 15, 2021).

———. "Former Pennsylvania Treasurer Bar- bara Hafer Sentenced for Lying to FBI." *Pittsburgh Post Gazette*, October 31, 2017. http://www.post-gazette.com/news/state /2017/10/31/Barbara-Hafer-sentencedlying -about-payments-FBI-former-treasurer /stories/201710310171 (accessed March 13, 2017).

Cowley, Stacy, and Jessica Silver-Greenberg. "Student Loan Collector Cheated Millions, Lawsuits Say." *New York Times*, January 19, 2017. https://www.nytimes.com/2017/01 /18/business/dealbook/student-loans-navient -lawsuit.html (accessed September 17, 2021).

Entin, Harry. "Ranking the States from Most to Least Corrupt." Fivethirtyeight.com, January 23, 2015. https://fivethirtyeight.com/features /ranking-the-states-most-to-least -corrupt/ (accessed March 13, 2018).

Friedman, Vanessa. "John Fetterman and the Remak- ing of Political Image." *New York Times*, May 26, 2022. https://www.nytimes.com/2022/05 /26/style/john-fetterman-hoodies-shorts .html (accessed June 8, 2022).

Goldmacher, Shane, Nick Corasaniti, and Nicholas Bogel-Burroughs. "Secretaries of State in Spotlight as Trump Ratchets Up Attacks to Sow Doubt." *New York Times*, November 5, 2020. https://www.nytimes .com/2020/11/05/us/politics/trump-vote -count.html? (accessed August 23, 2021).

"Governor Edward Martin." Pennsylvania Historical and Museum Commission, Pennsylvania Governors. http://www.phmc.state.pa.us /portal/communities/governors/1876-1951 /edward-martin.html (accessed June 14, 2017).

"Governor Mark Stephen Schweiker." Pennsylvania Historical and Museum Commission, Pennsylvania Governors. http://www.phmc .state.pa.us/portal/communities/governors /1951-2015/mark-schweiker.html (accessed June 14, 2017).

Greenblatt, Alan. "Lt. Governors on the Rise and out the Door." Governing, March 2016. http://www.governing.com/mag (accessed May 30, 2017).

———. "Why So Many Attorneys General Are Getting into Trouble." Governing, April 21, 2021. https://www.governing.com/now /why-so-many-attorneys-general-are-getting -into-trouble.html (accessed August 23, 2021).

Jacobson, Louis. "Secretary of State Seats Get Competitive." Governing, March 27, 2014. http://www.governing.com/topics/elections /gov-secretary-state-seats-get-competitive .html (accessed June 5, 2017).

Lavelle, Marianne. "Pennsylvania Gets F Grade in 2015 State Integrity Investigation." Public integrity.org, November 9, 2015. https:// www.publicintegrity.org/2015/11/09/18507 /pennsylvania-gets-f-grade-in-2015-state -integrity-investigation (accessed March 13, 2018).

Mayorquin, Orlando. "Who Is John Fetterman? The Democratic Nominee for Pennsylvania Senate." *USA Today*, May 19, 2022. https:// www.usatoday.com/story/news/politics /2022/05/13/pennsylvania-senate-race -2022-john-fetterman/9719427002 (accessed June 8, 2022).

McCoy, Craig. "Former AG Kane Released from Jail: 'Grateful' She Says." *Philadelphia*

Inquirer, July 31, 2019. https://www.inquirer
.com/news/kathleen-kane-released-jail
-attorney-general-pennsylvania-grand-jury
-leak-20190730.html (accessed July 31, 2019).
———. "With Jail on Hold, Former PA AG
Kathleen Kane Appeals Perjury Conviction."
Philadelphia Inquirer, January 17, 2018. http://
www.philly.com/philly/news/politics/state
/kathleen-kane-appealsperjury-prison
-pennsylvania-20180117.html (accessed January
31, 2018).
McCoy, Craig, and Mark Fazlollah. "Feds: Pa
Treasurer Rob McCord Secretly Taped Mil-
lionaire Pal Nearly 20 Times in Pay-to-Play
Scheme." *Philadelphia Inquirer*, January 9,
2017. http://www.philly.com/philly/news
/politics/Feds-Pa-treasurer-Rob-McCord
-secretly-taped-millionaire-pal-nearly
-20-times-in-pay-to-play-scheme
-.html (accessed March 13, 2018).
Ng, Alfred. "How the Equifax Hack Happened, and
What Still Needs to Be Done." CNET, September 7, 2018. https://www.cnet.com/news
/equifaxs-hack-one-year-later-a-look-back
-at-how-it-happened-and-whats-changed/
(accessed September 17, 2021).
"The Office." Pennsylvania Office of Attorney
General. https://www.attorneygeneral
.gov/the-office/ (accessed August 23, 2021).
Pennsylvania Department of Administration.
*Pennsylvania State Government Workforce
Statistics*. 2018. https://www.workforcereport
.oa.pa.gov (accessed September 29, 2021).

Pennsylvania Manual. Harrisburg: Commonwealth
of PA Books, 2017.
Renzi, Maureen. "An Independent View of
Pennsylvania Finances." *Pennsylvania CPA
Journal*, 2017, 12–15. https://www.cpajournal
.com/ (accessed October 7, 2021).
Schouten, Fredreka. "Secretary of State Races
Emerge as America's Newest Politi-
cal Flashpoint." CNN, August 11, 2021.
https://www.cnn.com/2021/08/11
/politics/secretary-of-state-races/index
.html (accessed August 23, 2021).
Singel, Mark S., Crystal Devine, Lawrence Knorr,
and Jennifer Cappello. *A Year of Change and
Consequences*. Mechanicsburg, PA: Sunbury
Press, 2016.
Skelley, Geoffrey. "Stepping Up: How Governors
Who Have Succeeded to the Top Job Have
Performed over the Years." Center for Politics,
May 18, 2017. http://www.centerforpolitics
.org/crystalball/articles/stepping-up-how
-governors-who-have-succeeded-to-the-top
-job-have-performed-over-the-years/
(accessed May 30, 2017).
Smith, Kevin, and Alan Greenblatt. *Governing States
and Localities: The Essentials*. Washington, DC:
CQ Press, 2014.
Thomson, Charles. "Whatever Happened to
Former State Treasurer Rob McCord? Here's
an Update." http://www.pennlive.com
/politics/index.ssf/2016/04/whatever
_happened_to_rob_mccor.htm (accessed
March 13, 2018).

CHAPTER 7

The Judicial Branch

Judges, the Law, and Pennsylvania's Court System

The Quaker State's court system is historic, intricate, and, too often for the average citizen, opaque and intimidating. Though its general organization is fairly standard, with trial and appellate courts and a single high court, its appellate level is distinctive in that Pennsylvania is one of only ten states with two *separate* appellate benches. Pennsylvania ranked fifth in 2018 in total number of judges and justices, behind Texas, New York, California, and Georgia, and eighth in 2013 in total trial court caseload. The caseload rankings appear consistent with the state's total population, which was fifth in the nation in 2020. In the following pages, Pennsylvania's court system is explained, with special attention given to each court's internal operation.[1]

HISTORY

Prior to independence, Pennsylvania's colonial court system was fragmented, part-time, and controlled by William Penn, the commonwealth's governors, or the Crown's representatives, none of whom were trained in the law. Efforts to bring coherence to the system in the seventeenth and early eighteenth centuries failed until the colonial assembly passed the Judiciary Act of 1722. The act created a three-person Supreme Court that met twice yearly in Philadelphia and "rode circuit"—judges literally rode from town to town—hearing appeals from lower courts, namely the Courts of Common Pleas in Philadelphia and Bucks and Chester Counties and county Courts of Quarter Sessions, which were also formed under the act. These courts remained in place until the 1776 constitution, which located Courts of Sessions and orphans' courts in every county. All judges were appointed to seven-year terms by a twelve-member, elected Executive Council, with each of the twelve counties represented by one member. Provision was also made for the election of justices of the peace "in every ward, township and district in the Commonwealth."[2]

The 1790 constitution brought more changes. The Courts of Oyer and Terminer and General Gaol Delivery (for criminal cases) and Register's courts and Courts of Quarter

Sessions of the Peace (for minor criminal and civil cases) were added in each county. All judges were appointed by the governor to life terms.

The 1838 constitution added Senate confirmation by simple majority vote to check the governor's appointment authority and limited Supreme Court justices' terms to fifteen years and common pleas judges to five years, though presiding judges could serve for ten years. Partisan judicial elections were adopted by an 1850 amendment, with any vacancies filled by gubernatorial appointment until the next election. The 1873 constitution incorporated partisan judicial election and also made the following changes: Supreme Court justices' terms were extended to twenty-one years without possibility of reelection, all other judges' terms were lengthened to ten years, and a two-thirds Senate vote to confirm interim judicial appointments replaced a simple Senate majority.[3]

In 1895, the legislature established a new appellate-level court, the Superior Court, to ease the Supreme Court's workload. Pennsylvania's Progressive Republicans, who controlled the legislature in 1913, passed a law requiring nonpartisan elections for Supreme Court justices and Superior Court judges. Candidates were forbidden to align with a political party, use partisan images in their campaign materials, or appear on the ballot with a party affiliation; however, Stalwart Republicans repealed the law eight years later.[4]

The adoption of the 1968 constitution brought extensive changes to the court system. It eliminated some courts and reorganized those remaining under the Unified Judicial

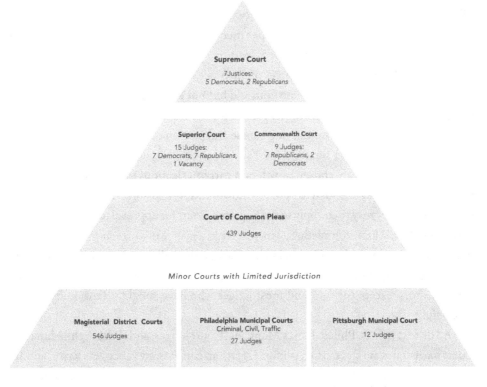

Supreme Court
7 Justices:
5 Democrats, 2 Republicans

Superior Court
15 Judges:
7 Democrats, 7 Republicans,
1 Vacancy

Commonwealth Court
9 Judges:
7 Republicans, 2
Democrats

Court of Common Pleas
439 Judges

Minor Courts with Limited Jurisdiction

Magisterial District Courts
546 Judges

Philadelphia Municipal Courts
Criminal, Civil, Traffic
27 Judges

Pittsburgh Municipal Court
12 Judges

FIG. 7.1 Pennsylvania court system. Source: compiled by the authors with data as of February 1, 2022.

System: minor courts (magisterial district courts, the Philadelphia Municipal Court, and a Pittsburgh Municipal Court created by the Supreme Court in 2004), Courts of Common Pleas, two appellate courts—the Superior Court and a new Commonwealth Court—and the Supreme Court.

To manage the new system, the Administrative Office of Pennsylvania Courts was established, with the court administrator of Pennsylvania serving as its director. With the new Unified Judicial System, there was an implicit understanding that the state's entire court system would be funded by the state government rather than as it had been, with the General Assembly funding the appellate courts and the district and magistrate courts funded by the county governments in which they were located. As we discuss later, the General Assembly has yet to fulfill this obligation.[5]

Partisan judicial elections continued, but retention elections were added for justices and judges wishing to remain on the bench after serving a ten-year term. Merit selection of judges was offered to the voters as an option during the 1969 primary election, but it was rejected, with voters retaining partisan elections.

JUSTICES, JUDGES, AND MAGISTRATES: QUALIFICATIONS, TENURE, AND ELECTIONS

All Pennsylvania justices and judges must be state residents for a minimum of one year, be less than seventy years old, hold state bar membership, and, for common pleas court judges, have been a district resident for at least one year. District judges, formally known as magisterial district justices or justices of the peace, are classified differently: they must be a state citizen, at least twenty-one years old but not older than seventy-five at time of election, and a district resident for one year, and either be a member of the Pennsylvania Bar or successfully complete a training course and pass an examination prepared by the Minor Judiciary Education Board.[6]

Justices and judges are chosen by voters in partisan elections to ten-year terms in odd-numbered years. They are not term-limited; however, at seventy-five they must retire from the bench, but they may then apply to the Supreme Court for approval to continue serving as senior judges.[7] Upon completing a ten-year term, a justice or judge may stand for retention election, in which the judge's name appears on the ballot without a party label and citizens vote simply yes or no to allow the judge to remain on the bench. All Supreme Court justices, except for one, and most judges who have sought retention have been successful.[8]

All district judges, Philadelphia's Municipal Court judges, and Pittsburgh's Municipal Court magistrates are elected in traditional, partisan contests, serve six-year terms, and are not term-limited; however, Philadelphia's municipal judges who wish to remain in office must run in retention elections as discussed above.

When a vacancy occurs on any bench, the governor may nominate an individual with appropriate qualifications, who then must be confirmed by a two-thirds vote of the Senate before completing the remainder of the term. There is no requirement that a governor solicit nominees or recommendations, though the Pennsylvania Bar independently evaluates and recommends justices and judges. Some governors, beginning with Scranton in 1964 and most recently Wolf, have empaneled nominating or advisory commissions to assess and rank judicial candidates. In periods of divided government, it is common for governors to negotiate with Senate leaders to win approval of nominees favored by both sides, which can appear to politicize the confirmation process.[9]

Judicial salaries are comparable to those in other northeastern states, with the highest earned by Supreme Court justices at $215,000 to Common Pleas judges at $186,700 to magisterial district judges at $91,597 in 2020. The chief justice and president judges receive slightly higher salaries.[10]

All justices and judges must conform to the Code of Judicial Conduct in the *Pennsylvania Rules of Court*, while magistrates follow the Rules of Conduct, Office Standards, and Civil Procedure for magisterial district judges. Justices, judges, and magistrates who violate the standards may be removed, suspended, or otherwise disciplined for misconduct in office.[11]

Currently, all appellate court justices and judges are elected statewide, but a constitutional amendment was introduced in 2021 to elect these judges from districts. Republicans advancing this proposal argue that candidates from two regions—the Philadelphia and Pittsburgh metropolitan areas—win the majority of seats on all three appellate courts. They contend that electing by region, with differently sized districts for each court reflecting the size of a court's bench—seven, nine, and fifteen—will provide all citizens an opportunity to feel represented on the appellate courts. Opponents respond that district elections are susceptible to gerrymandering and that appellate courts' jurisdictions are statewide and not limited to a county or region. They also argue that the amendment is a blatant political maneuver to restore Republican majorities on the Supreme Court. The amendment may appear on a ballot in 2023.[12]

Common pleas judges, district judges, and other minor court judges are elected from districts: 60 Courts of Common Pleas districts, 53 of which are a single county, while 7 districts join two counties, and 514 magisterial districts. Under article V, section 11, the General Assembly, with the Supreme Court's approval, has authority to alter the number and boundaries of Common Pleas districts, while magisterial districts are redrawn by the Common Pleas Court in which a district is located based on population and under the Supreme Court's supervision.

Because all judicial elections are partisan, all judicial candidates must first win a primary election before moving onto the general election. Judicial candidates circulate petitions to appear on the Democratic and Republican Parties' ballots. Each party has requirements for the number of voters' signatures and the number of counties that must

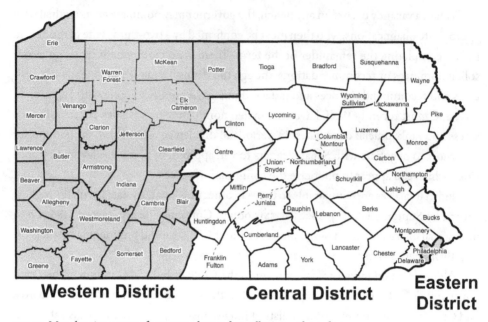

MAP 7.1 Map showing courts of common pleas and appellate court boundaries, 2020.

be represented among the total number of signatures. Candidates may cross-file in order to appear on both parties' ballots, but they must successfully meet each party's petition requirements. Though not as common in appellate court elections, cross-filing often occurs in common pleas and magistrate elections. Should a cross-filing candidate win both parties' primary elections, then the general election's outcome is a foregone conclusion.

Pennsylvania's judicial elections are frequently low-turnout affairs, barring some event that captures voters' attention, like a scandal. Citizens who do participate often have little knowledge of candidates beyond the candidates' names and party affiliations, even for incumbents standing for retention. In low-information elections, ballot position significantly affects a candidate's chance of winning, and in the Keystone State ballot position is literally the luck of the draw, as candidates' names are pulled from coffee cans, cigar boxes,

Table 7.1 Paired Common Pleas Court districts

Court district	Paired counties
17th	Snyder and Union
26th	Columbia and Montour
37th	Forrest and Warren
39th	Franklin and Fulton
41st	Juniata and Perry
44th	Sullivan and Wyoming
59th	Cameron and Elk

or hats in state and county election offices. Research strongly suggests that appearing at or near the top of a ballot's list or among the names in the first column of candidates when there are two or more columns is more important than a party, newspaper, or celebrity endorsement.[13]

Candidates may express their personal opinions broadly on issues, such as crime or taxes, during judicial campaigns; however, they may not "make any statement that would reasonably be expected to affect the outcome or impair the fairness of a matter pending or impending in any court." Typically, judicial candidates avoid taking controversial positions, preferring instead to speak about their qualifications, experience, and commitment to equality, justice, and the legal system.[14]

Judicial campaigns can be expensive, especially for the appellate courts. They require that candidates raise money like gubernatorial and legislative candidates. Pennsylvania's weak campaign finance rules also apply to judicial candidates, with one important exception: candidates are forbidden from personally soliciting contributions. Instead, their authorized campaign committees seek donations on a candidate's behalf or form a PAC that raises and spends money for a candidate. Additionally, individuals and groups may raise and spend money independently of a candidate's campaign. Many judicial candidates loan their campaigns money, which is legal, expecting that, upon winning, the debt will be repaid from the contributions that will roll in after the victory. And in a tradition unique to the Philadelphia Democratic Party, judicial candidates can pay the party $35,000 for the opportunity to be endorsed by the party, and they may also choose to hire "political consultants" to convince the city's sixty-nine ward leaders to support their candidacies, for which the ward leaders direct their committee people to distribute sample ballots at each voting precinct in their wards.[15]

Similar to other Pennsylvania elections, there is no limit on how much an individual or group may donate to a judicial campaign, and most candidates take advantage of donors' generosity. Hundreds of thousands of dollars have been raised for a single candidate, and millions have been spent on television ads alone in past elections. There is no requirement that candidates disclose their donations' sources beyond what the candidates include in their campaign finance reports, which lack detail. Most contributors to judicial elections are individual lawyers, law firms, or organizations and businesses with questions to be decided by the courts, and their contributions are legal, even if the lawyers appear before the judges to whom they have contributed. Such contributions raise legitimate questions about conflict of interest and judicial impartiality. Duquesne University law professor Bruce Ledewitz, however, has said that "he doesn't believe campaign dollars corrupt judges or taint their ability to make impartial decisions. But . . . it fuels what has been a long-standing debate in the state about whether judges should be elected or appointed."[16]

Men have held the vast majority of judgeships since the courts' first days, with even fewer people of color serving on its benches. The first woman elected to a judgeship was

Sarah M. Soffel in 1930, while the first African American, Herbert E. Millen, was elected in 1947. In 1959, Judge Juanita Kidd Stout was the first Black woman in the nation elected as a judge, to the Court of Common Pleas, and in 1988 she became the first to be appointed to the state's Supreme Court. In 1973, Genevieve Blatt became the first woman appointed to serve on the Commonwealth Court, while Phyllis Beck joined the Superior Court as its first woman in 1981, and Doris Smith-Ribner was the first *elected* to the Commonwealth Court in 1987. In recent years, the number of women and people of color who have attained judgeships has increased. An infographic released by the Pennsylvania Courts in 2022 revealed that 37 percent of all Pennsylvania's judges were women, with women comprising 36 percent of the Courts of Common Pleas, 27 percent of magisterial district judges, and 22 percent of Philadelphia Municipal Court judges.[17]

COURT STRUCTURE AND OPERATION

As discussed above, the Unified Judicial System established in the 1968 constitution created a four-tiered structure. Each level is defined by its jurisdiction, which is the authority assigned to a court, either by constitution or legislation, to hear cases and rule on legal matters. Two broad jurisdictional authorities are original and appellate. A court with original jurisdiction has the first right to hear a case, which is generally assigned to trial courts where evidence is presented, and a judge or jury renders a verdict. Appellate jurisdiction confers the right to review decisions made by lower courts. In appellate courts, cases are not retried; rather, judges are asked to resolve questions of law or procedure concerning a trial judge's decisions on, for example, the admission of evidence or jury instructions.

Within original and appellate jurisdiction, a court's jurisdiction is further defined by its geographic area, the particular types of cases it handles (such as those involving criminal or civil law), a case's parties (private individuals, a government entity), a case's substantive issue (contracts, estates, divorce), or the amount of money involved in a dispute. Referring to figure 7.1, we begin at the pyramid's base with the minor courts and move to the Supreme Court, describing each court's composition, jurisdiction, and operation.

Minor Courts: Magisterial Districts and the Philadelphia and Pittsburgh Municipal Courts

Magisterial district judges, once known as justices of the peace, are the presiding judges over all magisterial districts, except for those in the Philadelphia Municipal Court. There are 514 district judges, 13 of whom are in Pittsburgh's Municipal Court. As noted earlier, district judges need not be lawyers, but they must complete a special course and be certified. Philadelphia's 27 Municipal Court judges *must* be lawyers, for reasons discussed below.

Magisterial district courts have original jurisdiction to conduct nonjury trials of criminal summary offenses not involving delinquents and in civil disputes where the action's or material's value is less than $12,000. District judges may also preside over preliminary arraignments and hearings, set bail (except in murder or voluntary manslaughter cases), issue warrants, accept guilty pleas to DUI charges (if a first offense and no third party was injured), and accept guilty pleas for third-degree misdemeanors in special circumstances, among other matters. If either party is dissatisfied with a magistrate's verdict, the case is brought to a Common Pleas Court, where it is heard *de novo*, anew.

Philadelphia's Municipal Court is the state's only minor court that is a court of record—that is, one whose proceedings are recorded and maintained permanently and whose decisions can be formally appealed to a higher court—which is why its judges must be lawyers. When the city's courts were reorganized after the 1968 constitution, the Municipal Court was assigned original jurisdiction over all criminal offenses that carry a punishment of less than five years as well as all jurisdictions typical of any other state magisterial court. A separate Traffic Court system was also constructed alongside the Municipal Courts to handle parking and vehicular moving violations, but following several investigations that yielded indictments and convictions of magistrates for accepting bribes, the General Assembly in 2013 transferred Traffic Court's jurisdiction to the Municipal Court. Because Traffic Court was in the state constitution, however, voters needed to pass an amendment to officially remove it, which occurred in April 2016. Traffic Court is now a division of the Philadelphia Municipal Court, and magistrates hear its cases.[18]

In 2004, the Supreme Court formed Pittsburgh's Municipal Court to replace the city's Magistrate Courts. With criminal, traffic, and nontraffic divisions, the city's thirteen magistrates have original jurisdiction in the city to hear cases involving, among other things, nontraffic summary offenses, traffic offenses (other than parking), violations of Pittsburgh's ordinances, and preliminary hearings on misdemeanor and felony criminal cases, including all homicide cases in Allegheny County.[19]

Courts of Common Pleas

There are sixty Courts of Common Pleas across Pennsylvania, fifty-three of which are in a single county, including Philadelphia and Allegheny Counties, while seven combine two counties. Each court has at least one judge, ninety-three of whom are in Philadelphia, while twenty-three courts have just one or two judges. Where a district has more than one judge but fewer than eight, the jurist with the greatest seniority on the court becomes its president judge; if eight or more judges compose a court, the president judge is elected by the court's jurists to a single five-year term. A president judge may serve more than one term, but not consecutively.

Common pleas courts, often called trial courts, have original jurisdiction in all criminal and civil matters but hear appeals from the minor courts within their districts. They also have appellate jurisdiction in cases emerging from some state and most local government agencies. For example, should a planning authority deny a developer's request to construct houses in a community, the developer may appeal to the Court of Common Pleas to reverse the decision.

Candidates for common pleas judgeships frequently served first as a county district attorney or public defender or have been a prominent, successful local attorney. As suggested above, because judicial elections are low-information affairs, citizens typically cast their ballots for the candidate whose name they recognize. Well-known candidates are also better able to raise money from members of the local bar.

Electing women and minorities to the Common Pleas bench has been as challenging as wining seats in the General Assembly. As of 2022, approximately one in three trial court judges is a woman and fifteen of the president judges are women, but these figures are an improvement over 2018. Statistics for minority representation on the trial courts are difficult to acquire, but anecdotal evidence suggests that the total number of Black trial court judges has increased since 1970, most presiding in Philadelphia or Pittsburgh.[20]

Trial judges usually invoke precedent or the rules of trial procedure when deciding on attorneys' motions during a trial and instructing juries before their deliberations begin. Trial judges may follow state sentencing guidelines, as they are only advisory, when issuing sentences in criminal cases; however, should they depart from the guidelines, they must present their reasons on the record.

Appellate Courts: The Superior Court

Created by the General Assembly in 1895 to reduce the Supreme Court's caseload, the Superior Court originally had seven judges, but in 1979 voters approved a constitutional amendment increasing the bench to fifteen. The court's president judge is elected in the same manner as Common Pleas courts' presidents, with the same restrictions on term length.

By 2023, women held nine judgeships; however, the first woman, Phyllis W. Beck, was not seated on the court until 1981. Minority representation on the Superior Court has historically been low, with only one Black jurist currently a member and fewer than five in total since 2003 (table 7.3).

Referring to tables 7.2 and 7.3, though partisan balance on the court was relatively close during most terms between 2000 and 2020, Republicans held majorities sixteen times;

Table 7.2 Superior Court judges*

Judge and party affiliation	Sex	County
Bowes, Mary Jane (R)	F	Allegheny
Dubow, Alice Beck (D)	F	Philadelphia
Kunselman, Deborah A. (D)	F	Beaver
Lazarus, Anne E. (D)	F	Philadelphia
McCaffery, Daniel D. (D)	M	Philadelphia
McCarthy King, Megan (R)	F	Chester
McLaughlin, Maria (D)	F	Philadelphia
Murray, Mary (R)	F	Allegheny
Nichols, Carolyn H. (D)	F	Philadelphia
Olson, Judith Ference (R)	F	Allegheny
Panella, Jack A. (D) (President)	M	Northampton
Stabile, Victor P. (R)	M	Cumberland
Sullivan, Megan (R)	F	Chester

*Information as of April 2023; the court has two vacancies.

however, from the latter half of 2020 through 2022, vacancies created an evenly balanced court—seven Democrats and seven Republicans. In 2023, Democrats held a one-seat majority. As we discuss later, however, a judge's party affiliation is not usually a factor when Superior Court judges decide cases. Also interesting is that in 2020, eleven judges were elected from either Philadelphia or Allegheny County, suggesting that Pennsylvania's two largest cities exercise disproportionate weight in these elections.[21]

The court's appellate jurisdiction is extensive, hearing cases from district courts across the commonwealth in both criminal and civil law—for example, murders, contract disputes, contested wills, and medical malpractice. The court must accept *all* appeals filed with it, civil and criminal. The court does have original jurisdiction over issuing wiretaps and other electronic surveillance requested by the state attorney general and county district attorneys under the Wiretapping and Electronic Surveillance Control Act. Motions for wiretaps are processed in Harrisburg, Philadelphia, and Pittsburgh by the court's staff, which screens and reviews the requests. Individual Superior Court judges rotate through hearing these requests and rendering decisions.[22]

In recent years, the Superior Court has received over eight thousand appeals per year. Its fifteen judges have the highest caseload per judge of any appellate court in the nation. The court's prothonotary, or chief clerk, randomly assigns cases to three-judge panels in batches of forty-five cases from offices in Harrisburg, Philadelphia, and Pittsburgh. The prothonotary also randomly appoints judges to these panels for one year. Approximately 80 percent of the appeals are resolved as "submit cases"—that is, the opposing parties

Table 7.3 Party and sex of the Appellate Court judges and justices

	Supreme Court				Commonwealth Court					Superior Court				
	Party		Sex		Party			Sex		Party			Sex	
Year	D	R	M	F	D	R	NP	M	F	D	R	NP	M	F
2000	4	3	6	1	7	1	1	6	3	8	6	1	10	5
2001	4	3	6	1	7	1	1	6	3	8	7		10	5
2002	3	4	6	1	4	4	1	4	5	8	7		10	5
2003	2	5	6	1	4	4	1	4	5	7	8		10	5
2004	3	4	6	1	4	4	1	4	5	7	8		9	6
2005	3	4	6	1	5	3	1	4	5	7	8		9	6
2006	3	4	5	2	5	3	1	4	5	7	8		10	5
2007	3	4	6	1	5	3	1	4	5	7	8		10	5
2008	4	3	5	2	5	3	1	4	5	7	8		9	6
2009	4	3	5	2	4	4	1	4	5	6	9		7	8
2010	2	5	5	2	4	4	1	4	5	6	9		6	9
2011	2	5	5	2	2	6	1	4	5	6	9		5	10
2012	3	4	5	2	2	6	1	4	5	6	9		5	10
2013	3	4	6	1	1	6	2	3	6	5	9		4	10
2014	3	4	6	1	1	6	2	3	6	4	11		4	11
2015	1	4	4	1	1	6	2	3	6	5	10		5	10
2016	5	2	5	2	2	7		4	5	6	9		5	10
2017	5	2	4	3	2	7		4	5	6	7	1	5	9
2018	5	2	4	3	2	7		3	6	7	8		3	12
2019	5	2	4	3	2	7		3	6	8	6	1	6	9
2020	5	2	4	3	2	7		3	6	7	7		4	10
2021	5	2	4	3	2	7		3	6	7	7		1	10
2022	5	2	4	3	3	5		1	7	7	7		4	10
2023	4	4	3	3	2	6		1	7	7	6		3	10

This table's information assumes the constitutional complement for each court: seven Supreme Court justices, fifteen Superior Court judges, and nine Commonwealth Court judges. It does not include senior judges. Where the total number of judges for a court does not equal the constitutional number, a vacant seat occurred. Information as of April 2023. Source: compiled by the authors from *Pennsylvania Manuals*, Ballotpedia, and each court's webpage.

submit only briefs—while the remaining cases are "argument cases" that are decided following oral arguments for which briefs are also submitted.[23]

For hearing oral arguments, the panels sit for two days in one of three cities to consider their forty-five cases, allotting ten minutes per case—five minutes per side. In advance of arguments, judges read the briefs and other case materials and then meet with their chief clerk to discuss the cases, after which judges have their chief clerk write a bench memo summarizing the case and the judges' initial position. Few questions are posed by the judges during oral arguments, a function of the short time allotted and the judges' advance preparation. Panels are expected to render their decisions in ninety days, though delays are possible if a lawyer fails to submit all supporting documentation; however, in cases involving Children's Fast Track—custody, adoption, and so on—decisions are issued within sixty days.[24]

On a panel, the most senior judge or the president judge randomly assigns the task to write a first draft of an opinion, whether a case was considered by brief or oral argument. Typically, the president or most senior judge takes the first fifteen cases on the list, the next most senior judge receives fifteen cases, and the least senior judge accepts the last fifteen. A draft opinion circulates among all three judges until at least two judges agree with the opinion. Should the original draft opinion fail to gain a majority, a dissenting judge drafts an alternative opinion, which also circulates until at least two judges accept it. A judge signing on to the majority opinion may also write a concurring opinion, while a dissenting judge may write a separate opinion, but neither is not obliged to do so.[25]

The losing party in an appeal can request a reconsideration of the case by the full Superior Court, called an en banc session; however, for reconsideration to be granted, the party must present new evidence or demonstrate that a mistake was made by the hearing panel. En banc sessions are frequently held in Harrisburg, Philadelphia, and Pittsburgh, but, at the discretion of the president judge, a session may convene in another location. President Judge Correale Stevens explained that he enjoyed holding en banc sessions outside the major cities in order to educate the public about the court. En banc sessions are often broadcast on the Pennsylvania Cable Network (PCN).[26]

In our interviews with Superior and Commonwealth judges, we frequently heard that when deciding cases, they depend heavily on precedent cases as well as the relevant constitutional and/or statutory language, because these courts' responsibility is to correct errors and effectuate the law, not to make policy, which falls to the Supreme Court. Judge Panella stressed that the judges' life experiences and political opinions are set aside when considering the cases.[27] Judge Stevens added the importance of deference to Pennsylvania's constitution and existing laws to prevent the court from appearing "active or political."[28]

Appellate Courts: The Commonwealth Court

Legal contests involving the state government were handled by the Dauphin County Common Pleas Court from 1870 to 1970, but the 1968 constitution included language that created a new appellate court to handle these matters. In 1970, on the heels of the constitution's ratification, the General Assembly passed the Commonwealth Court Act, establishing the court with seven judges. The Act was amended in 1980 to add two judges. Its president judge is elected by the full bench to a five-year term, with the possibility for reelection but not consecutively. The Commonwealth Court has been likened to the US Court of Appeals for the DC Circuit.[29]

Women have fared better in gaining seats on Commonwealth Court than in Pennsylvania's other appellate courts. Since 2002, women have held a majority on the court, which elected its first female president judge in 2007. In 2023, seven of its nine judges were women, including the president (see tables 7.3 and 7.4). Judicial candidates of color, on the other hand, have had much less success winning election to this court. As with the Superior Court, statistical data are difficult to locate, but there have been fewer than six minority judges on the court in its relatively short history. Republicans have held a majority of the judgeships in every term from 2011 to 2023. From 2002 to 2010, however, parties' seat differential was relatively narrow. With only three Democratic judges on the court in 2023, the court appears to have a decidedly conservative orientation; however, a judge's political party carries less weight when deciding cases. Finally, the geographic balance on the Commonwealth Court, unlike that on the Supreme Court, does not favor the major cities.

The Commonwealth Court's jurisdiction is both original and appellate, though most of its caseload flows up from lower courts on appeal. As a trial court, it hears civil cases brought by or against the state government or a state official, except regarding cases where monetary damages are involved, challenges to state government policies, and all electoral disputes for local, state, or national offices. Its appellate jurisdiction extends to all cases beginning in the district courts in which the state or a county, city, or local government is a party as well appeals of decisions from agencies such as the Public Utilities Commission and Workers' Compensation Appeal Board.

Cases arriving under Commonwealth Court's original jurisdiction are handled in one of three ways, according to Judge Michael H. Wojcik. All cases are randomly assigned to a judge or panel by the court's prothonotary, except for en banc trials. The prothonotary also randomly places judges on panels. In the first and most frequently employed method, cases are heard by one judge as a bench trial or occasionally with a jury sitting in Harrisburg. Each judge serves for one week in the capital hearing original jurisdiction cases.

Table 7.4 Commonwealth Court judges*

Judge and party affiliation	Sex	County
Cannon, Christine Fizzano (R)	F	Delaware
Ceisler, Ellen (D)	F	Philadelphia
Covey, Anne E. (R)	F	Bucks
Dumas, Lori (D)	F	Philadelphia
Jubelirer, Renee Cohn (president) (R)	F	Centre
McCullough, Patricia (R)	F	Allegheny
Wallace, Stacy Marie (R)	F	McKean
Wojcik, Michael H. (D)	M	Allegheny

*Information as of April 2023 with one court vacancy.

While most cases are resolved in a week or less, should a trial go longer, the trial judge reschedules the remaining time to a date that fits the judge's calendar. The president judge may, however, reassign a lengthy case to a different judge. Second, when multiple briefs are filed, a three-judge panel hears the case. And when the court considers a case significant, it meets en banc to hear it, such as the 2016 ballot-access challenge to US Senate candidate Joseph Vodvarka.[30]

Every judge has a vote on every case heard under the court's original and appellate jurisdictions, whether the case is heard by one judge or a panel of three judges. An individual judge's decision or a panel's majority decision is filed with the court's clerk, who then circulates it among the other judges. Each judge reads, comments on, and votes in favor of or opposition to the opinion. If a majority agrees with the original decision and its reasoning, then the opinion is filed as submitted and announced as the Commonwealth Court's decision. When judges disagree, discussion occurs as the opinion circulates. The president judge may call an en banc session to decide the matter. The Court follows these procedures to ensure that it makes the right decision in each case, decisions that are consistent with precedent. "We all want to get it right, because the issues heard by the court often apply to more than just the litigants in the case; the decisions will ultimately affect everyone in the state somehow."[31]

Like its sister appellate court, the Commonwealth Court must accept all cases received on appeal, though not all receive oral argument. The vast majority of cases are filed as briefs, and parties may request oral argument. The prothonotary reviews and evaluates the cases and, in consultation with the president judge, selects those worthy of oral argument based on a case's broader legal implications for the commonwealth. Regardless of how a case is handled, the prothonotary randomly assigns the cases (roughly eighteen at a time), the judges, and the opinion-writing responsibilities to three-judge panels, balancing each judge's workload. For cases not involving oral arguments, the case's lead judge reviews all the case materials, writes the opinion, and circulates it to the other two judges. Comments and discussions occur until a majority agrees on a decision and opinion. A dissenting judge may write an opinion.[32]

For oral arguments, each case is allotted fifteen minutes evenly divided between the two sides to present their arguments. Judge Wojcik commented that, unlike the US Supreme Court, Commonwealth Court judges aren't strict about enforcing time limits and do not cut off attorneys in midsentence.[33] Judge Leavitt described oral arguments as a "conversation between lawyers and judges. You try to get right to the question because of time limits. . . . A judge has an obligation to tell the lawyers what the crux of the case is, what issues are of most concern for the court and the judges." Once a panel concludes hearing oral arguments, the opinion-writing process begins.[34]

Once a panel has its majority opinion, it is circulated among all court judges along with the dissenting opinion. If five or more judges agree with the decision and opinion, it is filed and announced as the court's decision; however, if a majority support the dissenting opinion, the case is then referred to a judicial conference in which all the court's judges meet to hear the authors of the majority opinion and minority opinions present their arguments, and at the conclusion the entire court votes to decide the case.

When deciding cases, appellate judges may bring their legal experience and political and judicial philosophies into the process, but we learned from our interviews that partisanship rarely is a factor. Judge Leavitt described her judicial philosophy as deferring to the laws made by the General Assembly, because laws reflect the will of the people; she stated she "will not make law from the bench" and was dismissive of employing legislative intent to aid in interpreting a law, arguing that legislative intent can be ambiguous; one cannot know the lawmakers' true intentions. The Commonwealth Court, she said, engages in "statutory construction," which is less intensively fact-based and more focused on the letter of the law and what the long-term consequences of the court's decision will have on those affected.[35]

Another judge described the Commonwealth Court as "an umpire: it calls the balls and strikes, and applies the right law in the right way, following precedent." The court rarely overturns its own precedents, because overruling prior decisions is not taken lightly. On the other hand, the court never overturns Pennsylvania Supreme Court decisions, because it would be difficult to defend; instead, if the Commonwealth Court thinks a prior Supreme Court decision is wrong, it can "hint at this diplomatically in the Court's decision."[36]

Appellate Courts: The Supreme Court

Pennsylvania's high court was established in 1684, making it the nation's oldest appellate court. In 1722, the Provincial Assembly passed the Judiciary Act and officially established a Supreme Court. Pennsylvania is one of eight states to elect its Supreme Court justices; the seven justices are chosen in statewide partisan elections to ten-year terms. Justices wishing to remain on the bench must run in a nonpartisan retention election. The justice with the most years of continuous service on the court becomes its chief justice for a five-year term, and the justice may become the chief again, but only after sitting out a full term.

Compared to Pennsylvania's other appellate courts, where women are well represented, their numbers on the Supreme Court are low, though they have been increasing slowly (see table 7.3). Minority representation, however, has lagged significantly. In the court's history, only one Black justice has been elected, Robert N. C. Nix, who served from 1972 to 1996 with the last five years as chief justice, while two have been appointed: Juanita Kidd Stout in 1988, serving to 1989, and Cynthia Baldwin in 2006, serving to 2007. All were Democrats from Philadelphia.

The court's geographic distribution appeared uneven in 2022, as six of the seven justices are from either the southeastern or southwestern corners.

The court's partisan composition shifted notably following the 2015 election, when three Democratic candidates were victorious, giving their party a majority for the first time

Table 7.5 Supreme Court justices*

Justice	Sex	County
Brobson, Kevin P. (R)	M	Dauphin
Donohue, Christine (D)	F	Allegheny
Dougherty, Kevin (D)	M	Philadelphia
Mundy, Sallie (R)	F	Tioga
Todd, Debra (D) chief justice	F	Allegheny
Wecht, David (D)	M	Allegheny

*Information as of April 2023. Court has one vacancy.

since 2001 (see table 7.3) Though a justice's party affiliation is not often a factor when deciding cases, it can be influential for some issues, particularly those that are politically charged or socially controversial, something we consider later in this chapter.[37]

The high court has both original and appellate jurisdictions. Its original jurisdiction covers requests for writs of *habeas corpus, mandamus,* and *quo warranto*; however, a party seeking any of these writs may also request them from lower courts.[38]

Under its appellate jurisdiction, the court has discretion in selecting most of the cases it hears using allocatur, a process similar to the US Supreme Court's writ of certiorari. From the thousands of appeals made each year since 2010, the court actually hears and decides fewer than three hundred cases.[39] Many of its cases are heard on appeal from the Superior and Commonwealth Courts, but the court also accepts direct appeals from the Courts of Common Pleas when the subject matter involves any of the following: the right to hold public office; the qualifications, tenure, and right and/or manner of service of members of the judiciary; a state attorney general or a court issuing a supersession (a stay of proceedings) against a district attorney; questions of incurring public debt by the state or any other level of government; a district court declaring a state statute or regulation unconstitutional; challenges to the right to practice law; and death penalty decisions, which are automatically appealed.[40]

The Supreme Court also hears appeals from several state boards and commissions—namely, Legislative Reapportionment Commissions (see chapter 4), the Minor Judiciary Education Board, the Pennsylvania Board of Law Examiners, the Disciplinary Board of the Supreme Court of Pennsylvania, the Pennsylvania Gaming Control Board, and the Court of Judicial Discipline.[41]

Finally, using its extraordinary jurisdictional authority, the court may take a case pending before a lower court, if the issue is deemed by the court to be of immediate and significant public import. The court can initiate this mechanism on its own or at the petition of one of the parties in the case.

When the court receives petitions for allocatur, they are handled by the Administrative Office of the Pennsylvania Courts (AOPC). Using a wheel, the AOPC's administrator randomly assigns the petitions to the justices, with each receiving up to four hundred a term. Working with their clerks, the justices review the material and write short, personal opinions, for internal use only, arguing to accept or reject each petition. The opinions are circulated, and if three justices agree to accept a petition, the AOPC schedules the case for oral argument before the full court. But, as indicated above, very few allocatur requests are granted; those not accepted do not receive an explanation.[42]

The court meets in Harrisburg, Philadelphia, and Pittsburgh for six-week oral argument sessions, hearing on average twelve cases per week. Both parties arguing before the court must submit briefs well in advance of their hearing date; the justices may also agree to accept *amicus curia*, or friend of the court, briefs. The court's chief clerk prepares a bench memo for each case, summarizing its facts and issues, which is distributed to every justice. Chief Justices Ronald Castille and Thomas Saylor both related that they met with their law clerks to discuss the cases to be heard each session day and how the justice might vote based solely on the briefs, a practice likely followed by other justices.[43]

The chief justice allots the time each argument receives, ranging from fifteen minutes to three hours, depending on the case's complexity, with time divided evenly between the litigants. Because the justices and their clerks are prepared, most oral arguments find the justices questioning the attorneys. After each day's arguments, the justices retire to their robing room, where they discuss and cast straw votes on each case, from most senior to least senior justice, with the chief justice voting last. These votes are not binding or permanent. When in the majority or minority, chief justices assign the writing of the majority or dissenting opinions, respectively, to themselves or another justice; when the chief justice is in the minority, the most senior justice voting with the majority may write the majority opinion or select another justice to draft it.[44]

Assigning an opinion is critical, as it may cause the justices to change their initial votes. As Chief Justice Castille described it, he selected justices for their "experience, expertise, and strengths. Who can write the best opinion?" Chief Justice Saylor also considered the justices' workload and if a justice wrote the recommendation for allocatur in the case. Both chiefs stated that they willingly took responsibility for drafting majority opinions in major cases—that is, those with significant consequences.[45]

Once drafted, a majority opinion circulates among the justices. If the straw vote is seven to zero, and the majority opinion fails to elicit any significant changes, then all the justices sign it and it is published quickly, usually in a month. When the straw vote is not unanimous, the circulating majority opinion is more likely to spur discussion and commentary as well as prompting some justices to write concurring and dissenting opinions. Justices can and do reconsider their original positions as they read the drafts. Should the majority opinion lose support, the majority opinion's author may adjust that opinion to accommodate those who no longer agree with it. If after further consideration the dissenting opinion achieves a majority, then the dissenting opinion becomes the new majority opinion. This extended deliberation adds time to the process, but once all the justices have settled on their positions, a final vote is taken and the decision is published.[46]

Both chief justices we interviewed were elected as Republicans and widely considered to hold conservative legal philosophies. But Justice Castille saw himself as "a middle of the road, practical jurist" who disagreed with Justice Scalia's application of original intent when interpreting the US Constitution, preferring to remain flexible when interpreting the state's constitution and laws. He offered several decisions in which he was in the majority with liberal justices, such as the 2015 gerrymandering case.[47] Justice Saylor, on the other hand, didn't place much stock in judicial philosophy. He "accords substantial deference to the political branches within their purview. The legislature has the tools that the judicial branch lacks, such as [the ability] to hold hearings and take testimony. The court's job is to discern what the legislature intended. Laws are the result of compromises and are not necessarily clear, making understanding legislative intent difficult. If the court gets it wrong, the legislature can fix the court's mistake by passing another law. In policy areas, the courts must defer to the legislative and executive branches."[48] He also exercises discretion in cases involving political questions, choosing to have the court avoid intruding in such matters; however, on constitutional questions where the legislature or executive have contravened constitutional principles, then the court must act, invoking precedent appropriately.[49]

Justice Saylor described four tools that he relied on to decide cases. He starts with history, asking what the people who wrote the constitution or law intended. Next, he searches for precedents to determine what, if anything, previous courts have written on the matter. Third, he turns to the document's plain text language to discern its meaning, and finally he asks what is the common understanding of the constitution's or law's language. He believes that incorporating all four tools has assisted him in writing decisions that meet the people's and government's needs.[50]

Because US Supreme Court decisions usually are the final word on major legal questions with important policy implications, much research has explored its justices' political ideologies. Few empirical quantitative or qualitative analyses, however, have focused on state high courts, despite their consequential role in protecting the rule of law, and none have focused specifically on Pennsylvania's highest court.[51] One fifty-state study that devised campaign contribution sources—CF scores—as an indicator for the judicial candidates' political orientation found that the Keystone State's court was slightly liberal (a CF score between 0 and -0.5) from 1979 to 2012.[52] As clever and sophisticated as the authors' methodology is, one must seriously question the CF score's validity, which raises concerns for the conclusions on the Pennsylvania court's political orientation.

Absent any empirical studies on Pennsylvania's highest court, legal commentators have offered their informed opinions on the subject. One of the most respected is Professor Bruce Ledewitz of Duquesne University's law school. According to Professor Ledewitz,

"When there was a Republican majority [from 2002 to 2015] there [weren't] any consistently conservative rulings." He noted the 2012 decision that tossed out the Republican gerrymander, the 2013 case that ruled against companies using fracking to extract natural gas, and the 2014 judgment that struck down a strict voter identification law that had passed a unified Republican government.[53]

But the 2015 election flipped the court's majority, and with it the court's Democratic majority issued some decidedly liberal decisions, such as upholding Philadelphia's soda tax, declaring that a clean environment is a right protected by the state constitution,[54] imposing new congressional districts over the General Assembly's objections,[55] and establishing a right for app-based gig workers to file for unemployment benefits.[56] Several challenges to Act 77 of 2019 are awaiting action by the Court as of 2023.

An article V responsibility that falls on the chief justice is oversight of the AOPC, which manages the entire Unified Court System. Both chief justices we interviewed stressed that nearly half of their workload involved supervising the court system, though day-to-day administration rests with the court administrator. In addition, there are nearly twenty boards and agencies that report to the chief justice, such as the Pennsylvania Board of Law Examiners, the Disciplinary Board of the Supreme Court, the Civil Procedures Rules Committee, the Minor Court Rules Committee, and the Interbranch Commission for Gender, Racial and Ethnic Fairness.

Court Ethics

The Quaker State's highest court has experienced more than its fair share of embarrassment and public derision over the last three decades. Beginning with the impeachment and removal of Justice Rolf Larsen in August 1994, and continuing through the indirect implication of Justice Dougherty in a federal investigation in 2019, the court's reputation has suffered.

Justice Larsen, first elected to the court in 1977, was embroiled in controversies during his time on the bench, but after his conviction for conspiring to obtain illegal drugs, suspension from the Supreme Court, and refusal to step down from the court, he was impeached by the House on a 199–0 vote and removed following a Senate trial on October 4, 1994, the first justice to be impeached in the court's history.[57]

In 2010, allegations swirled around Chief Justice Castille and Justice Sandra Shultz Newman for their personal relationships with lawyers and contractors involved in planning a new Family Court building for Philadelphia. Additional questions were raised about the propriety of gifts and trips accepted by Justice Castille over three years—2007 to 2009—from lawyers and large corporation valued at more than $14,000, all of which were legal.[58]

Justice Joan Orie Melvin was charged on April 7, 2010, along with her sisters, Jannine and Jane Orie, with using her Superior Court office staff and funds to campaign for seats on the Supreme Court in 2003 and 2009, winning the latter election. She was removed from the bench and later convicted on February 21, 2013.[59]

Following an investigation initiated by then–Attorney General Kathleen Kane, who claimed that the capital's male-dominated legal community had conspired to undermine her authority and complicate her office's investigation of Penn State's assistant football coach Jerry Sandusky for sexually assaulting minors, Justices Seamus McCaffery and Michael Eakin were found to have used government computers and email to share pornographic and racist materials. Justice McCaffery retired on October 27, 2014, rather face the ongoing investigation and possible charges. Justice Eakin fought the charges for almost two years even after his suspension by the court, and resigned on March 15, 2016.[60]

In 2018, investigative reports revealed that Chief Justice Saylor and Justices Donahue and Todd appeared to be spending court money lavishly for business activities, but no conclusive evidence could substantiate their allegations because detailed court expense reports were not made available.[61]

A federal district attorney's office in 2019 charged John "Johnny Doc" Dougherty, head of IBEW Local 98, and five other union members with embezzling over $600,000 from 2010 to 2016. Also listed, but not indicted or even named, was his brother, Justice Kevin Dougherty, as having been the recipient of personal work on his home paid for with the stolen money, bringing unneeded and unflattering attention to the court.[62]

THE ADMINISTRATION OF JUDICIAL CONDUCT

Pennsylvania created a sophisticated, professional, and coherent process for handling charges against any justice, judge, or magistrate in the state's legal system when the voters on May 18, 1993, ratified an amendment to article V that replaced the Judicial Inquiry and Review Board, which both investigated and tried cases, with two separate entities: the Judicial Conduct Board and the Court of Judicial Discipline. Both operate independently of all other courts and the legislative and executive branches to preserve the court system's integrity.

The Judicial Conduct Board receives information from all sources, including anonymous ones, concerning judicial misconduct. The Board's twelve members, six named by the governor and six appointed by the Supreme Court, serve without pay for a four-year term and may be reappointed after a one-year break. It must include equal numbers of Democrats and Republicans and be composed of three judges, three lawyers, and six nonlawyers. Everything associated with the Board's work is confidential, including the original complaint; any documents, records, or testimony collected; and activities associated with screening, verifying, and investigating the complaints. Following a comprehensive inquiry, should the Board determine that a complaint has merit, the Board's counsel files charges with the Court of Judicial Discipline.[63]

First seated by an act of the governor on August 11, 1993, the eight members of the Court of Judicial Discipline must hear and decide all misconduct charges referred to it by the Judicial Conduct Board. Four appointments are made by the Supreme Court: two judges, one magistrate, and one nonlawyer; four are named by the governor: one judge, two lawyers, and one nonlawyer. The court acts as a trial court, with a Conduct Board's attorney serving as prosecutor and the defendant represented by personal counsel; the burden of proof falls on the prosecution using compelling evidence. Should the court find that the charges are sustained, it has discretionary authority to decide the appropriate punishment under the Code of Judicial Conduct, from a reprimand to removal from office. If a convicted magistrate or judge wishes to appeal the court's verdict, the individual goes before the Supreme Court; however, a justice who appeals must appear before a special tribunal composed of seven judges chosen by lot from the judges of the Superior Court and Commonwealth Court who do not sit on the Court of Judicial Discipline or the Judicial Conduct Board. On appeal, "the scope of review is plenary on the law, clearly erroneous on the fact, and, as to sanctions, the scope of review is whether the sanctions imposed were lawful."[64]

Misconduct by justices, judges, and magistrates may never rise to meet official criteria that trigger formal charges or investigations, but they may be handled in other ways, as was the infamous "Kids for Cash" scandal. Two Luzerne County judges, President Judge Michael Conahan and Judge Mark Ciavarella, conspired to accept over $2.5 million from the owner of a for-profit juvenile detention center in return for convicting young defendants, most without lawyers and in hearings lasting minutes, and sentencing them to that facility. Though the Judicial Conduct Board had received complaints about Conahan's behavior between 2004 and 2008, the Board failed to take any action. But during the Board's investigation into Luzerne County Judge Ann H. Lokuta in 2006 for using court staff for personal work, Lokuta agreed to cooperate with FBI and IRS investigations of Conahan. A federal grand jury eventually brought charges against Conahan and Ciavarella in 2008. Conahan pleaded guilty, while Ciavarella went to trial and was convicted in 2010. This incident caused the General Assembly and the Supreme Court to perform a major overhaul of the state's juvenile justice system.[65]

Other examples of judicial misbehavior, such as the ticket-fixing scandal in Philadelphia's Traffic Court mentioned above, prompted actual changes, while a study of Philadelphia's Common Pleas Court system only recommended improvements to the court's culture and procedures. A report by the Center for Urban and Racial Equity (CURE) found "a culture of nepotism, mistrust and racial tension among the judges and staff" and recommended a long list of modifications.[66]

On the previous pages, several questions of major import for Pennsylvania's courts and judges were implied: how justices and judges should be selected and removed; whether judicial campaign contributions should be more closely regulated, if judicial elections are retained; and whether funding the state court system should be consolidated or shared. We consider each question below.

The Quaker State's judges have been chosen by partisan elections since 1850, and the method appears firmly entrenched despite calls for replacing it with merit selection. All of the justices and judges we interviewed voiced varying degrees of support for retaining partisan elections, with the most common themes being that elections express the public's will and give citizens control over their judges. They also argued that merit appointment is inherently a partisan process with less public accountability than elections. Judge Panella made a particularly compelling argument that appointing judges allows the other two branches too much influence over the courts, which must remain independent, and so he favored allowing voters to pick their judges.[67]

Those supporting merit selection, such as Pennsylvanians for Modern Courts, contend that partisan elections are fraught with problems that can undermine judges' legitimacy. For example, low voter interest in judicial elections and insufficient voter knowledge about judicial candidates can cause the election of unqualified or weakly qualified individuals. Judicial campaigns funded by lawyers, businesses, and corporations with cases before judges who accept the contributions raise serious questions about judicial impartiality. And subjecting judges to standing for retention following unpopular but legally correct decisions can and has contributed to some judges' defeat. Aware of the implications, judges may issue decisions that are popular rather than legally supported.[68]

Alternatives to partisan election are nonpartisan election, which is used in fifteen states; legislative appointment, which is found only in South Carolina and Virginia; gubernatorial appointment with or without confirmation, which is employed in twelve states; and the Missouri Plan, a system available in sixteen states. In the Missouri Plan, a recommending commission, appointed by the governor and/or other branches or organizations, screens and recommends a list of candidates to the governor, who nominates someone from the list to be confirmed by the Senate. Once confirmed, the judge serves a comparatively short initial term and then stands for retention for the full term of office.[69]

Each alternative has its advantages and disadvantages, which can be organized under two competing themes: maximum voter participation (elections) and limited voter involvement (appointment). The Missouri Plan falls somewhere between the two. No constitutional amendments designed to replace partisan elections have advanced beyond introduction in the General Assembly over many decades, and there is little reason to believe that any will clear the legislature in the future.

If elections, whether partisan or nonpartisan, continue as the method of selecting judges, then funding campaigns remain a concern. As we have repeatedly noted, Pennsylvania's lenient campaign finance laws leave judicial candidates open to accusations, fairly or unfairly, of rendering decisions that favor their contributors. Revisions to campaign finance rules meant to enforce strict contribution limits have been introduced for legislative and executive branch offices, but there is some question whether similar limits can be imposed on judicial candidates without the Supreme Court's blessing. Moreover, there is serious doubt that restricting who or what can donate to judicial candidates would pass US constitutional muster, because such checks can be viewed as limiting free speech.[70]

We discussed mechanisms for removing justices and judges above, including impeachment, yet steps taken in 2020 that threatened five Democratic justices for their 2018 redistricting decision suggest impeachment has become politicized. Impeachment is a legislative prerogative requiring action by both houses, which are obstacles to hasty or ill-considered impeachment motions. But in the hyperpartisan environment of the twenty-first century, either larger barriers must be erected or cooler heads must prevail to prevent impeachment from becoming a cudgel to intimidate the state's appellate justices and judges.[71]

Funding the state's entire court system has been a political football for decades. By statute, the state forced counties to assume their courts' financial burden, but a lawsuit heard by the Supreme Court in 1987 appeared to end this. The court ruled that the constitution requires that the state assume responsibility for the court system's operations. Yet the General Assembly failed to comply. Subsequent legal actions by the County Commissioners' Association in 1996 and again in 2009 were successful before the high court but did not lead to any action in the legislature. Chief Justice Castille believes that the state should fund all courts, because under the Unified Court System all court employees should be considered state employees. Resolving this dilemma will be expensive for the state should it ever agree to pay the full cost, but doing so would relieve financially stressed county governments and bring the Unified Court System into full compliance with the state's constitution.[72]

CONCLUSION

As one of three branches of Pennsylvania's government, the court system is possibly the least understood and appreciated by the public, even as it is viewed positively when compared to the other branches. In one survey, 54 percent expressed trust in the Supreme Court while 23 percent lacked trust and 24 percent were unsure. A national survey in 2007 found that people look more favorably upon their state courts than their executive or legislative branches.[73]

Despite their relatively low public profile, Pennsylvania's courts are a coequal branch that exercises their unique authority to check the powers of the other two. While the public may not pay close attention to their decisions, any single decision can have a dramatic impact on the political system. In like manner, actions by the governor and the General Assembly can significantly influence any and all elements of the state courts. Appreciating the interplay among the three branches is, therefore, essential for a more complete understanding of Pennsylvania's political system, as chapter 10's case study demonstrates.

NOTES

1. See Grey, Hanson, and Kousser, *Politics in the American States*; Smith and Greenblatt, *Governing States and Localities*.
2. *Pennsylvania Manual*, vol. 123, 5-3; Ballotpedia.
3. See Ballotpedia.
4. Ibid.
5. *Pennsylvania Manual*, vol. 123, 5-3.
6. Ibid., 5-6, 7.
7. The electorate approved a constitutional amendment in November 2016 that raised the retirement age to seventy-five. The amendment was not without controversy as two former Supreme Court justices joined a private attorney to challenge the amendment's wording, drafted by Secretary of State Pedro Cortes, which they argued was unnecessarily complex and confusing. The Wolf administration eventually agreed to simplify the language by removing any reference to the present retirement age of seventy. See Couloumbis, "Ballot Wording"; Caitlin McCabe, "Court Denies Effort"; Dent, "PA Ballot Question."
8. Justice Russel Nigro lost his retention election in 2005, a casualty of the General Assembly's 2005 midnight pay-raise vote. He became the first and only justice to date to lose a retention election. After the assembly repealed the pay raise, the Supreme Court ruled that the repeal did not affect any justices' or judges' salaries, further angering voters. Ironically, Nigro, a Philadelphia Democrat who voted with the minority, lost, while Justice Sandra Schultz Newman, a Philadelphia Republican also running for retention and who voted with the majority, won. See Barnes, "Anger over Pay"; Dao, "In a Rare Battle."
9. See Couloumbis, "Deal Put Judges on the Bench"; Krawczeniuk, "Wolf-Appointed Panel."
10. See the Pennsylvania Bulletin website.
11. *Pennsylvania Manual*, vol. 123, 5-3.
12. See Levy, "Pennsylvania Republicans Turn."
13. See Tannen, "Ballot Position Matters";

Brennan, "Ballot Crapshoot."
14. See Hall, "State Courts." On rare occasions, judicial candidates deploy negative attack ads to discredit their opponents, as happened in the race to fill a Supreme Court vacancy in the fall of 2021. Republican Commonwealth Court judge Kevin Brobson's ad claimed that Democratic Superior Court judge Marie McLaughlin "chose to void the guilty plea of a drunk driver who admitted to killing a pregnant woman and her unborn child," when, in fact, she voted with another judge to permit the defendant a new trial because of incompetent defense counsel. The Pennsylvania Bar Association declared that the ad's content had violated "standards of accuracy and integrity in campaign advertising that both campaigns agreed to follow as part of the bar's candidate evaluation process." Seidman, "Pa. Bar Association Criticizes TV Ad."
15. Seidman, "$2M Spent on TV Ads."
16. See Navratil and Couloumbis, "Justices Got Funds from Lawyers"; Seidman, "$2M Spent on TV Ads."
17. See Pennsylvania Courts, "Women on the Pennsylvania Bench."
18. See Roebuck, "For Traffic Court."
19. *Pennsylvania Manual*, vol. 123, 5-6.
20. See Erdley, "Women Hold Nearly a Third"; Pennsylvania Courts, "Women on the Pennsylvania Bench."
21. Jack Panella (president judge, Superior Court), interview with Baldino, August 17, 2020, by phone.
22. Title 18, chapter 57 of the Pennsylvania Code.
23. Panella, interview.
24. Ibid. Additionally, Superior Court justices individually hire either four clerks and two administrative assistants or five clerks and one assistant, with most choosing to do the latter. One clerk is appointed chief clerk, who coordinates the others' work. All clerks may be career clerks (that is, regular state employees), but a

judge may opt to reserve one clerkship—a step clerk—for a newly graduated lawyer, who may serve for up to two years.

25. Ibid.
26. See Light, "State Superior Court"; Correale Stevens (Superior Court judge), interview with the authors, May 24, 2016, by phone.
27. Panella, interview.
28. Stevens, interview.
29. Mary Hanna Leavitt (Commonwealth Court president judge), interview with the authors, September 20, 2016, by phone.
30. Michael H. Wojcik (Commonwealth Court judge), interview with the authors, July 14, 2016, by phone; see also IN RE: Nomination Petition of Joseph VODVARKA, March 30, 2016 https://caselaw.findlaw.com/pa-common wealth-court/1730728.html.
31. Traditions described here were initiated by the court's first president judge, James S. Bowman, according to interviews with Judges Leavitt and Wojcik.
32. Leavitt, interview.
33. Wojcik, interview.
34. Leavitt, interview..
35. Ibid.
36. Wojcik, interview.
37. See Jackson, "Democrats Gain Control"; Bishop, "Most Expensive Judicial Election."
38. A writ is a court order. A writ of habeas corpus is requested by a defense attorney to have a client brought before a judge, who compels the state to show cause for holding the client or release the client. Writs of mandamus are issued to lower courts or government officers to compel a government official to complete or halt official responsibilities. Writs of quo warranto question the authority of state government officials to engage in specific actions.
39. See 2018 Caseload Statistics of the Unified Court System.
40. Pennsylvania Manual, vol. 123, 5–4.
41. Ibid.
42. Each Supreme Court justice hires one chief clerk and three assistant clerks, who are permanent court employees. Four additional clerks are hired directly from law school and serve for up to three years.
43. Thomas Saylor (chief justice of the Supreme Court), interview with the authors, August 31, 2016, by phone; Ronald Castille (chief justice of the Supreme Court), interview with the authors, August 16, 2016, by phone.
44. Saylor, interview.

45. Saylor and Castille, interviews.
46. Ibid.
47. Castille, interview.
48. Saylor, interview.
49. Ibid.
50. Ibid.
51. Sutton, "States' High Courts."
52. Bonica and Woodruff, "State Supreme Court Ideology."
53. Caruso, "How Pa.'s Supreme Court Moved Left."
54. See Pennsylvania Environmental Defense Council v. Commonwealth of Pennsylvania, http://www.pacourts.us/assets/opinions /Supreme/out/J-35-2016m0%20-%201031 4240919600966.pdf.
55. See McCrystal, "Pa. High Court Upholds City."
56. See Reyes, "High Court Rules on Benefits."
57. See Brandolf and Bumsted, "Rolf Larsen"; Hinds, "Convicted Pennsylvania Justice."
58. See Fazlollah and Tanfani, "Lawyer for Court"; Heller, "Latest High-Court Fiasco"; Tanfani, "Ex-Justice Sought Project Fee."
59. See pennlive.com; IN RE: Jane Orie Melvin, August 30, 2012, http://www.pacourts.us /assets/files/setting-3437/file-4655.pdf ?cb=a64cdc.
60. See Esack and Hall, "Seamus McCaffery Retires"; Thompson, "Suspended Pa. Supreme Court Justice."
61. Knudsen and Bumsted, "High Priests of Secrecy."
62. See Baer, "Turmoil (Again)."
63. For a complete description of the Judicial Conduct Board's procedures, see its website, http://judicialconductboardofpa.org.
64. See Code of Judicial Conduct, effective July 1, 2014; Pennsylvania Manual, vol. 123, 5-7.
65. For the full story, see Ecenbarger, Kids for Cash. It is also worth noting that Judge Lokuta was removed from the bench. A few years later, Luzerne County judge Michael Toole was also removed for case fixing.
66. Roebuck, "Court Study Finds Nepotism."
67. Panella, interview.
68. See Pennsylvanians for Modern Courts website, https://www.pmconline.org; Gray, Hanson, and Kousser, Politics in the American States; also, Huntingdon County judge Morris Terrizzi related the story of his retention defeat following his correct decision (upheld on appeal) that allowed a county-wide property tax reassessment to proceed. Informal conversation with Baldino in 1991.

69. See Ballotpedia.com.
70. See *Buckley v. Valeo*, 424 U.S. 1 (1976). This is the US Supreme Court decision that ruled money donated to candidates is equivalent to speech and cannot be restricted under the First Amendment.
71. Seidman and Lai, "Impeach?"
72. *County of Allegheny v. Commonwealth*, 517 Pa.

65, 74–76, 534 A.2d 760, 764–65 (1987). See also Kennerly, "Can Philadelphia Sue Pennsylvania"; *Pennsylvania Association of County Commissioners v. Commonwealth of PA*, 617 Pa. 231 (2012).
73. See Institute of Public Opinion, "2020 Pennsylvania Post-Election"; Jamieson and Hennessy, "Public Understanding."

BIBLIOGRAPHY

Baer, John. "Turmoil (Again) for the State Supreme Court." *Philadelphia Inquirer*, February 11, 2019.

Ballotpedia. https://ballotpedia.org/Judicial_selection_in_Pennsylvania.

Barnes, Tom. "Anger over Pay Spelled Defeat for Justice Nigro." *Pittsburgh Post-Gazette* November 10, 2005. https://www.post-gazette.com/news/politics-state/2005/11/10/Anger-over-pay-spelled-defeat-for-Justice-Nigro/stories/200511100379.

Bishop, Tyler. "The Most Expensive Judicial Election in U.S. History." *Atlantic*, November 10, 2015. https://www.theatlantic.com/politics/archive/2015/11/the-most-expensive-judicial-election-in-us-history/415140.

Bonica, Adam, and Michael J. Woodruff. "State Supreme Court Ideology and 'New Style' Judicial Campaigns." SSRN.com, October 31, 2012. https://ssrn.com/abstract=2169664.

Brandolf, Adam, and Brad Bumsted. "Rolf Larsen, Impeached PA Supreme Court Justice, Dies at 79." TribLIVE.com, August 12, 2014. https://archive.triblive.com/news/rolf-larsen-impeached-pa-supreme-court-justice-dies-at-79-2.

Brennan, Chris. "Ballot Crapshoot for Would-Be Judges." *Philadelphia Inquirer*, February 3, 2017.

Caruso, Stephen. "How Pa.'s Supreme Court Moved Left, and What It Means for the GOP." *Philadelphia Tribune*, November 9, 2019.

Code of Judicial Conduct. Effective July 1, 2014. http://judicialconductboardofpa.org/code-of-judicial-conduct.

Couloumbis, Angela. "Ballot Wording Is Called Deceitful." *Philadelphia Inquirer*, July 22, 2016.

———. "Deal Put Judges on the Bench." *Philadelphia Inquirer*, November 22, 2019.

Dao, James. "In a Rare Battle, Justices Are Fighting for Their Seats." *New York Times*, November 6, 2005. https://www.nytimes.com/2005/11/06/us/in-a-rare-battle-justices-are-fighting

-for-their-seats.html?login=smartlock&auth=login-smartlock.

Dent, Mark. "PA Ballot Question About Judge Retirement Age Sparks Bitter Harrisburg Fight." BillyPenn.com, October 12, 2020. https://billypenn.com/2016/10/12/pa-ballot-question-about-judge-retirement-age-sparks-bitter-harrisburg-fight.

Ecenbarger, William. *Kids for Cash: Two Judges, Thousands of Children and $2.6 Million Kickback Scheme*. New York: New Press, 2012.

Erdley, Deb. "Women Hold Nearly a Third of Pennsylvania's Judicial Seats." Triblive.com, https://triblive.com/news/pennsylvania/women-hold-nearly-a-third-of-the-states-judicial-seats.

Esack, Steve, and Peter Hall. "Seamus McCaffery Retires Under Porn Email Scandal." *Allentown Morning Call*, October 27, 2014. https://www.mcall.com/news/pennsylvania/mc-pa-seamus-mccafery-retires-porn-emails-20141027-story.html.

Fazlollah, Mark, and Joseph Tanfani. "Castille Is Accepting of Litigants' Gifts, Trips." *Philadelphia Inquirer*, November 21, 2010.

———. "Lawyer for Court Also Aided Foxwoods." *Philadelphia Inquirer*, June 14, 2010.

Gray, Virginia, Russell L. Hanson, and Thad Kousser, eds. *Politics in the American States: A Comparative Analysis*. 11th ed. Washington, DC: Congressional Quarterly Press, 2018.

Hall, Melinda Gann. "State Courts." In Gray, Hanson, and Kousser, *Politics in the American States*, 288–97.

Heller, Karen. "Castille, Do Right Thing Now." *Philadelphia Inquirer*, November 28, 2010.

———. "The Latest High-Court Fiasco: Powerful, Plugged-in Lawyers Are Hired to Probe Power, Plugged-in Lawyers." *Philadelphia Inquirer*, June 20, 2010.

Hinds, Michael. "Convicted Pennsylvania Justice Is Facing Impeachment." *New York Times*, May 13, 1994.

Institute of Public Opinion, Muhlenberg College. "2020 Pennsylvania Post-Election Survey." December 2020.

Jackson, Peter. "Democrats Gain Control of Pennsylvania's Supreme Court." *Allentown Morning Call*, November 4, 2015. https://www.mcall.com/news/local/mc-pa-supreme-court-election-20151103-story.html.

Jamieson, Kathleen Hall, and Michael Hennessy. "Public Understanding of and Support for the Courts: Survey Results." *Georgetown Law Journal* 95, no. 4 (2007): 899–902.

Kennerly, Max S. "Can Philadelphia Sue Pennsylvania for More Court Funding?" litigation andtrial.com, May 18, 2009. https://www.litigationandtrial.com/2009/05/articles/the-law/for-non-lawyers/can-philadelphia-sue-pennsylvania-for-more-court-funding.

Knudsen, Paula, and Brad Bumsted. "The High Priests of Secrecy." *Citizens' Voice*, March 18, 2018.

Krawczeniuk, Borys. "Wolf-Appointed Panel Nearly Finished Screening for Judge Vacancies." *Citizens' Voice*, June 6, 2016.

Levy, Marc. "Pennsylvania Republicans Turn to Constitutional Amendment to Shake up Democratic-Majority on Supreme Court." *Allentown Morning Call*, January 18, 2020. https://www.mcall.com/news/pennsylvania/mc-nws-pa-redistricting-judges-20200118-xilsty3lurdlnoby6xmjm4p4pe-story.html.

Light, Mia. "State Superior Court Enrolls in High School." *Citizens' Voice*, March 8, 2011.

McCabe, Caitlin. "Court Denies Effort to Join Judicial Case." *Philadelphia Inquirer*, August 2, 2016.

McCrystal, Laura. "Pa. High Court Upholds City, Ending Case." *Philadelphia Inquirer*, July 19, 2019.

Navratil, Liz, and Angela Couloumbis. "Justices Got Funds from Lawyers in Report Fight." *Philadelphia Inquirer*, July 12, 2018.

Pennsylvania Bulletin. http://www.pacodeand bulletin.gov/Display/pabull?file=/secure/pabulletin/data/vol48/48-50/1921.html.

Pennsylvania Courts. "Women on the Pennsylvania Bench." Infographic publication of the Courts released on March 3, 2022.

Pennsylvania Manual. Vol. 123, 5-3, 5-4, 5-6.

Pennlive.com, February 21, 2013. https://www.pennlive.com/midstate/2013/02/pa_supreme_court_justice_joan.html.

Reyes, Juliana Feliciano. "High Court Rules on Benefits for Gig Workers." *Philadelphia Inquirer*, July 30, 2020.

Roebuck, Jeremy. "Court Study Finds Nepotism, Racial Rifts." *Philadelphia Inquirer*, July 10, 2020.

———. "For Traffic Court, Voters Decide the Fix Is Out." *Philadelphia Inquirer*, April 29, 2016.

Seidman, Andrew. "Pa. Bar Association Criticizes TV Ad by GOP Candidate for State Supreme Court." *Philadelphia Inquirer*, October 24, 2021.

———. "$2M Spent on TV Ads in Low-Key Judge Races." *Philadelphia Inquirer*, October 31, 2019.

Seidman, Andrew, and Jonathan Lai. "Impeach? A Rare Remedy for Courts." *Philadelphia Inquirer*, February 24, 2018.

Smith, Kevin B., and Alan Greenblatt. *Governing States and Localities*. 7th ed. Washington, DC: Sage, 2019.

Sutton, Jeffrey S. "States' High Courts Protect the Rule of Law, Too." *Philadelphia Inquirer*, September 16, 2018.

Tanfani, Joseph. "Ex-Justice Sought Project Fee for Her Son." *Philadelphia Inquirer*, December 6, 2010.

Tannen, Jonathan. "Ballot Position Matters." Econsultsolutions, February 19, 2017. https://econsultsolutions.com/ballot-position-matters-neighborhood-by-neighborhood.

Thompson, Charles. "Suspended Pa. Supreme Court Justice J. Michael Eakin Resigns from Bench in Email Scandal." pennlive.com, March 15, 2016. https://www.pennlive.com/news/2016/03/suspended_pa_supreme_court_jus.html.

Unified Court System. Caseload Statistics 2018. http://www.pacourts.us/assets/files/setting-768/file-8222.pdf?cb=2e094c.

CHAPTER 8

Pennsylvania and the Federal System

This chapter examines the complex relationship among the federal, state, and local governments in the United States. Pennsylvania exists within the limitations of the US Constitution and federal statutes. At the same time, Pennsylvania, like all states, has control over much of its state politics and policy, all while maintaining control over the actions of its local governments. The institutions, therefore, governing interstate relations are more numerous. These institutions at the federal level include Congress, the federal courts, and federal regulatory agencies. Likewise, Pennsylvania's legislature, court system, and regulatory system influence intergovernmental relations.

All states exist within the US federal system of government. Federalism is defined as a shared power structure between a national government and regional (state) governments with defined rules and responsibilities.[1] In the United States, the powers allotted to each level of government are strictly spelled out in the US Constitution. The federal government maintains supremacy over the state governments and is allotted both enumerated powers and a whole host of implied powers derived from specific expressed powers.[2] For example, the federal government has the right to create an army and a navy. The "necessary and proper" clause implies that Congress has the power to devise a national draft to populate that army and navy in times of war or even in peace. Likewise, state governments have specific constitutional rights under article IV and the Tenth Amendment. Article IV governs the territorial integrity of each state and the rules for making changes to any state boundaries. The Tenth Amendment gives rise to concurrent powers, those shared by both the federal and state governments, such as the power to tax. The US Constitution also addresses issues related to interstate rights and disputes. All states must honor other state laws and court decisions (article IV, section 1, clause 1) and grant "privileges and immunities" to other states' residents (article IV, section 2, clause 1). This means court decisions and legal contracts will be honored across state lines.[3]

The Supremacy Clause of the US Constitution (article VI, section 8) also gives rise to the doctrine of preemption—that is, federal laws preempt state laws. Federal courts can order states to change laws or policies that are in conflict with the federal government. This applies to federal regulatory agencies' decisions, which may be either explicit or implied.[4] In the case of *Pennsylvania v. Nelson* (1956), a state law making it a crime to seek to overthrow the federal government was struck down by the US Supreme Court because the court determined that Congress had already resolved the issue. Further, sedition was deemed to be a federal crime and, therefore, could only be addressed through federal law.[5]

Pennsylvania's role in the federal system historically has been much like that of all American states—that is, centered on regional issues. Not until the New Deal did the issue of federal intervention in state policies become apparent. Pre-1937, the Supreme Court applied a very narrow definition of interstate commerce that allowed the states a great deal of independence. However, the decades since have seen a gradual expansion of federal power over state statutes and policies. A broad definition of the interstate commerce clause has led to federal intervention in state labor and wage policies, land use and environmental policies, and criminal and civil legal standards. In short, the federal government's role throughout the twentieth century can be seen as one of imposing national standards and enforcing civil and individual rights in the states.[6]

A concrete example can be found in the imposition of the federal minimum wage, which applies across all states and includes wages paid to state and local government employees.[7] Other examples include prisoners' rights and due process rights for public employees. In *Hewitt v. Helms* (1983), the federal court ruled that Pennsylvania's prison administration rules had created a due process right for state prisoners within the state prisons.[8] Similarly, the decision in the case of *Cleveland Board of Education v. Loudermill* (1985) required a pretermination hearing (procedural due process) for state and local employees.[9]

Federal intervention into state and even local government policies has been further strengthened by the fiscal ties between the three levels of government. Beginning in the 1960s, federal grants have formed a strong source of income for both state and local governments. However, these federal dollars often come with many strings attached. The use of block grants, large chunks of federal dollars with fewer spending restrictions, was begun under President Nixon and expanded under Presidents Reagan and Bush; the practice continues today as a method of reducing federal management of state programs while also increasing state flexibility in the use of federal dollars. This policy approach, known as fiscal federalism, was greatly expanded in the 1990s under President Clinton to include most social welfare and entitlement programs such as food stamps, housing assistance, and Medicaid. The movement away from categorical grants and toward block grants was welcomed by the states but not widely lauded by the policy experts. When President Bill Clinton signed the Temporary Assistance to Needy Families (TANF) law, which replaced Aid to Families with Dependent Children (AFDC) in 1996, it was a dramatic shift in the way in which federal entitlements were provided.[10] Most recently, the Affordable Care Act provided vastly expanded federal block grant funding for Medicaid recipients up to 138 percent of the federal poverty line.[11]

Federal intervention in state policy areas does not, however, always come with matching dollars. One of the biggest issues in federalism over the past thirty years has been

Table 8.1 Medicaid funding at the state and federal levels

Location	Federal	State	Total
United States	64.4%	35.6%	100.0%
Alabama	72.2%	27.8%	100.0%
Alaska	72.8%	27.2%	100.0%
Arizona	76.8%	23.2%	100.0%
Arkansas	76.4%	23.6%	100.0%
California	60.2%	39.8%	100.0%
Colorado	57.7%	42.3%	100.0%
Connecticut	58.8%	41.2%	100.0%
Delaware	65.1%	34.9%	100.0%
District of Columbia	73.5%	26.5%	100.0%
Florida	60.9%	39.1%	100.0%
Georgia	67.8%	32.2%	100.0%
Hawaii	63.9%	36.1%	100.0%
Idaho	71.2%	28.8%	100.0%
Illinois	59.2%	40.8%	100.0%
Indiana	71.4%	28.6%	100.0%
Iowa	66.1%	33.9%	100.0%
Kansas	57.2%	42.8%	100.0%
Kentucky	78.0%	22.0%	100.0%
Louisiana	72.5%	27.5%	100.0%
Maine	65.7%	34.3%	100.0%
Maryland	60.2%	39.8%	100.0%
Massachusetts	55.4%	44.6%	100.0%
Michigan	71.0%	29.0%	100.0%
Minnesota	56.7%	43.3%	100.0%
Mississippi	76.5%	23.5%	100.0%
Missouri	65.6%	34.4%	100.0%
Montana	77.6%	22.4%	100.0%
Nebraska	53.0%	47.0%	100.0%
Nevada	74.0%	26.0%	100.0%
New Hampshire	55.3%	44.7%	100.0%
New Jersey	59.0%	41.0%	100.0%
New Mexico	78.9%	44.7%	100.0%
New York	70.2%	29.8%	100.0%
North Carolina	67.3%	32.7%	100.0%
North Dakota	59.6%	40.4%	100.0%
Ohio	68.2%	31.8%	100.0%
Oklahoma	64.2%	35.8%	100.0%
Oregon	73.4%	26.6%	100.0%
			(continued)

Location	Federal	State	Total
Pennsylvania	58.2%	41.8%	100.0%
Rhode Island	60.4%	39.6%	100.0%
South Carolina	71.3%	28.7%	100.0%
North Dakota	59.6%	40.4%	100.0%
Tennessee	66.2%	33.8%	100.0%
Texas	58.4%	41.6%	100.0%
Utah	69.8%	30.2%	100.0%
Vermont	59.3%	40.7%	100.0%
Virginia	56.0%	44.0%	100.0%
Washington	63.9%	36.1%	100.0%
West Virginia	78.7%	21.3%	100.0%
Wisconsin	59.7%	40.3%	100.0%
Wyoming	52.6%	47.4%	100.0%

Source: https://www.kff.org/medicaid/state-indicator/federalstate-share-of-spending/.

unfunded or underfunded federal mandates. The list of such mandates is extensive, covering everything from voter registration (Motor Voter Act of 1993) to disability rights (Americans with Disabilities Act of 1990) to the environment (Clean Air Act of 1963, Clean Water Act of 1972) to the aforementioned expansion of Medicaid, in which federal dollars did not pay the full cost of the program's administration.[12]

Federalism also applies to the relationship between state government and local government. Traditionally, local government has been controlled by state constitutions and state statutes. The concept of Dillon's rule, developed by the federal judiciary in the late nineteenth century, places local government in a subordinate role to the state government. This judicial rule gives states the authority to create and empower their local governments. In fact, local governments have no real constitutional roles other than those granted by each state.[13] This makes it difficult, if not impossible, for a local government to challenge its state on things like unfunded state mandates.

Interstate relations—that is, those between or among states—are governed by the Full Faith and Credit clause (article IV, section 1) and the Interstate Compact clause (article 1, section 23) of the US Constitution. According to the Full Faith and Credit clause, states are required to honor one another's laws and court decisions.[14] Prior to the 2015 Supreme Court decision on gay marriage, *Obergefell v. Hodges*, the Full Faith and Credit clause posed a real dilemma regarding the interstate legal recognition of gay civil unions.[15]

In general, interstate activities take three forms: interstate compacts, multistate legal action, and uniform state laws. Interstate compacts are formal agreements requiring approval by state legislatures. An example of an interstate compact is the multistate lotteries, such as Powerball, Mega Millions, and Megabucks. Multistate legal action increases the power of a lawsuit, such as the suits launched against the tobacco industry in the 1990s.

Lastly, the states have acted jointly to prohibit regulatory action by the federal government by establishing uniform laws like the Uniform Commercial Code, which has been adopted by all fifty states.[16]

States engage in joint activities such as environmental protection, transportation, and waterway controls. Examples include the Port Authority of New York and New Jersey, which runs all forms of transportation—land, sea, and air—in the New York City metropolitan region,[17] or the Chesapeake Bay program, which protects the Chesapeake Bay watershed.[18] Pennsylvania is similarly engaged in partnerships in the region to protect the use of joint waterways and to regulate transportation across these waterways. The Delaware River Joint Toll Commission maintains and regulates the bridges connecting New Jersey and Pennsylvania. The Commission does not receive any tax revenues from either state but rather relies entirely upon toll income for its operations. The Commission currently manages twenty bridges, eight of which are toll bridges. The Commission was created in 1934 with modifications to the agreement in the mid-1980s. In 1987, the Commission assumed ownership of the twelve non–toll bridges, two of which are foot bridges. These bridges had been maintained through equal funding from Pennsylvania and New Jersey. Today, they are the responsibility of the Commission. The Commission operates with ten commissioners, five from each state. The Pennsylvania commissioners are appointed by the governor and serve at the governor's discretion.[19]

The Commission has come under state scrutiny after a series of controversial rate hikes. In April of 2021, tolls on the Delaware River bridges rose substantially after ten years without any rate hikes. Commercial vehicles and non-E-ZPass holders took the brunt of the hike. The pandemic resulted in a decline of 11.8 million vehicles crossing the toll bridges from 2019 to 2020. In April 2021, the Pennsylvania House passed a bill requiring periodic state audits of the Commission's finances and allowed the governor to veto any rate hikes. This controversy illustrates the unique problems of interstate agencies or compacts that are not directly under state government control but that control joint state infrastructure and have widespread economic impact within the compact's member states.[20]

Pennsylvania has had a long and storied history of conflicts with federal mandates on everything from taxation to religious freedom to abortion to homeland security. Pennsylvania farmers most famously played a role in inciting the Whiskey Rebellion of 1791, protesting the imposition of a federal excise tax on whiskey.[21] In the early 1960s, the US Supreme Court struck down a Pennsylvania law requiring that the Bible be read in public schools.[22] Pennsylvania tested the very foundation of abortion rights with the passage of the Abortion Control Act of 1989 (P.L. 592), which requires a minor to gain parental permission or a court order to have an abortion. It also requires that the woman be provided with information related to the abortion and the alternatives to abortion twenty-four hours prior to the procedure (right to know or informed consent).[23] The abortion restrictions were upheld by the Supreme Court.[24] As recently as 2012, the Pennsylvania General Assembly rejected the Federal REAL ID Act of 2005 by passing the REAL ID Nonparticipation

Act (Act 38 of 2012). The federal law requires that state Departments of Motor Vehicles link to each other to create a de facto national database for identification. In the face of increased federal pressure, Pennsylvania finally began to implement the REAL ID law in March 2019. The COVID-19 pandemic gave the commonwealth some additional time to meet this federal mandate when the federal deadline for REAL ID was extended to May 3, 2023. After this date, a Pennsylvania driver's license was no longer valid form of identification for admission to federal military bases or nuclear installations or to board an airplane.[25]

Perhaps no single historical example better illustrates the complicated relationship between the federal government and the state of Pennsylvania than the Three Mile Island disaster. On March 29, 1979, the Three Mile Island (TMI) nuclear power plant experienced a problem with its vital cooling system. While a meltdown of the core did not occur, radiation did escape into the atmosphere. TMI was the worst nuclear commercial power accident of its time. As Governor Richard Thornburgh related in a personal interview, both the initial response and the cleanup involved federal, state, and interstate actors. At the federal level, the Nuclear Regulatory Commission (NRC) provided some initial support. However, after a year of inaction on the part of the NRC and the New Jersey–based utility company (General Public Utilities) that owned TMI, Governor Thornburgh's administration was forced to devise a plan to cover the roughly one billion dollars in cleanup costs. It was only through the urging of then Ohio governor Jim Rhodes at the National Governors' Conference that neighboring states were compelled to contribute to the cleanup. Governor Thornburgh himself had to lobby the federal government for its $190 million contribution to restore the site.[26]

The relationship between Pennsylvania's state government and its 4,678 local governments is outlined in the state constitution and state statutes.[27] Pennsylvania's court decisions have upheld Dillon's rule since 1870.[28] Local governments have only those powers granted by the state. An exception to Dillon's rule is the concept of home rule. Discussed in greater detail in chapter 9, home rule allows a local government to devise its own charter. Rather than authority coming from state law, local citizens create their government to meet their community's needs. Whether a local government adopts home rule or not, Pennsylvania's state government limits the ability of local government to tax, spend, and borrow and to legislate on issues involving land use, the environment, and public safety. The bottom line is that the state maintains the right to establish statewide standards on these issues, which is the power known as state preemption. It is basically the same as the federal power of preemption over the states. The main difference is that Pennsylvania's local governments, if empowered by the state legislature, can impose additional regulations in matters already covered by state law as long as those regulations are not incompatible with existing state statues or the state constitution.[29]

An example can be found in regard to local regulation of oil and gas drilling in the Marcellus Shale. According to the Oil and Gas Act of 1984, local governments could regulate wells but could not ban them entirely.[30] In a series of cases involving local governments' ordinances related to natural gas drilling (hydrofracking), the Pennsylvania Supreme Court found that local zoning regulations are constitutional under the Environmental Rights Amendment (Pa. Const. art I, § 27) as long as they pertain to location and not operation of the wells.[31] Act 13 of 2012, which replaced the Oil and Gas Act, attempted to force municipalities to include oil and gas drilling everywhere within their municipal boundaries. Again, the Pennsylvania Supreme Court sided with local municipalities, declaring that local property owners' rights must be protected. Local regulations and comprehensive municipal planning codes would be in addition to any state regulations and meet purely local needs to preserve land values and quality of life.[32] The following list illustrates the intersection of federal and state regulation of the hydrofracking industry, with statutes listed in order of importance.[33]

Safe Drinking Water Act of 1974
Clean Water Act of 1972
Clean Air Act of 1970
Comprehensive Environmental Response, Compensation, and Liability Act
    of 1980
Resource Conservation and Recovery Act of 1976
Endangered Species Act of 1973
Toxic Substances Control Act of 1976

Another area in which the state grants substantial power to local governments is police powers. Local governments have both specific grants of authority as well as general powers granted to them.[34] Pennsylvania's local governments can also engage in a variety of intergovernmental cooperative arrangements, which include things like police protection, ambulance services, and street maintenance. Pennsylvania local governments may also create Councils of Government (COG's). COG's are composed of multiple municipalities that can engage in activities such as regional planning, bulk purchasing, and training and continuing education for employees and elected officials.[35] Pennsylvania's municipalities can also create more formal structures for joint service provision. The most common of these is the joint municipal authority. Joint authorities can finance large-scale capital projects such as sewage and water treatment plants, airports, and transit systems.[36] Other types of cooperative entities include county-wide tax-collection districts for municipalities and school districts, transportation districts, and environmental improvement compacts.[37]

Probably one of the most complex intergovernmental relationships in Pennsylvania is the relationship between the commonwealth and its sixty-seven counties. Pennsylvania's counties are subdivisions of the state, and they encompass boroughs, cities, and townships.[38] According to Doug Hill, executive director of the County Commissioners Association of Pennsylvania (CCAP), Pennsylvania's counties struggle with both structural and financial issues. On the one hand, they are required to supply a long list of services; on the other hand, they are often underfunded to meet their obligations. One example is the provision of services to children and young people through county children and youth agencies. Counties provide monitoring, counseling, and placement of at-risk children and youth by paying for the services, based upon the current caseload, using county budget dollars. Legally, the state is obligated to reimburse the counties for 90 percent of the monies spent on the provision of these services. Counties, however, are often shorted on their reimbursement dollars or experience delays in reimbursement from the state.[39]

Other examples where the counties provide up-front services are mental health and intellectual disabilities. The state is obligated to reimburse the counties for up to 90 percent of the cost of such services, but counties have seen no increase in state funding in over a decade. There are long waiting lists for services, leaving the mental health population greatly underserved. This, in turn, has an impact on the county prison population, roughly two-thirds to three-quarters of which have substance abuse and mental health issues.[40]

Federalism is the intersection of federal constitutional power and law, states' rights as guaranteed by the Tenth Amendment, and service delivery and policy application by local governments. Nowhere is this mix more evident than in the creation and enforcement of immigration policy. The regulation of immigration and standards for US citizenship are the domains of the federal government, specifically the US Congress. The US Constitution assigns Congress the authority to determine the criteria for immigration and the natural-ization process for individuals not born on US soil.[41] But clear delineation of federal control has not stopped states from attempting to establish their own rules and regulations related to immigration. In 2010, Arizona passed the Support Our Law Enforcement and Safe Neighborhoods Act (SB 1070), which made it a state crime to be an undocumented person. State law-enforcement officers may demand proof of legal residency from anyone suspected of being in the country illegally. In 2012, the US Supreme Court struck down the provisions related to living or working in the United States as a state crime; however, the court did uphold the right of the state to demand proof of citizenship during routine traffic stops.[42]

The Arizona law included the issue of illegally working in the United States as a state crime. This issue of employer verification of the legal status of their employees dates back to 2006. Federal law penalizes an employer for knowingly hiring undocumented workers.[43] Employers can check their workers' social security numbers using the federal E-Verify site. This is currently a voluntary program.[44]

In 2006, a local government attempted to enter the sphere of federal control of immi-gration enforcement. The city of Hazleton, Pennsylvania, passed an ordinance that applied to all businesses and landlords within its limits. Under the Illegal Immigration Relief Ordi-nance, any business knowingly hiring undocumented workers would lose its license to operate in the city. Likewise, landlords knowingly renting to undocumented tenants would also remit their right to engage in real estate rentals in the city.[45] Legal commentators noted that the ordinance was "carefully crafted" in order to avoid conflict with federal law.[46] The city ordinance was originally ruled unconstitutional by a federal district judge in 2007.[47] After eight years of appeals, the US Supreme Court declined to hear the case in 2014, upholding the lower court's decision.[48]

CONCLUSION

The ongoing conflict between local needs and federal policies illustrates the complexities of America's federal system. The issues arising between the commonwealth of Pennsylvania and its numerous local governments highlight the balance between the rights of each state to impose statewide standards and local governments' dilemma, which is balancing their particular needs and regional demands while supported with barely adequate state funding. The future of American federalism has been further strained by the issues arising from the COVID-19 pandemic, which stretched the ability of state and local governments to address economic, health, and educational needs of their residents.

NOTES

1. Anton, *American Federalism.*
2. US Constitution, article I, section 8.
3. US Constitution, article IV; US Constitution, Tenth Amendment.
4. Linder, "Supremacy Clause."
5. *Pennsylvania v. Nelson,* 350 U.S. 497 (1956).
6. Byer Miller, "Burger Court's View."
7. *Garcia v. San Antonio Metropolitan Transit Authority,* 469 U.S. 528 (1985).
8. *Hewitt v. Helms,* 459 U.S. 460 (1983).
9. *Cleveland Board of Education v. Loudermill,* 470 U.S. 532 (1985); Ross, "Safeguarding Our Federalism."
10. McFarlane and Meir, "Do Different Funding Mechanisms"; Katz, "After 60 Years."
11. See http://www.ncsl.org/research /health/affordable-care-act-expansion .aspx.
12. Gormley, "Money and Mandates"; St. George, "Unfunded Mandates."
13. *City of Clinton v. Cedar Rapids and Missouri Railroad,* 24 Iowa 455 (1868).
14. US Constitution, article IV, section 1.
15. *Obergefell v. Hodges,* 576 U.S. (2015).
16. Bowman, "Horizontal Federalism"; Zimmerman, *"Trends in Interstate Relations."*
17. See https://www.panynj.gov/port -authority/en/index.html.
18. "Who We Are," https://www.chesapeakebay .net/about.
19. See https://www.drjtbc.org/about/.
20. Scott, "PA House Passes Bill"; Shortell, "Tolls Across the Delaware."
21. Brand, "Rye Whiskey."
22. *Abington School District v. Schempp,* 374 U.S. 203 (1963).
23. Pennsylvania General Assembly, Abortion Control Act of 1989, P.L. 592.
24. *Planned Parenthood of Southeastern Pennsylvania v. Casey,* 505 U.S. 833 (1992).
25. Blazina; "Long Delayed REAL ID"; Chinchilla, "After Pandemic Pause"; Department of Transportation, https://www.penndot.gov.
26. Richard Thornburgh, former governor, interview by the authors, July 22, 2016; Thornburgh, *Where the Evidence Leads.*
27. Department of Community and Economic Development, https://www.newpa.com.
28. *Philadelphia v. Fox,* 64 Pa. 169 (1870).
29. Local Government Commission, *Pennsylvania Legislator's Municipal*; Department of Community and Economic Development.
30. Pennsylvania Act 223.
31. *Huntley Inc. v. Borough of Oakmont,* 964 A.2d 855 (2009); *Range Resources Appalachia LLC v Salem Township,* 964 A.2d 869, 877 (2009).

32. *Robinson Twp. v. Commonwealth*, 83 A.3d 901 (Pa. 2013); Nolon and Gavin, "Hydrofracking," 1021–26.
33. Nolon and Gavin, "Hydrofracking."
34. Local Government Commission.
35. Ibid.
36. Municipal Authorities Act, 2001.
37. Local Government Commission.
38. See https://www.pacounties.org/PAsCounties/Pages/County-Information.aspx.
39. Doug Hill, former executive director, of County Commissioners Association of Pennsylvania, interview by author June 14, 2016.
40. Ibid.
41. US Constitution, article I, section 8.
42. *Arizona v. United States*, 587 U.S. 387 (2012), https://www.oyez.org/cases/2011/11-182 (accessed January 17, 2017).
43. 8 U.S. Code, section 1158, 2006.
44. "E-Verify," https://www.uscis.gov.
45. Hazleton, PA, Ordinance 2006-18.
46. Ting, "Case for Immigration Law Enforcement."
47. *Lozano v. City of Hazleton*, 496 F. Supp. 2d 477, 554–55 (2007).
48. Jackson, "Supreme Court Denial."

BIBLIOGRAPHY

"Affordable Care Act Medicaid Expansion." Updated October 14, 2021. http://www.ncsl.org/research/health/affordable-care-act-expansion.aspx (accessed January 14, 2014).

Aliens and Nationality. 8 U.S. Code §-1158 (2006).

Anton, Thomas Julius. *American Federalism and Public Policy: How the System Works*. New York: Random House, 1989.

Blanzina, Ed. "Long Delayed REAL ID Licenses Coming to Pennsylvania." *Pittsburgh Post Gazette*, December 31, 2018. https://www.post-gazette.com/news/transportation/2018/12/31/REAL-ID-Pennsylvania-new-cards-March-airport-security-federal-buildings/stories/201812310004 (accessed March 13, 2019).

Bowman, Ann O. "Horizontal Federalism, Exploring Interstate Interactions." *Journal of Public Administration Research and Theory* 14, no. 4 (2004): 535–46.

Brandt, Anthony. "Rye Whiskey, Rye Whiskey! When Frontier Whiskey Distillers Rebelled Against a Federal Liquor Tax, President George Washington Sent an Army to Quell the Protests—and Test the Strength of the New Constitution." *American History* 49, no. 3 (August 2014). http://www.historynet.com/magazines/american_history (accessed July 12, 2017).

Byer Miller, Louise. "The Burger Court's View of the Relationship Between the States and Their Municipalities." *Publius* 17, no. 2 (Spring 1987): 85–92. http://www.jstor.org/stable/3329936 (accessed February 9, 2015).

Chinchilla, Rudy. "After Pandemic Pause, PennDOT Once Again Issuing REAL IDs." September 17, 2020. https://www.nbcphiladelphia.com/news/coronavirus/after-pandemic-pause-penndot-once-again-issuing-real-ids/2536061/ (accessed July 7, 2021).

Christensen, Robert K., and Charles R. Wise. "Dead or Alive? The Federalism Revolution and Its Meaning for Public Administration." *Public Administration Review* 69, no. 5 (September/October 2009): 920–31. doi:40468971 (accessed February 9, 2015).

Department of Community and Economic Development. https://www.newpa.com (accessed September 16, 2016).

Gormley, William T. "Money and Mandates: The Politics of Intergovernmental Conflict." *Publius* 36, no. 4 (2006): 523–54.

Hazleton, PA. "Illegal Immigration Relief Act Ordinance." Ordinance 2006–18, September 12, 2006. http://clearinghouse.wustl.edu/chDocs/public/IM-Pa.

Jackson, Kent. "Supreme Court Denial Ends City's Illegal Immigration Case." *Standard Speaker* (Hazleton), March 4, 2014. http://standardspeaker.com/news/supreme-court-denial-ends-city-s-illegal-immigration-case-1.1644100 (accessed January 18, 2017).

Katz, J. L. "After 60 Years, Most Control Is Passing to States." *Congressional Quarterly* 54, no. 31 (1996): 2190–96.

Linder, Doug. "The Supremacy Clause and Federal Preemption." Exploring Constitutional Conflicts. http://law2.umkc.edu/faculty/projects/ftrials/conlaw/preemption.htm (accessed January 12, 2017).

Local Government Commission. *Pennsylvania Legislator's Municipal Deskbook*. 4th ed.

Harrisburg, PA: Local Government Commission, 2014.

McFarland, D. J., and K. J. Meier. "Do Different Funding Mechanisms Produce Different Results? The Implications of Family Planning for Fiscal Federalism." *Journal of Health Politics, Policy and Law* 23, no. 3 (June 1998): 423–54. doi:10.1215/0361 6878-23-3-423.

Nolon, John R., and Steven E. Gavin. "Hydro-fracking: State Preemption, Local Power, and Cooperative Governance." *Case Western Reserve Law Review* 63, no. 4 (2013): 995–1039.

Pennsylvania General Assembly. Pennsylvania Oil and Gas Act (Act 223), 58 PA. CONS. STAT. ANN. § 601.602 (West 1996) (repealed 2012).

Pennsylvania General Assembly. Abortion Control Act of 1989, P.L. 592, no. 64.

Pennsylvania General Assembly. Municipal Authorities Act of 2001, P.L. 287, no. 22.

Ross, Douglas. "Safeguarding Our Federalism: Lessons for the States from the Supreme Court." *Public Administration Review* 34 (November 1985): 723–29. doi:156.12.36.144 (accessed September 23, 2015).

Scott, Andrew. "Pa. House Passes Bill to Reign in Delaware River Joint Bridge Toll Commission." *Allentown Morning Call*, April 19, 2021. https://www.mcall.com/business /transportation/mc-biz-joint-delaware -river-toll-bridges-hike-20210329-ys7tj

ptwb5cjhgjhygqutavyoi-story.html (accessed August 15, 2021).

Shortell, Tom. "Tolls Across the Delaware River on Route 22 and I-78 Will Climb Next Month." *Allentown Morning Call*, March 29, 2021. https://www.mcall.com/business/trans portation/mc-biz-joint-delaware-river-toll -bridges-hike-20210329-ys7tjptwb5cjhgj hygqutavyoi-story.html (accessed July 12, 2021).

St. George, James R. "Unfunded Mandates: A Balancing State and National Needs." *Brookings Review* 13, no. 2 (Spring 1995): 12–15. doi:10.2307/20080550 (accessed February 9, 2015).

Ting, Jan C. "The Case for Immigration Law Enforcement in the United States and in Hazleton, Pennsylvania." *Widener Law Journal* 17, no. 383 (2008): 383–90.

Thornburgh, Richard. *Where the Evidence Leads: An Autobiography.* Pittsburgh: University of Pittsburgh Press, 2010.

"Who We Are." Chesapeake Bay Program, 2021. https://www.chesapeakebay.net/about (accessed August 15, 2021).

Zimmerman, Joseph F. State-Local Relations: A Partnership Approach. 2nd ed. Westport, CT: Praeger, 1995.

———. "Trends in Interstate Relations." In State and Local Government, edited by John R. Baker. Baltimore: Lanahan Press, 2010.

CHAPTER 9

The Commonwealth of Pennsylvania

State Government Relations with Its Counties, Local Governments, and Special Districts

Pennsylvania has a long history of local government, stretching back to its colonial foundations. Citizens of the commonwealth are invested in local decision-making on issues such as land use, taxation, and education. This chapter will outline the many types of local government found in Pennsylvania and the issues related to a decentralized approach to governance and planning. The diversity of institutional structures found in Pennsylvania's local governments complicates the ability of these institutions to create fiscal policy and to deliver constituent services such as mental health care, child welfare, environmental planning, and traditional infrastructure like roads, water, and sewer. The positive aspects of citizen participation at the local level are offset by the difficulties in addressing regional issues facing the state in the twenty-first century.

Pennsylvania has the most local government units of any state in America. There are 4,678 different units of local government in the Quaker state, encompassing counties, municipal governments (both incorporated and unincorporated), and special districts, including 500 school districts.[1] Table 9.1 gives a breakdown of these local governments.

Local governments are creations of state government. Dillon's rule, a legal principle named for Iowa Supreme Court justice John F. Dillon, whose decision first pronounced it, means that local governments have limited rights and powers.[2] They are governed by state constitutions and statutes and are not covered by the US Constitution's Tenth Amendment, regarding reserved powers.[3] Pennsylvania's local governments are specifically governed by the provisions of article IX of the Pennsylvania constitution, which grants authority to the state legislature to create the types and powers of local government while also prescribing rules regarding options for alternative types of governance structures, such as home rule and optional plans, and addressing other issues such as municipal debt limits.[4] Article III of the Pennsylvania constitution classifies counties and other local governments by population.[5] The majority of the day-to-day operations of local government, however,

Table 9.1 Pennsylvania's local governments

Type	Number
First class city	1 (Philadelphia)
Second class A city	1 (Scranton)
Second class city	1 (Pittsburgh)
Third class city	53
Town	1 (Bloomsburg)
Borough	959
First class township	92
Second class township	1454
County	67
School district	500
Authority	1525 (active)

Source: *Pennsylvania Legislator's Municipal Deskbook*, 4th ed. (Harrisburg: Local Government Commission General Assembly of the Commonwealth of Pennsylvania, October 2014).

are determined by state statutes, such as county codes, borough codes, and township codes.[6] A quick overview of the types and powers of local government highlights the differences among local government in Pennsylvania.

TO HOME RULE OR NOT TO HOME RULE?

A short explanation of local government structure is needed before discussing each type of government. As noted above, state statutes or codes provide for a certain type of governance structure for each local government subdivision. However, revisions to the state's constitution in 1968 allowed the General Assembly to pass legislation permitting local governments to adopt home rule. Under the Home Rule Charter and Optional Plans law, all local governments, except Philadelphia, can either create a new form of local governance or choose from one of the optional plans. The process involves a study commission and a public referendum to approve the final plan.[7]

COUNTIES

Pennsylvania's sixty-seven counties are grouped into nine classes based upon county population. Philadelphia is the only first-class county and the only consolidated city-county. A first-class county must have a minimum population of 1.5 million to receive this designation.[8] Counties are actually subdivisions of state government, and as such they are responsible for record keeping, administration of justice, and provision of social services, such as welfare, protection of children and youth, and services for the elderly. Since the mid-1970s, counties have been authorized to take on additional activities such as land use and environmental planning, emergency response, health services, and local economic development. The default form of government is the three-person commission, with two majority commissioners and one minority commissioner. These counties typically elect numerous "row" officers, who oversee departments responsible for managing particular county functions, including district attorney, sheriff, coroner, prothonotary, and register of wills.

Counties that have chosen the home rule option design their own governance structures—for example, an elected council and elected executive (Northampton and Lehigh Counties), or an elected council and appointed county manager (Luzerne County). Home rule counties have often also opted to eliminate elected row offices in favor of appointed administrators for some or all the county offices, except for district attorney, which the state requires to remain an elected position.[9]

Because counties function as the state government's most important unit at the local level, they are faced with unique challenges and opportunities. Doug Hill, former executive director of the Pennsylvania County Commissioners Association, laid out some of the major issues facing the Keystone State's counties. He noted that counties face both structural and financial challenges. Counties are required by the commonwealth to provide certain basic services but are dependent upon the state for funding. As Mr. Hill noted, the state has not met its fiscal or statutory obligations for over a decade. An example can be found in Children and Youth Services. According to the law, counties must budget for projected needs, and the state should provide a 90 percent match to county funds. However, while county Children and Youth offices must operate on a daily basis, payments from the state come on a quarterly basis after county money has been expended. The legislature and the governor can delay payments to the counties, thereby creating the illusion of a balanced state budget, but counties must still meet payroll.

Another example can be found in mental health and intellectual disabilities services. Again, the state must provide a 90 percent match to county spending, but there have been no increases in the state's contribution for the past decade. The result is long waiting lists for treatment and services exacerbated by the opioid addiction crisis within the state.[10]

Beyond these immediate fiscal issues, Mr. Hill expounded on the pervasive structural issues related to the counties' abilities to function. Some of these issues are inherently political. He specifically cited transportation, criminal justice, and aging. While counties continue to struggle to repair roads and bridges and to fund mass transportation, $100 million from the vehicle license fund, which was expected to pay for these projects, has instead ended up funding the state police. Additionally, the criminal justice system, which includes county prisons, continues to incarcerate large numbers of nonviolent criminals, most on drug-related charges, without commensurate increases in the state's contribution.

Lastly, an aging state population has severely restricted services for the elderly while impacting the available workforce. As Mr. Hill explained, the perennial issue is "the incapacity of the state legislature to match income with expenditures."[11] These county issues require both political will and increased expenditures.

Ultimately, counties have decided that they are the best equipped to provide regional services such as emergency planning and response. Counties actually engage in planning, training, and response in keeping with the old adage that "all disasters are local." The state's role is one of coordination among the federal and state governments and the local municipalities.[12]

CITIES

Cities are corporate entities. They can own property, sue and be sued, and make contracts. Like any corporation, they exist in perpetuity.[13] Pennsylvania's cities are divided into four classes based upon population. The only first-class city in Pennsylvania is Philadelphia, followed by Pittsburgh (second class) and Scranton (second class A). The commonwealth's fifty-three remaining cities are designated as third-class cities. Philadelphia adopted a home rule charter in 1951, creating a seventeen-member council, elected by district and at-large, and an elected mayor. The city is usually classified as a strong-mayor system because the mayor appoints the managing director, who oversees the city departments, and all the other row officers, except the district attorney, who is elected separately. Pittsburgh and Scranton, likewise, have strong mayoral systems with appointment, veto, and fiscal powers.[14]

The third-class cities' default form of government under the Third-Class City Code of 1931 is the commission form, under which the mayor acts as the president of the council and each of the four commissioners leads a city department. A controller and treasurer are also elected separately, with additional officials appointed by the elected commissioners. From 1957 to 1972, the Optional Third-Class City Charter Law allowed cities to choose from two plans: the strong mayor–council form of government or the council-manager form of government.[15] Thirteen cities continue to operate under this statute, with nine cities using the strong mayor–council format, including Bethlehem, Erie, Harrisburg, and York. Other cities, such as Titusville and Lock Haven, chose the council-manager structure.

Third-class cities seeking to change their form of government are covered by the Home Rule Charter and Optional Plans Law of 1972,[16] which allows voters to elect a commission to draft their own local charter. After voter approval, the charter acts, in effect, like a local constitution. The types of local government vary greatly among the nineteen cities that have adopted charters, including strong-mayor, manager-council, and modified commissions. In addition, the law offers the optional plans to any municipality in the state.

Table 9.2 Forms of government in Pennsylvania cities

Home rule charter municipalities		
Commission	Council manager	Mayor-council
Chester, Greensburg	Clairton, Coatesville, Farrell, Franklin, Hermitage, Johnstown, Nanticoke, Pittston, St. Marys, Warren	Allentown, Altoona, Carbondale, Easton, Lebanon, McKeesport, Philadelphia, Pittsburgh, Reading, Scranton, Sharon, Wilkes-Barre

Optional plans under Act 62		Optional third class city charter law	
Council-manager	Mayor-council	Council-manager	Mayor-council
Dubois	Hazleton		Lock Haven, Bethlehem, New Castle, Meadville, Erie, Williamsport, Oil City, Harrisburg, York, Titusville, Lancaster

Third class city code
Commission
Aliquippa, Lower Burrell, Arnold, Monessen, Beaver Falls, Monongahela, Braford, New Kensington, Butler, Pottsville, Connellsville, Shamokin, Corry, Sunbury, Duquesne, Uniontown, Jeannette, Washington

Special legislation
Parker City operates under a weak mayor-council form of government established by Act 184 of 1873

Source: Department of Community and Economic Development, *Home Rule in Pennsylvania*, 10th ed. (Harrisburg: Governor's Center for Local Government Services, 2018).

However, they do not receive the same local powers as home rule. Only three municipalities have opted for the optional plans.[17]

All classes of Pennsylvania cities, but especially the third-class cities, have been buffeted by economic and social changes in the twenty-first century. The Pennsylvania Municipal League is an association advocating for Pennsylvania's third-class cities, larger boroughs, and urban townships. Executive Director Richard J. Schuettler identified the major issues confronting its membership, listing pension funding, tax-exempt properties, property tax reform, and binding labor arbitration among them.[18]

BOROUGHS

Boroughs are also incorporated entities. The default form of government for Pennsylvania's boroughs is the weak mayor–council structure, in which council members are elected to handle finances and service delivery such as streets and police protection. The mayor, whose position is largely ceremonial, votes only in the case of a tie. The council appoints a secretary and treasurer and may choose to hire a borough manager to administer day-to-day affairs. Boroughs can adopt home rule charters or choose from optional plans like cities. Boroughs may also use consolidation to change their government structure, though consolidation plans were recently voted down by both DuBois and State College Boroughs.[19]

TOWNSHIPS

Townships are municipal governments created by the state to provide local government services in unincorporated areas of the state. In theory, townships are rural in nature, but in reality many townships provide services that rival their adjacent cities and boroughs. Townships are designated as first class or second class depending upon population density. First-class townships need to reach a population density of three hundred people per square mile and require a vote of the residents to be reclassified. First-class townships operate under the commissioner form of government, with at least five elected commissioners, an elected tax collector, and an elected auditor. Townships may appoint a manager to handle daily administrative chores. The default status of Pennsylvania's townships is second class. These townships have three to five elected supervisors and an elected tax collector.[20]

First-class townships tend to operate much like their urban municipal counterparts in nearby cities and boroughs. They provide an array of services, from police and fire protection to land-use planning to recreational services. Second-class townships offer few direct services beyond road maintenance. Police protection is often provided by the state police, and planning falls to the county. But while second-class townships provide fewer services, they also have lower taxes.[21]

SPECIAL DISTRICTS

Special districts may be formed by one or more political subdivisions, such as cities, boroughs, or townships, to provide specialized services to the people in the district's area in a more cost-efficient manner than any individual government unit could deliver. Services may include water and sewer, public transit, airports, and economic development. They are usually single-purpose in nature, and they rely upon fees or loans to fund their activity rather than taxes. In fact, one of the main reasons for the creation of special districts is to circumvent the strict debt and tax limitations placed on Pennsylvania's local governments by code. Despite being created by local governments, special districts are independent legal entities. They are governed by individuals appointed to boards or commissions by local elected officials in the participating municipalities.[22]

SCHOOL DISTRICTS

School districts are also special districts, but they are tasked with a single function: public education. They are governed by nine-member elected boards whose members serve as unpaid volunteers. School boards hire a superintendent of schools, a business manager, and other administrative personnel to deliver education to students and comply with numerous federal and state mandates and regulations regarding public education. There are currently five hundred school districts in Pennsylvania, which are categorized into five classes based on population. The number of students per district ranges from just two hundred students in Austin Area in Potter County to more than one hundred and forty thousand students in Philadelphia.[23]

According to Nathan Mains, executive director of the Pennsylvania School Boards Association, Pennsylvania has a "world class education system across the state led by an incredible group of elected volunteers." He noted that these volunteer school board members are "unlike any other elected officials in the commonwealth" and include approximately 4,500 school directors, career center boards, intermediate center boards, and community college boards, who all serve without pay. However, he cautioned that the commonwealth's school districts face some major challenges, among them funding, employee pensions (more on this later), property taxes, charter schools, and consolidation of districts.[24]

The state legislature revised and adopted its funding formula, which allocates a fixed percentage of available state dollars for each school district rather than a set dollar amount. The formula is based upon a complex algorithm of student population adjusted for poverty rate and number of English as a second-language learners, plus a weight for the effect of charter schools and the local funding, which comes from property taxes. Pennsylvania's "hold harmless" provision requires that a school district cannot receive less money than in previous years, so schools with declining enrollments compete with schools with larger student populations for the same state dollars. The revised funding formula will eventually eliminate this practice, but as of the 2017–2018 fiscal year, only 7.6 percent of total education funding was distributed using the revised funding formula.[25]

While education appropriations have increased in recent budgets, state funding accounts for only about 20 percent of the actual cost of running a school district.[26] By comparison, in Vermont state funds make up 90 percent of education funding, while in New York and New Jersey state funding accounts for 40 percent of educational funding.[27] The primary source of revenue for school districts remains locally generated, primarily from property taxes. Most school districts can expect to experience shortfalls, with 70 percent of Pennsylvania's school districts operating at a deficit through 2019–20. School

School District Projections: Annual Changes in Revenues, Expenditures; Shortfall/Surplus

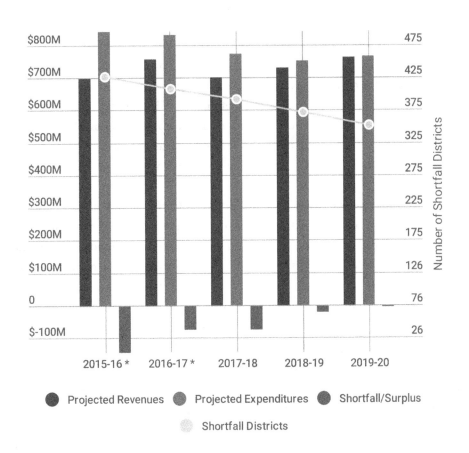

FIG. 9.1 School district projections: annual changes in revenues, expenditures; shortfall/surplus. Source: Center on Regional Politics, Temple University.

districts must operate with balanced budgets, which can be achieved by raising taxes, reducing programs, cutting teachers and staff, or all three. And while the pension burden for local districts will decrease, health-care expenses continue to increase at an estimated cost of $200 million annually.[28]

Charter schools, especially cyber schools, remain an issue both in terms of cost and performance. Because local districts are required to pay tuition for each student attending a Pennsylvania charter school, charter school expenses are currently tied with pension contributions as the second-highest expenditure for local school districts, yet charter schools are not held to the same testing and performance requirements as regular district schools.[29]

ISSUES FACING PENNSYLVANIA'S LOCAL GOVERNMENTS

In interview after interview with government officials, policy think tank analysts, local government advocacy groups, and local government managers, the same issues were repeatedly cited: the challenges of providing the best services to residents and paying for them. These issues are complicated by population growth in suburban areas, aging populations in rural areas, and structural limitations inherent in Pennsylvania's constitution and statutes. Throw in the need to meet increased federal and state mandates and the power of local identity and local political culture, and one uncovers a huge fiscal and political dilemma.

Phil Klotz, former executive director, and David Green, current executive director and former assistant director and legal counsel at the Local Government Commission, point to the slow pace of legislative change for local governments. It took eleven years to make changes to the Third-Class City Code (2003 to 2014) and fifteen months to amend the County Code, despite being initiated by county elected officials. Article IX of the Pennsylvania constitution enshrines the existing, antiquated local government structures, while home rule remains underutilized. And while the means for functional consolidation of service areas such as police, fire, water, and sewer exist, consolidations do not always result in cost savings. Councils of governments (COG's) or intergovernmental cooperation agreements can alleviate service delivery issues, but the public often complains about subsidizing other municipalities. In the end, Phil Klotz states, "The growing pains would be substantial."[30]

Analysts at the Pennsylvania Economy League (PEL), an independent nonprofit research organization, identify similar issues for local governments. In an interview with Gerald Cross, former executive director, Joseph Boyle, senior research associate, and Lynne Shedlock, communication director, they discussed the "life cycle of municipalities." Because the funding model for municipalities relies on growth in real estate tax revenues, cities, boroughs, and townships eventually reach their maximum funding capacity. Revenue sources that depend on real estate, earned income, and real estate transfer taxes remain stagnant while service demands increase. As they stated, "provision and receipt of municipal services is an accident of where you live," meaning that one might have full-time police and fire protection while neighboring communities rely on state police coverage and volunteer fire companies.[31] Eliminating such differences may rely on increased cooperation and the creation of special municipal districts that provide services, for example the solid waste compacts formed in the mid-1980s. Storm water management may provide the next opportunity for regional cooperation, but, as they suggested, people prefer their local government and feel strongly connected to it, as illustrated by their bond with the local school district sports teams.[32]

Possibly no issue has plagued the Quaker State's elected officials, policy-makers, and academics more than the ongoing pension crisis at the local level. According to a 2019 report from the Pennsylvania auditor general's office, there are 3,300 local government pension plans that cover employees in cities, boroughs, townships, special districts, and counties. Since 1974, the number of pension plans at the local level has more than doubled. Nearly 70 percent of these plans are self-insured, defined benefit plans—that is, employees are guaranteed a certain income upon retirement—for which local governments are financially responsible, guaranteeing that the benefits are received. Ninety-eight percent of Pennsylvania's pension plans are categorized as small, containing fewer than one hundred members. Seventy percent of the state's pension plans have ten or fewer members. Most municipalities establish separate pension plans for police and fire. Counties generally have one plan for all employees, ranging in size from twenty-nine members to over 7,100.[33]

The real issue, however, is not just the sheer number of pension plans in the commonwealth but the fiscal instability of these plans. As the vast majority are self-insured, they must have enough money invested in the pension plan to pay current and future retirees. As of 2018, municipal pension plans had unfunded liabilities of 8.8 billion dollars, while counties had unfunded liabilities of $1.6 billion. Act 44 of 2009 requires that municipal pension plans be rated on a point scale from 0 to 3 according to their level of unfunded liability. Examining the ratings, plans range between those that are not distressed (funded at 90 percent or more) to those severely distressed (less than 50 percent funded). Plans that are rated 1 (minimally distressed) can participate in voluntary fixes such as requirements for total member contributions or increased contributions from the municipality. Moderately and severely distressed plans must take mandatory actions such as revising

Table 9.3. Local government pension plans

	Police	Fire	Nonuniformed	Total
County	0	0	71	71
City	59	45	65	169
Borough	462	22	610	1,094
First class township	89	6	122	217
Second class township	301	10	890	1,201
Authority	0	0	515	515
Regional	34	3	26	63
Total	945	86	2,299	3,330

Source: PA Auditor General. Eugene A. DePasquale, Susan Hockenberry, Mary Soderberg, and Janet Yeomans, "Pennsylvania's Municipal Pension Challenges" (2015). http://www.paauditor.gov/Media/Default/Print /2015/FINAL_Pension_Taskforce_Report_June%2030_FINAL2.pdf (accessed December 4, 2021).

their benefit plans for new hires or aggregating all pensions funds for administration and investment purposes. For example, new hires may take longer to be vested in the plan.[34]

School District Pension Plans

The fiscal outlook for school district pension obligations is based more on long-term contractual obligations than fund management. All teacher pension funds are managed by the Pennsylvania Public Schools Employees' Retirement System (PSERS). Districts are responsible for contributing to PSERS based upon individually negotiated contracts within each school district. As of 2018, PSERS is 56.3 percent funded, with an unfunded liability of $44.5 billion. PSERS's troubles lie with school districts and the commonwealth underfunding pension programs in the early 2000s, coupled with the effects of the Great Recession in 2008. The vast majority of the unfunded debt (75 percent) is the result of previously accrued pension obligations. As of 2017, school districts are now fully funding their current pension obligations. Act 5 of 2017 further addresses the pension problem by modifying the types of pension plans available to new members to include a mix of defined benefit and defined contribution plans.[35]

Pension Solutions

With the passage of Act of 2009, the total number of distressed pension plans has dropped slightly since 2014. But what are the real answers to this long-term drag on municipal and school district finances? The Governor's Task Force on Municipal Pension Plans and Temple University's Center on Regional Politics have made some specific recommendations for change. These include increasing transparency and accountability of the current pension plans and reforming past pension fund obligations, strike such as by shifting these plans to a shared benefits manager. Nationally, reforms have included increasing employee contributions, moving toward defined contribution plans, and changing the way in which members are vested or extending the retirement age.[36] Pennsylvania's Act 5 is the first step in adopting long-term reforms that will eventually lower the burden of pension costs for the commonwealth's taxpayers.

THE FUTURE OF PENNSYLVANIA'S LOCAL GOVERNMENTS

Pennsylvania's local governments remain under fiscal stress due to declining populations and changing demographics. Issues such as infrastructure, taxes, opioid and heroin addiction, and service delivery to an aging population will continue to plague Pennsylvania's numerous local governments but will be especially stressful for rural entities. Pennsylvania's constitutional mechanisms and current state law do not make it easy for local government consolidation. Citizens do not favor losing their local identity, yet they tend to oppose increasing their tax burden. Informal cooperation and innovation at the lowest level of government may be the best answer to Pennsylvania's local government challenges. Scores of local nonprofits and community foundations, along with school district–based outreach programs, seek to address the social issues faced by local government. Barring a major shift in state politics, local governments will continue to be a powerful interest group in Harrisburg and the strongest political and social identity for the commonwealth's residents.[37]

NOTES

1. Local Government Commission, *Pennsylvania Legislator's Municipal.*
2. *City of Clinton v. Cedar Rapids and Missouri Railroad*, 24 Iowa 455 (1868).
3. Ibid.; Smith and Greenblatt, *Governing States and Localities.*
4. PA constitution, article IX.
5. PA constitution, article III, section 20.
6. Local Government Commission.
7. 53 Pa.C.S. § 2901 et seq.
8. County Code, 1955.
9. Local Government Commission, *Pennsylvania Legislator's Municipal*; Department of Community and Economic Development, *Citizen's Guide*; League of Women Voters, *Key to the Keystone.*
10. Doug Hill, former executive director, of County Commissioners Association of Pennsylvania, interview by author June 14, 2016.
11. Ibid.
12. Ibid.
13. Smith and Greenblatt, *Governing States and Localities.*
14. Local Government Commission, *Pennsylvania Legislator's Municipal*; Department of Community and Economic Development, *Citizen's Guide*; League of Women Voters, *Key to the Keystone.*
15. 53 P.S. § 41101 et seq.
16. 53 Pa.C.S. § 2901 et seq.
17. Department of Community and Economic Development, *Citizen's Guide*; Department of Community and Economic Development, *City Government*; Local Government Commission, *Pennsylvania Legislator's Municipal*; League of Women Voters, *Key to the Keystone.*
18. Richard J. Schuettler (executive director of the Pennsylvania Municipal League), interview with authors, August 3, 2015, by phone.
19. Department of Community and Economic Development, *Citizen's Guide*; Department of Community and Economic Development,

Home Rule; League of Women Voters, *Key to the Keystone.*
20. Department of Community and Economic Development, *Citizen's Guide*; League of Women Voters, *Key to the Keystone*; Local Government Commission, *Pennsylvania Legislator's Municipal.*
21. Ibid.
22. 1 PA.C.S. § 1991; Local Government Commission, *Pennsylvania Legislator's Municipal.*
23. Pennsylvania Department of Education, https://www.education.pa.gov; Public School Code of 1949.
24. Mains, interview.
25. Pennsylvania Basic Education Funding Commission, *Basic Education Funding*; House Appropriation Committee (D).
26. Hartman and Schrom, "Tale of the Haves."
27. Maciag, "States That Spend."
28. Hartman and Schrom, "Hard Choices Still Ahead"; Hartman and Schram, "Tale of the Haves."
29. Mains Interview; Hartman and Schram "tale of the Have." Nathan Mains, CEO, Pennsylvania School Boards Association Interview by author, Februray 17, 2017.
30. Philip H. Klotz (former director of the Local Government Commission) and David Green (staff member), interview with the authors, August 5, 2015.
31. Gerald Cross (executive director of the Pennsylvania Economy League), Joseph Boyle (PEL staff member), and Lynne Shedlock (PEL staff member), interview with authors, August 10, 2015, in the office of the Pennsylvania Economy League, Wilkes-Barre, PA.
32. Ibid.
33. Auditor general, *Status Report.*
34. Ibid.; Preveti and Lazarski, "Mapping Out Pennsylvania's Distressed."

35. Esack, "From Boom to Bust"; PSERS, *On Point Budget*; Act 5, 2017.
36. Center on Regional Politics, "Problem of Funding Pensions"; DePasquale et al.,

"Pennsylvania's Municipal Pension."
37. Schuetter, interview; Klotz and Green, interview; Cross, Boyle, and Shedlock, interview.

BIBLIOGRAPHY

Act 5 of 2017. Amendments Education (24 PA.C.S.), Military and Veterans Code (51 PA.C.S.) and State Government (71 PA.C.S.)—Omnibus Amendments, P.L. 11, no. 5.

Act 44 of 2009. Municipal Pension Plan Funding Standard and Recovery Act, P.L. 396, no. 44.

Auditor General. *Status Report on Local Government Pension Plans in Pennsylvania*. Harrisburg: Municipal Pension Reporting Program, 2019.

Center on Regional Politics. "The Problem of Funding Pensions: An Update." No. 4, June 2016. Philadelphia: Temple University Center on Regional Politics.

County Code. Act 130 of 1955.

Department of Community and Economic Development. *A Citizen's Guide to Pennsylvania Local Government*. 11th ed. Harrisburg: Governor's Center for Local Government Services, 2018.

———. *City Government in Pennsylvania Handbook*. 3rd ed. Harrisburg: Governor's Center for Local Government Services, 2013.

———. *Home Rule in Pennsylvania*. 10th ed. Harrisburg: Governor's Center for Local Government Services, 2018.

DePasquale, Eugene A., Susan Hockenberry, Mary Soderberg, and Janet Yeomans. "Pennsylvania's Municipal Pension Challenges." 2015. http://www.paauditor.gov/Media/Default /Print/2015/FINAL_Pension_Taskforce _Report_June%2030_FINAL2.pdf (accessed December 4, 2021).

Esack, Steve. "From Boom to Bust: A Timeline of Pennsylvania's Public Pension Systems." *Allentown Morning Call*, January 10, 2019. https://www.mcall.com/news/nation world/pennsylvania/mc-nws-pennsylvania -pension-time-line-20190110-story.html (accessed April 13, 2019).

Hartman, William, and Timothy J. Schrom. "Hard Choices Still Ahead: The Financial Future of Pennsylvania's School Districts." Philadelphia: Temple University Center on Regional Politics, March 2017.

———. "A Tale of the Haves and Have Nots: The Financial Future of Pennsylvania's School Districts." Philadelphia: Temple University

Center on Regional Politics, January 2019.

Home Rule Charter and Optional Plans Law Act 62 of 1972. 53 Pa.C.S. § 2901 et seq.

League of Women Voters. *Key to the Keystone State, Pennsylvania*. University Park: Pennsylvania State University Press, 1989.

Local Government Commission. *Pennsylvania Legislator's Municipal Deskbook*. 4th ed. Harrisburg: Pennsylvania General Assembly, 2014.

Maciag, Michael. "States That Spend the Most (and the Least) on Education." *Governing*, June 3, 2019. https://www.governing.com/archive /gov-state-education-spending-revenue-data .html (accessed December 4, 2021).

Markosek, Joe. "PA's Fair Funding Formula Explained." http://www.pahouse.com/Files/Documents /Appropriations/series/3013/BEFC_BP _011018.pdf (accessed January 10, 2018).

"Municipal Statistics." https://dced.pa.gov/local -government/municipal-statistics (accessed May 21, 2018).

Optional Third Class City Charter Law. Act 399 of 1957, 53 P.S. § 41101 et seq.

Pennsylvania Basic Education Funding Commission. *Basic Education Funding Commission Report and Recommendation*. Harrisburg: Pennsylvania Department of Education, June 18, 2015.

Pennsylvania Public Schools Employees' Retirement System (PSERS). *On Point Budget Report Highlights, 2018–2019*. https://www.psers.pa .gov (accessed October 13, 2019).

Preveti, Emily, and Lindsay Lazarski. "Mapping out Pennsylvania's Distressed Municipal Pension Plans." April 9, 2015. https://whyy.org/articles /mapping-out-pennsylvanias-distressed-muni cipal-pension-plans (accessed March 11, 2019).

Public School Code of 1949. Act of March 10, 1949, P.L. 30 no. 14.

Smith, Kevin, and Alan Greenblatt. *Governing States and Localities*. Thousand Oaks, CA: CQ Press, 2014.

Third Class City Code. Act 317 of 1931, § 203.1, 53 P.S. § 35203.1. https://pennreporter.wordpress .com/city-council/third-class-city (accessed May 22, 2018).

CHAPTER 10

Pennsylvania Politics in the Time of a Pandemic and a Presidential Election

In January 2019, the world first learned of COVID-19, a highly contagious, deadly virus. As the pathogen spread in the following months, governments at all levels—national, state, and local—mobilized to limit its transmission, treat those infected, and, when a vaccine became available, administer it expeditiously to as many people as possible. Concurrently, the United States was in the throes of an unusually heated presidential election that began with a multicandidate Democratic primary and ended with an unprecedented general election in which the incumbent president and his followers contested the outcome.

These two events occurred in a political environment poisoned by sectarian partisanship. Recalling the discussion in chapter 3, the distance between Republicans and Democrats in the electorate had been expanding to Grand Canyon dimensions since 2010, leaving the opposing sides exhibiting such visceral animosity that finding common ground on any subject was nearly impossible. Traditional political partisanship had devolved into sectarian partisanship, creating a toxic political atmosphere.

But conducting elections and responding to emergencies are basic services that citizens expect their governments to deliver. Pennsylvania's government had routinely managed federal, state, and local elections without serious disagreements over their procedures or results. Similarly, during floods, snowstorms, or catastrophes like the Three Mile Island incident, the government had mobilized in response as its parties and citizens united in support of the governor's leadership, placing the community's needs over those of individual citizens and partisan interests. Even during periods of divided government, the parties and the branches had operated to conduct elections and manage crises. The responses to the COVID pandemic and the 2020 presidential election, however, were decidedly less than harmonious and distinctively dysfunctional.

Complicating a coherent, routine government response to the pandemic and the presidential election was President Donald J. Trump, who initially downplayed COVID-19's severity and questioned Pennsylvania's election rules and procedures. Prior to the November election, Trump claimed without evidence that his victory in the Keystone State would be stolen from him because tens of thousands of illegal votes would be cast for Biden and many of Trump's votes would be invalidated by rigged voting machines. Trump and his followers repeated his "Big Lie" at every opportunity after November 3, claiming that the election had been stolen from Trump and that Pennsylvania's twenty electoral votes would have been his if not been for the chicanery of Democratic politicians and the judges who conspired against him.

The pandemic and the presidential election strained Pennsylvania's institutions' ability to operate efficiently and effectively in 2020. The General Assembly, the executive branch—the governor and the secretaries of Health and State—and the courts were pressured to handle the health emergency and the election in ways that favored partisan interests rather than those of the entire commonwealth. The stress placed on the political system resulted in the branches often appearing to work at cross-purposes and scrambling to justify their actions.

Because we believe that institutions matter, that how they are structured and how they operate affect public policy, it is imperative that we understand the response of Pennsylvania's institutions to the twin trials of a health emergency and divisive election. In searching for explanations, we turned to Madison's *Federalist Papers* No. 10 and No. 51, in which he argued that infusing the three branches of the federal government with separate and overlapping powers created a system of checks and balances that prevents the government from abusing the people's liberties while protecting the government from itself. Madison described how those holding positions in each branch would be driven by their personal ambitions to use their offices' constitutional powers to defend their respective branches against attempted encroachments by other branches. He assumed that this would prevent one branch from dominating the others.

If one applies Madison's logic—the Madison Model—to Pennsylvania in 2020 and beyond, one could explain the General Assembly's resistance to the governor's emergency disaster declarations as a collective effort by its members to preserve the assembly's voice in the government's operation. Similarly, when the legislature challenged state court decisions in *federal* court that permitted the adjustment of voting rules by the secretary of state to accommodate the pandemic, the assembly claimed that it was protecting its constitutional authority to determine voting procedures. Likewise, the governor's refusal to release information to the General Assembly about the criteria used to grant exemptions to business closures and the extent of COVID-19 fatalities in nursing homes were examples of the executive branch defending its power to carry out its duties in an emergency.

But what if the defenses offered by the General Assembly and governor were less about maintaining their constitutional authority and more about retaining power for partisan reasons, which we label the Partisan Model? One could argue that by weakening the governor and the states' courts, Republicans in the legislature hoped to recapture the governorship and gain a majority on the state's high court. Likewise, the governor's resistance to legislative requests for information may have been intended to shield the next

Democratic gubernatorial candidate from attacks by a Republican opponent on Governor Wolf's response to the pandemic.

While the federal government and other states' governments were also dealing with the same problems that pitted executive against legislative branches, Pennsylvania's experience was distinctive, as we demonstrate in the following pages. Governmental institutions under stress reveal their best and worst features when elected and appointed leaders confront legal, moral, and ethical questions.

PRE-PANDEMIC POLITICAL LANDSCAPE

Entering 2020, the Quaker State's government was divided, with Republicans holding majorities in both chambers of the General Assembly: 110 Republicans and 93 Democrats in the House, and 28 Republicans, one Independent who caucused with the GOP, and 21 Democrats in the Senate. Republicans also held seven of the nine seats on the Commonwealth Court. Meanwhile, the governor, lieutenant governor, attorney general, treasurer, and auditor general were all Democrats, as were five of the seven justices of the Supreme Court. (The Superior Court was not significantly involved in these issues.)

In 2016, Democrats swept the elected executive offices—attorney general, treasurer, and auditor general—with no winner receiving more than 51 percent of the popular vote. These positions were up for grabs again in 2020. Governor Wolf won reelection in 2018, defeating Republican Scott Wagner 58 percent to 41 percent. Referring to figure 5.1, approximately 42 percent of Pennsylvanians approved of Wolf's performance in office in October 2021, lower than his high point of 52 percent in July 2020, suggesting that the public was unsatisfied with the governor's management of the pandemic and the state's slow economic expansion.

Governor Wolf and the General Assembly's GOP leadership frequently disagreed about annual budget and appropriations bills, school funding, the use of federal COVID relief funds, and other matters, but they did manage to find common ground to address the opioid epidemic and to repair the state's election laws with the passage of Act 77 of 2019, discussed in chapter 3.

With a divided government, a lame-duck governor, and an economy slowly recovering from the severe blow it suffered during the Great Recession, Republicans and Democrats prepared for a full slate of primary and general elections with the presidency at the top of the ballot, US congressional elections, the entire state House and half of the state Senate, and the three executive offices all occurring under Act 77's new rules. The venomous political environment, already a noxious cauldron nearly boiling over, augured an exceptionally ugly 2020 campaign season, with the incumbent president stirring in unsupported accusations about his opponent's business interests and unfounded claims of fraud and corruption in the nation's and Pennsylvania's electoral processes. As the new year began, however, few could foresee how everything would change when the World Health Organization (WHO) announced on January 9, 2020, that a coronavirus-related pneumonia had appeared in Wuhan, China. The CDC revealed on January 21 that the United States had its first COVID-19 case. On January 31, the WHO issued a global health emergency, followed by the Trump administration's pronouncement on February 3 of a US health emergency. On March 11, the WHO officially proclaimed COVID-19 a pandemic. Two days later the Trump administration declared a national health emergency and imposed a ban on all non-US citizens traveling into the United States from twenty-six countries.

In the next two sections, we consider the pandemic and the 2020 presidential election separately. Rather than describe in detail specific events that occurred over two years, in appendices C, D, E, and F we provide chronologies of actions and decisions taken by each branch. The tables do not list every action or decision but rather those that were, in our opinion, significant to the flow of events or illustrative of a branch's pattern of behavior.

THE PANDEMIC

Governor Wolf's emergency disaster declaration on March 6, 2020, officially put Pennsylvanians on notice that the state was mobilizing to confront COVID-19. According to the Emergency Powers Act of 1978, the governor had the authority to issue emergency declarations that have the force of law, including limiting the sale of alcohol and firearms, imposing travel restrictions, and suspending state regulations.[1] In May 2021, Pennsylvanians approved two constitutional amendments that limited these emergency powers to twenty-one days, unless extended by the General Assembly. Previously, the governor's declarations were effective for sixty days.[2]

Wolf renewed the disaster declaration five more times. The public's initial reaction was resigned acceptance, as news from places hard hit by the virus, like New York City, made the seriousness of the contagion a reality. A week later, the governor ordered schools to be closed temporarily, only to extend the closure for the remainder of the school year. Then, on March 19, Wolf issued a stay-at-home order for all nonessential workers, essentially closing all private business and government offices until further notice. Despite the severity of the restrictions, there was little resistance to the governor's actions from the General Assembly.

The first indications of defiance by the legislature began in late April 2020, when it passed, mostly along party lines, a series of bills allowing small businesses to reopen after their owners had been denied a designation as essential businesses after seeking such approval from the Wolf administration. They complained to their state legislators that the Wolf administration's criteria for exempt status were opaque, arbitrarily applied, or unnecessary. Thereafter, through April 2021, the General Assembly's GOP leadership continued to introduce and pass bills, with little or no Democratic support, to overturn elements of

Wolf's emergency disaster declaration, only to have the governor veto them. The General Assembly failed to override any veto.

The legislature's efforts to remove the emergency declaration continued even as Wolf announced steps to reopen the state's businesses gradually. The most serious legislative measure came in July 2020 with passage, along straight party-line votes, of several constitutional amendments whose purpose was to give lawmakers the authority to end any emergency declaration by a simple majority vote without possibility of a governor's veto. In May 2021, two amendments passed with 52 percent of the vote but what was actually equivalent to about 13.5 percent of all registered Pennsylvanians. The General Assembly ended the emergency on June 10, with twelve House Democrats and no Senate Democrats voting in support.

With the success of their amendment to restrict the governor's emergency powers, Republican legislative leaders began the process of placing many more amendments before the voters. Designed to limit the governor's authority to issue executive orders and regulations, the amendments would grant the legislature the power, by majority vote only and without the possibility of veto, to strike down executive orders and regulations within twenty-one days of issuance (see appendix D).

Efforts by the GOP to have Pennsylvania's Supreme Court find Wolf's emergency disaster declaration unconstitutional were unsuccessful. On April 13, 2020, the high court unanimously upheld the governor's constitutional authority to issue emergency declarations, and the US Supreme Court declined to hear the appeal of *Friends of Danny DeVito, et al. v. Wolf and Levine*. A case filed in federal district court, *County of Butler, et al. v. Wolf*, challenging the governor's emergency powers went against the governor, but on appeal the Third Circuit overturned the lower court's decision. Another suit, this one filed by student athletes, was filed in federal district court, but the judge dismissed it (see appendix C).

Pennsylvania's Supreme Court was again involved in pandemic-related litigation when the General Assembly passed a concurrent resolution to end the emergency disaster declaration on June 10, 2020, with twelve Democrats joining all Republicans. The GOP leadership refused to send the resolution to the governor, claiming the concurrent resolution did not require any action by him. The Wolf administration appealed to the Supreme Court (see appendix C), which voted 5–2 along party lines and declared that concurrent resolutions *do* require an action from the governor.

A series of spikes in COVID-19 infection rates began in the winter of 2020, but the vaccine's arrival in early 2021 brought some relief. Resistance to the vaccine, however, contributed to virus's spread among the unvaccinated. In an attempt to slow the contagion, Wolf and acting Secretary of Health Alison Beam issued health warnings. In August 2021, Wolf asked the Republican legislative leaders to pass a mask mandate for all schoolchildren, but they refused. Acting Secretary Beam then issued a mask mandate for children in all schools, K-12, and all pre-K and child care centers. Several suits were filed in Commonwealth

Court (see appendix C) challenging the constitutionality of Beam's orders. A five-judge panel of the Commonwealth Court voted 4–1 (the dissenting judge was a Democrat) that Beam did not have the authority to issue the mandate under the 1955 Disease Prevention and Control Act. On appeal, the state's Supreme Court upheld the lower court's decision (see appendix C).

Considering the behavior of the three branches in this matter, we believe the partisan model provides the better explanation for what occurred. The lopsided partisan votes in both chambers of the General Assembly against a governor of the opposing party, as well as the partisan votes in the appellate courts, strongly suggest that the motivating force was attaining or holding political advantage rather than preserving constitutional authority. In addition, the GOP's strategy of proposing constitutional amendments to limit the governor's powers and to elect appellate judges and justices by district (see below), and threatening impeachment of Democratic justices on the Supreme Court, cannot be interpreted any other way than how Governor Wolf described it: "a naked power grab" by Republicans, and hence a strictly partisan endeavor.[3] Since January 2022, the Republican-controlled General Assembly has introduced at least fifteen amendments that would, if approved, significantly weaken the executive branch's powers, particularly the governor's, and undermine the independence of the state's appellate courts.

THE 2020 PRESIDENTIAL ELECTION

Because elections by their very nature are partisan affairs, explicating the branches' decisions during this particular election is challenging. In recent history, processing and counting ballots had become routinized, professionalized, and depoliticized. One expects controversy to surround candidates and their campaigns, but not necessarily ballots and how and where they can be cast and counted. Nevertheless, the disputes that arose in 2020 were mostly over technical issues that previously would not have drawn scrutiny or been challenged.

The 2020 presidential election in Pennsylvania and the nation might not have devolved into a series of skirmishes fought among the three branches had it not been for the inflammatory public statements made by President Trump, but we will never know. We can, however, set aside President Trump's role in the matter as much as possible and focus instead on what happened in the Keystone State.

Recall that the General Assembly passed Act 77 of 2019 with overwhelming support from both parties and the governor. Touted as modernizing Pennsylvania's elections, the bill allowed, among other reforms, anyone to vote by mail for any reason. The presidential primary was the first scheduled to take place under the Act but was postponed from April until June due to the pandemic. Many voters took advantage of the mail ballot option, causing county election offices to scramble to meet the demand. Though there were some small glitches, the primary was successful. As county election offices prepared for the general election, they asked the legislature to allow for precanvassing of mailed ballots and clarification on the use of drop boxes. The General Assembly failed to act on their requests, leaving Secretary of State Boockvar to provide guidance, which she did by extending the deadline to receive mailed ballots and approving the use of drop boxes. Republican lawmakers then acted quickly to reverse the secretary's directions by introducing a number of bills to amend Act 77 to limit the use of drop boxes while also requiring more stringent identification criteria to vote. Bills that cleared the General Assembly were passed on straight party-line votes, only to be vetoed (see appendix E).

The GOP then went to the courts—state and federal—beginning in September 2020. In case after case, the Pennsylvania Supreme Court's five (and sometimes four) Democratic justices ruled against the Republicans, occasionally overturning decisions by the Republican-dominated Commonwealth Court. In federal courts, the GOP fared no better, regardless of which president had appointed the judges (see appendix C).

The Democratic Party, however, was more successful in its litigation when Pennsylvania's highest court approved a revised deadline for the acceptance of mailed ballots, the use of drop boxes, and the requirement that poll watchers reside in the county in which they observe. The party failed to convince the court to approve counting third party–delivered ballots (which Republicans derisively call "ballot harvesting") and "naked" ballots, those ballots arriving without a security envelope.

After the November 3 election, the pace of litigation increased dramatically, as Pennsylvania Republicans and the Trump campaign sought to reverse *only* the presidential election's outcome, as Republicans won two of three statewide offices and increased their majority in the House while maintaining their margin in the Senate. The GOP raised no objections to races where they were victorious. In all but one of their suits, Republicans lost their challenges, with the one victory occurring in the matter of the positioning of partisan observers counting Philadelphia's votes.

Failing in the courts, the GOP's legislative leaders held a series of hearings and investigations, searching for possible voter fraud, voting equipment malfunctioning or tampering, and malfeasance by election workers (see appendix E). As of publication, no evidence of fraud or abuse has been discovered, though three men were caught and pleaded guilty to fraud for casting a deceased relative's mail-in ballot for Trump. A "forensic audit" of the presidential vote of all sixty-seven counties was initiated in the Senate, but Democrats challenged this, and as of publication no findings have been released.

Utilizing a strategy that had succeeded for them in dealing with the governor's pandemic management, Republicans began the constitutional amendment process to eliminate no-excuse mailed ballots, to require voters to present identification (type unspecified) when voting in person or when requesting an absentee ballot for a constitutionally specified reason, and to elect all appellate judges and justices by districts. The latter would allow the legislature to gerrymander judicial districts to ensure that the majority party would win a majority of seats on the three appellate courts, but especially the Supreme Court.

Once again, we think that the partisan model offers a more plausible explanation for the institutions' actions than the Madisonian. Both parties used their offices—for the Democrats, the executive branch and Supreme Court, and for the Republicans, the legislature—to either defend the presidential election's result or overturn it. Failing to persuade the vast majority of the appellate judges and justices at the state and federal levels that heard their cases, Republicans sought to amend Pennsylvania's constitution. By our count since January 2022, at least fifteen amendments targeting elections have been introduced by Republicans. In our minds, this is a clearly partisan tactic employed to retain the GOP's legislative majority, retake the governorship, and gain a majority of seats on all three appellate benches. Scant evidence suggests that either party intended to preserve the constitutional independence of any branch, though the Democrats' efforts to resist Republican attempts to throw out tens of thousands or even millions of legally cast ballots because of rumors of fraud were appropriate given the lack of evidence of election fraud.

CONCLUSION

Pennsylvania's experience managing the pandemic and a complicated presidential election was not unique. Other states, many with divided governments, also faced these challenges, but no other state's drama played out exactly as it did in Pennsylvania. Obviously, the Quaker State's cast of characters was different, as were the tactics they chose, the resources available, the closely divided citizenry, and the tools Pennsylvania's constitution made available to them. The state's institutions—and the actors within them—each contributed to the outcomes discussed in these pages. For example, Pennsylvania's seven-member Supreme Court, with a five-to-two Democratic majority, exercised its constitutional authority to mostly support the governor's decisions dealing with the virus and those of the secretary of state when advising county election officers on how to run an election during a pandemic. Had the partisan balance favored Republicans, the court's rulings might have been different, resulting in drastically different outcomes. Likewise, if the governor's emergency powers were less expansive, the legislature might have assumed a leadership position managing the pandemic. We could speculate different scenarios, but our point is that institutions matter. In a crisis, institutional stability, dependability, and continuity are vital and expected; learning from past experiences, one of the features of an institution, is essential if societies dependent on institutions are to function during crises. Without institutional memory, governments are doomed to fritter away valuable time as they devise solutions that failed in the past. The performance of Pennsylvania's governmental institutions during difficult times raises serious questions about their fitness to deliver basic, routine services under "normal" conditions.

We leave the reader with a series of questions to consider about Pennsylvania's political system, based on observations gleaned from our combined eighty-five years of experience studying politics and governments.

To what lengths should the state's representatives and senators go to meet their constituents' demands when those demands are without merit, are based on false information, or would cause a majority of the state's residents harm?

Should the constitutional amendment process be used by one party controlling the legislature to circumvent a governor's veto? More generally, should the amending process be employed to address a problem that could otherwise be resolved through negotiation between the parties? Is Pennsylvania's amending process too easy? Should it be amended to make it more difficult to initiate and pass amendments?

Are the governor's powers under an emergency disaster declaration too broad? Are they too ambiguous? Should the issuance of an emergency disaster declaration require action by both the governor and the General Assembly?

How much more transparency should be expected and required of governors and the legislature when making decisions? Are current sunshine laws sufficient to satisfy citizens, interest groups, and journalists who have access to contemporary technological devices and social media?

When the state's constitution is silent or vague on matters dealing with elections, how far can the state's courts go in either expanding or contracting voters' rights? Should courts be able to use an emergency as justification to expand or constrict the powers of another branch?

What are the ethical and moral responsibilities of political parties to speak factually at all times about public issues? Do party leaders bear any responsibility to all of Pennsylvania's residents for the ethical and moral behavior their members?

When seeking favorable treatment from government, do special interest groups have any responsibility to consider the harm that achieving their objectives might have on a majority of the state's people?

Do political journalists have a responsibility to provide accurate, objective information in the face of challenges from those in office who question journalists' legitimacy, competence, and professional practices? When those holding positions of authority in government lie or dissemble in their public statements, what is a journalist's responsibility, if any, to correct the statements and to identify the statements as lies or falsehoods? In an age of journalists as celebrities, what is their responsibility, if any, to challenge those in power as well as their audience? What duty do journalists have, if any, to uphold and protect democratic values?

Regardless of how the reader decides to answer these questions, we hope that we have provoked the reader to think critically about Pennsylvania's political system. We believe that those interested in improving the Keystone State should ask their own questions of elected and appointed government officials and challenge them and hold them responsible for their behavior.

NOTES

1. PA Code 35, chapter 73.
2. Associated Press, "Pennsylvania Becomes 1st in Nation to Curb." https://www.marketwatch.com/story/pennsylvania-becomes-1st-in-nation-to-curb-governors-emergency-powers-01621451442.
3. Finnerty, "Capitolwire."

BIBLIOGRAPHY

Albiges, Marie. "GOP Seeks More Control over Courts." *Philadelphia Inquirer*, January 14, 2021.

———. "Pa. Could Become Outlier on How Judges Are Elected." *Philadelphia Inquirer*, February 5, 2021.

Associated Press. "Pennsylvania Becomes 1st in Nation to Curb Governor's Emergency Powers." May 19, 2021. https://www.marketwatch.com/story/pennsylvania-becomes-1st-in-nation-to-curb-governors-emergency-powers-01621451442.

———. "State Lawmakers Vote for Package of 5 Constitutional Amendments." *Citizens' Voice*, December 15, 2021.

Barry, Ellen. "Pennsylvania Bans Alcohol Sales on One of the Busiest Nights of the Year." *New York Times*, November 25, 2020.

Caletati, Jessica. "GOP Mostly Mum on Vaccine Hesitancy." *Philadelphia Inquirer*, May 6, 2021.

Caruso, Stephen. "In Late Night Debate, House Votes to Undo Wolf's Emergency Declaration." *PA Capital-Star*, May 29, 2020.

Corasanti, Nick. "Pennsylvania Court Says State's Mail Voting Law Is Unconstitutional." *New York Times*, January 28, 2022.

Coston, Ethan Edward. "Vetoes v. Constitutional Amendments." *Philadelphia Inquirer*, January 17, 2022.

Couloumbis, Angela. "Auditor Calls Waiver Program Inconsistent." *Philadelphia Inquirer*, October 7, 2020.

———. "ELECTION: Pa. Could Be Challengers' 'Ground Zero.'" *Philadelphia Inquirer*, October 19, 2020.

———. "LEGAL DRAMA: As Trump's chances Dwindle, GOP Targets Top Election Officials." *Philadelphia Inquirer*, November 7, 2020.

———. "Pa. Businesses Are Challenging Wolf's Emergency Powers. So Far, Governor Is Winning." *Pittsburgh Post-Gazette*, March 25, 2020.

———. "Pa. Lawmaker Tests Positive." *Philadelphia Inquirer*, May 28, 2020.

Couloumbis, Angela, and Cynthia Fernandez. "GOP Bars Senator, Ousts Fetterman." *Philadelphia Inquirer*, January 6, 2021.

———. "GOP v. Wolf: A Year of Acrimony." *Philadelphia Inquirer*, February 4, 2021.

Couloumbis, Angela, and Sam Janesch. "Pa. Legislature's Redacted Legal Bills Flout Court Ruling, Leaving Taxpayers Guessing." *Philadelphia Inquirer*, January 11, 2022.

Fernandez, Cynthia. "EMERGENCY: GOP and Some Democrat Lawmakers Approve Resolution to End It." *Philadelphia Inquirer*, June 11, 2020.

———. "High Court Says Legislature Can't End Wolf's Disaster Declaration." *Philadelphia Inquirer*, July 2, 2020.

———. "Pa. GOP Aims to Limit Wolf's Authority." *Philadelphia Inquirer*, January 14, 2021.

———. "Pa. House Bill on Voting Advances." *Philadelphia Inquirer*, September 2, 2020.

Finnerty, John. "Capitolwire: Republicans Propose Constitutional Changes to Limit Executive Orders." Capitolwire.com, November 10, 2021. https://www.senatoraument.com/2021/11/10/capitolwire-republicans-propose-constitutional-changes-to-limit-executive-orders.

Gabrielle, Trip. "Even in Defeat, Trump Tightens Grip on State GOP Lawmakers." *New York Times*, December 9, 2020.

———. "GOP Defiance of Pennsylvania's Lockdown Has 2020 Implication." *New York Times*, May 14, 2020.

———. "A GOP Lawmaker Had the Virus. Nobody Told Democrats Exposed to Him." *New York Times*, May 28, 2020.

———. "Pennsylvania GOP Refuses to Seat Democrat Lawmaker in State Legislature." *New York Times*, January 5, 2021.

Gardner, Amy, Josh Dawsey, and Rachel Bade. "Trump Asks Pennsylvania House Speaker for Help Overturning Election Results, Personally Intervening in Third State." *Washington Post*, December 7, 2020.

Hanna, Maddie. "Pa. Mask Mandate Fails to Quiet Rancor." *Philadelphia Inquirer*, September 5, 2021.

Helderman, Rosalind S. "It Was Like This Rogue Thing: How the Push by Trump Allies to Undermine the 2020 Election Results Through Ballot Reviews Started Quietly in Pennsylvania." *Washington Post*, June 6, 2021.

Hughes, Sarah Anne. "Voters Back Curtailing Governor's Emergency Powers." *Philadelphia Inquirer*, May 20, 2021.

Hughes, Sarah Anne, and Marie Albiges. "Senator Backs Election Audit." *Philadelphia Inquirer*, June 19, 2021.

Jaafari, Joseph Darius. "Wolf Inmate Cuts Fell Short." *Philadelphia Inquirer*, June 17, 2020.

Lai, Jonathan. "Election Audit Stirs Budget Dispute." *Philadelphia Inquirer*, June 29, 2021.

———. "Election Officials Warned on Ballots." *Philadelphia Inquirer*, May 29, 2021.

———. "Election System Mired in Conflict." *Philadelphia Inquirer*, November 25, 2021.

———. "GOP Fights for Bigger Role in State Map." *Philadelphia Inquirer*, January 10, 2022.

———. "Last Pa. Election Challenge Tossed." *Philadelphia Inquirer*, April 20, 2021.

———. "Pa. Ballot Mail Date Key to Vote Being Cast." *Philadelphia Inquirer*, July 31, 2020.

———. "Pa. Still Has a Ballot Issue." *Philadelphia Inquirer*, March 19, 2021.

———. "Primary Reveals Bugs in Election System." *Philadelphia Inquirer*, May 29, 2021.

———. "Rules Up in the Air As Election Day Nears." *Philadelphia Inquirer*, September 2, 2020.

———. "What Trump Got Wrong, Again, in Pa." *Philadelphia Inquirer*, January 7, 2021.

———. "Wolf Now Open to Voter ID Changes." *Philadelphia Inquirer*, July 21, 2021.

———. "Wolf: Pa. Election Audit Would Be a 'Disgrace.'" *Philadelphia Inquirer*, July 9, 2021.

———. "Wolf Vetoes Fund for Vote Audit Bureau." *Philadelphia Inquirer*, July 1, 2021.

Lai, Jonathan, and Marie Albiges. "Pa. GOP Proposes Election Overhaul." *Philadelphia Inquirer*, June 11, 2021.

Lai, Jonathan, and Chris Brennan. "Republicans Offer Mail Ballot Plan." *Philadelphia Inquirer*, August 25, 2020.

Lai, Jonathan, Chris Brennan, Jonathan Tamari, and Cynthia Fernandez. "Pa. Court Extends Mail-in Time." *Philadelphia Inquirer*, September 18, 2020.

Lai, Jonathan, and Ellie Rushing. "USPS: Can't Make Pa. Ballot Times." *Philadelphia Inquirer*, August 14, 2020.

Lai, Jonathan, and Rob Torne. "Pa. Leads Suit Against Post Office." *Philadelphia Inquirer*, August 22, 2020.

Lai, Jonathan, and Andrew Seidman. "Pa. Court Overturns Mail Vote Law." *Philadelphia Inquirer*, November 25, 2022.

———. "Pa. GOP Outlines Voter Law Proposals." *Philadelphia Inquirer*, May 11, 2021.

Levy, Marc. "Mailed Ballots Can't Be Tossed over Signatures." *Philadelphia Inquirer*, January 29, 2020.

———. "Pa. Won't Block Entire Subpoena in Election Probe. However, the Order Did Not Immediately Allow the Release of Protected Voter Information." *Philadelphia Inquirer*, January 11, 2022.

Levy, Marc, and Mark Scolfaro. "Another County Balking at Election Audit." *Philadelphia Inquirer*, July 16, 2021.

———. "GOP Clash Brews in Pa. over Audit of 2020 Results." *Philadelphia Inquirer*, June 4, 2021.

———. "Pa. Decertifies County's Voting Machines." *Philadelphia Inquirer*, July 27, 2021.

Liptak, Adam. "A Deadlocked Supreme Court Allows Extra Time for Some Pennsylvania Ballots." *New York Times*, October 19, 2020.

———. "Supreme Court Rejects Republican Challenge to Pennsylvania Vote." *New York Times*, December 8, 2020.

Lisi, Tom. "Provisional Ballots Delay Pa. Vote Count." *Philadelphia Inquirer*, November 7, 2020.

Mahon, Ed. "DEMOCRATS: Despite Biden Surge, Party Lost Races Up and Down the Pa. Ballot." *Philadelphia Inquirer*, November 7, 2020.

Martines, Jamie. "Levine Pressed About Nursing Homes." *Philadelphia Inquirer*, March 22, 2021.

———. "Lockdowns in Pa. Not the Answer, Experts Say." *Philadelphia Inquirer*, November 11, 2020.

Martines, Jamie, and Angela Couloumbis. "Pennsylvania Gov. Tom Wolf Asks Republican Leaders to Return to Harrisburg and Pass School Mask Mandate." Allentown Morning Call, August 25, 2021.

———. "GOP on Brink of Keeping Control of Pa. Senate." *Philadelphia Inquirer*, November 5, 2020.

McCoy, Craig, and Jamie Martines. "Trump Team Vows to File Suit in Pa. over Ballots." *Philadelphia Inquirer*, November 9, 2020.

McDaniel, Justine, Allison Steele, and Erin McCarthy. "Wolf Fears Strain on Hospitals." *Philadelphia Inquirer*, December 8, 2020.

McDaniel, Justine, and Erin McCarthy. "Pa. House: Let Counties Run Sites." *Philadelphia Inquirer*, March 25, 2021.

———. "Wolf Halts Indoor Dining, Gyms." *Philadelphia Inquirer*, December 11, 2020.

———. "Wolf Orders Masks in All Pa. Schools." *Philadelphia Inquirer*, September 1, 2021.

McDaniel, Justine, Elle Silverman, and Allison Steele. "THE REGION: State Considers New Limits. Wolf Tests Positive." *Philadelphia Inquirer*, December 10, 2020.

McLaughlin, Jason. "Doctors Say School Mask Mandate Is a Good Move." *Philadelphia Inquirer*, September 2, 2021.

———. "Lockdowns in Pa. Not the Answer, Experts Say." *Philadelphia Inquirer*, November 11, 2020.

Moss, Rebecca. "CARE HOMES: The Virus Exploited Problems State Had Failed to Address." *Philadelphia Inquirer*, June 14, 2020.

Murphy, Jan. "Pa.'s Lawmakers Question Gov. Wolf's Authority to Extend Mailed Ballot Deadlines in 6 Counties." *PennLive/Patriot News*, June 1, 2020.

———. "Should Pa.'s Appellate Court Judges Be Term-Limited? A House Panel Thinks So." *PennLive/Patriot News*, December 13, 2021.

Ohl, Danielle. "Pa. Voters Could Be Flooded with Choices." *Philadelphia Inquirer*, January 18, 2022.

———. "Top Pennsylvania House Republican Want to Expand Lawmakers' Power over Governor, Executive Branch." *Spotlight*, November 9, 2021.

PA Code 35, Chapter 73. https://www.legis.state.pa.us/cfdocs/legis/LI/consCheck.cfm?txtType=HTM&ttl=35&div=0&chpt=73.

Parish, Marley. "Pa. Court Declines Request to Quash Senate GOP Election Investigation Subpoena, Needs More Time for Review." *Pennsylvania Capital-Star*, January 10, 2022.

Pattani, Aneri. "Decades Old Law Hides State's Response." *Philadelphia Inquirer*, August 20, 2020.

Previti, Emily. "Trump Campaign Sues Pennsylvania over Mail-in Voting and Other Election Issues." *PA Post*, June 29, 2020.

Prose, J. D. "GOP State Lawmakers File Suit to Have Mail-in Voting Tossed Out. Who Is Suing Who?" *GoErie*, September 3, 2021.

Roebuck, Jeremy. "GOP Files Late Flurry of Challenges." *Philadelphia Inquirer*, December 8, 2020.

———. "Where Trump's Legal Challenges Stand." *Philadelphia Inquirer*, November 10, 2020.

———. "A Wider, Wilder Attack." *Philadelphia Inquirer*, December 8, 2020.

Roebuck, Jeremy, and Sean Collins Walsh. "Trump's Team Takes Its Battle to Gettysburg." November 26, 2020.

Roebuck, Jeremy, Jonathan Lai, and Maddie Hanna. "CHALLENGES: Early Courtroom Win for the President Gives Way to a Slow Steady Count." *Philadelphia Inquirer*, November 6, 2020.

Scolfaro, Mark. "House Votes to End Disaster Order." *Philadelphia Inquirer*, June 9, 2021.

Seidman, Andrew. "Growing Push for a Pa. Vote Audit." *Philadelphia Inquirer*, June 5, 2021.

Seidman, Andrew, and Chris Brennan. "Pa. Treasurer Torselli Falls in Upset to Garrity." *Philadelphia Inquirer*, November 11, 2020.

Seidman, Andrew, and Jonathan Lai. "Senator Wants Vote 'Audit' in 3 Counties." *Philadelphia Inquirer*, July 8, 2021.

Seidman, Andrew, and Jonathan Tamari. "Pa. GOP Congressmen Are Standing by Trump." *Philadelphia Inquirer*, January 13, 2021.

Simon, Sarah. "Health Officials Failed to Safeguard Trust in Pa.'s Coronavirus Data, Sowing Confusion." *Philadelphia Inquirer*, June 14, 2020.

Stinelli, Nick. "Gov. Wolf Outlines Color-Coded Plan to Begin Reopening." *Pittsburgh Post-Gazette*, April 22, 2020.

Tamari, Jonathan. "In Pa., a Voting Rights Battle." *Philadelphia Inquirer*, January 25, 2022.

———. "Quiet After High Court Loss." *Philadelphia Inquirer*, December 16, 2020.

Tamari, Jonathan, and Andrew Seidman. "STICKING WITH TRUMP: Most Pa. Republicans Continued Challenge." *Philadelphia Inquirer*, January 8, 2021.

Vadala, Nick. "How a Proposed Amendment to the State Constitution Could Affect Abortion Access in Pennsylvania." *Philadelphia Inquirer*, January 27, 2022.

Viebeck, Elsie. "In Latest Bow to Trump, GOP Lawmakers in Pennsylvania Plan to Launch Hearings on 2020 Vote." *Washington Post*, August 25, 2021.

Wines, Michael. "State Lawmakers Take Aim at the Emergency Powers Governors Have Relied on in the Pandemic." *New York Times*, March 27, 2021.

Appendix A

People Interviewed

METHODOLOGY

Our goal was to interview people who served in elected and appointed positions in Pennsylvania's government, whose experiences would illuminate its intricacies, revealing details not often made available to the general public. We also included public figures whose work either affected or was affected by government, namely party officials, lobbyists, think tank scholars, and members of the media who reported on Harrisburg's politics.

We began with individuals known to us, such as our local representatives and senators, and then asked for their assistance in introducing us to legislative leaders. In similar fashion, we contacted individuals in the executive branch and the courts, who held important positions—for example, a chief of staff to the governor or a clerk to a judge or justice—who could give us entree to a governor or appellate judge. In this manner, we were able to interview over sixty individuals.

When requesting an interview, we explained our project and assured the person that we were not interested in politicizing the information provided by the interviewee. We provided subjects with a list of open-ended questions, and offered each person the opportunity to review the book's text where the person was quoted for accuracy. Most people who reviewed the material found nothing objectionable, and those who offered corrections did so to make their contributions clearer and more informative.

Interviews were conducted in person or by phone, Skype, or Zoom. For most of the interviews, both authors were present, and six interviews were attended by one or two undergraduate research assistants. Detailed notes were taken during all interviews by the authors and assistants, and transcribed quickly thereafter. Consolidating the notes ensured as complete a record of each interview as possible.

We want to express our deepest appreciation for all those who agreed to be interviewed, generously giving of their time and expertise to our project.

INTERVIEWEES IN ALPHABETICAL ORDER

Acker, Michael   Interviewed by phone on June 29, 2016. Mr. Acker is a partner and senior vice president of Triad Strategies, a Harrisburg government relations / lobbying firm. Prior to joining Triad, he was executive deputy secretary at the Department of Labor and

Industry during the Ridge administration as well as in the Thornburgh/Schweiker administrations and an aide to US Senator John Heinz.

Aichele, Steven   Interviewed in person at Baldino's home. Mr. Aichele is an attorney with a major Philadelphia firm. He was active in politics at the local and county levels when he was asked by Governor Corbett to be his chief legal counsel and then his chief of staff for a year.

Atkinson, David   Interviewed by phone on June 8, 2016. Mr. Atkinson was State Senator Robert Jubelirer's chief of staff for much of the senator's time in office, and a coauthor along with Jubelirer and Vincent Carocci of *The Senate Will Come to Order, but the Politics May be Messy*. He is currently a consultant at DAA Consulting.

Baer, John   Interviewed by phone on May 25, 2016. Mr. Baer was a long-time columnist for the *Philadelphia Daily News* and then for the *Philadelphia Inquirer* based in Harrisburg.

Baker, Lisa   Interviewed in person on August 11, 2015, in her Dallas, Pennsylvania, office. Ms. Baker is a Republican state senator who has served continuously in the Senate since 2007.

Barr, Gene   Interviewed by phone on July 11, 2016. Mr. Barr was the director of government relations for the Pennsylvania Chamber of Commerce at the time of the interview. He worked for the Chamber for over twenty years but has had over forty years of work experience in government, including his time with the Chamber.

Bumsted, Brad   Interviewed by phone on May 25, 2016. Mr. Bumsted became a reporter in 1974, and began covering Harrisburg in 1983 for the *Pittsburgh Tribune Review*. He is currently a reporter and editor for the *Caucus*.

Burn, James   Interviewed by phone on September 9, 2016. Mr. Burn was the state Democratic Party chair from 2010 to 2015. He previously served as chair of the Allegheny County Democratic Party from 2006 to 2012.

Castille, Ronald D.   Interviewed by phone on August 16, 2016. Mr. Castille, a Republican, was elected district attorney in Philadelphia in 1986 and served until 1991. He was elected to the Supreme Court, serving from 1994 until 2014. He was the chief justice from 2008 until his retirement in 2014.

Corbett, Tom   Interviewed by Skype on July 18, 2016. Mr. Corbett served as governor from 2011 to 2015. He previously served as an assistant US district attorney for Pennsylvania's Western District from 1988 to 1995. He then was appointed as Pennsylvania's attorney general to fill the unexpired term of Ernie Preate in 1995 and held the post until 1997. He was elected the state's attorney general in 2004 and served from 2005 until his election as governor.

Costa, Jay Interviewed by phone on September 16, 2016. Mr. Costa, a Democrat, was first elected to the state Senate in 1996, where he has served as the minority leader since 2011.

Couloumbis, Angela Interviewed on June 1, 2016. Ms. Couloumbis has over twenty-five years of experience as a reporter for the *Philadelphia Inquirer* covering Harrisburg before joining *Spotlight PA*.

Cross, Gerald Interviewed on August 10, 2015, in the Wilkes-Barre, Pennsylvania, office of the Pennsylvania Economy League. Joining Mr. Cross for the interview were Ms. Lynne Shedlock and Mr. Joseph Boyle, PEL staff members. At the time of the interview, Mr. Cross was the executive director of the PEL's Central Division. He joined the PEL in 1988 and became executive director in 2010; he currently is a senior research fellow.

Delano, Jon Interviewed by phone on August 10, 2016. Mr. Delano has served as a chief of staff to former Democratic representative Doug Walgren; as a reporter for KDKA-TV, a columnist for the *Pittsburgh Business Times,* and an adjunct professor at Carnegie Mellon University.

Groen, Marcel Interviewed by phone on July 6, 2016. Mr. Groen was the state Democratic Party chair from 2015 to 2018.

Hayes, Samuel E., Jr. Interviewed by phone on July 18, 2016. Mr. Hayes was first elected to the House in 1970, where he served until 1992. He was majority leader for two years, 1981–82; minority whip from 1979-1980 and again from 1983–88. He also served as secretary of agriculture from 1997 to 2003 under Governor Tom Ridge.

Hill, Doug Interviewed by phone on June 14, 2016. Mr. Hill was the Executive Director of the County Commissioners Association of Pennsylvania. He retired in 2019 after thirty-five years with the Association.

Jackson, Peter Interviewed by phone on June 1, 2016. Mr. Jackson was an AP reporter for thirty-eight years, with over twenty years in Harrisburg before his retirement.

Jubelirer, Robert Interviewed by phone on June 8, 2016. Mr. Jubelirer was first elected to the Pennsylvania Senate in 1974 and served continuously until 2006, when he was defeated in a primary election. He served as president pro tempore from 1984 to 2006, and as lieutenant governor from 2001 to 2003.

Klotz, Philip H. Interviewed on August 3, 2015, in the Local Government Commission's office in Harrisburg. Mr. Klotz was the director of the Local Government Commission from 2015 to 2019. Joining Mr. Klotz for the interview was a staff member, David A. Greene. Mr. Klotz is currently director of government and community affairs and a research associate at the Pennsylvania Economy League, Central Division.

Krawczeniuk, Borys Interviewed by phone on May 24, 2016. Mr. Krawczeniuk has been a reporter for the *Scranton Times Tribune* for over thirty-five years, covering politics at the state and local levels.

Leavitt, Mary Hanna Interviewed by phone on September 20, 2016. Ms. Leavitt, a Republican, was first elected to the Commonwealth Court in 2001, where she served until her retirement in 2021. She served as the court's president judge from 2016 through 2021.

Mains, Nathan Interviewed by phone on February 17, 2017. Mr. Mains is the chief executive officer of the Pennsylvania School Boards Association, a position he has held since 2013.

McLaughlin, Joseph Interviewed by phone on August 18, 2016. Mr. McLaughlin began his career as a political reporter coving Illinois politics before returning to Pennsylvania to become press spokesperson for the House from 1974 to 1977, followed by a stint as press person for the National Governor's Association. He worked for Philadelphia mayor Bill Green from 1982 to 1983, then as a lobbyist for S. R. Wojdak Associates from 1983 to 2003. He joined the Rendell administration as a senior advisor for one year in 2004 before joining the political science department of Temple University, where he directed the Institute for Public Affairs and the Center for Regional Politics, from which he retired in 2020.

Novak, Alan Interviewed by phone on July 6, 2016. Mr. Novak was the state Republican Party chair from 1996 to 2005. He is the founder and president of Novak Strategic Advisors and cofounder of the RooneyNovak Group, both Harrisburg-based lobbying organizations.

Oleksick, Jerry Interviewed in his Harrisburg office on September 28, 2018. He was the acting secretary of labor and industry in the Wolf administration. Previously, he was the president of the Pennsylvania State Education Association (PSEA).

Panella, Jack A. Interviewed by phone on August 17, 2020. At the time of the interview, Mr. Panella was the president judge of the Superior Court, a position he attained in 2014. Previously, he was the solicitor for Northampton County from 1987 to 1991 and served as a Common Pleas Court judge in Northampton County from 1991 to 2003, when he was first elected to the Superior Court.

Pashinski, Eddie Day Interviewed on August 17, 2015, in person at his Wilkes-Barre, Pennsylvania, office. Mr. Pashinski is a Democratic representative who was first elected in 2004.

Rademan, Nicole Interviewed by phone on July 15, 2016. At the time of the interview, Ms. Rademan was clerking for Superior Court judge Platt. She had previously clerked for

Superior Court judges Ford Elliott, Freedberg, Ott, Panella, and Stevens. She currently clerks for Judge Murray.

Rendell, Ed   Interviewed in person on December 18, 2015, in his Philadelphia office. Mr. Rendell served as governor from 2003 to 2011. Previously, he served two terms as Philadelphia's district attorney from 1978 to 1986, and as mayor from 1992 to 2000.

Rooney, T. J.   Interviewed by phone on July 1, 2016. Mr. Rooney held the post of state Democratic Party chair for seven years: 2003 to 2013. He was also managing director of Tri State Strategies PA, LLC and a founder of RooneyNovak Group, both lobbying firms.

Saylor, Thomas G.   Interviewed by phone on August 31, 2016. Mr. Saylor, a Republican, was Somerset County district attorney from 1972 to 1982; first deputy state attorney general, 1983 to 1987; and a Superior Court judge from 1993 to 1997. He served as a Supreme Court justice from 1998 until 2021, during which he was chief justice from 2015 until 2020.

Schuettler, Richard J.   Interviewed by phone on August 3, 2015. Mr. Schuettler was the executive director of the Pennsylvania Municipal League, an organization that represents the interests of large boroughs, some metropolitan townships, and other municipalities in Harrisburg.

Schweiker, Mark   Interviewed in person on May 27, 2016, at his company's office. Mr. Schweiker served as lieutenant governor under Tom Ridge from 1995 to 2001 before becoming governor in 2001 to complete Ridge's second term. Ridge was offered a position in the Bush administration following 9/11.

Scranton interview (see pg. 116n35) missing from appendix.

Shapiro, Joshua   Interviewed in Harrisburg on October 24, 2017 while serving as Attorney General. Mr. Shapiro, a Democrat, served as a representative from 2005 to 2012, Montgomery county commissioner, 2012 to 2016, attorney general, 2017 to 2023, and currently serves a governor.

Singel, Mark   Interviewed in his office at the Winter Group, Harrisburg, on June 21, 2017. Mark Singel was lieutenant governor from 1987 to 1995 with Governor Casey. Singel is currently employed as a lobbyist with the Winter Group.

Stafford, Richard   Interviewed in person on August 8, 2016 at Temple University's Harrisburg campus with a second interview by phone on August 17. Mr. Stafford is the Heinz College Distinguished Service Professor of Public Policy. He worked on Governor Thornburgh's first gubernatorial campaign as director of research, then served on his transition team, eventually joining his administration as secretary of legislative affairs. For one and one-half years he also served as chief-of-staff.

Stevens, Correale   Interviewed by phone on May 24, 2016. Mr. Stevens, a Republican, served in the House from 1981 to 1988 before being elected to serve as district attorney and then a Common Pleas Court judge in Luzerne County. In 1997, he was elected to the Superior Court, where he served until 2013, with two years as president judge. In 2013, he was appointed to fill a vacant seat on the Supreme Court by Governor Tom Corbett, where he served until 2016.

Sturla, Michael   Interviewed by phone on August 18, 2016. Mr. Sturla was first elected to the House in 1990. He was a member of the House Democratic Policy Committee from 1991 until 2020, and served as chair from 2016.

Swift, Robert   Interviewed by phone on May 24, 2016. Mr. Swift was a reporter for the Times Shamrock newspaper chain based in Harrisburg for over forty years until his retirement.

Thornburgh, Richard   Interviewed in his summer home in Ligonier, Pennsylvania on July 22, 2016. Mr. Thornburgh served as governor from 1979 to 1987 and as US Attorney General from 1988 to 1991 during President George H.W. Bush's administration.

Vaughan, James   Interviewed by phone on August 9, 2016. Mr. Vaughan began his career as a lobbyist in 1999. At the time of the interview, he was the executive director of the Pennsylvania State Education Association (PSEA). Previously, he was the chief government relations person for the PSEA.

Walsh, Dennis   Interviewed by phone on June 9, 2016. Mr. Walsh worked in and around government for over forty years, including serving as Governor Ridge's secretary to the legislature from 1995 to 2000. At the time of the interview, he was a government relations specialist with the Bravo Group, a Harrisburg lobbying / government relations firm.

Williams, Anthony Hardy   Interviewed by phone on September 9, 2016. Mr. Williams, a Democrat, served in the House from 1989 to 1998, and was first elected to the state Senate in 1998. He was serving as the Democratic Minority Whip at the time of the interview.

Wojcik, Michael H.   Interviewed by phone on July 14, 2016. Mr. Wojcik, a Democrat, was elected to the Commonwealth Court in 2016, where he continues to serve.

Wolf, Tom   Interviewed by phone on March 22, 2016. First elected in 2010, Mr. Wolf is completing his second term as governor.

Young, Mary   Interviewed by phone on July 8, 2016. Ms. Young was the director of government relations for the Association of Independent Colleges and Universities of Pennsylvania, a position she held for over seventeen years. She worked in various state government offices for nearly thirty-five years before joining the AICUP.

Yudichak, John   Interviewed in person on August 10, 2015, in his Nanticoke, Pennsylvania, office. At the time of the interview, Mr. Yudichak was a state senator elected as a Democrat. He was elected to the state House as a Democrat, where he served from 1999 to 2010. Elected to the state Senate in 2011 as a Democrat, he left the Party in 2019 to become an Independent, here he caucused with the Republican Party until his retirement in December 2022.

Appendix B

Statewide Election Results, 1932–2020

Year	Office	Republican	%	Democrat	%
1932	President	Hoover	51	Roosevelt	45
1932	Senate	Davis	49	Rupp	43
1932	Treasurer	Waters	52	Shannon	42
1932	Auditor general	Baldwin	52	Sarig	42
1934	Senate	Reed	47	Guffey	51
1934	Governor	Schnader	48	Earle	50
1934	Internal affairs	Taylor	47	Logue	50
1936	President	Landon	41	Roosevelt	57
1936	Treasurer	Pinola	44	Ross	55
1936	Auditor general	Sweeney	40	Roberts	60
1938	Senate	Davis	55	Earle	43
1938	Governor	James	53	Jones	46
1938	Internal affairs	Livengood	53	Logue	46
1940	President	Wilkie	46	Roosevelt	53
1940	Senate	Cooke	47	Guffey	52
1940	Treasurer	Malone	35	H.G. Wagner	65
1940	Auditor general	Gelder	46	Ross	54
1942	Governor	Martin	54	Ross	45
1942	Internal affairs	Livengood	54	Hess	45
1944	President	Dewey	48	Roosevelt	51
1944	Senate	Davis	49	Myers	50
1944	Treasurer	Baird	49	Black	50
1944	Auditor general	Watkins	49	Rosenberg/Wagner	50
1946	Senate	Martin	59	Guffey	40
1946	Governor	Duff	59	Rice	41
1946	Internal affairs	Livengood	58	Schmid	41
1948	President	Dewey	47	Truman	51
1948	Treasurer	Barber	70	Lane	30
1948	Auditor general	Heyburn	70	Black	30
1950	Senate	Duff	51	Myers	48
1950	Governor	Fine	51	Dilworth	48
1950	Internal affairs	Livengood	53	Ruth	47
1952	President	Eisenhower	53	Stevenson	47
				(continued)	

Year	Office	Republican	%	Democrat	%
1952	Senate	Martin	52	Bard	48
1952	Treasurer	Heyburn	62	Leader	48
1952	Auditor general	Barber	52	Blatt	48
1954	Governor	Wood	46	Leader	54
1954	Internal affairs	Dixon	48	Blatt	52
1956	President	Eisenhower	57	Stevenson	43
1956	Senate	Duff	49.6	Clark	50
1956	Treasurer	Kent	52	Knox	47
1956	Auditor general	C. Smith	53	F. Smith	47
1958	Senate	Scott	51	Leader	48
1958	Governor	McMonigle	49	Lawrence	51
1958	Internal affairs	Gleason	48	Blatt	52
1960	President	Nixon	49	Kennedy	51
1960	Treasurer	C. Smith	49	Sloan	51
1960	Auditor general	Kent	48	Minehart	51
1962	Senate	VanZandt	49	Clark	51
1962	Governor	Scranton	52	Dilworth	46
1962	Internal affairs	Kelly	49	Blatt	51
1964	President	Goldwater	35	Johnson	65
1964	Senate	Scott	51	Blatt	49
1964	Treasurer	Fleming	44	Minehart	56
1964	Auditor general	Helm	43	Sloan	57
1966	Governor	Shafer	52	Shapp	46
1966	Internal affairs	Tabor	51	Blatt	49
1968	President	Nixon	44	Humphrey	48
1968	Senate	Schweiker	52	Clark	46
1968	Treasurer	Pasquerilla	47	Sloan	51
1968	Auditor general	Depuy	44	Casey Sr.	54
1970	Senate	Scott	51	Sesler	45
1970	Governor	Broderick	42	Shapp	55
1972	President	Nixon	59	McGovern	39
1972	Treasurer	Williams	46	Sloan	52
1972	Auditor general	McCorkel	43	Casey Sr.	55
1974	Governor	Lewis	45	Shapp	54
1974	Senate	Schweiker	53	Flaherty	46
1976	President	Ford	48	Carter	50
1976	Senate	Heinz	52	Green	47
1976	Treasurer	Crawford	47	Casey Sr.	52
1976	Auditor general	Gleason	45	Benedict	50
1978	Governor	Thornburgh	53	Flaherty	46
				(continued)	

Year	Office	Republican	%	Democrat	%
1980	President	Reagan	51	Carter	43
1980	Senate	Specter	50	Flaherty	48
1980	Attorney general	Zimmerman	51	O'Pake	48
1980	Treasurer	Dwyer	49	Casey Sr.	48
1980	Auditor general	Knepper	48	Benedict	50
1982	Senate	Heinz	59	Wecht	39
1982	Governor	Thornburgh	51	Ertel	46
1984	President	Reagan	53	Mondale	46
1984	Attorney general	Zimmerman	49.7	Ertel	49.3
1984	Treasurer	Dwyer	54	Benedict	46
1984	Auditor general	Shanaman	48	Bailey	52
1986	Senate	Specter	56	Edgar	43
1986	Governor	Scranton III	48	Casey Sr.	51
1988	President	Bush	51	Dukakis	48
1988	Senate	Heinz	66	Vignola	32
1988	Attorney general	Preate	50	Mezvinsky	47
1988	Treasurer	English	43	Knoll	57
1988	Auditor General	Hafer	49	Bailey	48
1990	Governor	Hafer	32	Casey Sr.	68
1991	Senate*	Thornburgh	45	Wofford	55
1992	President	Bush	36	Clinton	45
1992	Senate	Specter	49	Yeakel	46
1992	Attorney general	Preate	50	Kohn	48
1992	Treasurer	Henry	35	Catherine Knoll	65
1992	Auditor general	Hafer	53	Lewis	47
1994	Senate	Santorum	49	Wofford	47
1994	Governor	Ridge	45	Single	40
1996	President	Dole	40	Clinton	49
1996	Attorney general	Fisher	50	Kohn	48
1996	Treasurer	Hafer	49	Minna Baker Knoll	48
1996	Auditor general	Nyce	42	Casey Jr.	58
1998	Senate	Specter	61	Lloyd	35
1998	Governor	Ridge	57	Itkin	31
2000	President	Bush	46	Gore	51
2000	Senate	Santorum	52	Klink	46
2000	Attorney general	Fisher	54	Eisenhower	43
2000	Treasurer	Hafer	49	Catherine Knoll	47
2000	Auditor general	True	40	Casey Jr.	57
2002	Governor	Fisher	44	Rendell	53
2004	President	Bush	46	Kerry	51
				(continued)	

Year	Office	Republican	%	Democrat	%
2004	Senate	Specter	53	Hoeffel	42
2004	Attorney general	Corbett	51	Eisenhower	48
2004	Treasurer	Pepper	37	Casey Jr.	61
2004	Auditor general	Peters	45	Wagner	59
2006	Senate	Santorum	41	Casey Jr.	59
2006	Governor	Swann	40	Rendell	60
2008	President	McCain	44	Obama	55
2008	Attorney general	Corbett	52	Morganelli	46
2008	Treasurer	Ellis	43	McCord	55
2008	Auditor general	Beller	38	Wagner	52
2010	Senate	Toomey	51	Sestak	49
2010	Governor	Corbett	55	Onorato	45
2012	President	Romney	47	Obama	52
2012	Senate	Smith	46	Casey, Jr.	54
2012	Attorney general	Freed	42	Kane	56
2012	Treasurer	Vaughn	44	McCord	53
2012	Auditor general	Maher	46	DePasquale	50
2014	Governor	Corbett	45	Wolf	55
2016	President	Trump	48.1	Clinton	47.4
2016	Senate	Toomey	49	McGinty	47
2016	Attorney general	Rafferty	49	Shapiro	51
2016	Treasurer	Voit	44	Torsella	51
2016	Auditor general	Brown	45	DePasquale	50
2018	Senate	Barletta	43	Casey Jr.	55
2018	Governor	Wagner	41	Wolf	58
2020	President	Trump	49	Binden	50
2020	Attorney general	Heidelbaugh	46	Shapiro	51
2020	Treasurer	Defoor	50	Ahmad	46
2020	Auditor general	Garrity	49	Torsella	48
2022	Senator	Oz	46	Fetterman	51
2022	Governor	Mastriano	42	Shapiro	56

*A special election to fill the seat of Senator Heinz, who died in an accident

Appendix C

Legal Actions Filed in State and Federal Courts Related to the Pandemic and 2020 Presidential Election

Date	Court and Case	Comments
2020		
April 14	PA Supreme Court: *Friends of Danny DeVito, et al. v. Wolf and Levine*	In a unanimous vote, the court upheld the constitutionality of Gov. Wolf's emergency disaster declaration issued as appropriate under his police powers. Petitioners were businesses that were deemed nonessential; they challenged the authority of Wolf and Levine to issue the declaration.
May 6	US Supreme Court: *Friends of Danny DeVito, et al. v. Wolf*	The court declined to hear the appeal of Pennsylvania's high court decision in *Friends of Danny DeVito, et al. v. Wolf and Levine.*
June 10	Commonwealth Court: *Scarnati, Corman and the Senate Republican Caucus v. Wolf*	The General Assembly passed a concurrent resolution, HR 836, declaring an end to the governor's emergency disaster declaration. The petitioners asked the court to issue a writ of mandamus to compel the governor to follow the legislature's resolution and lift his declaration. This court never issued a ruling because of *Scarnati et al. v. Wolf* (below).
July 1	PA Supreme Court: *Scarnati, Corman and the Senate Republican Caucus v. Wolf*	Gov. Wolf asked the court to use its King's Bench power (extraordinary jurisdiction) to take the case described above from the Commonwealth Court and decide it. In a 5–2 vote, it ruled that the legislature's resolution to end the disaster required an action, either a signature or veto, by the governor. As the legislature had not submitted the resolution to the governor, the court ruled the resolution a "legal nullity," that is, it had no legal value or significance, as if it had never happened.
September 14	Federal Court, PA Western District: *County of Butler, et al. v. Wolf*	The suit, brought by several counties, businesses, and elected officials, sought to remove provisions in the governor's emergency disaster declaration, particularly those limiting the size of indoor and outdoor gatherings and the closure of "non-life-sustaining" businesses. Judge William S. Stickman IV's decision limited some provisions in the declaration.
		(continued)

Date	Court and Case	Comments
September 14	PA Supreme Court: *Democratic Party of PA v. Boockvar*	The Democratic Party's suit sought to expand voters' opportunities during the pandemic, specifically to allow more time for mailed ballots to be counted if they are postmarked by election day, to use drop boxes to collect mailed ballots, to count "naked ballots," that is, mailed ballots without security envelopes, and to allow third parties to deliver mailed ballots to election offices or drop boxes. In advance of the suit, the party and Boockvar had negotiated a solution. The court approved the three-day extension for the receipt of mailed ballots, if properly postmarked, the use of drop boxes, and removed the Green Party candidate from the presidential ballot, but it rejected third-party delivery of mailed ballots and the counting of "naked ballots."
September 17	PA Supreme Court: *Jake Corman, et al. v. Democratic Party of PA*	Corman and other Republican legislative leaders challenged Boockvar's election guidance, particularly the deadline extension for receiving absentee ballots and permitting the use of drop boxes. The Court ruled 4–3, with one Democratic justice joining the two Republicans, that the state constitution's free and equal elections clause supported Boockvar's decisions. It found that the existing seven-day gap between the last day to request and absentee ballot and election day deadline to return a ballot was inadequate during an election strained by the pandemic and the US Postal System's expected delivery delays. It also approved the use of drop boxes.
September 28	Federal Court, PA Eastern District: *Commonwealth of PA, et al. v. Louis Dejoy and the USPS*	Pennsylvania and six other states sought an injunction in civil court to compel the USPS to deliver mailed ballots in a timely manner. Mr. Dejoy had announced that he was implementing new postal procedures that would cause the mail to be processed and delivered more slowly, which would affect mailed ballots. Judge Gerald A. McHugh granted the injunction, ordering the USPS to prioritize election mail.
October 1	Federal Court, PA Western District: *A.M., et al. v. Pennsylvania Interscholastic Association*	Judge Susan Baxter dismissed the student athletes' claim that they were denied access to a PIAA-approved golf tournament when it limited the number of golfers who could participate because of the governor's emergency disaster declaration.
October 2	US Third Circuit Court of Appeals: *Wolf v. County of Butler*	The Court overturned the decision of Judge Stickman in *County of Butler v. Wolf*, reinstating all provisions of the governor's emergency declaration.
October 10	Philadelphia Common Pleas Court: *Donald J. Trump for President, Inc. v. Philadelphia County Board of Elections*	The Trump campaign sought to have its poll watchers gain access to satellite election offices where voters obtained or submitted their mailed ballots. Judge Gary S. Glazier denied the request.
		(continued)

Date	Court and Case	Comments
October 10	Federal Court, PA Western District: *Donald J. Trump for President, Inc. v. Boockvar*	The Trump campaign sought the following: to ban the use of drop boxes for mailed ballots; to not count "naked ballots"; to allow poll watchers in polling places regardless of where in PA the poll watchers resided. Judge J. Nicholas Ranjan ruled against the Trump campaign on all points.
October 11	Federal Court, PA Western District: *Donald J. Trump for President, Inc. v. Philadelphia County Board of Elections*	The Trump campaign appealed Judge Glazier's decision (see above). Judge Ranjan upheld Judge Glazier's decision.
October 18	US Supreme Court: *Republican Party of PA v. Boockvar*	The court was asked to hear an expedited appeal of the PA Supreme Court's decision in *Jake Corman, et al. v. Democratic Party of PA* (see above). The court refused.
October 22	Federal Court, PA Middle District: *Pennsylvania Voters Alliance, et al. v. Centre County, et al.*	A suit brought by a group of conservative voters and state Republican legislators to bar six counties' election offices from accepting grant money from a philanthropic organization, the Center for Technology and Civic Life, to help pay for elections. Judge Matthew W. Braun dismissed the suit, writing that the arguments were "unpersuasive."
October 23	PA Supreme Court: *In Re: November 3, 2020 General Election*	Secretary of State Boockvar asked the court to use its King's Bench power to take this case from Commonwealth Court. The question posed by the Trump campaign was whether mailed ballots should be counted if the voter's signature on the envelope did not match the signature on file with the county election office. The court accepted the case and ruled 7–0 to permit the ballots to be counted.
October 28	US Third Circuit Court of Appeals: *Pennsylvania Voters Alliance, et al. v. Centre County, et al.*	Republicans appealed Judge Braun's decision of October 22 (see above). The court ruled that the appellants had no standing to challenge the constitutionality of the grants.
October 28	US Supreme Court: *Republican Party of PA v. Boockvar*	Republicans asked the court for an expedited hearing for a writ of certiorari and to stay the PA Supreme Court's decision in this case. The Court refused the request, voting 4–4, which allowed the PA Supreme Court decision to stand.
November 6	Commonwealth Court: *In Re: Canvassing Observation*	The Trump campaign asked to have its poll watchers moved closer to election workers who were counting mailed ballots in Philadelphia. The court ruled that the watchers relocated closer to counters. Unsatisfied with their watchers' new position, the Trump campaign appealed in federal court.
November 7	Federal Court, PA Eastern District: *Donald J. Trump for President, Inc. v. Philadelphia County Board of Elections*	The court allowed the Commonwealth Court decision in *In Re: Canvassing Observation* to stand, ruling that the poll watchers' new location was adequate for observing and for the safety of election workers.
		(continued)

Date	Court and Case	Comments
November 11	Commonwealth Court: *Donald J. Trump for President, Inc. v. Boockvar*	The Trump campaign asked the court for injunctive relief to block the state and counties from counting provisional ballots of voters who failed to provide proper identification by the official deadline, the Monday following the election. Secretary of State Boockvar had extended the deadline three days because of the pandemic. The Trump campaign argued that Boockvar lacked the authority to issue this guidance. The court ruled to enjoin the counties from counting any ballots that arrived late as well as the provisional ballots.
November 13	US Third Circuit Court of Appeals: *Bognet, et al. v. Boockvar, et al.*	Bognet appealed Judge Gibson's decision (see October 28 above). The court upheld Judge Gibson's decision.
November 18	Montgomery County Court of Common Pleas: *In Re: Canvass of Absentee and Mail-in Ballots of the November 3, 2020 General Election*	The Trump campaign filed similar suits in six other counties to halt the counting of ballots on which voters had not written their addresses beneath their signatures on the security envelope. The judge denied the request and the Trump campaign withdrew its suit.
November 20	PA Supreme Court: *Ziccarelli, et al. v. Allegheny County Board of Elections*	Ziccarelli, a defeated Republican state House candidate, along with several others, sued in state district court to prevent counties from counting "undated ballots." The trial court found for the county. On appeal to Commonwealth Court, it overturned the district court decision. On appeal to the Supreme Court, it reversed Commonwealth Court's decision and allowed the ballots to be counted.
November 21	Federal Court, PA Middle District: *Donald J. Trump for President, Inc. v. Boockvar*	Judge Matthew W. Braun dismissed with prejudice a request by the Trump campaign to block the certification of PA's election results. Mr. Rudy Giuliani represented the Trump campaign. In his decision, the judge wrote that the argument was "unsupported by evidence" and that the evidence that was presented was a "Frankenstein monster."
November 23	PA Supreme Court: *In Re: Canvass of Absentee and Mail-In Ballots of November 3, 2020 General Election*	The Trump campaign asked the court for an emergency appeal to challenge a decision by the Allegheny County Board of Elections to count 2,349 mailed ballots without dates, addresses, or printed names on the ballot envelopes. The court, voting 5–2, denied the request for an emergency appeal.
November 25	Commonwealth Court: *Kellym, Parnell, et al. v. Pennsylvania, Wolf, et al.*	Several Republican congressional candidates filed suit to disqualify all mailed ballots cast in PA, claiming Act 77 of 2019 (see chapter 3) was unconstitutional. Judge Patricia McCullough issued an injunction to halt the certification of mailed ballots. Wolf and others appealed to the PA Supreme Court.
		(continued)

Date	Court and Case	Comments
November 26	Federal Court, PA Middle District *Pirkle, et al. v. Wolf*	PA voters sought to halt the certification of the state's presidential election results in certain counties. They claimed that "illegal ballots" were counted. The plaintiffs withdrew their suit when they were unable to produce evidence. The case was dismissed.
November 27	US Third Circuit Court of Appeals: *Donald J. Trump for President, Inc. v. Boockvar*	The Trump campaign appealed Judge Braun's decision (see November 21 above). The court upheld Judge Braun's decision.
November 28	PA Supreme Court: *Pennsylvania, Gov. Wolf, et al. v. Kelly, et al.*	The appellants sought to overturn Judge McCullough's decision (see November 25 above). The court vacated the judge's decision and allowed the ballots to be counted and certified. The court determined that the plaintiff's case was filed too late, over a year and two election cycles after Act 77 of 2019 was passed.
December 8	PA Supreme Court: *Donald J. Trump for President, Inc. v. Bucks County Board of Elections*	The Trump campaign challenged the Election Board's decision to count "naked ballots" (those submitted without a security envelope) or with incomplete dates and addresses. Previously, a state trial court and the Commonwealth Court upheld the Election Board's decisions. The Supreme Court rejected the Trump campaign's argument and found for the Board of Elections.
December 10	Commonwealth Court: *Metcalfe, et al. v. Wolf, et al.*	Appellants requested an emergency injunction to decertify the 2020 presidential election results. The court denied the request, finding it was an "improper and untimely election contest."
December 11	Federal Court, PA Middle District: *Parker v. Wolf*	Judge John E. Jones III ruled against the petitioners, private citizens who filed suit to block mask mandates and contact tracing. They claimed that the governor's emergency disaster declaration was a "unilateral exercise of power" that violated their rights under the First, Fourth, and Fourteenth Amendments. Judge Jones found no merit in their argument.
December 11	US Supreme Court: *Texas v. PA*	Texas attorney general Paxton and eleven other state attorneys general asked the court to throw out all of PA's Electoral College votes due to alleged election irregularities. The Court found that the plaintiffs lacked standing and that PA's electoral votes were to be counted.
		(continued)

Date	Court and Case	Comments
December 20	US Supreme Court: *Donald J. Trump for President, Inc. v. Boockvar and County Boards of Election*	The Trump campaign asked the court for an expedited review of three PA Supreme Court decisions: *In Re: November 3, 2020 General Election*; *In Re: Canvassing Observation*; and *In Re: Canvass of Absentee and Mail-In Ballots in the November 3 General Election*. The Trump campaign alleged that county election officials across the state violated the state's election code by not enacting "procedural safeguards to deter fraud and ensure transparency" of mailed ballots, as well as a failure to allow poll watchers to observe voters casting mail-in ballots at satellite election offices. The court declined an expedited review, but it set a deadline of January 22, 2021 for the respondents to submit briefs to the court.
2021		
January 8	Federal Court, PA Eastern District: *Donald J. Trump for President, Inc. v. Philadelphia County Board of Elections*	The Trump campaign sought an emergency injunction to stop the counting of all the city's ballots because its poll watchers were not close enough to the election workers counting ballots. Judge Paul S. Diamond denied the request.
January 11	US Supreme Court: *In Re: Canvassing Observation*	The Trump campaign appealed Judge Diamond's ruling (above). The Court declined to hear the case.
January 12	Federal Court, PA Western District: *Ziccarelli v. Allegheny County Board of Elections*	Plaintiff, a Republican congressional candidate, asked the court to prevent the county from counting "undated" ballots (see November 23 above). Judge J. Nicholas Ranjan ruled against the plaintiff.
January 22	US Supreme Court: *Kelly, et al. v. Pennsylvania, Gov. Wolf, et al.*	Plaintiffs, Republican congressional candidates, asked the court to block the certification of all the state's Electoral College votes because mailed ballots were not excluded. The PA Supreme Court had vacated the Commonwealth Court's decision in this case (see November 28 above). The Court denied the plaintiffs' request.
February 22	US Supreme Court *Donald J. Trump for President, Inc. v. Boockvar and County Board of Elections*	The court dismissed the suit without comment following the receipt of the briefs requested by the court on Decembe 20 (see above).
April 19	US Supreme Court *Bognet v. Degraffenreid*	Bognet filed an appeal of the Third Circuit decision (see November 13 above). The court dismissed the case.
July 26	Commonwealth Court: *Doug McLinko v. Pennsylvania, Department of State and Degraffenreid*	The petitioner, a Bradford County commissioner, filed suit on July 26 to have the court declare Act 77 of 2019 unconstitutional. The court consolidated with *Bonner* (see Jan. 28, 2022 below). The petitioner's arguments were the same as those in *Bonner*.
		(continued)

Date	Court and Case	Comments
September 17	Commonwealth Court: *Costa, et al. v. Corman, et al.*	Democratic senators sought a court order to block the Senate Intergovernmental Affairs Committee's subpoena seeking data and voter information on the 2020 presidential election. (See also January 10, 2022, below.)
November 10	Commonwealth Court: *Corman, individually and on behalf of two minor children, et al. v. Acting Sec. of Health Beam*	A suit originally filed on September 8 by the students' parents was joined by Corman and others. They argued that Acting Secretary of Health Beam did not have the authority under the 1955 Disease Prevention and Control Act to require students to wear face masks without a gubernatorial emergency declaration in force. A five-judge panel for the Court, 3 Republicans and 2 Democrats, voted 4–1 that Beam did not have the authority to issue the mask mandate, but Judge Cannon ordered that the mandate remain in place while the decision was appealed by the Wolf administration to the PA Supreme Court (see immediately below).
December 10	PA Supreme Court *Corman, et al. v. Beam*	The court ruled that the Acting Sec. of Health Beam lacked the authority to impose the mandate. It vacated the mandate, which allowed school districts to set their own masking rules free of state control.
December 15	Commonwealth Court: *Commonwealth of PA, Dept. of State, Degraffenreid v. Corman, et al., Costa, et al. v. Corman, et al. , and Haywood and Haywood v. Degraffenreid*	Attorney General Shapiro, the Department of State, and Degraffenreid, along with the Senate Democrats, asked the court to block a subpoena issued by the Senate Intergovernmental Affairs Committee investigating the 2020 presidential election. The subpoena sought personal voter information not generally available to the legislature. A five-judge panel consolidated these cases, but no decision was rendered at this time.
2022		
January 10	Commonwealth Court: Same case as December 15	The five-judge panel heard testimony and issued an unsigned decision saying that the court needed more time and information before it could render a decision. Both sides claimed victory.
January 28	Commonwealth Court: *Bonner, et al. v. Dept. of State and Degraffenreid* and *McLinko v. Dept. of State and Degraffenreid* (cases consolidated)	Bonner and thirteen other Republican lawmakers filed suit on September 2 to have Act 77 of 2019 declared unconstitutional. They argued that the Act (see chapter 3) violates the state constitution, Article VII, sec. 14, which authorizes the legislature to create a means of voting for people who are unable to vote in person for specific reasons on election day. However, the constitution does not specifically preclude the legislature from extending absentee voting to citizens for other reasons. The court's five-judge panel voted 3–2 along party lines to strike down Act 77 in its entirety. The governor immediately appealed the decision (see below).
		(continued)

Date	Court and Case	Comments
May 27	US Third Circuit Court of Appeals: *Ms. Linda Migliori, Francis J. Fox, Richard E. Richards, Kenneth Ringer and Sergio Rivas v. Lehigh County Board of Elections*	On appeal from the Federal Court, PA Eastern District, this court decided that ballots cast in Lehigh County on November 2, 2021, that were received without dates adjacent to the voter's signature on the security envelope, should be counted, reasoning that the "dating provisions in 25 PA. Cons. Stat., sections 3146.6(a) and 3150.16 are immaterial to a voter's qualifications and eligibility." The court also ruled that the plaintiffs, all private citizens, had the right to challenge the Board of Elections decision to not count the undated ballots.
August 2	PA Supreme Court: Consolidated cases	On appeal from the Commonwealth Court, the Court voted 5–2 along party lines to uphold Act 77 of 2019's constitutionality. The majority opinion states, "Our General Assembly is endowed with great legislative power, subject only to express restrictions in the Constitution. . . . We find no restriction in our Constitution on the General Assembly's ability to create universal mail-in voting." The majority rejected the Commonwealth Court's argument that the constitution limited mail-in ballots to absentee voters, saying that absentees are the minimum protected class of voters and that nothing prevents the legislature from expanding this method to other voters.

Appendix D

Pandemic-Related Actions of the General Assembly

Date	Bill	House Action	Senate Action	Comments
2020				
April 21	HB 2376: bill to allow businesses to operate using curbside delivery during the emergency disaster declaration	April 21 vote: 112–90	No Senate floor vote taken by publication	
May 13	SB 327: bill to authorize counties to develop their own mitigation plans allowing businesses to reopen	May 13 vote: 108–94	May 13 vote: 28–20	Vetoed May 19
June 9	HR 836: concurrent resolution to end the pandemic emergency declaration	June 9 vote: 121–81	June 9 vote: 31–19	Vetoed July 14. House override attempt failed on September 9: 118–84.
June 10	HR 106: a concurrent resolution to end the governor's pandemic emergency declaration	Floor vote, June 10, 121–81	Floor vote, June 10, 30–20	Republican leaders chose not to send this to the governor for a signature or veto. Matter settled by state Supreme Court (see appendix C)
July 14	HB 2541: a bill authorizing all counties to reopen	Floor vote, July 14, 114–87	No action taken by publication	
July 15	HB 2463: a bill requiring state agencies to respond to requests for public records made during the governor's pandemic emergency declaration	Floor vote, July 15, 202–0	Floor vote, July 15, 50–0	July 27, bill became law without the governor's signature
				(continued)

Date	Bill	House Action	Senate Action	Comments
July 15	HB 1166: a concurrent resolution to amend the constitution. Four individual amendments included, two of which limit the time period of a governor's emergency disaster declaration by a vote of the General Assembly	Floor vote, July 14, 114–86	Floor vote, July 15, 33–17	The governor has no role in amending the constitution.
September 2	HB 1566: a bill to permit the state's professional licensing agencies to issue advice to professionals seeking guidance on how to conduct their businesses under the emergency disaster declaration	Floor vote, September 2, 115–87	No action taken by publication	
September 9	HB 2787: a bill to allow school districts to conduct their sports and extracurricular activities during the lockdown despite the governor's emergency declaration forbidding this	Floor vote, September 15, 149–53	Floor vote, September 9, 39–11	September 21, vetoed
September 15	HB 2530: a bill to amend the state's religious freedom act to permit churches to conduct services during the governor's health emergency, which specifically included religious services	Floor vote, September 22, 145–56	No action taken by publication	
September 23	HB 2513: a bill to allow bars and restaurants to operate indoors without the purchase of food at 50 percent capacity and with social distancing, despite health emergency declaration	Floor vote, Sept. 22, 145–56	Floor vote, September 23, 43–6	October 16, vetoed; House override attempt failed on Oct. 20, 133–69
October 21	SB 1164: a bill to change coroner's requirements for determining and listing COVID-19 as a cause of death	Floor vote, October 21, 132–69	Floor vote, October 22, 39–10	Nov. 1, vetoed
				(continued)

Date	Bill	House Action	Senate Action	Comments
November 18	HB 1747: a bill to limit the governor's power to regulate firearms during an emergency disaster declaration	Floor vote, November 18, 127–74	Floor vote, November 18, 29–20	Nov. 25, vetoed
2021				
March 24	HB 63: a bill to require additional COVID vaccine shipments to Philadelphia's suburban counties for the counties to distribute	Floor vote, March 24, 135–66	No action taken by publication	
April 6	HB 605: a bill to limit the liability of businesses to certain COVID related lawsuits	Floor vote, April 6, 107–94	No action taken by publication	
April 21	HB 747: a bill authorizing retail stores to remain open with one staff person and one customer during the emergency declaration thereby circumventing the governor's small business closure	Floor vote, April 21, 117–84	No action taken by publication	
April 27	SB 106–see Appendix D			
June 10	HR 106: a concurrent resolution to end Governor Wolf's last extension of his emergency declaration pursuant to constitutional amendment allowing the General Assembly to end the emergency declaration	Floor vote, June 10, 121–81	Floor vote, June 10, 30–20	No gubernatorial action permitted
June 24	SB 618: a bill to limit the power of the secretary of health to permit the use of vaccine passports by state government and private businesses	Floor vote, June 23, 112–89	Floor vote, June 24, 29–21	July 1, vetoed
				(continued)

Date	Bill	House Action	Senate Action	Comments
September 28	SB 846: a bill to allow parents to decide whether their children will wear masks in school, removing the state Department of Health, county health, departments, and local school boards from the decision	No action taken by publication	Education Committee, September. 28, 7–4 (straight party line vote)	
September 29	HB 1861: a bill to allow all waived regulations contained in the governor's March 6, 2020, emergency disaster declaration that apply to the Department of Health and Human Services and the Bureau of Professional and Occupational Affairs to remain in place until March unless the governor and the agencies decide to terminate them. Waiver examples include allowing out-of-state doctors to treat patients in PA, allowing retired or lapsed professionals to return to practice medicine, and for patients to continue to telemedicine	Floor vote, September 29, 200–0	Floor vote, September 29, 48–0	September 30, signed by the governor
September 29	SB 397 and 398: the bills allow the governor's March 6 emergency disaster declaration provisions that permitted physician assistants to practice to the full extent of their training while removing barriers that delay their entrance into full practice	Floor vote, September 29, 200–0	Floor vote, September 29, 48–0	Sept. 30, signed by the governor
				(continued)

Date	Bill	House Action	Senate Action	Comments
October 4	HB 1893: a bill requiring more transparency from the Department of Health by expanding the public access to data compiled by the department about diseases, including case numbers, deaths, and possibly personal medication information as the bill does not specifically restrict such access	Floor vote, Oct. 4, 113–87	No action taken by publication	
December 15	SB 106: House amends and votes on constitutional amendments (see appendix D)			

Appendix E

Election-Related Actions of the General Assembly

Date	Bill	House Action	Senate Action	Comments
2020				
September 2	HB 2626: a bill to amend the state election code to eliminate the use of drop boxes and satellite offices, permit people from outside a county to serve as poll watchers, shorten the time period that voters can request mail-in ballots and increase penalties for anyone convicted of violating the Election Code	Floor vote, Sept. 2, 112–90	No action taken by publication	
November 19	HR 1100: a resolution to permit the Legislative Budget and Finance Committee to contract with a private company to conduct a forensic audit of the 2020 presidential election	Floor vote, November 19, 112–90	No action taken by publication	
November 23	Rep. Seth Grove, House State Government Committee chair, releases a report, conducted by the committee, on voting in the 2020 election. The report chronicles those gubernatorial actions, guidance issued by the secretary of state and court decisions that the Committee believes adversely affected the election			
November 25	House Republicans hold a special committee hearing in Gettysburg to take testimony on alleged fraud during 2020 presidential election. Among the witnesses were Rudy Giuliani and President Trump, by phone.			
				(continued)

Date	Bill	House Action	Senate Action	Comments
2021				
January 13	HB 38: a joint resolution proposing a constitutional amendment to require all state appellate judges and justices to be elected by district rather than in statewide elections	January 13, introduced but no floor vote taken	No action taken by publication	
January 26	HB 263: a joint resolution proposing a constitutional amendment to create a mixed system of selecting all appellate judges and justices, that is, some by appointment and some by election from newly created judicial districts	January 26, introduced and referred to Judiciary Committee	No action taken by publication	
April 13	SB 529: a constitutional amendment to prevent the state (more particularly, the governor) from entering any interstate compacts longer than ten years	No floor action taken by publication	April 13, referred to committee; no further actions taken by publication	
April 27	SB 106: a constitutional amendment to change the method of selecting lieutenant gubernatorial candidates to allow a party's gubernatorial nominee to choose the person rather than have the candidate elected in a separate primary election	No floor action taken by publication	Floor vote, April 27, 43–4	Two Democrats and two Republicans voted against it
May 5	HR 91: a resolution to establish a task force to investigate the failure to properly advertise the constitutional amendment that would have extended the time period for child sexual abuse victims to file legal claims	Floor vote, May 5, 111–90	No Senate action necessary	
May 24	HB 1010: a concurrent resolution proposing a constitutional amendment to transfer responsibility for advertising state constitutional amendments from the Secretary of State to another department	Floor vote, May 24, 113–88	No action taken by publication	
				(continued)

Date	Bill	House Action	Senate Action	Comments
June 23	SB 735: a joint resolution to amend the constitution to require voter identification (type unidentified) be presented when casting an in-person or mailed ballot	No action taken by publication	Floor vote, June 23, 30–20	
June 25	HB 1300: a bill to amend the election code with provisions to create a separate election audit bureau within the auditor general's office and more stringent voter ID requirements	Floor vote, June 22, 110–91	Floor vote, June 25, 29–21	June 30, vetoed
June 28	HB 1717: a constitutional amendment to repeal Act 77 of 2019	June 28, referred to committee	No action taken by publication	
July 8	State Senator Doug Mastriano requests that three counties—Philadelphia, Tioga, and York—send his committee their election records so that the Committee can conduct a forensic audit of the 2020 presidential election.			
August 4	State Senator Doug Mastriano seeks authority for his committee to issue subpoenas to compel testimony and the release of county election records to the Senate.			
August 24	Senate president pro tempore Jake Corman replaces Senator Doug Mastriano with Senator Cris Dush as chair of the Senate Intergovernmental Operations Committee investigating the 2020 presidential election and leading a forensic audit. SB 106 (see Appendix D)			
September 9	State Senator Dush officially announces that his committee will conduct a forensic audit of the 2020 presidential election.			
				(continued)

Appendix E   223

Date	Bill	House Action	Senate Action	Comments
September 15	Senate Intergovernmental Operations Committee votes to issue subpoenas to the Secretary of State to send to the committee following: lists of all registered voters who voted in the 2020 primary and general elections; voters' names, addresses, dates of birth, driver's license numbers, the last four digits of their Social Security numbers; and whether they voted in-person, by mail, or provisionally. All communications between the state and county election officials during the primary and general elections, including any guidance and directives regarding the administration of elections and training materials for election workers. The committee voted along party lines, 7–4 to approve.			
September 16	Senate Democrats seek a court injunction to block the subpoenas from being issued and enforced.	No action taken by publication	September 17, referred to committee	
September 17	SB 878: a bill to make uniform and clarify the state's election procedures as requested by county election officials	September 27, State Government Committee voted, 10–5	No action taken by publication	
				(continued)

Date	Bill	House Action	Senate Action	Comments
September 27	HB 1596: a joint resolution proposing a constitutional amendment to do the following: require all voters casting in-person ballots or by mail to present "valid identification" (details on what constitutes valid identification to be described in future legislation); ban counties from accepting donations that help pay for elections; make the secretary of state an elected office, rather than appointed; require paper ballots to have a watermark; allow people to inspect paper ballots for up to two years after an election; require the auditor general to conduct audits of all elections before the election results are certified			
September 27	HB 1800: a bill to require voters to present valid identification to vote in-person or by mail; new security measures for drop boxes; allow voters to repair ("cure") their mailed ballots if submitted without proper signature; and many other provisions in the constitutional amendment discussed above	September 27, referred to State Government Committee	No action taken by publication	
September 27	HB 1904: a constitutional amendment to eliminate retention elections for all justices and judges; instead, all justices and judges would stand for reelection in general elections	September 27, referred to committee	No action taken by publication	
September 27	HB 1910: a constitutional amendment to limit the Supreme Court's rule-making abilities	September 27, referred to committee	No action taken by publication	
				(continued)

Date	Bill	House Action	Senate Action	Comments
October 18	SB 551: a constitutional amendment to eliminate all judicial retention elections; instead, justices and judges would stand for reelection in a general election.	No action taken by publication	October 18, referred to Appropriations Committee	
November 17	HB 2069: a constitutional amendment to limit the executive branch's power to issue regulations	November 17, referred to committee	No action taken by publication	
November 17	HB 2070: a constitutional amendment to limit the governor's authority to issue executive orders	Novemer 17, referred to committee	No action taken by publication	
November 19	SB 946: a constitutional amendment to limit the governor's powers and those of any executive branch agency to sustain orders or proclamations that have the force of law	No action taken by publication	November 19, referred to committee	
November 19	SB 947: a constitutional amendment to remove the governor's power to veto legislative resolutions that disapprove of state regulations	No action taken by publication	November 19, referred to committee	
December 13	HB 1880: a constitutional amendment to limit the term of all appellate justices and judges to two, six-year terms	December 13, Judiciary Committee voted, 15–8	No action taken by publication	
December 13	HB 2141: a constitutional amendment to eliminate appellate court retention elections; instead, appellate court justices and judges would stand for reelection against an opponent when their terms end.	December 13, Judiciary Committee voted 13–10 (party line)	No action taken by publication	
				(continued)

Date	Bill	House Action	Senate Action	Comments
December 15	SB 106: the House took up and added four amendments to SB 106 (see April 27 above): to empower the auditor general to conduct audits of all elections (an audit can include an election's administration, voting machine certification, the accuracy of voter registration lists, and an election's final results); a twenty-one-day time limit on all executive orders and proclamations with the force of law issued by a governor, unless the General Assembly votes to approve the order or proclamation; legislative disapproval of all regulations issued by the executive branch by a simple majority vote not subject to the governor's veto; a requirement that all voters present "valid identification" (type not specified) when casting ballots in-person or by mail	December 15, floor votes on each amendment, two passed 113–90 and two passed 114–90, final floor vote, 113–87	Returned to Senate for its consideration of the amended bill	
2022				
January 11	HB 38: a constitutional amendment to elect all appellate justices and judges by districts drawn by the legislature rather than the election at-large	January 11, referred to the Judiciary Committee	No action taken by publication	
April 28	SB 1209: a constitutional amendment to require that the Legislative Reapportionment Commission count prisoners as residents of the county in which they are incarcerated rather than in their home counties	No action taken by publication	April 28, referred to Judiciary Committee	
				(continued)

Date	Bill	House Action	Senate Action	Comments
June 28	SB 1182: a constitutional amendment to revise how the chair of the Legislative Reapportionment Commission is selected. Requires that if the four appointed members of the LRC cannot elect their chair, the Supreme Court must name the chair by randomly selecting from among all active senior appellate court judges	No action taken by publication	June 28, first floor consideration, no floor vote taken by publication	
July 8	SB 106 (see December 15 above): Senate considers and amends bill returned from House. The five final amendments are: declares that the state constitution does contain a right to abortion, including publicly funded abortions; increases the powers of the General Assembly to reject vetoes issued by the governor; additional voter identification requirements; changes voter residency requirements, increasing from thirty days to ninety days to vote in a state election and sets the voting age at twenty-one; requires that all elections be audited by the auditor general; removes the lieutenant governor's power to cast a tie-breaking vote on final passage of a bill and to allow a party's gubernatorial candidate to choose the lieutenant governor rather than have the voters select one in a primary election. After the Senate vote, the resolution was sent immediately to the House, which voted on the same day.	July 8, floor vote, 107–9	July 8, floor vote, 28–22	

Appendix F

Election- and Pandemic-Related Actions of the Executive Branch

Date	Action
2020	
March 6	Governor Wolf issues his first emergency disaster declaration in response to the COVID-19 pandemic.
March 13	The governor issues a temporary emergency school closing.
March 19	The governor issues a stay-at-home order for all state residents and closed all nonessential businesses.
March 23	School closure extended
April 9	The governor orders all schools closed through the end of the school year for in-person instruction.
April 27	The governor announces his plan for a phased reopening of businesses beginning May 8 with counties moving from red to yellow to green based on COVID infection rates and hospitalizations in each county
June 3	The governor renews his emergency disaster declaration for an additional ninety days.
July 2	Secretary of Health Rachel Levin expands the order requiring all people to wear masks in all public places, indoors and outdoors, and in private businesses.
July 2	The governor and Secretary Levine recommend that all people who enter the state from a list of fifteen states with high COVID infection rates self-quarantine.
July 15	The governor and Secretary Levine issue new statewide limits for occupancy rates for restaurants, bars, nightclubs, and gyms, but not churches. The governor also announces a plan to reopen schools in the fall.
August 6	Secretary Levine recommends that all school sports programs be postponed for the entire school year.
August 19	The Department of Education issues mask mandates for all students over age two in public and private schools as well as social distancing in classrooms, cafeterias, etc., while in school.
September 1	The governor renews his emergency disaster declaration for ninety days
September 7	The governor and Secretary Levine issue an order allowing restaurants to increase their maximum seating capacity to 50 percent, effective September 21.
October 6	The governor and Secretary Levine issue an order increasing outdoor gatherings to a maximum of 7500 and indoor gatherings to 3750, effective October 9.
October 7	Auditor General Eugene DePasquale announces the findings of his investigation into how business waivers were granted by the Wolf administration. While inconsistencies in applying criteria and confusion over those criteria created an unfair playing field for businesses applying for a waiver were uncovered, no evidence of illegal activities was found.
	(continued)

Date	Action
November 18	Secretary Levine orders new COVID-19 mitigation rules: masks required indoors, including gyms and public transportation facilities, whenever people from separate households are in the same space; masks required in all outdoor spaces unless social distancing for non–household members can be always maintained; all out-of-state travelers required to show a negative coronavirus test from the last seventy-two hours before they arrive in the state.
November 30	The governor renews his emergency disaster declaration for another ninety days.
December 10	The governor announces that he tested positive for COVID-19.
December 11	The governor announces a three-week ban on indoor dining, indoor entertainment, most social gatherings, and indoor school sports
2021	
January 11	The governor announces his COVID vaccine-distribution plan.
January 15	The governor announces that the Capitol building will close for two days during the new president's inauguration in anticipation of protests and potential violence similar to what occurred in Washington on January 6.
February 4	Secretary of State Kathryn Boockvar resigns.
February 19	The governor renews his emergency disaster declaration for another ninety days.
March 1	The governor reduces some travel restrictions on out-of-state visitors.
March 16	The governor lowers restrictions on businesses and indoor and outdoor events.
April 1	Acting Secretary of Health Alison Beam announces that more people will be eligible for vaccines.
May 5	The governor announces that all restrictions on businesses, events, and other activities, except for mask mandates, will expire on May 31.
May 17	Acting Secretary Beam announces that vaccinated people no longer need to wear masks indoors.
May 20	The governor renews his emergency disaster declaration for another ninety days.
May 28	Acting Secretary Beam announces that the mask mandate will be lifted for everyone on June 28.
July 1	The governor reinstates a mask mandate for all people in all public places.
July 22	Acting Secretary of State Veronica Degraffenreid decertifies Fulton County voting machines after they were "inspected" by an uncertified company at the request of the county commissioners.
August 10	The governor issues an executive order requiring all health care workers at state-run facilities to be vaccinated. Workers requesting exemption must be tested regularly.
August 25	The governor asks the leaders of the General Assembly to pass legislation to require masks for all students in public and private schools, pre-K to high school, and for children in day care facilities over two years old. The leaders, all Republicans, refused the request on August 27.
September 1	Acting Secretary Beam issues a mask mandate for all students and children as requested by the governor on August 25.
September 14	The governor withdraws his nomination for Acting Secretary Degraffenreid to become the secretary of state, fearing her nomination hearing would serve as a vehicle for Senate Republicans to question the legitimacy of the 2020 election.
	(continued)

Date	Action
September 15	Republican auditor general Timothy DeFoor releases a report of his investigation into the business waivers issued during the lockdown's earliest days. His findings are similar to those of Secretary DePasquale's report: no criminal wrongdoing.
September 23	Attorney General Josh Shapiro files suit against Senate President Pro Tempore Jake Corman and Senator Cris Dush in Commonwealth Court to block the subpoena issued by the Senate Intergovernmental Operations Committee.
November 8	The governor announces that on January 17, 2022, his statewide mask mandate for all schoolchildren will end and that school districts will be permitted to determine for themselves whether to require children in grades K through 12 to wear masks. The mask mandate remains in effect for early learning programs and child care providers.

Index

References in *italic* refer to figures. Referneces in **bold** refer to tables.

material groups, 57
Maverick Finance, 62
Maverick Strategies, 62
May, Cornelius, 6
McCaffery, Seamus, 149
McClure, Alexander, 15
McCord, Rob, 124, 125
McGinty, Katie, 113
media, 2, 63–64, 112
    See also social media
Medicaid, 158, 159–60, 160
Medicare for All, 50
Mellow, Robert, 96
Melvin, Joan Orie, 148–49
mental health services, 164, 170
Metcalfe, Daryl, 91
Me-Too movement, 96
Miccarelli, Nick, 96
Michael Turzai et al. v. League of Women Voters et al.,
    79
Michener, James, 17, 71
Midlands political culture, 33
Mifflin, Thomas, 108
Millen, Herbert E., 136
minimum wage, 158
minor courts, 132, 136–37
Minuit, Peter, 6
Missouri Plan, 151
Monongahela people, 5
moralist culture, 32
    See also political culture
municipalities
    funding model, 176
    pension plans, 177
    revenue sources, 176
Munsee, 5
Muslims, 10
Musto, Raphael, 96

"naked" ballots, 187, 208, 209, 211
National Conference of State Legislatures (NCSL),
    72
Native Americans, 4–7, 22
    agriculture, 5
    Europeans and, 5, 6–7
    government, 5–6
    hunter-gatherers, 4–5
    populations, 5
    trade with, 5, 11
    use of force against, 11
natural gas, 24–25
naturalization process, 164
natural resources, 24–25
Navient scandal, 123
negativism, 35
Neuman, Brandon, 62

Neustadt, Richard, 93
New Amsterdam, 6, 7
    See also New York
New Deal, 26, 29, 158
Newman, Sandra Shultz, 148
New Netherlands, 7
New School Democrats, 13
newspapers, 63
New Sweden Company, 6
New World, 5, 6, 8
New Yankeedom, 33, 35
New York, 5, 7, 9
Nix, Robert N. C., 144
Nixon, Richard, 55, 158
Noti, Adav, 62

Obama, Barack, 31, 47, 49, 75
O'Bannon, Helen, 113
Ocasio-Cortez, Alexandria, 50
Oil and Gas Act of 1984, 162–63
    See also Act 13 of 2012
oil/oil production, 24, 25
    discovery, 24
    drilling, 24
Old School Democrats, 13
Optional Third-Class City Charter Law, 171
Orban, Frank A., 17
organizations
    General Assembly, 83–88
    political parties, 50–53
Orie, Jane, 96, 148
Orie, Jannine, 148

Packard, Asa, 24
pandemic. *See* COVID pandemic
Panella, Jack A., 141, 151
Partisan Model, 182, 186, 188
Pashinski, Eddie Day, 86, 87, 89, 91
Patriot News, 63
patronage, 33, 34, 52
    See also political culture
pay-to-play scheme, 124–25
Pecora, Frank, 85
Penn, William, 1, 2, 4, 7–11
    agreement with Duke of York, 8
    charged with treason, 9
    debt, 7, 8
    First Frame, 1, 8, 70
    Great Laws, 8
    Lower Colonies, 8, 9
    persecution, 7, 9
    petition, 8
    proprietary charter, 8
    as Quaker missionary, 7
    recruiting people of all faiths, 8
    Second Frame, 8–9, 10

Penn, William (*continued*)
    Third Frame, 10
    Treaty Elm, 9
Penn, William, Jr., 7
PennFuture, 58
Pennsylvania
    climate, 25
    constitutions (*see* constitution[s])
    Declaration of Independence and, 11
    founders and foundation of, 1, 8–11
    historical development, 4–18
    natural resources, 24–25
    physical geography, 23
    political culture, 2, 22, 31–36
    political geography, 26–30
    population, 25–26, 27, 28, 73
    as proprietary colony, 4, 7–11
Pennsylvania Association of Government Relations, 61
Pennsylvania Bar, 133
Pennsylvania Cable Network (PCN), 141
Pennsylvania Economy League (PEL), 176
Pennsylvania Emergency Management Agency (PEMA), 122
Pennsylvania Historical and Museum Commission, 109
Pennsylvania Liquor Code, 109
Pennsylvania Municipal League, 172
Pennsylvania Public Schools Employees' Retirement System (PSERS), 124, 178
Pennsylvania Racehorse Development and Gaming Act, 95
Pennsylvania Rules of Court, 133
Pennsylvania Society, 53
Pennsylvania Supreme Court. *See* Supreme Court (Pennsylvania)
Pennsylvania v. Nelson, 157–58
Penrose, Boies, 45, 95
pension plans, 177–78
    distressed, 177–78
    school district, 178
    solutions, 178
Persily, Nate, 79
Perzel, John, 60, 96
Philadelphia, 6, 7, 11, 12, 26–27
    as a dog whistle, 36
    as first-class city, 171
    as first-class county, 169
    home rule charter, 171
    knowledge economy, 25
    machines, 34
    population growth, 26
    resentment toward, 36
    riot of 1779, 12
    students, 174
    television market, 30
    ticket- fixing scandal, 150
Philadelphia Inquirer, 31, 63
Philadelphia's Municipal Court, 136, 137

physical geography, 23
    See also political geographies
Pileggi, Dominic, 49
Pinchot, Gifford, 55, 109
Pittsburgh, 23
    knowledge economy, 25
    population growth, 26, 27
    racial diversity, 27
Pittsburgh Post-Gazette, 63, 114
Pittsburgh's Municipal Court, 136, 137
Pittsburgh Tribune-Review, 63
polarization, political/partisan, 112, 181
    sectarian polarization, 66
political action committees (PAC), 44, 45, 62
political culture, 2, 22, 31–36
    components, 31
    concept, 32
    individualistic, 32, 33, 34, 96–97
    moralist, 32
    patronage, 33, 34
    subcultures, 33
    traditional, 32, 33
political geography, 26–30
    sports markets, 30
    "T," 26, 28, 29–30, 54
    television markets, 30
political parties, 2, 41, 47–57
    control and domination, 47, 48–49
    in electorate, 53–55
    in government, 55–57
    internal discord, 50
    local organizations (machines), 34
    organizations and leadership, 50–53
    platforms, 52–53
    voters registration and affiliation, 45, 53–55
    See also Democrats/Democratic Party; Republicans/Republic Party
Pontiac's War, 11
Popular faction, 10, 11
population, 25–28, 73
Port Authority of New York and New Jersey, 161
Postage and Communications Expense Account, 77
Potter, Ellen, 109
Preate, Ernie, 45, 123
presidential election of 2016, 30
presidential election of 2020, 2, 186–88
    bills (General Assembly actions), 221–28
    disputes, 186
    executive branch actions, 229–31
    legal actions filed, 207–14
    mail ballots and voter fraud, 42
    secretaries of state and, 120
    Trump and, 42, 120, 181–82, 186
principals, 61
Printz, Johan, 6–7
prisoners' rights, 158
Proclamation of 1763, 11